READING DIAGNOSIS AND INSTRUCTION
Theory Into Practice

Robert J. Marzano
Mid-Continent Regional Educational Laboratory

Patricia J. Hagerty
Adams County School District #12, Colorado

Sheila W. Valencia
Center for the Study of Reading

Philip P. DiStefano
University of Colorado, Boulder

PRENTICE-HALL, INC., Englewood Cliffs, New Jersey 07632

Library of Congress Cataloging-in-Publication Data

Reading diagnosis and instruction.

   Bibliography: p.
   Includes index.
   1. Reading (Elementary)—United States.
2. English language—Study and teaching
(Elementary)—United States.   I. Marzano, Robert J.
LB1573.R2786   1987   372.4   86-25386
ISBN 0-13-755836-8

Editorial/production supervision and
  interior design: Edie de Coteau
Cover design: Wanda Lubelska
Manufacturing buyer: John Hall

Printed in the United States of America

10 9 8 7 6 5 4 3 2 1

ISBN 0-13-755836-8   01

Prentice-Hall International (UK) Limited, *London*
Prentice-Hall of Australia Pty. Limited, *Sydney*
Prentice-Hall Canada Inc., *Toronto*
Prentice-Hall Hispanoamericana, S.A., *Mexico*
Prentice-Hall of India Private Limited, *New Delhi*
Prentice-Hall of Japan, Inc., *Tokyo*
Prentice-Hall of Southeast Asia Pte. Ltd., *Singapore*
Editora Prentice-Hall do Brasil, Ltda., *Rio de Janeiro*

To my brother, Louie: R.J.M.

To my parents, Janet and Jack: S.W.V.

To my husband, Tom: P.J.H.

To my family: P.P.D.

Contents

v

DIAGNOSTIC TECHNIQUES

READING INSTRUCTION

Chapter 11:
READING AND THINKING SKILLS **225**

INSTRUCTIONAL PEDAGOGY AND CLASSROOM MANAGEMENT

Chapter 12:
EFFECTIVE READING INSTRUCTION: MANAGEMENT AND INSTRUCTION IN THE REGULAR CLASSROOM **245**

Chapter 13:
THE MANY ROLES OF THE READING SPECIALIST **277**

Chapter 14:
QUESTIONS TO TEACH BY **299**

Preface

Given the plethora of reading diagnosis textbooks currently in use, a logical and perhaps necessary question is "Why another?" In other words, what is the justification for writing and producing *Reading Diagnosis and Instruction: Theory into Practice*? We believe that there are three main justifications for its development and use:

1. It Weaves Theory into Practice: There are many reading textbooks currently on the market which do an exemplary job of *describing* diagnostic techniques and their related instructional activities. However, what is not easily found within reading textbooks is a thorough discussion of how the various theories of reading can and should be used to "shape" the interpretation of specific diagnostic devices and a concomitant discussion of how reading theory can and should be used as the backdrop for planning reading instruction. This is precisely the intent of *Reading Diagnosis and Instruction*—it overlays theory into practice. A useful metaphor is that the text uses theory as a latticework on which to hang decisions related to diagnosis and instruction in reading.

To this end four major theories of reading are developed in Part I of the text: the bottom-up theory, the top-down theory, the interactive theory, and the production system theory. These theories are presented along with a discussion of current research in language and cognition. Part I of *Reading Diagnosis and Instruction* is meant to provide the framework for much of the discussion in the remainder of the text.

2. It Emphasizes the Fluid and Dynamic Nature of Diagnosis and Prescription: Some reading textbooks either directly or indirectly portray reading diagnosis as a fairly straightforward, linear process of giving tests, interpreting results and then prescribing instruction. This is not consistent with either the research on diagnosis or our experience with it. Diagnosis, in most fields (e.g., medicine, auto mechanics), is usually more of a holistic process which involves the use of formal assessment techniques, informal techniques, hypothesis generating, hypothesis testing, intuition, and sometimes even guessing. Reading diagnosis and instruction, then, is much like the process engaged in by the ethnographic researcher. The ethnographer has a theory from which she/he operates. In *Reading Diagnosis and Instruction*, reading teachers and reading specialists are strongly encouraged to select one of the four theories presented in Part I as the framework they will use to diagnose student strengths and weaknesses and then plan instruction.

The ethnographer uses new information to restructure old hypotheses and formulations. The diagnostic/prescriptive process as described in Part II of the text, is a dynamic interplay between assessment and instructional activities. The reading teacher or reading specialist engages in brief but informative assessment activities; from this, hypotheses are generated and instruction planned. During instruction, hypotheses are confirmed, changed or dropped and new ones generated. New assessment activities are planned and, as a result, new instructional activities. The process, then, is recursive and dynamic, new information always being used to structure future activities and restructure old conclusions.

3. It Frames Reading Instruction and Learning to Read in the Context of General Instructional Pedagogy and General Principles of Learning: It is our contention that the good teacher of reading is first a good teacher. Consequently, throughout the text, instructional strategies are discussed in light of current research on instructional pedagogy. This is evident in the discussion in Part III on instructional techniques designed for specific reading competencies and in the discussion of general instructional heuristics found in Part IV of the text.

It is also our contention that the process of reading is a subset of more general cognitive processes that relate to learning of all types. Techniques are presented which help students bridge their learning about the reading process to other academic skills and content areas. Similarly, techniques are presented to make students aware of general dispositions necessary for efficient learning within any environment. Some of these general metacognitive strategies include the generation of positive attitudes about the task at hand and about self, setting goals, managing time and resources, etc.

Thoughtful use of this textbook should provide the tools and experience necessary to become a highly effective reading teacher, reading specialist, or content area teacher interested in improving students' abilities to process, analyze, and retrieve information. The text can be used at the graduate or undergraduate levels. At the undergraduate level the selection of a theoretical framework (theory of reading) by students should be done with a strong guiding hand from the instructor. Also students should be provided with a maximum number of opportunities to field test the various diagnostic and instructional techniques presented. At the graduate level students should be allowed more freedom in their selection of a theory base and in their selection of diagnostic and instructional techniques which complement that framework.

In writing a text such as this there are always many more people involved than those whose names appear on the cover. We would like to express our gratitude to Dr. Patricia H. Duncan, Virginia Commonwealth University, and Professor Dixie Lee Spiegel, University of North Carolina.

Robert J. Marzano
Patricia J. Hagerty
Sheila W. Valencia
Philip P. DiStefano

1

INTRODUCTION AND OVERVIEW

Reading is a highly valued skill in a literate, technically advanced society such as ours. It wasn't too long ago that formal education was organized around reading instruction. For example, in the 1800s Boston's grammar schools were organized into two departments, each with its own master and his two or three assistants: The reading department and the writing department each enrolled students for its half-day course (Clifford, 1984). Despite the fact that we hear and read so much about functionally illiterate adults in our society and are told "Johnny still can't read" (Flesch, 1981), our society is among the most literate in the world. Similarly, in spite of claims by such noted literary figures as T.S. Eliot that the growth of picture-oriented media has lessened the need for reading (Kandel, 1950, p. 348), the number of books purchased each year is on the increase, attesting to the fact that Americans are reading, and reading more than they ever have before.

It is not an exaggeration to say that reading is at the core of a technical society. Some economists and economic historians contend that a 40% literacy rate in the population is a necessary but not sufficient condition to initiate or maintain economic development (C.A. Anderson & Bowman, 1976). For example, Cipolla (1969) stated that "technical advances in open-sea navigation, map and clockmaking and production of firearms and precision instruments in the 16th century rested on a growing supply of literate craftsmen" (p. 49).

Those who can't read are placed at a serious disadvantage in our society.

Table 1.1 Categories Used by Reading Educators to Define Reading Instruction

LABEL	DEVELOPMENTAL	CORRECTIVE	REMEDIAL
Grade-level reading ability	On grade	1 year below grade level	2 years below grade level

They face the social stigma of being different. They face years of repeated failure in school, because almost all knowledge imparted in school is dependent on the ability to read. They face serious problems in obtaining a driver's license, navigating in their physical environment, learning a skill, obtaining a job. In short, they are handicapped in their ability to lead normal, productive lives.

A primary purpose of schooling is to teach children to function as literate citizens in our society. As teachers, we recognize this important purpose, and we seek to help all children read at a level at which they can function successfully in society. Fortunately, many children learn to read successfully with a minimal amount of instruction. Many others succeed with teacher guidance and instruction. Commonly we call such students *developmental readers*. Still others have a great deal of difficulty, even with the best instruction that we can provide for them.

In this book we want to impart to teachers knowledge about "the best instruction" to provide for those children for whom reading presents some difficulty. These children lie on a continuum in their reading deficiency. Those reading approximately *one year below grade level* are referred to as *corrective*; that is, the reading problem is regarded as being correctable in the regular classroom by the regular classroom teacher. Other children have more serious reading problems, reading *two or more years below grade level*, and are referred to as *remedial*. For these readers the reading problem is regarded as serious enough to be in need of remediation, usually by a special reading teacher in a resource room where children are "pulled out" of the regular classroom for a specific period each day. Table 1.1 summarizes the different categories of readers.

School districts vary in their interpretation and handling of corrective and remedial readers, particularly as budget restraints force districts to use classroom teachers to correct and remediate reading problems. In this book we will present the knowledge and skills necessary for working with *both* types of reading problems and demonstrate how to work effectively in both the resource room and the regular classroom.

BASIC ASSUMPTIONS

In developing this textbook we have made some basic assumptions that have guided what we present and how we present it. These are discussed next.

Assumptions About Reading

Reading Is a Cognitive Process. Reading is fundamentally a process of thinking, cognition. Therefore, a knowledge of reading must include a knowledge of basic cognitive processes. Even at the beginning of the 20th century such theorists as Thorndike and Huey were attesting to the cognitive complexity of the reading process. Experiments in perception and memory have suggested that reading is a process of selectively attending to information in the form of written language, of taking in certain components of that information, of storing those components in certain ways, and of recalling them under certain conditions. Today much of our knowledge about reading comes from such diverse cognate fields as developmental psychology, cognitive psychology, clinical psychology, psycholinguistics, and artificial intelligence. To be an effective reading teacher-diagnostician requires general knowledge of how the mind functions and specific knowledge of how it functions during reading.

Reading Is a Language Process. The strong relationship between reading and language seems obvious, yet, before the late 1960s, linguists took little interest in studying the reading process. Today much of reading diagnosis and instruction is based on such complex linguistic concepts as case grammars, discourse theory, phonology, and generative grammars. Studies in these areas have provided reading teachers with invaluable instructional techniques and reading diagnosticians with new insights into possible causes of reading difficulty.

Reading Is Part of a Larger System of Behavior. The more human behavior is studied, the more it appears to be integrated. That is, we do not separate our lives into categories, or discrete events. Rather, what happens to us one day affects what happens the next. As it relates to reading, this assertion implies that reading behavior cannot be studied in isolation. Instead, the reading teacher must view reading behavior as a subset of a much larger system, taking into account the student's attitudes, home environment, and instructional setting.

Assumptions About Diagnosis

Reading Diagnosis Is an Inexact Process of Ethnographic Research. Some reading textbooks portray reading diagnosis as a linear process of giving tests, interpreting results, and prescribing instruction. This is a model taken from the hard sciences (e.g., chemistry, physics). Even the word *diagnosis* implies a well-defined scientific problem.

> **diagnosis 1a:** the art or act of identifying a disease from its signs and symptoms **2:** a concise technical description of a taxon **3 a:** investigation or analysis of the cause or nature of a condition, situation, or problem (e.g., of engine trouble)

b: a statement or conclusion from such an analysis. (*Webster's Ninth New Collegiate Dictionary*, 1983, p. 349)

In fact, reading diagnosis is not concise or linear, as would be diagnosis of the misworkings of a malfunctioning gas engine. A better metaphor for reading diagnosis is that it is a process of ethnographic research. Ethnographic research (also called *qualitative* or *phenomenological* research) is an approach to scientific inquiry that has become popular in education from the mid-1970s on. According to Fetterman (1984), the ethnographer is a human instrument, testing and shaping ideas and insights on the basis of objective data and a conscious subjective stance. The shape of the ethnographer's conclusions is based as much on his or her evaluation design as on his or her personality and training. In other words, the ethnographic approach to diagnosis calls on the reading teacher to use objective test data, along with informal observation and even intuition, to generate hypotheses about why a student is having difficulty reading. These initial hypotheses constitute a starting place from which to plan instruction. Diagnosis does not end after the formal tests have been administered. Rather, it continues throughout the entire time the teacher and student interact. As new information is acquired, new hypotheses are generated and tested. Ethnographic diagnosis is a dynamic, generative process.

Reading Diagnosis Must Be Model Driven. *Model* here refers to a theory of how reading works. A good automobile diagnostician can pinpoint an engine's trouble because she or he knows how an engine works. The diagnostician operates from some model of the inner workings of an automobile. A physician does the same. She or he spends years learning the theory of the interworkings of the human body and then creates a model used to generate guesses about why a patient is having a particular problem. Similarly the reading teacher must have a model of the reading process from which to diagnose reading difficulties and plan instruction. We believe that, without a strong model of the reading process, the reading teacher runs a strong risk of giving unnecessary tests and prescribing unnecessary instruction.

Assumptions About Instruction

The major assumption made about reading instruction is that it occurs within the framework of a more generalized system of instructional pedagogy. That is, good reading instruction occurs when the reading teacher is aware of good general instructional practices. A good reading teacher is, first, a good teacher and, second, a specialist in reading. The period since the mid-1970s has seen a tremendous growth in our knowledge of the art and science of teaching. For the first time in the history of education, we are beginning to pinpoint practices that have measurable effects on learning. Sound reading instruction is necessarily circumscribed by a knowledge of these more general instructional procedures.

EFFECTS OF ASSUMPTIONS ON TEXT ORGANIZATION

The content and organization of this textbook springs directly from the assumptions we have made. Because reading involves cognitive processes, language processes, and more generic behaviors, we have devoted a section of the text to explaining current research and theory in those areas. That section is entitled "Language, Cognition, and Reading" and contains three chapters (2, 3, and 4). Given the importance which we attribute to a knowledge of the basic principles in these reading-related areas, we consider this section a key to understanding the remaining chapters in the book. Chapters 2, 3, and 4 set the stage for the subsequent discussion of diagnostic and instructional practices.

The assumption that reading diagnosis is a process of ethnographic research manifests itself in our recommendations for collecting, organizing, and interpreting data. Specifically, chapter 7, entitled "Synthesizing and Integrating Test Data: An Ethnographic Approach," discusses such ethnographic processes as data display, data reduction, hypothesis generation, and triangulation as they relate to reading diagnosis. Chapter 7 is found in the second section of the text, entitled "Diagnostic Techniques." That section also contains two chapters that treat informal and formal tests of reading.

The assumption that reading diagnosis is model driven sets the tone for the entire text. In chapter 4 we present a number of models of the reading process—theories about how reading works. From that chapter on, our discussions about diagnostic and instructional techniques occur in the context of these models. That is, we attempt to identify how each technique, diagnostic or instructional, relates to these models. We also strongly recommend that the readers of this text either select one of the models discussed in chapter 4 or develop their own models as soon as possible as an organizing structure for selecting which information within this text is most relevant. Another way of saying this is that we are not so much concerned about which model you use to diagnose and teach as we are about whether or not you have a model.

Finally the assumption that reading instruction is a subsystem of more generalized instructional techniques translates into two sections devoted to instruction. Section III, entitled "Reading Instruction," contains chapters on instruction at the word level (chapter 8), on instruction at the syntactic and discourse levels (chapter 9), on instruction at the schema level (chapter 10), and on instruction that goes beyond comprehension (chapter 11). Section IV, entitled "Instructional Pedagogy and Classroom Management," contains a chapter summarizing the most current theory and research on effective instructional techniques that generalize to all content areas (chapter 12). It also contains a chapter on the management of instruction in regular classrooms and resource room settings (chapter 13).

A thoughtful reading of this textbook will provide the theoretical and practical knowledge with which to implement a sound diagnostic and instructional program for remedial and corrective readers.

SUMMARY

In this chapter we have discussed the importance of reading in a technological society such as ours. We have also identified the basic assumptions that are the foundation of this textbook:

I. About reading
   A. Reading is a cognitive process.
   B. Reading is a language process.
   C. Reading behavior is part of a larger system of behavior.
II. About diagnosis
   A. Reading diagnosis is a process of ethnographic research.
   B. Reading diagnosis should be model driven.
III. About instruction
   A. Good reading instruction is part of a system of more generalizable instructional practices.

We have used these assumptions to organize the information presented in this text. Based on these assumptions about reading, we present chapters that discuss the various theoretical approaches to reading and the relationship of reading theory to research and practice in language and cognition. Because of our assumptions about diagnosis, we interpret the various informal and formal assessment techniques in reading in light of the various theoretical approaches to reading. We also describe how to use assessment information in a holistic, dynamic manner. Finally, based on our assumption about instruction, we present instructional techniques specific to reading, along with more general techniques that apply to a wide variety of content and educational settings.

2

LANGUAGE AND THOUGHT

A knowledge of reading necessarily involves a knowledge of language and how it works. A knowledge of language involves a knowledge of how the mind operates. The purpose of this chapter is to provide an overview of language and its place in cognition. We begin with a brief discussion of some working principles of thought and memory. We should note here that this is a very complex topic, which we will be dealing with only superficially. However our discussion is detailed enough to provide insight into the various aspects of language use.

What type of information is stored in the mind, or what type of information is found in memory? Although we tend to use the word *memory* to represent a unitary process, at least three different stages of memory have been identified: (a) sensory information storage, (b) short-term memory, and (c) long-term memory. Figure 2.1 depicts the three memory systems.

Sensory information storage, sometimes called *immediate perceptual memory*, basically contains raw information from the senses. The duration of this raw information is quite short, anywhere from 0.1 to 0.5 seconds. You can observe your sensory information storage by performing one or more of the following tasks:

1. Stare at an object for awhile and then close your eyes tightly and keep them closed. Notice that the sharper images you see linger for awhile after you have closed your eyes. This is because it takes from 0.1 to 0.5 seconds for your sensory information storage to clear and make itself ready for new information.

SENSORY SYSTEMS   MEMORY SYSTEMS

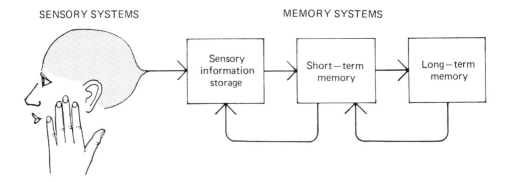

Figure 2.1

From *Elementary Language Arts* (p. 15) by P. DiStefano, J. Dole, and R. Marzano, 1984,
New York: Macmillan. Originally published by John Wiley and Sons. Reprinted by permission.

2. Clap your hands a few times very loudly. Notice that you will retain the memory
   of the sound for a brief period of time after the clapping has stopped.
3. Wave a pencil back and forth in front of your eyes. The shadowy image you see
   is, again, your sensory information storage of the image of the pencil slowly
   fading.
4. Press the index finger of one hand against the back of the wrist on your other
   hand. Notice that the sensation of being touched lingers briefly even after you
   remove your index finger. (DiStefano, Dole, & Marzano, 1984)

Once the information in sensory information storage fades or decays,
you are left with a representation, or analog, of what you actually perceived (J.R.
Anderson, 1980).

Information in sensory information storage is translated into information in short-term memory. Short-term memory has greater capacity than sensory information storage (Klausmeier & Goodwin, 1975). Moreover, it appears
that a person has a certain amount of control over how long information is
stored in short-term memory. You have probably been in a number of situations
where you have artificially kept information in short-term memory; for example,
after looking up a telephone number in the directory, you subvocally repeated
it until you dialed the number. Chances are that, soon after the number was
dialed, it was forgotten. The available evidence suggests that, without rehearsal
(subvocally repeating the information), information is lost from short-term memory in about 15 to 30 seconds. Short-term memory is also limited in the amount
of information that can be stored. To illustrate, briefly look at the following
letters; then close your eyes and see if you can recall them:

p   n   l   z   r   t   v

If you used rehearsal as a device to keep these letters in short-term memory, you probably could recall them. Now try recalling the following letters:

b   x   c   w   v   t   r   z   l   n   p

You probably could not recall these letters. This is because they exceed the amount of information that can be stored in short-term memory. The first list of consonants contained seven letters. This is the average number of random pieces of information that can be recalled using short-term memory. The second list contained 11 letters. Unless reorganized in some more efficient way, they overload the short-term memory system.

Short-term memory is sometimes referred to as *working memory* or *buffer memory*. You use it to retain in the forefront of your mind whatever it is you are attending to at a particular moment. According to F. Smith (1978), short-term memory is of central importance in reading specifically and in language processing in general. The contents of short-term memory are usually the last few words you have read or listened to. It contains what you are about to say or write, and it is where you lodge the traces of what you have just read.

Of course we know far more information than we are consciously aware of. This information is housed in long-term memory. Whereas short-term memory is very limited in its capacity, long-term memory appears to be almost limitless. Dyer (1976) stated that long-term memory has enough storage capacity to accept 10 new facts every second: "It has been conservatively estimated that the human brain can store an amount of information equivalent to one hundred trillion words, and that all of us use but a tiny fraction of this storage space" (p. 42).

Whereas there is generally no difficulty retrieving information from short-term memory, our ability to retrieve information from long-term memory is limited. Sometimes it is very difficult to get ahold of information from long-term memory. An illustration of this is provided by the "tip-of-the-tongue" phenomenon (R. Brown & McNeill, 1966). You know a person's name is medium length and begins with an H, and you're sure it's not Halper, Herndon, or Hinkle. Suddenly the name pops into your head—Horowitz! The information was there in long-term memory but not immediately accessible.

Our ability to retrieve information from long-term memory depends on the clues we have to it. The number of clues we have to information depends on how the information has been stored. Underwood (1969) has identified nine types of clues, or *attributes*, that can be associated with information in long-term memory. When remembering something, we might use any one, or a number, of these attributes to "pull up" the information into consciousness. The nine attributes are

1. *Temporal:* Recalling the time in which an event occurred
   Example: Remembering that the school picnic happened right before July 4

2. *Spatial:* Recalling where objects are in relationship to each other
   Example: Remembering that you sat in front of a boy with blond hair in the second grade
3. *Frequency:* Recognizing that an event occurs frequently or infrequently
   Example: Remembering that your teacher used to say "ah" whenever she paused
4. *Modality:* Recalling an event because it made a strong impression on you visually, auditorily, or tacitly
   Example: Remembering an event because it was associated with a loud noise
5. *Acoustic:* Recalling a piece of linguistic information because of how it sounded when it happened
   Example: Recalling the form of a word or a phrase on the basis of its sound
6. *Visual:* Recalling the visual mental image associated with information
   Example: Remembering a word on the basis of the mental image representing it
7. *Affective:* Recalling an event because of an emotion attached to it
   Example: Recalling the day you were not picked to be a cheerleader because of how sad it made you feel
8. *Context:* Recalling information because of the general context in which it appeared
   Example: Recalling the context in which you first learned the difference between the words *there* and *their*
9. *Verbal:* Recalling information because of a word associated with it
   Example: The word *number* generally cuing the retrieval of numerals

These attributes are "entry points" to information stored in long-term memory. To illustrate, at any time, you are constantly being bombarded with information to your consciousness, or short-term memory. As you walk down the street you hear noises, see objects in relationship to other objects, hear words and sentences being spoken, feel emotion, and on and on. If you attend to any one piece or attribute of this incoming information, that attribute can cue any other piece of information in long-term memory that has a similar attribute. This explains why, as you walk down the street, you might find yourself thinking of your family reunion 10 years earlier. A smell, a taste, a noise you processed in your short-term memory while walking down the street cued a similar attribute you had stored with the remembrance of the family reunion.

Information in long-term memory is constantly being used to interpret the outside world. That is, we use it to make sense out of what we perceive in sensory information storage and short-term memory. For a moment reconsider Figure 2.1. Notice that the three memory systems have arrows connecting the boxes in both directions, incoming and outcoming information. Sensory information storage feeds short-term memory, which, in turn, feeds long-term memory. Long-term memory enables us to interpret information that is being processed in short-term memory, which helps us interpret information in sensory information storage. The whole process feeds back on itself in a mutually dependent system. To illustrate this, consider Figure 2.2. It could not possibly exist in three dimensions. Yet, as you look at it, it appears to make sense as a three-dimensional object. This is because your long-term memory is sending your short-term memory and sensory information storage messages that the object is three dimensional.

But how does language come into play in this complex system? Essentially language is a very abstract level of coding or labeling of information in long-term memory. Most thoughts begin as remembrances of nonverbal attributes. Flower and Hayes (1984) reported that, when people write, they first begin by tapping the nonverbal information stored in long-term memory. This information includes "knowledge that is stored as a perceptual experience—these nonverbal representations constitute a rich body of knowledge that is difficult but sometimes necessary to capture in words" (p. 130). J.R. Anderson (1980) called this type of information *spatial images*. Bryden and Ley (1983) called it *visuospatial information*. This nonverbal information is an elementary form of information storage. It is raw information, raw building material, that will be shaped and molded by language.

Language is essentially the labeling of visuospatial and other types of nonverbal information. For example, when we have a set of internal chemical reactions that produces pleasant bodily sensations, we label this set of experiences *liking*. Funkenstein (1967) reported that the set of experiences we call *fear* is produced by the secretion of adrenalin; the set of experiences we call *anger* is produced by a similar hormone called *noradrenalin*.

Naming, or labeling, is perhaps the fundamental characteristic of language. The actual labels we select are fairly arbitrary cultural decisions. As Condon (1968) stated,

> If we desired, and everybody agreed to the change, we could call this book a "spaghetti" and could call spaghetti "book." If the change were consistent, no

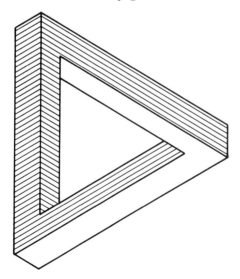

Figure 2.2

confusion would result. Indeed over many years referents for certain sounds (words) do change, but because speakers learn the changes at the same time, there is no confusion. That the word *girl* once meant a young person of either sex or that the word *coast* formerly applied to any border (Switzerland used to have a "coast") says something about converting the convention of naming and not about the history of girls, boys and borders. (p. 29)

This propensity for naming apparently exists among higher animal forms. For example, Washoe is a chimp who was taught the American Sign Language (Gardner & Gardner, 1971). At one time this was considered impossible for all forms of life other than humans. As R. Brown (1973, p. 32) stated, when the teachers of Washoe began their experiments, they must have felt no lack of doubters. Noam Chomsky, in *Language and Mind* (1968), had written "Anyone concerned with the study of human nature and human capacities must somehow come to grips with the fact that all normal humans acquire language whereas acquisition of even its barest rudiments is quite beyond the capabilities of an otherwise intelligent ape" (p. 59). Similarly Eric Lenneberg, in *New Directions in the Study of Language* (1964), wrote, "There is no evidence that any nonhuman form has the capacity to acquire even the most primitive stages of language development" (p. 67). In spite of these warnings, Washoe was able to learn the rudiments of American Sign Language using essentially a naturalistic training method similar to that used with well-tended children. By age 4 Washoe was making approximate use of 85 different signs and producing strings or sequences in sentence format up to 5 signs long. An analysis of Washoe's language indicated that she was performing much in the manner of a child of 16 to 27 months (R. Brown, 1973).

The propensity for human beings to name things has at least two consequences (Condon, 1968). The first consequence is that we begin to notice those things for which we have created names. Condon used the example of taking a course in astronomy. Before taking the course you look up at the sky and see only stars. After a few weeks you do not just see stars; indeed, you see super novae, white dwarfs, galaxies. "Thus, for better or for worse, when names are learned we see what we had not seen, for we know what to look for" (p. 31).

The second result of labeling our experiences is that we begin not to notice certain things. This sounds like a contradiction of the first result, and in a paradoxical sense it is. Once we have learned to make distinctions among things, we tend to highlight the differences and ignore the similarities. Before you knew the distinctions among, and established names for, galaxies, super novae, white dwarfs, and other celestial bodies, you saw the stars as a sea of light, a unified body of glittering particles. Once distinctions have been made through labeling, it is difficult to see the stars in this manner.

These two seemingly paradoxical outgrowths of our ability to label experience via language are at the core of a deep philosophical question related to language, namely: Does language shape perception and consciousness? This question is commonly called the *issue of linguistic relativity*.

On one side of the issue are those who believe that language is simply a representation of thought. That is, the language we use is determined by the thoughts we have. This is basically the position held by Piaget. He theorized (1965) that children's acquisition of langue is dependent on the presence of mental patterns for specific motor behaviors and for internalized concepts or generalizations. Language for Piaget was simply the representation via speech patterns of these internalized structures. As described by Waterhouse (1980), Piaget posited that, after the initial stages of development, the child goes through the acquisition of social language and finally is able to use language to create complex abstract and logical structures.

Somewhat in the middle of the controversy is the semiotic extension theory (McNeill, 1975), which posits that language forces us into certain modes of expression but does not shape perception. McNeill posited that, at the level of what we might call a single thought, we are forced into expressing perception as objects, actions, states, and events. He argued

> Relying on the semiotic extension of the basic speech mechanism, speech production is organized around such conceptual entities as Objects, Agents, States and Events, regardless of the level of mental processing behind the content being expressed. Even abstract content, where there may not be real objects, actions, states or events at all, must be organized into these sensory-motor structures. (pp. 1–2)

This assertion about predetermined modes of expression is supported by the linguist Schlesinger (1971).

On the other side of the issue are those who assert that language dictates perception. Best known for this position is Benjamin Whorf, who was a student of the famous linguist Sapir. Building on the teachings of Sapir (1921), Whorf (1956) developed the principle of linguistic relativity.

> We are thus introduced to a new principle of relativity, which holds that all observers are not led by the same physical evidence to the same picture of the universe, unless their linguistic backgrounds are or can in some way be calibrated. (p. 214)

Whorf proposed that we dissect nature along the lines laid down by our native languages. The thoughts we isolate from the world of perception are not there because they stare every observer in the face; "on the contrary, the world is presented in a kaleidoscopic flux of impressions which has to be organized by our minds—and this means largely by the linguistic systems in our minds" (p. 213). Whorf's writings have commonly been interpreted as saying that language governs perception. That is, we are capable of perceiving only what our language dictates. In recent years Clarke, Losoff, and Rood (1982) have shown that this is an exaggeration of Whorf's hypothesis. More accurately, Whorf's hypothesis is an extension of phenomenology. Clark, Losoff, McCracken, and Rood (1984) explained that "a fundamental assumption of phenomenology is that there is no 'objective' reality which exists independent of our apprehension of it. That is to say, reality is socially constructed; our ability to function in society and to interact successfully with other human beings is a result of our assumption that everyone agrees with our interpretation of reality" (p. 51).

But how do the hypotheses of Whorf, Piaget, and the others affect you, the teacher of reading? They underscore the importance of language and its relationship to thought. A fundamental awareness for a teacher of reading is that language is a window to cognition. Observing a child's language is observing the child's interpretation of reality. Listening and observing from this perspective make a powerful and insightful teacher. They provide information that could never be obtained from a test.

THE STUDY OF LANGUAGE

Given the importance of language, it is no wonder that it has been the subject of intense study for centuries. In this section we will consider four areas of language study: (a) syntax, (b) phonology, (c) semantics, and (d) pragmatics. More and more the teaching of reading demands a working knowledge of complex areas of language study. Here we provide an overview of four of the most important areas of language study relative to reading.

Syntax

The study of syntax is the study of the structure of language, or why we put words together the way we do. It was once theorized that people generated sentences on a word-to-word basis. That is, one word cued the speaker to the next word, which cued the speaker to the next word. This model was called a *chain model*. In his discussion of the development of chain models, Slobin (1979) explained that the simplest way to account for sequential acts was to propose that each response becomes, in turn, a stimulus for the following response. Each word in a sentence determined the next word. This notion appealed to traditional behaviorist or stimulus-response psychology.

In 1951 Karl Lashley presented strong arguments and evidence against chain models. He claimed that the temporal sequence of words was determined by underlying structures that span more than two word chains. He wrote of a "schema of order" that accounted for the way we organize words. He found evidence for this underlying schema of order in slips of the tongue, errors in typewriting, and people's ability to comprehend some words in some situations only after they had heard them spoken. As an example Lashley offered the following. (To understand Lashley's point, you should imagine hearing these words rather than reading them.)

> Rapid righting with his uninjured hand saved from loss the contents of the capsized canoe.

When this sentence is listened to, the correct meaning of the word *righting* is determined a few seconds *after* the word is heard. This implies that, when processing the sentence, the hearer might be trying possible structures into which the words can fit. We might say that the study of syntax is the study of these possible structures.

In 1957, in his book entitled *Syntactic Structures*, Noam Chomsky began what might be called a revolution in linguistics by hypothesizing that the structure, or syntax, of a language is at the core of its production and comprehension. More specifically, Chomsky hypothesized that we have an innate sense of a sentence. As we comprehend or produce language, we constantly use this innate sense to derive and produce meaning. To illustrate, consider the sentence "They were visiting professors." This sentence is ambiguous; it can mean two different things. Another way of saying this is that it has two possible structures that can be depicted by bracketing the groups of words that go together as phrases:

1. (They)   ([were visiting] [professors])
2. (They)   ([were] [visiting professors])

One method linguists use to study the structure of language is through phrase-structure grammars. Phrase-structure grammars attempt to systematize the intuitive awareness we have for the grouping of ideas. For example, consider the sentence "the old man watched the young girl playing on the swing." If you were asked to divide this sentence into parts, which division would sound the most reasonable?

1. The old man watched —— the young girl playing on the swing.
2. The old man watched the young girl —— playing on the swing.
3. The old man —— watched the young girl playing on the swing.

An analytic tool commonly used within phrase-structure grammars is *constituent analysis*. Slobin (1979) demonstrated the use of constituent analysis with the sentence "The boy hit the ball." Linguistic intuition tells us that some words go together; *the ball*, for example, seems like a unit. One way of expressing this intuitive notion is that *the ball* can be substituted for by a single word, *it*; likewise, *the boy* can be substituted for by *he*. Table 2.1 demonstrates the levels of substitution for this sentence.

Table 2.1

The boy	hit	the ball
He	hit	it
He		acted

In Table 2.1 words that go together are called *constituents*. For example, *the ball* is a constituent; *hit the* is not.

Another way to describe the constituent structure of a language is to use a generative grammar. Generative grammars are derived from formal logic. With formal logic you start with a basic axiom and then apply rules for rewriting the axiom. With a generative grammar, you begin with the symbol for a sentence and then use "rewrite" rules to generate the words in the sentence. Slobin (1979) offered the following rewrite rules as an example of a generative grammar:

1. S   → NP + VP
2. NP → T + N
3. VP → V + NP
4. T   → the, a
5. N   → boy, girl, ball
6. V   → hit

Using these rewrite rules in a sequence of steps allows us to generate the sentence "The boy hit the ball."

Step 1:   S   → NP + VP
Step 2:   NP → T + N
Step 3:   T   → the
Step 4:   N   → boy
Step 5:   VP → V + NP
Step 6:   V   → hit
Step 7:   NP → T + N
Step 8:   T   → the
Step 9:   N   → ball

In 1965 Noam Chomsky published *Aspects of a Theory of Syntax* and again changed the world of linguistics. Chomsky hypothesized that not all of the structure of an utterance is evidenced on the "surface." To illustrate, consider the following:

1. The boy hit the ball.
2. What did the boy hit?

These sentences are obviously related, but their similarities would not be represented in a phrase-structure grammar or a generative grammar. To account for the underlying similarity of these utterances, Chomsky developed a transformational grammar. One assumption of transformational grammar is that sentences begin with an underlying deep structure that goes through a series of transformations to become the surface structure—that which we read or hear. Transformational grammars would posit that both sentences just listed have the same underlying deep structure. The difference is that the second sentence went through a series of transformations. In greatly simplified form, the transformation of Sentence 1 to Sentence 2 might be depicted in the following way (note that the symbol $\Longrightarrow$ stands for *transformed into*):

$$\text{The boy hit the ball} \Longrightarrow \text{The boy hit what} \Longrightarrow \text{What did the boy hit?}$$

The development of transformational grammars greatly expanded the power and sophistication of the study of syntax. It also introduced many perplexing questions, one of the primary ones being, if all of the structures of English are not evident in surface forms of sentences, how do children learn them? This question supported the assertion that language ability is innate and greatly weakened the stimulus-response theory of language acquisition (e.g., the chain model).

The final type of grammar we will consider in our discussion of syntax is traditional grammar. Traditional grammar is sometimes called *school grammar* because it is the type of grammar commonly taught in school. Traditional grammar dates back to the work of Lindley Murray (1795) and Alexander Bain (1869). The teaching of traditional grammar is generally associated with the presentation of rules as prescriptions for students to follow. There is a misconception among many teachers that teaching prescriptive rules helps students' speaking and writing abilities. Research has never supported the contention that teaching traditional grammar in any way aids language or thinking ability. For example, Briggs (1913) reported that grammar did not improve students' ability to reason logically. Hoyt (1906), Boraas (1917), and Asker (1923) found very low correlations between knowledge of grammar and a variety of scores associated with usage tests, poetry interpretation, and writing ability. There have also been a number of studies suggesting that the prescriptive nature of traditional grammar can negatively affect language use (Catherwood, 1932; Cutwright, 1934; Symonds, 1931). As an end in itself, the teaching of traditional grammar has some merit. It is a detailed system for describing language, although it is not as powerful as generative or transformational grammars. However, it is logical and, if reinforced, can provide a common vocabulary between teacher and students with which to discuss language.

Phonology

Phonology is the study of the sound system of a language. There are approximately 44 speech sounds, or *phonemes*, in the English language. These are not all of the sounds we can make, only those used in the English language. According to Lindfors (1980),

> The human being is capable of making a wide range of sounds with his vocal apparatus. He can cough, whistle, sing, sneeze, and wheeze. He can also talk. Considering the diverse set of sounds all human beings can make so easily by means of an air stream passing through the vocal tract and out through the mouth and/or nose, it is interesting that only a subset are the sounds of talk in any language. (p. 67)

The most commonly used phonemes in the English language are displayed in Figure 2.3.

The study of the physical properties of phonemes and the manner of their articulation is called *phonetics*. Linguists studying phonetics seek to determine how the various phonemes of a language are produced. They study the similarities and differences among sounds, the physical movements necessary for their articulation, and the vibrations that account for their acoustic effect.

Human sounds are produced by the passage of air from the lungs through the vocal cords in the throat and then out of the body through either the mouth or the nose. In the process the sounds are intensified and shaped in different ways. The pharynx (or pharyngeal cavity), the mouth (or oral cavity), and the nose (or nasal cavity) are used to intensify sound. For this reason they are sometimes called the *resonators*. The soft palate (or velum), the hard palate, the tongue, the teeth, and the lips are used to shape sounds. They are sometimes referred to as the *articulators*. In phonetics the sounds of English are described in terms of how the resonators and articulators are used to produce them. Figure 2.4 illustrates how the common phonemes are produced.

The terms *bilabial*, *labiodental*, and so on along the top row of the consonant chart refer to specific parts of the nasal, oral, and pharyngeal cavities. The line leading from each term identifies the specific location to which the term refers. For example, there is a line leading from the term *bilabial* to the two lips. This indicates that bilabial refers to the use of the lips in the production of a phoneme. Note that there is only one line leading from the vowel chart to the diagram. This line leads to the center of the tongue. This indicates that vowels are produced primarily by the position of the tongue within the oral cavity. *High,*

Vowels	Consonants	Liquids	Glides
/i/ beat	/b/ bat	/r/ ring	/w/ wow
/I/ bit	/p/ pat	/l/ lazy	/y/ yen
/e/ bait	/f/ fat		
/ɛ/ bet	/v/ van		
/š/ bat	/θ/ breath		
/ə/ roses	/ð/ breathe		
/ʌ/ but	/t/ ted		
/u/ cooed	/d/ dead		
/ʊ/ could	/s/ same		
/o/ code	/z/ zest		
/ǫ/ cawed	/č/ chop		
/ā/ cod	/ǰ/ jam		
	/š/ shut		
	/ž/ vision		
	/k/ cake		
	/g/ get		
	/h/ hen		
	/n/ neat		
	/m/ map		
	/ṇ/ ring		

Figure 2.3

From *Elementary Language Arts* (p. 28) by P. DiStefano, J. Dole, and R. Marzano, 1984, New York: Macmillan. Originally published by John Wiley and Sons. Reprinted by permission.

mid, and *low* refer to the tongue's position in a vertical direction; *front, central*, and *back* refer to the tongue's position in a horizontal direction. You can obtain a "feel" for these positions by pronouncing some of the vowels on the vowel chart. For example, if you say the vowel sounds in the words *beat, bet*, and *bat* in that order, you should feel your tongue drop vertically. If you pronounce the vowel sounds in the words *bat, cold*, and *cawed*, you should feel your tongue move backward on a horizontal plane.

In the consonant chart the words *stops, fricatives, sibilants, affricates, nasals*, and *liquids* refer to the changes made in the flow of air by different parts of the mouth. When the air flowing from the lungs through the mouth is abruptly stopped and then let go, the resulting phoneme is called a *stop*. Note that the phonemes /b/ and /p/ are stops; more specifically they are bilabial stops. This means that, in their production, the air flowing from the lungs is stopped by the two lips (hence, *bilabial*) and then abruptly let go. The phonemes /t/, /d/, /k/, and /g/ are also stops, but the airflow is impeded by an area of the mouth other than the lips. Fricatives are produced by stopping the air and letting it escape gradually rather than abruptly. For example, the fricatives /f/ and /v/ are produced by obstructing the air using one lip and the upper teeth (hence, *labiodental*).

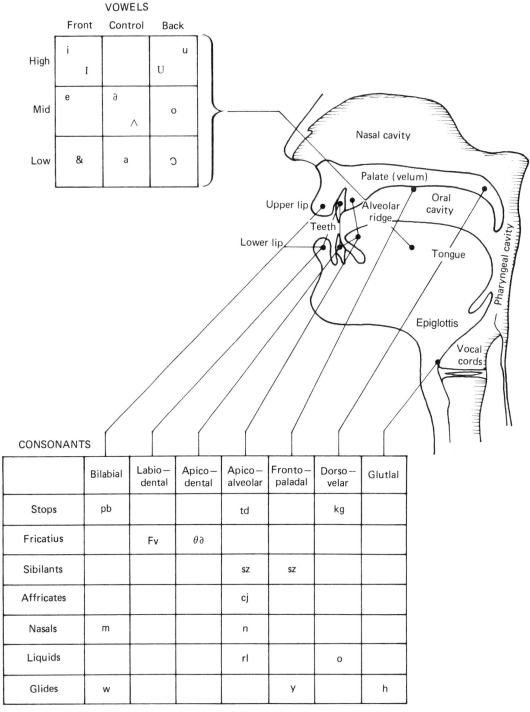

Figure 2.4

From *Elementary Language Arts* (p. 30) by P. DiStefano, J. Dole, and R. Marzano, 1984, New York: Macmillan. Originally published by John Wiley and Sons. Reprinted and adapted with permission of Macmillan Publishing Company.

When considering the sounds of a language, it is useful to also consider the symbol system used to represent those sounds, or the orthography of the language. The orthography of a language is its writing system. Writing systems can be of three different types: pictographic, ideographic, and alphabetic. Pictographic systems use pictures to represent concepts and ideas. Pictographic systems were the earliest form of writing and date back to prehistoric times. The pictures representing hunts and social activities found in the caves of early man are examples of pictographic systems. The major drawback to pictographic systems is that all ideas are not representable by pictures. Pictographic systems led to the development of ideographic systems. In ideographic systems each word in the language is assigned to a specific symbol that shows no relationship to the way the word is pronounced. The Chinese and the Japanese have very well developed ideographic writing systems. English, although not ideographic in nature, does employ some ideographs—mathematical signs (+ , =), numerals (1, 2, 3), and abbreviations (Mr., Mrs.). With an ideographic system the reader either knows or doesn't know what the symbol means. There can be no "decoding" as we know it in the reading of English.

With an alphabetic system there is correspondence between the sounds of the language and the written symbols. English is an alphabetic system. Problems occur with an alphabetic system when there is not a one-to-one correspondence between the sounds in the language and the symbols used to represent those sounds. For example, in English there are approximately 44 sounds, yet we have a 26-letter system to represent those sounds. Consequently many letters stand for more than one sound. This lack of sound-symbol correspondence creates problems in learning to read and write. To compensate, alternate orthographic systems that have one symbol for each sound have been developed. One of the more well-known alternate orthographic systems is the Initial Teaching Alphabet (i.t.a.) developed by Pitman and St. John (1969) in England. That orthography is presented in Figure 2.5.

Using the i.t.a., children learn to read and write very quickly because of the close sound/symbol match. Unfortunately, when they transfer to traditional orthography, most, if not all, of the gains they have made vanish.

Semantics

Semantics is the study of meaning within a language. Before discussing semantics, we should note that it is a misrepresentation to consider meaning in language as independent from syntax, phonology, or pragmatics. We have already seen that syntax is intimately tied to meaning. Indeed the deep structure of an utterance *is* the underlying meaning. Syntax signals meaning, as do phonological and pragmatic aspects of language.

Semantics is concerned "with the meaning of words, the meaning of relations among words, sentences and other linguistic entities" (Bryen, 1983,

Figure 2.5

From *Elementary Language Arts* (p. 32) by P. DiStefano, J. Dole, and R. Marzano, 1984, New York: Macmillan. Originally published by John Wiley and Sons. Reprinted by permission.

p. 19). Semantic structure, even at the word level, is one of the most difficult aspects of language to analyze. How do we attach meaning to words? What do we know when we say we know a word? J. Katz and Fodor (1983) proposed the semantic-feature model for answers.

The semantic-feature model asserts that words are known or comprehended by specific semantic features they possess or do not possess. Figure 2.6 illustrates semantic features.

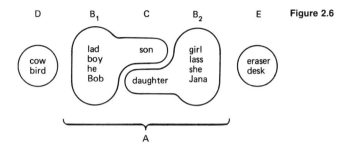

Figure 2.6

The words in set A are all human, animate, and two-legged. These are semantic features. The words in B_1 and B_2 are differentiated by the fact that all B_1 words contain the added semantic feature of *male*; all B_2 words have the semantic feature *female*. Words in set C do not share a male-female distinction, but they do share a semantic feature that might be called *siblings*.

Semantic-feature theory posits that, for each word we know, we associate a number of semantic features with it.

Cow: [animate] [concrete] [four-legged] [milk-producing] . . .
Girl: [animate] [concrete] [two-legged] [human] [female] . . .
Desk: [inanimate] [concrete] [four-legged] . . .

When we use a word or hear a word used we are aware of its semantic features. This explains why using some words together simply does not make sense. For example, Bryen (1983) stated that each of the sentences in the following list is anomalous because words with incompatible semantic features are used in conjunction with one another:

1. The chair drank some water.
2. The dog thought about his bone.
3. My son was angry at herself.
4. Her husband is a bachelor.

The study of semantics goes beyond the single-word level to groups of words in sentences. Words used in sentences have distinct semantic roles. To illustrate, consider the sentence "Stephen opened the door with a key." There are four distinct roles played by the words in this sentence:

SEMANTIC ROLE	DESCRIPTION	EXAMPLE
Agent	The person who causes the action to occur	Stephen
Action	The action that occurs	opened
Object	The receiver of the action generated by the agent	door
Instrument	The object used to facilitate the action	key

The study of the semantic roles of words in sentences has been formalized in various *case grammars*. Case grammars have been developed by such noted linguists as R. Brown (1973), Fillmore (1968), and Chafe (1970). For a moment recall McNeill's (1975) assertion that language organizes perception into objects, actions, states, or events. Case grammars might be viewed as the study of those organizational mental predispositions determined by language.

Case grammars have also been a powerful tool in explaining how we might store linguistic information in long-term memory. As an illustration, consider the following sentences:

1. Bill went to the drugstore.
2. There he met his sister.
3. They bought their father a coat.

Using case grammar categories, we can map how the information contained in these sentences might be organized in memory. Figure 2.7 contains such a mapping.

Finally, semantics extends to the study of broad frameworks in which words and sentences are used. D. Olson (1970) stated that words are not simply the names of things. Rather they "designate, signal or specify an intended referent relative to the set of contextual alternatives from which it must be differentiated" (p. 264). The speaker or writer must always contend with making clear the specific meaning of the words being used, reducing if possible all alternative meanings of the words except those intended. For example, the word *fair* can denote a carnival-like event, a description of the weather, one's hair coloring or skin pigment, or evenhanded behavior (Bartel, 1975). It is this broader context of meaning that is the focal point for the next area of linguistic study, pragmatics.

Pragmatics

Pragmatics is an extension of semantics. It is a relatively new area of linguistic study. According to van Dijk (1980), pragmatic theory is in its infancy. The attempt in pragmatics is to study the broadest framework in which language is produced and interpreted. One useful framework linguists employ is the *speech act*. A speech act, also called an *illocutionary act*, is the social act accomplished by the utterance of a meaningful expression in a given context (van Dijk, 1980, p. 175). It is the context in which speech acts occur that determines to a great extent the meaning being conveyed. To illustrate, consider the many meanings of the salutation "good morning." If said while walking out of a tent in the early morning in Yellowstone National Park, it can mean "It's probably not going to rain today." If said by one office mate to another in downtown Manhattan, it can be a substitute for "Hello." If said by a salesman over the telephone, it can

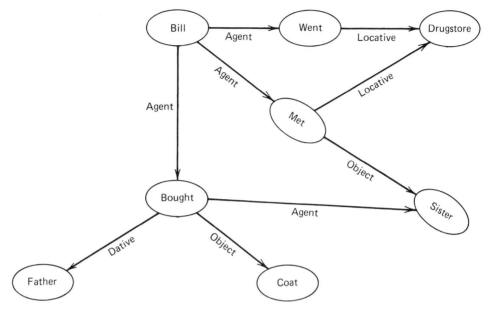

Figure 2.7

Note. From *Elementary Language Arts* (p. 40) by P. DiStefano, J. Dole, and R. Marzano, 1984, New York: Macmillan. Originally published by John Wiley and Sons. Reprinted by permission.

mean "Are you willing to have a discussion about what I would like to sell you?" We might say that pragmatics is the study of the messages behind the words, the identification of the intent behind the interaction.

According to Bruce (1980), the ability to express intention begins before a child can speak. It is evident at the single-word level (Bruner, 1973; Dore, 1974) and is elaborated over many years of development to the complexities of adult language (Shatz, 1977). Van Dijk (1980) asserted that there are seven basic intentions, or messages, behind language:

1. *Assertions:* statements of what the speaker considers to be fact
2. *Questions:* statements that indicate missing pieces of information for the speaker
3. *Requests:* statements that solicit specific action from the listener
4. *Promises:* statements that assert that the speaker will perform specific actions
5. *Commands:* statements that specify actions to be taken by the listener
6. *Threats:* statements that specify consequences to the listener if commands are not carried out
7. *Congratulations:* statements that indicate the value the speaker puts on actions performed by the listener.

In a somewhat different vein, Halliday (1975) has identified seven purposes for the use of language:

1. *Instrumental:* Language as a means of getting things. *Examples:* I want. I need.
2. *Regulatory:* Language as a means of controlling behavior or attitudes of others. *Examples:* Do as I tell you. Bring me this thing.
3. *Interactional:* Language as a means of getting along with others in a social context. *Examples:* It is nice to see you. Pleased to meet you.
4. *Personal:* Language as a means of expressing individuality or self. *Examples:* Here I come. I don't like this.
5. *Heuristic:* Language as a means of finding out new information. *Examples:* Tell me why. What is this called?
6. *Imaginative:* Language as a means of creating new worlds, making up stories or poetry. *Example:* Let's pretend.
7. *Informative:* Language as a means of telling someone something. *Examples:* I've got something to tell you. I want to report on something.

From these models of the pragmatic function of language we can see that the study of pragmatics is quite varied. However, it is one of the most promising areas of language research because it deals with the basic motivation and intentions of language use.

THE LINGUISTICALLY DIFFERENT

The family we are born into represents the linguistic environment in which we develop. Even within a given culture, these environments differ from region to region. These variations are manifested in many ways. Children from Boston learn to pronounce *car* as *cah*; children from Georgia say *y'all*.

Variations in the use of a language are called *dialect*. A given language typically consists of many dialects, or systematic variations in phonology, syntax, and semantics. In English, one of these dialects is accepted as most appropriate for classroom use. We call this *Standard English*. Standard English is that variation of spoken English considered to carry the most prestige within the American community (E.B. Smith, Goodman, & Meredith, 1976). The language of national TV broadcasters most closely represents this dialect. A problem arises when children who speak nonstandard English enter school and are confronted with a different dialect and a subculture supporting that dialect (Dole, 1981). The new subculture of the school rejects the child's language and attempts to eradicate it and replace it with the language of the classroom (Meier & Cazden, 1982). Shuy (1969) called this the "Bonnie and Clyde" tactic of teaching English. He quoted from one observation of how English was being taught to the Pine Ridge Sioux Indians:

Teachers are trained to criticize (the local dialect) as "bad English," and so, no sooner does the Indian child open his mouth to speak English, than he is branded publicly as speaking incorrectly. (p. 78)

The belief that standard English is better than other nonstandard dialects spawned the language-deficit hypothesis (Bereiter & Englemann, 1967), which was most prominent in the late 1960s. Proponents of the language-deficit hypothesis argued that a nonstandard dialect was actually an example of an under-developed dialect. Consequently it was "incorrect" (Cullinan, 1974). This hypothesis was supported by studies of nonstandard-English-speaking children that found their IQ scores below those of standard-English speakers. Several classic studies by sociolinguists such as Labov (1966) and Shuy, Wolfram, and Riley (1968) refuted the language-deficit hypothesis. They demonstrated that nonstandard dialects such as black English were systematic, rule governed, and logical variations of English. It was also found that many nonstandard-English-speaking children are highly verbal with their peers, "nonverbal" only in the more formal, standard-English-speaking classroom. Shuy (1977) summarized:

> . . . there is no problem internal to any language or dialect that affects intellectual development. The variation within a language and the way people evaluate this variation reflect the organization of the community, geographically and socially. (p. 106)

The past 15 years have seen a great deal of research on language differences. Box 2.1 portrays some common differences between black English and standard English.

One area of study that has greatly added to our knowledge of language differences is *social registers*. DeStefano (1973) defined registers as "a set of linguistic forms used in given social circumstances" (p. 191). Shuy (1977) demonstrated the continuum of language forms used in different social registers with a single sentence:

1. Hey! Don't bring no more a dem crates over here!
2. Hey! Don't bring no more a dose crates over here!
3. Hey! Don't bring no more of those crates over here!
4. Hey! Don't bring any more of those crates over here!
5. Please don't bring any more of those crates over here!
6. Gentlemen, will you kindly desist in your conveying those containers in this general direction? (p. 85)

Sociologists argue emphatically that there are no rights or wrongs associated with the continuum of registers, just differences. We all use different registers as we communicate with different people in different social situations. DeStefano (1973) gave an example of a teacher who was upset with the behavior

Box 2.1 *Some Phonological and Syntactic Differences Between Standard English and Black English*

Phonological

Feature	Standard English = Black English
1. r'lessness	tore = toe
	sore = so
2. l'lessness	toll = toe
	tool = to
3. th	mother = muvver
	tooth = toof
4. ing	going = goin
	hearing = hearin
5. ed	jumped = jump
	missed = miss
6. s, es	10 cents = 10 cent
	Mary's hat = Mary hat
7. sk	desk = des, desses
sp	wasp = was, wasses
st	test = tes, tesses

Syntactic

1. Double negation	Tom doesn't have = Tom ain't got no
2. Verb to be	She is always here = She be always here
	or She always here
3. past tense	He walked = He walk
4. Plurals and possessives	10 cents = 10 cent
	Mary's hat = Mary hat
5. Subject/verb agreement	John walks = John walk

Note. From *Elementary Language Arts* (p. 53) by P. DiStefano, J. Dole, and R. Marzano, 1984, New York: Macmillan. Originally published by John Wiley and Sons. Reprinted by permission.

of one of her students. "Hubert is a constant disrupter in class," she said to her principal. "Hubert has some difficulty settling down to do his work," she said to Hubert's parents. To her fellow teachers she said, "That kid's driving me nuts with his yackity-yacking," and to Hubert she said, "Hubert, be quiet" (p. 190).

Despite the fact that we know one dialect is not better than another dialect, many teachers still believe it is their duty to teach and reinforce "good English" (Standard English). The National Council of Teachers of English (NCTE) responded to this assertion by defining good English in the following way: "Good English is that form of speech which is appropriate to the speaker, true to the language as it is, and comfortable for the speaker and listener. It is the product of custom, neither cramped by rule nor freed from all restraint; it is never fixed, but changes with the organic life of the language" (see Lightner, 1965, p. 86). Paraphrased, good English, according to the NCTE, is the use of the appropriate register for the social situation in which language is being used.

When discussing language differences we refer not only to those children who speak nonstandard dialect but also to those children whose English is influenced by another language. These children come from homes and families in which English might not be spoken at all. The children of these families, in turn, might have limited English proficiency or none at all; they might be bilingual or even speak English only. Nevertheless, their home language and experiences are influenced by a culture and a language different from that of the Anglo, middle-class school. Many of these children, like nonstandard-English-speaking children, achieve at a slower rate than their white Anglo peers. Thonis (1976) listed four conditions that contribute to failure and confusion for these children:

1. Lack of experiences in the dominant culture from which concepts specific to the English-speaking community may be acquired
2. Inadequate oral command of the English language, which is the language of the instructional program
3. Lowered sense of self-esteem resulting from repeated feelings of inadequacy
4. Unrealistic curriculum, which imposes reading and writing English before listening comprehension and speaking fluency have been established (p. 1)

In 1974 a landmark U.S. Supreme Court decision, *Lau v. Nichols*, ruled that instruction in English to children who could not understand English was discriminatory. The Court argued that schools had to provide children with training in the English language because they could not understand the "language of instruction" of the classroom and were being deprived of their basic right to education. Guidelines for training were established by the former Department of Health, Education and Welfare.

Given that the target children represented a fairly heterogeneous group, Lau categories were established to help identify and serve these children. In all, five categories were established (see Box 2.2).

Teaching a heterogeneous group of language speakers is an incredible challenge, one many reading teachers face daily. To meet this challenge a teacher must be well trained, well informed and, above all, understanding of differences among children because of their varied language backgrounds. Recall from our discussion of linguistic relativity at the beginning of this chapter that language very possibly shapes perception. Those students in your class with a nonstandard or non-English-speaking background might have not only a different language but also a different reality from which they interpret the world. Meeting the needs generated by these differences requires a level of consciousness and sensitivity demanded in few other professions. As summarized by Dawson (1974).

The conflict that faces teachers in multra-cultural school settings is basically one of misunderstanding and lack of knowledge of the culture children bring to school. To work successfully, teachers need empathy, cultural understanding and all those qualities that characterize the best in humans in any vocation. (p. 54)

Box 2.2   *Lau Categories*

Degrees of Linguistic Ability to Speak English

A. *Monolingual* speaker of a language other than English (no English spoken).
B. *Dominant* speaker of a language other than English (speaks some English, but mostly speaks another language).
C. *Bilingual* (speaks both English and another language equally well).
D. *Dominant* speaker of English (speaks mostly English, but some of a language other than English).
E. *Monolingual English* (speaks only English, but comes from a home where another language is spoken).

Note. From *Elementary Language Arts* (p. 56) by P. DiStefano, J. Dole, and R. Marzano, 1984 New York: Macmillan. Originally published by John Wiley and Sons. Reprinted by permission.

SUMMARY

In this chapter we have discussed language and its relationship to cognition. At a very basic level, language is a labeling of perception. Some theorists suggest that language actually controls perception. There are four areas of language study that particularly relate to reading instruction: syntax, phonology, semantics, and pragmatics.

Syntax is the study of the structure of language. At a surface-structure level, syntax deals with word order; at a deep-structure level, syntax conveys meaning. A sense of syntax is so basic that many theorists consider it an innate quality of human beings. Phonology is the study of the sound system of a language. The human body is capable of making many different sounds. Any given language uses only a small subset of these sounds. Difficulty with learning to read occurs with English because its sound system does not match well with its symbol system (its orthography). Semantics is the study of meaning in a language, specifically the meaning conveyed by words. Words have semantic features that determine their meaning. When we know a word, we are aware of its semantic features and the various case forms it can take within an utterance. Pragmatics is the study of the contextual variables surrounding the use of language and their influence on the meaning of language. Pragmatics is primarily concerned with the various intentions of language.

In this chapter we also discussed the linguistically different, those students who speak a nonstandard dialect or who have learned English as a second language. The language of these students is not incorrect, only different. The teacher should be aware of these differences when planning instruction and be sure not to convey a message that a different dialect or language is wrong or substandard in any way.

3

ASPECTS OF READING

In this chapter we will consider some of the components of the reading process. We will not attempt to combine these into any unified theory of reading (we will do that in chapter 4); rather our purpose here is to begin laying the theoretical groundwork for describing the reading process. In this chapter we will consider six aspects of reading, or six types of analysis present in reading: (a) letter recognition, (b) phonemic analysis, (c) word identification, (d) syntactic analysis, (e) discourse-level analysis, and (f) schema-level analysis.

LETTER RECOGNITION

There has been a great deal of research on letter recognition. Probably the most well-known summary and discussion of the findings of that research is an article by Gough (1976) entitled "One Second of Reading." Gough described the myriad processes that probably occur within a single second of reading. Briefly, Gough asserted that reading begins with an eye fixation; the reader's eyes focus on a point slightly indented from the beginning of the line. The eyes remain in that fixation for about a quarter of a second or 250 milliseconds (msec). They then sweep 10 to 12 letter spaces to the right in what is called *saccadic* movement. (This term is derived from the French *saccade*, which, translated into English, means "jerk"). Saccadic movement, then, is rapid, irregular, spasmodic jumps from one position to another. This sweep consumes about 0.2 seconds or 200 msec. A new fixation then begins. When the end of a line is reached, the eye focuses on a slightly indented point at the beginning of the next line. This movement is called a *return sweep* and lasts about 400 msec. With each fixation, a visual pattern is reflected onto the retina. This sets in motion an intricate sequence of activity resulting in the formation of an icon.

An icon is a representation of the image on the retina. As Gough said, an icon is not a "little picture in the eye but a little picture in the head." (p. 511) These images are stored in what is called an *iconic buffer*. Studies have shown (Sperling, 1963) that this buffer can hold up to 17 unrelated letters. Gough further stated that an icon is an unidentified or unrecognized image, "a set of bars, slits, edges, angles and breaks" (p. 510).

An icon is recognized as a letter via the application of a letter-recognition mechanism. It is not known exactly what process this mechanism employs. There are two predominant theories: template matching and feature analysis. The template-matching theory postulates that we have an internal representation for each letter we can recognize; that is, we have a template for each letter. When we see a letter, we match its lines and shapes with our stored templates. Letters are simply compared to each stored template until a match is made.

The problem with the template-matching theory is that it does not adequately explain how we are able to recognize variant forms of letters. For example, how are we able to recognize that *a*, *a*, and *a* all belong to the same category? The obvious answer is that we have different templates for each of the various forms. Given the number of potential forms for letters, this explanation does not seem feasible.

The feature-analytic model asserts that we test each letter for critical features that distinguish it from others. As F. Smith (1982) stated, "the results of each test eliminate a number of alternatives until, finally, all uncertainty is reduced and identification is achieved" (p. 104). Each test is conducted by a feature analyzer, which looks for (is sensitive to) just one kind of feature. That is, one feature analyzer might determine if the configuration is round; another might determine if the configuration has a straight line at a particular angle. With this system, a letter would be recognized by matching the identified features with those critical to each letter.

This model seems much more feasible than the template model because it requires a less complex system for recognition. That is, relatively few operations are needed to finally recognize a letter. With the template-matching model, each template must be considered, until a match is made. With the feature-analytic model, a decision that a configuration has no curved shapes eliminates the possibility of certain letters such as *a*, *b*, *c*, and *d*.

Regardless of how it is accomplished, it is generally agreed that letter recognition is a key component of the reading process. Nicholson (1958), for example, concluded that knowledge of the names of letters is the best guarantee that a child will learn to read. This conclusion was based on the finding that tests measuring ability to associate the name of a letter with its form showed a high correlation with the learning of words. A.V. Olson's work (1958) implies that, while a knowledge of letter names does not assure success in learning to read, lack of that knowledge assures failure.

PHONEMIC ANALYSIS

Phonemic analysis refers to the act of translating or transcribing printed symbols (letters) into the sounds they represent. It has been hypothesized that letters and groups of letters, once recognized, are translated into a phonemic representation called *systemic phonemes* (Chomsky & Halle, 1968). Dechant and H.P. Smith (1977) stated that, to do this, the reader must first be able to discriminate between the sounds and the phonemes of a language. They stated that

> If the child cannot hear the sounds correctly, he normally cannot learn to speak them correctly. Furthermore, if he confuses or distorts sounds in speech, it frequently is impossible for him to associate the correct sound with the visual symbol. Thus, inadequate auditory discrimination leads to improper speech and ultimately to an incorrect association of sounds and printed symbols. (p. 105)

The Soviet psychologist Elkonian used the term *phonetic hearing* (1973) to describe the act of discriminating among the various phonemes of a language. Berry and Eisenson (1956) stated that it is the high-wavelength frequency sounds (/f/ /v/ /s/ /z/ /zh/ /sh/ /th/ /t/ /d/ /p/) that determine whether an individual can discriminate well among the sounds of English. That is, an individual who can discriminate among the high-frequency sounds in a language is also able to distinguish among the low-frequency sounds.

That phonemic transcription is a part of the reading process is generally accepted by most theorists. However, the importance of the process and how it is accomplished are debated. LaBerge and Samuels (1974) felt that phonemic transcription occurs at close to a letter-by-letter level. But it occurs so quickly that it is imperceptible at a conscious level. F. Smith (1982) felt that phonemic transcription occurs only as a "mediated" word-recognition process. That is, an individual attempts to decode at the phoneme level only if he or she cannot recognize the word as a unit.

WORD IDENTIFICATION

The next level of processing generally considered when studying reading is the word. How is a word identified during reading? The seminal study in the area of word recognition was conducted in 1969 by Reicher, whose subjects viewed words, geometric shapes, and single letters for brief durations and were then tested on their recall. In general, Reicher found that subjects recalled whole words better than familiar shapes or single letters. Put another way, subjects were more accurate in reporting what they saw when the stimulus was a word than when it was either a single letter or a shape. Reicher's results were later replicated by Cosky (1976). These findings have been taken as strong evidence that we do not read in a letter-by-letter fashion. If we did, it would be very strange that we would be more accurate at perceiving many units (in this case, the many letters in a word) than one unit.

Given that we recognize a word as a unit (at least at some level), we are faced with the same question encountered with letter recognition: How is it done? One common theory is analogous to the template theory of letter recognition. That is, we have an internal representation, or template, for each word. It has been estimated that the fluent reader is able to recognize about 50,000 different words on sight (F. Smith, 1982). Does this mean that the fluent reader has 50,000 pictures or representations of words? Even if the fluent reader did, this would not account for his or her ability to recognize variant forms. For example, if we have a mental picture for *cat*, do we also have one for *cat*, CAT, and cat?

A more plausible theory of word recognition is that it is done via the identification of spelling patterns. To illustrate: You probably have little trouble recognizing the nonsense words *vernalt* or *miper*. Readers have little difficulty identifying sequences of letters that are not English, providing they are close approximations to English (F. Smith, 1982). This indicates that there are some highly frequent letter combinations in the English language that might be used as part of the word identification process (Miller, Bruner, & Postman, 1954).

A common belief among reading teachers is that affixes (prefixes and suffixes) represent one general category of easily recognized spelling patterns. Johnson and Pearson (1984) discussed techniques for teaching various affixes under the assumption that a knowledge of them increases a student's chances of recognizing words. They cited research by Deighton (1959) that highlights 10 common prefixes with invariant meanings:

INVARIANT PREFIXES

apo	—	apoplexy, apogee
circum	—	circumnavigate, circumvent
equi	—	equidistant, equilibrium
extra	—	extracurricular, extrasensory
intra	—	intravenous, intramural
intro	—	introspection, introvert
mal	—	maladjusted, malapropism
mis	—	misapply, misunderstand
non	—	nonentity, nonprofit
syn	—	synagogue, synapse, synonym

Another unit of spelling, or unit with which to describe spelling patterns, is the morphograph (Dixon, 1977; Dixon & Engelmann, 1979). The study of morphographs was generated from the perceived inadequacy of the morpheme as a unit of study (Becker, Dixon, & Anderson-Inman, 1980). As Becker et al. explained (p. 2), the majority of English words are actually composites of smaller units of meaning. These smaller units are referred to by linguists as *morphemes*. Morphemes are irreducible units of meaning, each carrying a distinct semantic message. For example, the word *renovate* is comprised of three morphemes: *re* meaning "again"; *nov* meaning "new"; and *ate* meaning "to make or cause." At first glance, morphemes would appear to be a potentially rich source, in terms of their contribution to reading instruction. However, as Becker et al. pointed out, they do pose many procedural problems. For example, it is commonly accepted that the suffix *-tion* exists and is widely used to form nouns from Latin verbs and stems (e.g., *revolution*, *agitation*). However, a thorough analysis of all words ending in *-tion* reveals that the first letter, *t*, is actually a part of the original verb; the correct suffix is *-ion*. The study of morphographs is an attempt to improve upon, in an instructional sense, the study of morphemes. A morphograph is an irreducible unit of meaning in written English that adheres to a common spelling pattern within the words in which it is found. In their study of 26,000 high-frequency words, Becker et al. (1980) identified those morphographs they considered useful as instructional tools for reading and spelling.

A final unit used to analyze spelling patterns in words is the phonogram. A phonogram is a spelling pattern that always begins with a vowel (e.g., *ate*, *ole*, *aid*). Whereas morphemes and morphographs have some inherent meaning, phonograms are pure spelling patterns. Other than affixes, phonograms are probably the most common instructional tool for improving word recognition through spelling patterns.

Even though theorists cannot agree on the precise process of word identification, it is clear that it involves meaning. That is, even though we may use spelling patterns (e.g., affixes, morphographs) in the process, fundamentally it involves attaching meaning to words. Recall that in chapter 2 we emphasized the point that language is a process of labeling phenomena. The words in a language are those labels. When we recognize a word we activate or recall the experiences we have associated with the word. Figure 3.1 is a fanciful depiction of this point.

Figure 3.1

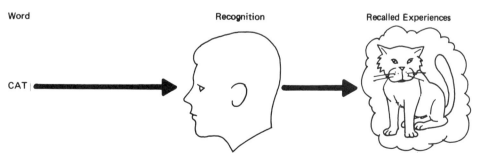

Word   Recognition   Recalled Experiences

CAT

From this perspective it can be said that you cannot "identify" a word for which you have no associated meaning (recalled experiences). This is particularly important to remember as a teacher of reading. *Word identification is not recognizing spelling patterns.* It is attaching meaning to a symbol (a word). Spelling patterns can aid in this process, but they are only a means to an end, not the end in themselves.

SYNTACTIC ANALYSIS

If independent unrelated words were presented to a person at the normal rate of reading, she or he would lose track very quickly. The fact that we can follow normal speech or read written information indicates that we must be organizing or "reading" the information we hear and read into large chunks. These larger chunks are determined by our internalized set of rules for syntax.

As we saw in chapter 2, it has been hypothesized that the rules governing syntax are innate, that is, we are born with them. Stated in other words, a child enters the world with a built-in disposition for language that he or she adapts to the language being learned (Chomsky, 1957). To obtain a sense of the innateness of syntactic rules, consider Table 3.1, taken from a study by R. Brown (1972).

In this table, Brown described children's imitations of model sentences spoken by their mothers. In their imitations, children preserved the word order of the modeled sentences and were highly systematic in their selection of words to be retained. These constructions by children were not simply rote imitations. Children also exhibited the ability to produce novel sentences not heard of in adult speech, for example, "gone milk," "more story," "off coat." These novel sentences contained the same structure as the children's imitations.

Over time, these early structures expand until they take on the more

Table 3.1

MODEL UTTERANCE	CHILD'S IMITATION
Tank car.	Tank car.
Wait a minute.	Wait a minute.
Daddy's briefcase.	Daddy briefcase.
Fraser will be unhappy.	Fraser unhappy.
He's going out.	He go out.
That's an old-time train.	Old-time train.
It's not the same dog as Pepper.	Dog Pepper.
No, you can't write on Mr. Cromer's shoe.	Write Cromer shoe.

Note. From *Pycholinguistics: Selected Papers* (p. 81) by R. Brown, 1972, New York: Macmillan Publishing Co., The Free Press. Copyright © 1970 by the Free Press. Reprinted by permission.

familiar characteristics of adult syntax. Ringler and Weber (1984) stated, "The development of this rule-governed grammar by children is first evident with the production of two-word constructions at about eighteen months to two years and continues with the production of three-word constructions in the second year" (p. 57). By the time a child has reached 3 ½, she or he has mastered the basic syntax of a language and can produce sentences of indefinite length (Crystal, 1976).

The reader, then, uses his or her knowledge of syntax to organize information into units of meaning larger than the word. Experiments by Bever, Lackner, and Kirk (1969) indicate that we tend to chunk semantic information, using syntactic boundaries. That is, the reader uses his or her knowledge of syntax to organize information or predict what information will come next. For example, Mehler and Carey (1967) found that, when readers expected one sort of structure (e.g., *They are buying gloves*), this expectation interfered with their ability to identify a sentence with a structure that looked identical but was in fact different (e.g., *They are boxing gloves*).

Huggins and Adams (1980) reported that there is a great deal of research evidence to indicate that clausal units form very strong boundaries for language processing. For example, Garret, Bever, and Fodor (1966) asked subjects to identify where they heard an extraneous noise (a click) in recorded sentences. Regardless of where the clicks were placed, subjects tended to hear them at clause boundaries in sentences. Although the methodology and interpretations of such click experiments have been criticized (G.M. Olson & Clark, 1976; Watt, 1970), the vast majority of research in syntax strongly suggests that we use clausal boundaries as an aid to decoding (Carroll, & Bever, 1976; Fodor, Bever, and Garrett, 1974).

Another way of considering the role of syntax in language processing is to start with the observation that the vehicle of language permits a message to be expressed only in sequential fashion. Our knowledge of, and expectations about, syntax help us unravel the meaning of the sequential representation of the information. If the sequential information is not presented in a familiar structure, we have difficulty interpreting it. To illustrate, Huggins and Adams (1980) reported that most children are able to understand the sentences "The dog chased the cat," "The cat killed the rat," "The rat ate the malt" even when they are combined into a single sentence with embedded clauses.

[This is] the dog, that chased the cat that killed the rat, that ate the malt.

Such a structure is called a *right-branching structure* (clauses are embedded to the right) and is very common in English. However, if we take these same sentences and combine them in what is called a *center-embedding fashion*, the construction is almost unintelligible.

[This is] the malt, that the rat, that the cat, that dog chased killed ate.

This is because right-branching embeddings are quite common within English syntax, whereas center embeddings are not.

We might say, then, that syntactic analyisis is the use of our knowledge of syntax to set up expectations about the way information will be presented in oral and written language.

DISCOURSE-LEVEL ANALYSIS

Discourse-level processing refers to recognition of the overall structure and format of the information being read or heard. It might be likened to recognizing the syntax for an entire passage, not just a sentence. To illustrate discourse-level processing, observe your thoughts as you read the following:

Once upon a time . . .

What do you expect to come after this phrase? Most likely you expect to read about a story. Something will happen to someone. The story will describe how the person reacted, whether or not the person's goal was accomplished. The story will occur during a particular time and in a particular place. It will have different characters; some of them will be "good guys," some will be "bad guys." All of this and more is part of your set of expectations accompanying the phrase *once upon a time*.

The reason you have this set of expectations is that you have an internalized grammar, so to speak, relative to discourse structure. This grammar tells you that information you read or hear will generally be organized in specific structures. One such structure is narration. Consequently, when you read the phrase *once upon a time*, you expect a narrative structure to follow.

It has been hypothesized (Rumelhart, 1975) that the processing of information at the discourse level probably occurs in a hierarchial fashion, or what is called a *top-down* manner, in which the larger structures activate the smaller structures. (We will consider top-down processing in more depth in chapter 4.) Commonly, theorists make distinctions among three types, or layers, of discourse-level structures: (a) simple relationships between ideas, (b) basic patterns among ideas, and (c) superstructures.

To facilitate the discussion of the three different types of discourse structures, we will first consider the concept of a proposition. Most theories of long-term memory posit that linguistic information is stored in a propositional format. Roughly speaking, propositions are conceptual structures that are the minimal bearers of truth or satisfaction. Thus, "John" is a concept but is not information that can be true or false, whereas "John is ill" would be a proposition because it could be true or false (van Dijk, 1980, p. 207). Propositions, then, are sets of concepts that together make up information that can be true or false, or example, satisfied and dissatisfied. We should note here that we are defining propositions in a restricted manner, one that equates a proposition with a linguistic clause. Propositions have also been used to describe units larger and smaller than clauses.

There is ample research evidence to show the primacy of proposition recognition in information processing. For example, Bransford and Franks (1971) found that comprehension could be characterized as a process of synthesizing information into semantic chunks that are propositional in nature. Sachs (1967) found that, although memory for specific aspects of a sentence faded quickly, memory for the propositional gist of a sentence was remarkably stable. Working with children, Pearson (1974/75) obtained results corroborating the findings of Bransford and Franks and Sachs. Propositions are so basic to the processing of information that we might say that a proposition is a good operational definition of an *idea*.

Simple relationships, as defined here, address the issue of how one proposition might be related to another proposition. To illustrate, consider the following:

> It's a nice day but . . .
> I'm in a bad mood.

Here there are two propositions: (a) "It's a nice day," and (b) "I'm in a bad mood." There is a relationship between these two propositions signaled by the linguistic connective *but*. *But* commonly signals what is known as a *contrastive relationship* between propositions. Many researchers and theorists have identified different types of relationships between propositions. Halliday and Hasan (1976) identified five major classes of relationships: reference, reiteration, ellipsis, conjunction, and lexical reiteration and collocation. Meyer (1975) listed 17 types of relationships or "rhetorical predicates," some of which are listed in Table 3.2. In a similar fashion, Pitkin (1977) has identified 12 types of relationships, Turner and Greene (1977) 8, and deBeaugrande (1980) 8.

Table 3.2

RELATIONSHIP	DESCRIPTION	EXAMPLE
Alternative	Equally weighted options	Sue is short, and Sally is short.
Response	Equally weighted questions, remarks, replies, or problems, solutions	What is life? What is death?
Equivalent	Restatement of information in a different way	Mark was tired. He was exhausted.
Adversative	Relating what did not happen to what did happen	Bill went to the store. He did not buy anything.
Covariance	Cause and effect, reason and result	Steve left because Brian left.

As it relates to reading, we are suggesting that a crucial component of the reading process is the identification, or recognition, of these relationships among propositions. There is ample research evidence to support this assertion. For example, it has been found that, when a reader or listener comprehends information presented in linguistic form, there is a strong drive to identify the referential links between ideas (propositions). If the reader or listener cannot identify these referential ties, she or he backtracks until a "link" is identified or inferred. If no linkage is found, processing breaks down (Kintsch, 1979; Kintsch & van Dijk, 1978; Meyer, 1975; Waters, 1978).

One of the primary ways an individual recognizes relationships between propositions is by linguistic cues or signals. Many of the relationships have explicit words and phrases that signal their presence. For example, following are some of the words and phrases that signal what has been called an *equality relationship* (Marzano, 1983):

> and, moreover, equally, too, besides, furthermore, likewise, similarly, as well, in addition, besides

It has been shown that a knowledge of these connective devices is an important factor in the reading process (Robertson, 1968). Similarly, E. Katz and Brent (1968) found that both first and sixth graders preferred descriptions of causal relationships that were made explicit by a linguistic connective. These findings were corroborated by Marshall and Glock (1978–79), who found that explicitly stated relationships facilitated the recall of information. We will consider the use of relationship signals as instructional tools in chapter 9.

The recognition of relationships among propositions accounts for the comprehension of what is referred to as the *microstructure of information*, the meaning of those explicitly stated propositions and their relationships to one another. However, the efficient processing of information demands that ideas be organized into more global structures. It has been suggested that the process of comprehension is that of identifying "models" or embedded "pattern" structures that fit the information (Schank, Goldman, Reiger, and Reisbeck, 1975). It is this type of processing that we refer to as *pattern level analysis*. Patterns are groups of propositions that have some distinct ordering of relationships. In chapter 9 we will consider five basic pattern types. However, as a brief illustration, consider the following:

> Let me tell you about my car.
> It has whitewall tires and is painted red.
> It has a 430 horsepower engine.
> It can do the quarter mile in 9.6 seconds.
> It has . . .
> It . . .

You would expect most of the statements that might follow to be about the author's car. Another way of saying this is that all of the statements except the first perform a specific function; they provide information about the concept *car*. When a group of statements performs a specific function, we call that group of statements a *pattern*.

It has been shown that the more organizational patterns are made salient in information to be read, the easier the information is to process and retrieve (Frederiksen, 1975; Kintsch, 1974; Meyer, 1975). It has also been suggested that textbooks be written in more explicit patterns, to facilitate comprehension, and that students be given more direct instruction in pattern-level analysis (J.R. Anderson, 1976; Pearson, 1981). Supporting this suggestion is a rapidly growing body of research that indicates that patterns can be explicitly taught to, and used by, students to facilitate the processing and retrieval of information (P. Alexander, Goetz, Palmer, & Mangano, 1983; Greenwald & Pederson, 1983; Leslie & Jett-Simpson, 1983; Taylor & Samuels, 1983).

At a very high level of discourse organization are superstructures, "patterns of patterns" if you will. Whereas a basic pattern of information might span a few sentences or even a few paragraphs, a superstructure might encompass an entire chapter or an entire book. DeBeaugrande (1980) listed eight types of superstructures: descriptive, narrative, argumentative, literary, poetic, scientific, didactic, and conversational. Van Dijk (1980) listed four types of superstructures: narratives, arguments, scholarly reports, and newspaper articles. A superstructure is simply a large pattern a reader or listener can expect to find when processing information. For example, when you read a novel, you expect the first part of the book to provide some background information (e.g., the setting, characteristics of characters). Not far into the story, you expect some event to occur that will cause a reaction by the characters. Finally, you expect a conclusion or ending to the story. These expectations are generated by your internalized superstructure for a story.

As is the case with basic patterns, a very consistent finding within the research literature is that readers of all ages tend to recall the major parts of the superstructure for information read (Mandler & Johnson, 1977; Meyer, 1975; Thorndyke, 1977; van Dijk & Kintsch, 1976).

Before leaving this discussion of discourse-level processing, we should cite one piece of research that highlights the importance of the whole domain of relationship, pattern, and superstructure recognition. In 1965, deGroot tested the hypothesis that chess masters were better at chess than nonmasters because they had better memories. DeGroot presented the masters and nonmasters with chessboards on which the pieces were arranged as you might find them in the middle of a chess game, and then took them away. He then asked the subjects to reconstruct the arrangements of the boards after a sufficient amount of time had passed for the information to be wiped from short-term memory. As expected, the masters had almost total recall; the nonmasters had virtually no recall. However, when the masters and nonmasters were presented with a random arrangement of chess pieces, the masters could do no better than the nonmasters. These findings were interpreted as evidence that the masters had, over time, internalized patterns of chess arrangements that they recognized during play and used as a basis for strategy planning. In effect, it was their ability to recognize many different types of patterns that made them masters at chess. Likewise, students' ability to recognize relationships, patterns, and superstructures within information they read and hear determines, at least partially, the extent to which the information is efficiently processed. We will consider how to use relationships, patterns, and superstructures as instructional tools in chapter 9.

SCHEMA-LEVEL ANALYSIS

Schema-level analysis refers to understanding information as an organized whole. It is perhaps the highest level of information organization. We might say that relationships represent one level of information organization. Patterns are a level higher in terms of amount of information organized. Superstructures are at still a higher level. Finally schemata (the plural of schema) are at the highest level of information organization. To obtain a sense of what is meant by schema-level analysis, try reading the following passage:

> If the balloons popped the sound wouldn't be able to carry since everything would be too far away from the correct floor. A closed window would also prevent the sound from carrying, since most buildings tend to be well insulated. Since the whole operation depends upon a steady flow of electricity, a break in the middle of the wire would also cause problems. Of course, the fellow could shout but the human voice is not loud enough to carry that far. An additional problem is that a string could break on the instrument. Then there could be no accompaniment to the message. It is clear that the best situation would involve less distance. Then there would be fewer potential problems. With face to face contact, the least number of things could go wrong.
> (Bransford & Johnson, 1972, p. 719)

No doubt you understand whole sentences and phrases in this passage. You might even recognize some patterns, but you probably do not get the gist of the passage. In other words, it makes no sense as a whole. This is because you have no schema for the information. Now consider Figure 3.2 and then reread the passage. Figure 3.2 should provide the necessary schema with which to interpret the passage.

Schemata are the largest organizational blocks used to store information, and, as we shall see in chapter 4, they play a fundamental role in the reading process. Rumelhart (1980) stated that schemata are fundamental elements upon which all information processing depends. "Schemata are employed in the process of interpreting sensory data (both linguistic and nonlinguistic), in retrieving

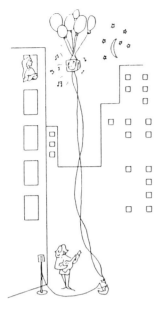

Figure 3.2

From J.D. Bransford and M.K. Johnson, Contextual Prerequisites for Understanding: Some investigations of comprehension and recall. *Journal of Verbal Learning and Verbal Behavior 11*, pp., 717–726. Copyright 1972 by Academic Press. Reprinted by permission.

information from memory, in organizing actions, in determining goals and subgoals, in allocating resources, and, generally in guiding the flow of processing in the system" (pp. 33–34).

To illustrate the use of schema at a nonlinguistic level, consider the example by Palmer (1975). As reported by Rumelhart (1980, p. 46), the object on top (A) in Figure 3.3 is easily recognizable as a face but not when the parts

A.

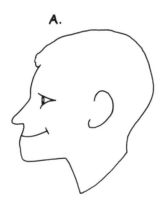

B.

Figure 3.3

are out of sequence (B). Consequently, it cannot be that we recognize the parts first and then the whole. Rather, the parts suggest possible schemata. When we settle on a schema that seems to fit the data, we use that schema to interpret the remaining information.

When comprehending information heard or read, you not only recognize the general structure of the information (discourse-level processing) but also identify the general background of the information (Brewer, 1980). In short, your schema for a given piece of information contains all the pertinent world knowledge about the information: the different nuances of meaning, the purpose of the message, the appropriateness of the information. We might say that human beings organize the world in schemata. Obviously schemata play a central role in an individual's interaction with the world. We will discuss the instructional use of schemata in chapter 10.

SUMMARY

In this chapter we have discussed six components of the reading process: (a) letter recognition, (b) phonemic analysis, (c) word identification, (d) syntactic analysis, (e) discourse analysis, and (f) schema analysis. Letter recognition is the process of discriminating among different letters, probably by analyzing the distinctive features for each letter. Phonemic analysis is the recognition of the select sounds used within a particular language, as distinct from the many possible sounds the human voice can make. Word recognition is the identification of words either immediately or through recognizing common spelling patterns or smaller units of meaning within a word. Syntactic analysis is the use of the structure of the language to identify clause and sentence boundaries within oral and written language. Knowledge of syntax is used to select which information to read and to predict forthcoming information. Discourse-level analysis is the identification of basic relationships, patterns, and superstructures of ideas. Discourse-level analysis can be described as the identification of the structure of large blocks of information. Schema-level analysis is the use of the remaining background information about a passage not covered by the other types of analysis. Schemata contain the information that unifies topics. Information in schemata creates the framework to organize what is read into a unified whole.

MOI

ies about the reading process. We
nd theory on brain behavior and
fect reading instruction.

uld first acknowledge the difficulty
Huey stated that

nen we read would almost be the acme
vould be to describe very many of the
nind, as well as to unravel the tangled
rformance that civilization has learned

for a reading teacher to consider
es that a teacher's beliefs about the
ght and how it is taught (Shavelson
id Kamil (1978) have suggested that
ts the type of activities the teacher
her believes that the reading process
begins with the printed word and then goes to meaning, then she or he emphasizes basic decoding skills. If the teacher believes that reading is basically a

search for meaning, then she or he teaches children to generate meaningful hypotheses about what to expect next in the text. Barr's (1975) case study found that teachers varied greatly in the amount and timing of their grouping practices in reading. She postulated that this was due to their varying beliefs about the reading process and how it should be taught and reinforced. For example, teachers whose model for reading was basically comprehension oriented rather than decoding oriented were more likely to group students for basal reading activities than for phonics instruction.

In this section we will consider four views about reading, or four models of reading: (a) the top-down model, (b) the bottom-up model, (c) the interactive model, and (d) the production-system model. These models will form the framework for our discussion throughout the text of various diagnostic and instructional techniques.

Prior to the mid-1960s, the commonsense view of reading was that it is a precise process involving exact, detailed sequential perception and identification of letters, word spelling patterns, and larger units. Ken Goodman (1967) challenged this commonsense perspective, speculating that reading is an inexact process of predicting what will come next and then confirming or disconfirming those predictions. Goodman developed his theory of reading by studying the mistakes or "miscues" of children as they read aloud. He noticed that, when children were reading for meaning, they would make errors that were logical but did not necessarily follow the letter-sound patterns associated with the word they were reading. For example, they might say the word *boat* for *ship* or *car* for *automobile*. From this, he reasoned that children were using information from their schemata to interpret print, rather than relying on bits of information about letters or words. In other words, reading was a search for meaning or a process of matching the information in the text to the reader's knowledge base.

Such a notion is called a top-down model of reading. That is, relative to the aspects of reading discussed in chapter 3, the top-down model assumes that reading begins at the schema level and works down to the letter level, as in the diagram.

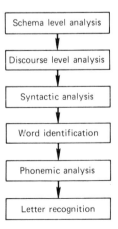

The reader generates guesses using his or her higher level knowledge. The flow of information runs from the top down. As described by Ken Goodman (1967), reading is a psycholinguistic guessing game. It involves an interaction between thought and language.

> Efficient reading does not result from precise perception and identification of all elements, but from skill in selecting the fewest, most productive, cues necessary to produce guesses which are right the first time. The ability to anticipate that which has not been seen, of course, is vital in reading, just as the ability to anticipate what has not yet been heard is vital in listening. (p. 468)

The top-down model of reading was also popularized by Frank Smith (1975).

The bottom-up model asserts that there is an opposite flow of information. The assumption is that the processing of information proceeds from the smallest unit to the largest, as in the next diagram.

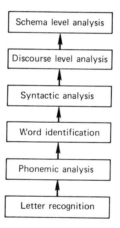

Gough (1976) is commonly cited as one of the major proponents of the bottom-up approach. As Ringler and Weber (1984) characterized Gough's bottom-up model of reading, processing proceeds step by step to higher stages, moving from letter recognition to decoding at the phoneme level, to word recognition, to syntactic and semantic characteristics (discourse- and schema-level analyses). The reader uses the information at one level to move up to the next level. The act of reading is one in which the reader plods through sentences letter by letter, word by word, building comprehension "brick by brick."

To compromise with the bottom-up versus top-down debate, interactive models have been developed. Basically an interactive model posits that a reader uses both bottom-up and top-down strategies when reading. Rumelhart (1977) is usually credited with the early development of interactive models. McNeil (1984) described the interaction between top-down and bottom-up processes in the following way. The top-down process calls for activating schemata and applying them when setting expectations for reading and making inferences. The reader's goals and expectations strongly influence what is read and selected for reading. In contrast, bottom-up processing occurs when the reader attends to the text and then searches for structures (schemata) within which to fit the incoming information. The reader monitors information from the bottom up, replacing initial expectations with new ones signaled by the text (p. 4).

In other words the interactive model asserts that a reader commonly begins with one approach; if this does not work, the reader shifts to another. To illustrate the interaction between top-down and bottom-up processes, read the following passage and try to observe your thoughts as you do so.

> The procedure is actually quite simple. First you arrange things into different groups. Of course, one pile may be sufficient depending on how much there is to do. If you have to go somewhere else due to lack of facilities, that is the next step, otherwise you are pretty well set. It is important not to overdo things. That is, it is better to do too few things at once than too many. In the short run, this may not seem important but complications can easily arise. A mistake can be expensive as well. At first, the whole procedure will seem complicated. Soon, however, it will become just another facet of life. It is difficult to foresee any end to the necessity for this task in the immediate future, but then, one can never tell. After the procedure is completed, one arranges the materials into different groups again. Then they can be put into their appropriate places. Eventually they will be used once more, and the whole cycle will then have to be repeated. However, that is part of life. (Bransford & Johnson, 1972, p. 400)

Most people find this passage difficult to read until they are given the information that it is about washing clothes. Given that you did not know what the passage was about, you probably began with a bottom-up strategy. As you read you were searching for a schema with which to interpret the passage. Within the first few seconds of reading, you probably generated a number of possible schemata with which to interpret the passage, most likely schemata about different procedures you are aware of. You then read to confirm your hypothesis, using a top-down approach. You kept on reading until you realized that you had selected an inappropriate schema; at that time you shifted to a bottom model in search of another schema. You probably read through the entire paragraph, continually switching back and forth between top-down and bottom-up strategies and never identifying the appropriate schema with which to interpret the paragraph.

The final model of reading we will consider is the production-system model. It represents an entirely different way of looking at reading. The production-system model of reading is based primarily on the work in artificial intelligence of John Anderson (1983). Anderson postulated that we store information in cognitive structures called *productions*. These operate much like computer programs in the mind. Anderson postulated that we have productions that allow us to perform very simple tasks and productions that allow us to perform highly complex tasks. Complex tasks are accomplished by stringing together single productions to form production networks, or production systems.

Reading is one of those complex processes that requires individual productions connected into a complex system.

The important distinction made by the production-system theory is that between procedures and the information necessary to carry out a procedure. As an illustration, consider the following example of a production:

IF   person 1 is the father of person 2
        and person 2 is the father of person 3
THEN   person 1 is the grandfather of person 3.

To complete this production an individual must know (a) the concepts *person*, *father*, and *grandfather*; and (b) the order of conditions and consequent action within the production. Another way of saying this is that an individual must know factual information and strategies for using that factual information. In more technical terms, factual information is sometimes referred to as *declarative information*; strategies for using declarative information are called *procedural information*. As Sywlester (1985) pointed out, declarative information contains the who/what/where/when/why facts about the world. Procedures tell us how to use those facts. The two are inexorably linked. Procedures are built on facts. Without them there could be no procedures; without procedures, facts are relatively useless. The accomplishment of a goal is a constant interplay, via production systems, between declarative and procedural information. This is particularly true about reading; it is a constant interplay between strategies for understanding the printed word and the necessary factual information for activating those strategies. Without both components, reading is inefficient. Top-down, bottom-up, and interactive models of reading do not make this distinction clearly, although the use of factual versus procedural information is implied in each of the models. We introduce the production-system theory of reading as a model that cuts across the other models; it adds a distinction (that between declarative and procedural information) to the other models that we find very useful for instructional purposes.

TRANSLATING READING MODELS INTO INSTRUCTION

Although section two of this text deals specifically with the instructional implications of each of the four models, we should note here that there have been attempts to translate some of them into instructional pedagogy. For example, the bottom-up model of reading is commonly translated into what is called a *skills approach*. The skills approach is characterized by the belief that the reader must master all the subcomponents of the reading process before reading can be fluent. This is usually done via drill and practice exercises. For example, Gross, Carr, Dornseif, and Rouse (1974) wrote: "A critical part of any reading or language arts program is the teaching of the skills underlying the reading process. Without the basic skills of word discrimination, vocabulary development and comprehension, it is virtually impossible for a student to read new material with success" (p. 782).

Within the skills model of instruction, the teacher progresses through a set of skills that, for the most part, can be written in behavioral form. For example, Gross et al. (1974) listed a set of behavioral objectives constituting a skills program: "Given a sentence with a heteronym, the student will identify, correctly from the context, the syllable that is accented" (p. 784). Box 4.1 lists some of the subskills commonly identified in skills approaches.

The top-down model of reading is commonly translated into what is called the *whole-language* approach to reading. Here the emphasis is on having the child (a) recognize that reading is a process of obtaining meaning, and (b) utilize his or her knowledge of the world and of information in print to extract

---

Box 4.1 *Partial List of Subskills Commonly Found in Skills Approaches*

Word Recognition

  Basis sight vocabulary
  Direction words
  Abbreviations
  Contractions
  Common signs

Word Analysis

  Auditory discrimination
  Initial consonant sounds auditorily
  Substitution of initial consonant sounds
  Ending sounds
  Vowels
  Short vowel sounds
  Long vowel sounds
  Initial clusters
  Diagraphs and diphthongs
  Phonetic irregularities
  Common endings of thyming words
  Suffixes
  Prefixes
  Syllabication

Vocabulary

  Context clues
  Classification
  Analogies
  Antonyms
  Homonyms

meaning. Underlying the whole-language approach is the assumption that children will naturally learn the necessary subskills of reading if their attention is on generating meaning while they read. We might say that the whole-language approach emphasizes the *gestalt* of reading. Commonly, proponents of the whole-language approach use language-experience activities to teach beginning reading, although the language-experience approach (or LEA) was developed long before whole-language instruction became popular.

During the 1960s, Doris Lee and Roach Van Allen (1963) extended the work of Sylvia Ashton-Warner (1963) to develop the language experience approach. Allen (1976) later described the philosophy of the language experience approach.

> I can think about what I have experienced and imagined.
> I can talk about what I can think about.
> What I talk about I can express in some other form.
> Anything I record I can recall through speaking or reading.
> I can read what I can write by myself or what other people write for me to read.

When practiced, the LEA has children talk about their experiences. This is translated to print and then becomes the subject matter for the students' reading. We will consider the language-experience approach in greater depth in chapters 8, 9 and 10.

Another technique commonly associated with the top-down model is the Directed Reading-Thinking Activity (DR-TA) (Stauffer, 1970). With the DR-TA, children are asked to identify what they already know about a story or topic before they begin reading. They then make predictions about the story and read to confirm or disconfirm their predictions. We will discuss the DR-TA process in more depth in chapter 10.

The interactive model of reading has no strong instructional derivative. Commonly, proponents of this approach rely heavily on whole-language techniques but supplement their instruction with selected skills. The strong emphasis, however, is on meaning. Because of this we will generally combine the interactive approach with the top-down model as we discuss instructional techniques throughout the text.

Production-system theory is new enough within reading education that no distinct instructional programs have been developed. However, production-system theory does have some fairly straightforward instructional implications. One is that "factual" information relative to reading should be explicitly taught to students. For example, we might conclude that such elements as letter-sound relationships, phonograms, sight words, discourse patterns, and superstructures should be overtly taught to students. From this perspective we might conclude that the production-system model is aligned with the skills, or bottom-up, approach. However, in addition to factual knowledge pertinent to reading, the production-system model implies that specific strategies for reading should be taught. A fairly consistent finding in the research has been that good readers use explicit strategies that they can articulate (A. Brown & Smiley, 1977; Di-Stefano, Noe, & Valencia, 1981; Pressley, Levin, & Bryant, 1983). Recently it has been found that explicit instruction in reading strategies can significantly improve a reader's comprehension (Pressley & Levin, 1983a, 1983b). It has also been hypothesized that good readers bring different strategies to different types of discourse. For example, van Dijk and Kintsch (1983) suggested different reading strategies for different types of material.

Translated into instruction, then, the production-theory model would identify specific declarative information and procedures, or strategies, important to reading. As mentioned previously, production theory is new enough that no complete model of reading has been developed. However, with some fore-thought, many of the skills and competencies mentioned thus far can be categorized into declarative versus procedural information. For example, the levels of analysis used to describe the top-down and bottom-up models can be described in terms of the necessary declarative and procedural knowledge. This is done in Table 4.1, which implies a two-pronged approach to reading instruction. One prong would emphasize declarative information, the other the procedures or strategies that utilize the declarative information. Such an approach would also have implications for diagnosis. Using a production-theory model, the reading specialist would try to identify whether a student was lacking the declarative information necessary to perform a reading skill, the skill itself, or both. As we discuss diagnostic and instructional techniques in later chapters, we will consider their utility with a production-theory model and the other models presented here.

OTHER CHARACTERISTICS OF READING

Although not explicitly stated in reading-process models, there are a number of characteristics that are integral parts of reading. Here we will consider four essential characteristics: (a) inference, (b) attention and capacity, (c) metacognition, and (d) attitudes and motivation.

The Role of Inference

One characteristic of the reading process that is implied in all models is the role of inference. We might say that most of the information we think we comprehend is actually inferred. As an illustration, consider the following:

> The two children saw the book of matches and immediately began thinking of games to play. By midafternoon the house was engulfed in flames.

If you observed your thoughts as you read these two sentences, you probably noticed that you made many inferences regarding what happened between the

Table 4.1 Declarative and Procedural Knowledge Necessary for Various Levels of Analysis

LEVEL OF ANALYSIS	DECLARATIVE KNOWLEDGE	PROCEDURAL KNOWLEDGE
Schema-level analysis	General background information obtained from life experiences	Strategies for indentifying the general idea of what is to be read Predicting what will happen next
Discourse-level analysis	Superstructures of information organization Patterns of information organization Types of relationships between ideas (propositions) Linguistic signals for patterns and relationships	Strategies for identifying superstructures, patterns, and relationships in written information
Syntactic analysis	Syntactic rules of English	Strategies for using syntax to identify an unknown word Strategies for predicting what will come next within a sentence
Word identification	Basic sight vocabulary Spelling patterns, affixes, morphographs, and phonograms	Strategies for identifying words using spelling patterns, affixes, morphographs, and phonograms
Phonemic analysis	Phonemes of the English language Auditory discrimination among phonemes Letter/sound relationships	Phonics strategies
Letter recognition	Lines and shapes used in English orthography The alphabet	Strategies for recognizing unknown letters

events stated in the first sentence and the events stated in the second sentence. Specifically, you might have inferred that the children began playing with the matches and accidentally caught the house on fire. In a propositional sense, the information that was stated and the information that was inferred might be represented in the following way:

Proposition 1: The children saw the matches (stated).
Proposition 2: The children began thinking of games (stated).
Proposition 3: The games included using the matches (inferred).
Proposition 4: While the children were playing games with the matches, the house caught on fire (inferred).
Proposition 5: The house caught on fire in the early afternoon (inferred).
Proposition 6: By midafternoon the house was engulfed in flames (stated).

As you can see, much of the information that was "comprehended" about the two sentences was an "elaboration" on what was actually stated. It might have been that the children decided to play with the matches outside and the house was struck by lightning, or that the children's games had nothing to do with the matches.

Kintsch (1979) has hypothesized that, when we read or listen to something, we form a mental representation of the information stated and the information we think should be stated. That is, we fill in the blanks.

There are certain types of information that we commonly fill in or infer. For example, when you read or hear about a person you tend to infer information about the person's

1. Appearance
2. Background experience
3. Personality

Our ability to fill in information comes from our knowledge base about what we are reading and the way we expect information to be "chunked." Van Dijk (1980) hypothesized that one "chunk" of information is the "fact." According to van Dijk, a fact contains

1. An event
2. Participants in the action
3. Goal of the action (why it was done)
4. Time and duration of the action
5. Location of the action

When we read or hear any portion of a fact, we automatically infer the remaining parts. For example, when you read the sentence "The boy hit the girl," you are given information about parts 1 and 2 of a fact. However, you infer the goal or reason for the event (e.g., The girl was bothering the boy); you infer the time of the event (e.g., The boy hit the girl during recess); and you infer the location of the event (e.g., It probably happened on the playground).

Warren, Nickolas, and Trabasso (1979) distinguished among three general types of inferences: logical, informational, and value. Logical inferences are those inferences of relationships between ideas. For example, the inference that one event caused another or the inference that one statement is an example of another. Informational inferences refer to background information not stated in the passage. They deal with the type of information in van Dijk's fact—the who, what, where, and when of an event. Value inferences require the reader to infer the purpose or intentions of the author and make value judgments about the thoughts and actions of the characters. Ringler and Weber (1984) gave very explicit examples and suggestions for the application of the Warren et al. (1979) model. Table 4.2 illustrates Ringler and Weber's description of the different inference categories.

Table 4.2

INFERENCE CATEGORIES	DESCRIPTIONS
Logical Inferences	
a. Motivational	a. Inferring the reasons for a character's voluntary thoughts, actions, or goals (or vice versa)
b. Psychological	b. Inferring the reasons for a character's involuntary thoughts, actions, or feelings
c. Physical	c. Inferring mechanical or nonhuman causes for given actions or events
Informational Inferences	
a. Pronominal	a. Stating the antecedents or pronouns
b. Referential	b. Specifying the related antecedents of actions or events when the referents are not pronominally marked
c. Elaborative	c. Adding information which does not contribute to the story
d. Spatial-temporal	d. Locating events or series of events in place or time
Value Inferences	
Evaluative	Reacting critically to story characteristics inherent in narratives

Note. From *A Language-Thinking Approach to Reading* (p. 198) by L.H. Ringler and C.K. Weber, 1984, New York: Harcourt Brace Jovanovich. Copyright 1984 by Harcourt Brace Jovanovich. Reprinted by permission.

Inference is actually symptomatic of a much more global process that we constantly engage in, that of interpretation based on our expectations. About expectation, the linguist Deborah Tannen has said

> I have been struck lately by the recurrence of a single theme in a wide variety of contexts: the power of expectation. For example, the self-fulfilling prophecy has been proven to operate in education as well as in individual psychology. I happened to leaf through a how-to-succeed book; its thesis was that the way to succeed is to expect to do so. Two months ago at a conference for teachers of English as a second language, the keynote speaker explained that effective reading is a process of anticipating what the author is going to say and expecting it as one reads. Moreover, there are general platitudes heard every day, as for example the observation that what is wrong with marriage today is that partners expect too much of each other and of marriage.
>
> The emphasis on expectation seems to corroborate a nearly self-evident truth: in order to function in the world, people cannot treat each new person, object, or event as unique and separate. The only way we can make sense of the world is to see the connections between things, and between present things and things we have experienced before or heard about. These vital connections are learned as we grow up and live in a given culture. As soon as we measure a new perception against what we know of the world from prior experience, we are dealing with expectations. (1979, p. 137)

Hart (1983), in his explication of the PROSTER theory of brain behavior, defined learning as the extraction from confusion of meaningful patterns. That is, we make sense of the sensory information in working memory by looking for expected patterns of information. Frank Smith (1982) referred to this phenomenon as using the "theory of the world in our heads."

> What we have in our heads is a theory of what the world is like, a theory that is the basis of all our perceptions and understanding of the world, the root of all learning, the source of all hopes and fears, motives and expectancies, reasoning and creativity. And this theory is all we have. If we can make sense of the world at all, it is by interpreting our interactions with the world in the light of our theory. The theory is our shield against bewilderment. (p. 57)

The importance of this concept goes far beyond reading pedagogy. As Tannen stated, it is found in almost all fields of study. Throughout the text, we will consider ways of helping students see the role of their expectations and interpretations in the reading process and in their general academic behavior.

Attention and Capacity

Attention and capacity are essential components of all models of reading, although few people explicitly consider them. Attention is the act of focusing perception on selected sensory information. For example, when reading, you focus attention on the visual information contained on the printed page and dampen the attention paid to other sensory stimuli (e.g., the temperature of the room, noises, physical sensations). Capacity refers to the amount of attention given to a cognitive task. It is assumed that capacity is limited. Attention and capacity are perhaps best illustrated by early listening experiments. Broadbent (1958) found that people select one ear at a time to use when listening, in order to focus the limited capacity of attention. However, it was also found that, while listening, people can recognize their own names and other familiar signals with the nonattending ear (Moray, 1959). This points to the existence of possible unconscious automatic processes (e.g., an unconscious operating production that might be stated as "If my name is stated, then I should interpret this as important information") that are always in operation but require little of the limited attention capacity.

La Berge and Samuels (1974) stated that, during the execution of a complex skill, it is necessary to coordinate many component processes within a short period of time. If each component requires attention, performance of the complex skill is impossible because the capacity for attention is excluded. But, if enough of the components can be processed automatically, then the load on attention is within tolerable limits, and the skill can be successfully performed (p. 548). Although La Berge and Samuels are commonly associated with a bottom-up model, we feel that the concepts of attention and capacity are useful additions to the production-system model of reading. That is, our ability to constantly shift back and forth between factual information and procedures used in the reading process is dependent on the automaticity of the procedures and retrieval of the factual information. When procedures and factual information are automatic, they take up little room in short-term memory (they require little capacity), leaving room for the reader to attend to more complex aspects of reading. When a procedure is not automatic or factual information is not easily retrieved, attention must be focused on the needed fact or procedure. If this happens too frequently the comprehension process is "short circuited" and gradually breaks down.

Metacognition and Reading

Metacognition refers to the deliberate conscious control of one's own cognitive actions (A. Brown, 1980). The Russian psychologist Vygotsky (1962) felt that knowledge moves from the automatic unconscious level to the gradual increase in active conscious control over knowledge. Flavell (1976) defined metacognition in the following way:

> Metacognition refers to one's knowledge concerning one's own cognitive processes and products or anything related to them, e.g. the learning of relevant properties of information or data. For example, I am engaging in metacognition (metamemory, metalearning, meta-attention, metalanguage, or whatever) if I notice that I am having more trouble learning A than B; if it strikes me that I should double-check C before accepting it as a fact; if it occurs to me that I had better scrutinize each and every alternative in any multiple-choice type task situation before deciding which is the best one. . . . Metacognition refers, among other things, to the active monitoring and consequent regulation and orchestration of these processes in relation to the cognitive objects or data on which they bear, usually in the service of some concrete goal or objective (p. 232).

As it relates to reading, metacognition is translated into many different abilities. A. Brown (1980) listed the following metacognitive reading abilities:

1. Clarifying the purposes of reading, that is, understanding the task demands, both explicit and implicit
2. Identifying the aspects of a message that are important
3. Allocating attention so that concentration can be focused on the major content area rather than trivia
4. Monitoring ongoing activities to determine whether goals are being achieved
5. Engaging in review and self-interrogation to determine whether goals are being achieved
6. Taking corrective action when failures in comprehension are detected
7. Recovering from disruptions and distractions—and many more deliberate, planful activities that render reading an efficient information-gathering activity. (p. 456)

Within reading education, metacognition is a relatively new area of study. Yet it appears to have a bright future. For example, Resnick (in press) has cited the metacognitive reading strategy developed by Palincsar and Brown (1984) as one of the most promising instructional techniques to be derived from the research literature in years. That technique, called *reciprocal teaching*, has long-term effects and transfers to a variety of academic contexts. We will consider reciprocal teaching along with other metacognitive strategies in chapter 10.

Attitudes and Motivation

Most teachers intuitively sense that motivation is a key component of the reading process. In Asher's (1980) review of the research on topic interest and reading comprehension, he stated that motivation is responsible for much of the performance relative to reading.

As important as motivation is, its dynamics have not been well understood within education. However, recent years have seen somewhat of a breakthrough in our understanding of motivation. Specifically, research indicates that motivation is strongly influenced by attitudes. If certain attitudes are present in certain situations, then people are motivated; if these attitudes are not present, then people are not motivated. To illustrate, Harter and Connell (1981), basing much of their work on that done by White (1959, 1960), found that, unless a student believes that she or he is in control of the outcome of a task, the student will not be highly motivated to engage in the task regardless of how well she or he performs. This flies in the face of the more traditional approach to motivation, which assumes that if a student is successful at a task she or he will be motivated to perform the task in the future. We might depict the traditional view of motivation in the following way:

The current research suggests that a person's attitudes intervene in the relationship between success and motivation; in more technical terms, attitudes mediate the relationship between achievement and motivation. This might be depicted in the following way:

This new model of motivation implies that teachers should be aware of their students' attitudes toward specific academic tasks (e.g., reading) and try to foster attitudes that will stimulate motivation. In chapter 11 we will consider some attitudes that have been found to be important to motivation, and we will discuss ways of fostering these attitudes as a part of reading instruction.

NEW THEORIES ABOUT COGNITION: THEIR ROLE IN READING INSTRUCTION

It is becoming increasing difficult to read about educational theory or practice without encountering some mention of brain lateralization or learning styles. In this section we briefly consider each area and discuss its implications for reading.

Brain Lateralization

In its simplest form, the lateralization movement within education asserts that each hemisphere of the human brain processes information in distinct ways. The left hemisphere is primarily responsible for the processing of linguistic information. This is done in a fairly linear or sequential fashion. Information that is visuospatial and affective in nature is processed in the right hemisphere. This is done in a more holistic manner than the processing of linguistic information. For example, Hart (1983) claimed that information processed in the right hemisphere is holographic, that is, any piece of information contains components of all other pieces. Much of the impetus for the brain lateralization movement in education springs from the work of Roger Sperry, a Nobel Prize winner in medicine. Sperry's first experiments were conducted on animals (1964). In these experiments he found that, if all connections were cut between the two hemispheres of the brain, it was possible to train each side of the brain separately, so that the right side would learn one response whereas the left side could be taught a contradictory response.

This split-brain operation, called a *commissurotomy*, was also commonly conducted on patients suffering from severe cases of epilepsy. After the commissurotomy, the patients seemed surprisingly normal. Akelaitis (1944), studying the reactions of split-brain patients, stated that there was almost no change in their mental ability. In Sperry's work with human subjects, he began conducting experiments similar to those done with animals. He found distinct hemispheric abilities. For example, if the word *pencil* were flashed to the left visual field (which sends messages to the right hemisphere), the patient could select a pencil from among a group of objects. However, when asked why he did so, the patient would respond that he didn't know. From such experiments it has been extrapolated that the left hemisphere is responsible for the processing of certain types of information in certain ways, as is the right hemisphere.

Based on this research, some educators have developed lists of skills associated with each hemisphere. For example, relative to reading and writing ability, Sinatra (1982, pp. 208–209) offered the list of right-brain and left-brain skills found in Table 4.3.

Table 4.3 Contribution of Each Brain Hemisphere to Reading and Writing

LEFT HEMISPHERE VERBAL MEDIATION	RIGHT HEMISPHERE NONVERBAL MEDIATION
Phonemic discrimination; grapheme to phoneme correspondence; analytic processing of parts to name word	Grapheme array perceived in gestalt; deriving meaning directly from spoken or printed word; image produced
Learning rules of syllabification and identification of word parts (structural analysis) such as prefixes and suffixes; applying rules to lists of words	Learning new words holistically, in "natural" content areas such as music, gym, shop, the arts, and some sciences; associating real experience with word meaning
Memorizing words of songs such as the "Star Spangled Banner"	Feeling memory of melody patterns through chanting, jingling, and singing to induce words
Using nonsense syllables and nonsense words to teach word attack skills	Teaching concrete, image producing words and building associative webs (synonym, antonym, classification) amongst word meanings
Naming and describing objects and parts of space though verbal mode	Finding way in space; tracing route, touching and holding objects to label and describe; arousing associations with object
Identifying and naming words using denotative meanings such as dictionary definitions	Identifying and naming words using connotative, associative, image producing strategies through figures of speech, metaphor, simile, and analogy; using the context to arrive at an intelligent guess of a word's meaning
Sequencing events or numbering in order; arranging from part to whole	Relating events to a whole theme; associating ideas to central image which may or may not have sequence orientation
Locating the main idea sentence in a paragraph and constructing an outline of parts	Forming key image of a paragraph (or theme) and visualizing details in relationship to central image
Reading and following verbal directions	Looking at a plan, blueprint, map, or picture; tracing route, internally verbalizing, and then reading or writing directions
Reading and writing exercises which emphasize denotative language and literal comprehension such as getting the facts, "locating the answer," etc.	Obtaining meaning from the visual (pictorial), and structural (webs and semantic maps); personalized, affective associations (emotion) made with theme and ideas in passage
Subskill approach to reading and writing development such as occurs in skills management systems, criterion reference systems, diagnostic-prescriptive programs, etc.	Whole discourse mode or whole language approach; presenting schema or nonverbal representation of whole discourse scope, such as semantic mapping, arousing personalized association to theme
Attention to mechanics of writing, i.e., spelling, punctuation, and agreement	Attention to the gestalt of writing coherent sentences in meaningful sequences

Table 4.3 continued

LEFT HEMISPHERE VERBAL MEDIATION	RIGHT HEMISPHERE NONVERBAL MEDIATION
Analyzing and labeling parts of speech, finding subjects and predicates, telling functional use of sentence parts	Composing and writing sentences through intermediary steps such as sentence combining or through whole composition involvement in prewriting (composing), writing, editing, and refining
Analyzing literary works, separating parts and passages to isolate content or intent of author	Literary synthesizing by discovering relationship between two or more disparate themes, events, characters, etc.
Writing compositions from lists of facts and information given on a topic; constructing outlines following teacher prearranged format	Writing from visual compositions, which are sequences of pictures arranged to infer a story or stories
Writing answers to specific questions or topics where information is generally given in text and needs to be located and copied; summarizing a work; adding to existing information	Synthesizing several works or passages to relate meaning in a novel way; creating new ideas not there before

Note. From "Learning Literacy in Nonverbal Style" by R. Sinatra, 1982, *Student Learning Styles and Brain Behavior*, pp. 208–209. Copyright 1982 by National Assn. of Secondary School Principals. Reprinted by permission.

In a more general vein, Marilee Zdenek in her book, *The Right-Brain Experience* (1983, pp. 13–14) stated that the two hemispheres are responsible for the following sets of activities:

LEFT HEMISPHERE

Language
Analytic reasoning
Literal interpretations of words
Linear processing of information

Mathematics
Control of movement on the right side
of the body

RIGHT HEMISPHERE

Images
Perception of spatial relationships
Metaphoric reasoning
Music
Imagination
Artistic reasoning

Sexual responses
Spirituality
Dreaming
Emotions
Control of movement on the left side
of the body

Some researchers have taken great exception to the identification of skills based on lateralization research. In an article entitled "Dichotomania: An Essay on Our Left and Right Brains," Whitaker (1981) likened the current split-brain educational movement to the dubious practice of phrenology popular in the late 1800s. Phrenology was the science, or art, of determining personality traits, intellectual capacity, and other matters by examination of skull configurations. Whitaker also likened the educational split-brain emphasis to the ambidextral-culture movement also begun in the late 19th century. With the discovery in the 1860s of the correlation between language localization in the left hemisphere and right-handedness, the left hemisphere was soon touted as the "learning hemisphere." This resulted in the ambidextralist movement. Whitaker stated that

> The ambidextralists believed that great things were in store for mankind if only the neglected right hemisphere could be properly stimulated by training the left hand. The ills of contemporary society, the shortcomings of the educational system, in sum the imperfection of man and woman, were all attributed to lop-handedness and the assymetries of the human brain. (p. 2)

That there are differences between the two hemispheres is undeniable. Hemispheric differences have been shown in the processing of verbal information (Thatcher, 1977), in the processing of music with and without lyrics (Gardiner & Walter, 1977), and in the expression and evaluation of human emotions (Bryden & Ley, 1983). However, the extent to which we can generalize to instructional activities is still unclear.

In this text we take the position that there are certain nonverbal or nonlinguistic aspects of thinking that are important to the processing of information. Although we do not necessarily agree with the lists of skills developed by some educators, we do feel that lateralization research supports the exploration of some of these nonlinguistic components of thought. In chapter 11 we will discuss techniques for fostering "wordless thinking" as it relates to reading.

Learning Styles

Although they are derived from different research bases, the split-brain movement and the learning-styles movement have had a similar impact on education. Much of the current theory on learning styles stems from the early work of Carl Jung. In his book entitled *Psychological Types* (1976), first printed in 1921, Jung identified four basic types of people relative to the way they perceive and process information:

> Feelers: Feelers assign value to what they perceive. Things are good or bad. The act of assigning value is a conscious one based on an internalized set of rules.
> Thinkers: Thinkers are concerned with organizing information. How does one idea relate to another. This too is a conscious, rational process.
> Sensors: Sensors are primarily conscious of their sensations. They interpret the world as a set of smells, tastes, feelings, etc. Although this is a conscious process,

sensors do not assign value to their sensations nor do they categorize and label them like feelers and thinkers do respectively. Instead they are simply aware of their sensations and do not impose a great deal of control over them.

Intuitors: Intuitors are the opposite of sensors. They are aware of sensations but attempt to impose control over them and understand them. Where sensors are simply aware of their sensations, intuitors try to interpret their sensations.

Since Jung's original work, a number of models of personality and learning types have been developed: (Dunn & Dunn, 1978; Gregoric, 1979; Kolb, Rubin, & McIntyre, 1974; Letteri, 1982). One of the more widely used models of learning styles for educational purposes is that developed by McCarthy (1980), who based much of her work on that of Kolb. McCarthy identified two basic dimensions of learning style: (a) whether individuals are concrete or abstract in terms of how they process information and (b) whether individuals are active or reflective in terms of how they process information. Relative to the concrete versus abstract dimension, abstract processors are best described as thinkers, whereas concrete processors are best described as sensors or feelers. Relative to the active versus reflective dimension, active processors can be described as doers; reflective processors can be described as watchers. These two dimensions can be combined into a scheme for classifying people as one of four different learning-style types. The four types are illustrated in Table 4.4.

McCarthy has developed an instructional system that insures that learning activities come from all four quadrants of Table 4.4, thus covering all the different learning styles a child might have.

What do the learning-style theorists have to offer the reading teacher? Again, although we do not agree with the specific skills identified by proponents of the learning-style movements, we do feel that they bring a useful new per-

Table 4.4

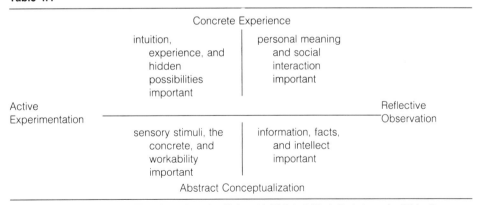

Note. From *The 4Mat System: Teaching to Learning Styles with Right/Left Mode Techniques* (p. 35) by B. McCarthy, 1980, Barrington, IL: Excel, Inc. Copyright 1982 by Excel Inc. Reprinted by permission.

spective to reading instruction. For example, McCarthy (1980) suggested reading comprehension activities as diverse as

> Determining how you would get on the right bus in an unfamiliar city without being able to read
> Describing how you would feel if you were the main character in a story
> Listing the vocabulary words that seem to be the most heavily laden with emotional overtones
> Describing what you would have done had you been able to jump into a story

Such diverse activities broaden students' awareness of reading and can add variety and spice to the curriculum. We might say that one of the most important contributions that both the brain lateralization and learning-style movements have made to education is to highlight the importance of the nonverbal aspects of learning. As mentioned previously, we will consider some of these aspects in chapter 11.

SUMMARY

In this chapter we presented four models of reading and described them in terms of the aspects of reading mentioned in chapter 3. The top-down model of reading assumes that information is processed from the schema level down. The bottom-up model assumes that processing proceeds from the letter-recognition level up to the schema level. The interactive model asserts that both directions of information flow are used in reading. Finally, the production-system model emphasizes the declarative and procedural aspects of the reading process. Instructional implications were briefly mentioned for each model.

Four other aspects of reading were also mentioned: inference, attention and capacity, metacognition, and attitudes. Inference refers to the constant interpretations we make about information read or heard. Attention and capacity relate to the information-processing need to attend to selected stimuli because of the limitations of short-term memory. Metacognition refers to the awareness of, and control over, cognition during the processing of information. Attitudes are those beliefs an individual has that affect motivation and other aspects of learning. Finally, we considered the brain lateralization and learning-style movements within education and discussed their applications to reading instruction.

5

INFORMAL ASSESSMENT

In the last section of the text, we presented a theory base for discussing reading and different models of the reading process. In this section, we focus on diagnostic procedures to assess reading ability. As we consider different assessment tools, we will discuss how they relate to the theory presented in chapters 1–4.

In this chapter, we discuss informal assessment techniques; in the next chapter we will present formal techniques. The informal methods of assessment that you will use will depend upon your model of reading and on whether you are a classroom teacher or a reading teacher in a special class.

OBSERVING AND INTERVIEWING

As a classroom teacher, you are probably constantly monitoring the progress of your students. By systematizing your monitoring procedures, you will be able to diagnose strengths and weaknesses of your students' reading ability. Y.M. Goodman (1978) described a procedure of naturalistic assessment she called *kid watching*. The advantage of using naturalistic assessment rather than a more formal type of assessment is that you are able to see how your children read and use language in realistic settings.

Naturalistic assessment is based on four simple elements: (a) observing, (b) interacting, (c) documenting, and (d) interpreting. The procedure is quite simple. Your first observe students' behaviors while interacting with them in a variety of circumstances and with various materials. For example, you might observe students during reading groups, during silent reading, during journal writing, during assigned reading, during reading conferences, and during writing conferences. You then attempt to document and interpret your observations. One method of documenting and interpreting your naturalistic assessment is through anecdotal records. Keeping anecdotal records allows you to (a) evaluate students' progress in a nonthreatening, unobtrusive manner; (b) note changes and growth in reading and general language development; (c) maintain a readily accessible data bank for evaluation; and (d) review more aspects of reading than can be done using standardized tests.

When you conduct naturalistic assessment, you should follow some guidelines to insure that your anecdotal records provide a reliable picture of your students' strengths and weaknesses. The first guideline is that your assessment should take place as a part of the instruction process, not as a separate activity. That is, you want to observe your students as they are working in real reading and language situations rather than in testing situations. As you observe students in these natural settings, you should try to observe the procedures they use as well as their knowledge of important facts (declarative information) relative to reading.

When you observe students making mistakes or "miscues" in reading, you should try to assess the quality of the miscues rather than their quantity. Later in this chapter, we will describe fairly detailed procedures for determining the quality of miscues students make in reading. However, for now, we are simply stressing the fact that naturalistic assessment involves judgments on your part as to the quality of students' reading. This is far more important than simply listing errors.

Finally, a third principle of naturalistic assessment is that what you look for should be guided by your model of reading. For example, if you subscribe to a top-down approach, you should look for student behaviors that indicate strengths and weaknesses in the skills implicit in that model. Conversely, you ignore behaviors that cannot be interpreted within that model.

Naturalistic assessment, then as described by Y.M. Goodman (1978), is a very loose, informal technique requiring a great deal of interpretation of student behaviors. However, its informality does not mean it is not a powerful assessment tool. In chapter 7 we will provide guidelines for the integration of formal assessment with naturalistic assessment.

Many teachers augment their naturalistic assessments by obtaining feedback from students. One way of obtaining feedback is through the Reading Interview (Burke, 1980). The reading interview (Figure 5.1) is designed to provide insight into a reader's perceptions of the reading process. A student's responses to the questions on the reading interview should reveal the student's strategies for dealing with difficult reading material, his or her conception of a good reader, and a self-assessment.

The reading interview is meant to be used with one student at a time.

Figure 5.1   Reading Interview by Carolyn L. Burke. From *Reading Comprehension: An Instructional Videotape Series Resource Guide* (p. 71) by B.P. Farr and D.J. Strickler, 1980, Bloomington, IN: Indiana University Press. Copyright 1980 by Carolyn L. Burke. Reprinted by permission.

Name _____ Age _____ Date _____

Occupation _____ Education Level _____

Sex _____ Interview Setting _____

1. When you are reading and you come to something you don't know, what do you do?
   Do you ever do anything else?

2. Do you think that (ask teacher's name) is a good reader?
   or Who is a good reader that you know?

3. What makes her/him a good reader?

4. Do you think that she/he ever comes to something she/he doesn't know when she's/he's reading?

5. Yes   When she/he does come to something she/he doesn't know, what do you think she/he does about it?

   No   Suppose Pretend that she/he does come to something that she/he doesn't know. What do you think she/he does about it?

6. If you knew that someone was having difficulty reading how would you help them?

7. What would a/your teacher do to help that person?

8. How did you learn to read?

   What did (they/you) do to help you learn?

9. What would you like to do better as a reader?

10. Do you think that you are a good reader? _____   _____   Why?
                                              Yes   No

Additional Notes:

In situations where you do not have the time to interview all of your students individually, you might use an interest inventory that you can give to the entire class. Although interest inventories are not designed to yield the same diagnostic information as the reading inventory, they can be quite useful if you "read between the lines." As an illustration, consider the secondary-level inventory in Figure 5.2 developed by W.H. Miller (1978). Students' responses to the questions on the inventory can tell how much students read, what they read, and even when and why they read. This information, coupled with that gleaned from classroom observation, can tell you a great deal about students' knowledge of declarative and procedural information relative to reading.

Figure 5.2 INTEREST INVENTORY (Secondary-school level). *Note.* From *Reading Diagnosis Kit* (p. 292–293) by W.H. Miller, 1978, West Nyack, NY: The Center for Applied Research in Education. Copyright 1978 by Center for Applied Research in Education, Inc. Reprinted by permission.

Written Form

Name _____ Grade _____ Teacher _____

1. What is the title of the book which you have read recently that you liked the best?

2. What is the title of the best book which you have ever read?

3. How much do you like to read for pleasure during your spare time?

   very much _____
   somewhat _____
   not very much _____
   not at all _____

4. What are the titles of some of the books in your home?

5. Do you read a newspaper every day?

6. What part of the newspaper appeals the most to you?

   news section _____
   editorial page _____
   society page _____
   teen-age page _____
   sports section _____
   comic section _____
   agriculture section _____

Figure 5.2 continued

7. What type of comic books do you enjoy reading?

8. How many books have you borrowed from the public library during the last month?

9. What magazines do you read regularly?

10. What kind of things do you usually do after school?

11. What kind of things do you usually do on a weekend?

12. What subjects do you like best in school?

13. What hobbies or collections do you have?

14. What clubs or groups do you belong to?

15. What sports do you enjoy watching?

16. What are the titles of the last few movies which you have seen?

17. What living person do you admire the most?

18. What person from history do you admire the most?

19. What do you like to do during summer vacation?

20. Of the following kinds of books, which ones would you like to read for pleasure?

sport stories _____

adventure stories _____

historical novels _____

adult novels _____

probelms of teen-agers _____

biographies and autobiographies of famous people _____

mystery stories _____

career stories _____

science-fiction _____

scientific experiments _____

stories about minority groups _____

nature stories _____

poetry _____

INFORMAL GROUP TESTS

Some classroom teachers desire more structure to diagnosis than is provided by naturalistic assessment. Their reasoning is that additional data besides their own observations are needed for diagnosing the strengths and weaknesses of their students. In this section, we present diagnostic tools that use classroom materials. We are not considering commercially prepared tests. The advantage to using informal group tests over commercially prepared reading inventories and standarized tests is that students are assessed on material they will actually be using in class. We will consider three types of informal group tests: cloze, maze, and group reading inventories.

Cloze Tests

The cloze technique has for years been an important and versatile informal assessment tool. Cloze refers to the psychological principle of closure. Closure is a *gestalt* term that applies to the human tendency to complete a familiar but "not quite finished" pattern.

The cloze procedure was originated by W. Taylor in 1953, but its roots can be traced to Ebbinghaus, who developed a "completion method" test in 1897. Simply stated, the cloze procedure is a method by which you systematically delete words from a text passage and evaluate students' ability to accurately supply the deleted words. Cloze tests can be developed with relatively little effort and without special training in test construction. To develop and administer a cloze test, gather reading selections from textbooks, basal readers, or any other materials that students will be using and follow these steps:

1. Select a passage of approximately 250–300 words on a level at which the students should be reading.
2. Retype the passage. Beginning with the second sentence, delete every fifth word. Replace each deleted word with a 12-space line, no matter how long or short the word is. Do not delete words from the first or last sentences. There should be approximately 50 blank spaces in the selection.
3. After making copies for the students, direct them to fill in each blank with the words they think best fit.
4. Score the students' papers by counting as correct only those responses that *exactly* match the original selection. Synonyms are not counted as correct. Each correct response is given two points.

Bormuth (1968) developed cloze cutoff scores for determining students' independent, instructional, and frustration levels. We will discuss these levels in more depth later in this chapter. Briefly, though, a student's independent level of reading is that at which she or he can read with full comprehension without help. A student's instructional level is that at which she or he comprehend the material but might need outside help (e.g., from the teacher). Finally, the frustration level is that at which comprehension is not possible for the student even with outside help. Bormuth's cloze cutoff scores for these levels are

$$56\%-100\% = \text{Independent Level}$$
$$44\%-55\% = \text{Instructional Level}$$
$$0\%-43\% = \text{Frustration Level}$$

Many teachers question the directive of not counting synonyms as correct when scoring a cloze test. Given that meaning is the most important aspect of reading, they naturally assume that any word that makes sense in the context of the passage should be given credit. However, Bormuth's intent was not to penalize students, but to develop a scoring system that was objective. We recommend a compromise position. Briefly, after you have finished scoring the students' papers using the Bormuth criteria, identify those papers that fall into the "frustration" category. For these students, rescore synonyms as correct, to see how many students would move up to another level. In this way, you are not penalizing students for using synonyms. You might want to follow the same procedure for the instructional level group. Box 5.1 contains a partial cloze test, with the deleted words presented below the paragraph.

If you choose not to use the Bormuth method of scoring, you might want to use a modified miscue format. This modified method takes into account the different responses a student could make to a blank. There are four possibilities: correct word (CW), synonym (SYN), syntax correct/semantics incorrect (SC/MI), and syntax incorrect/semantics incorrect (SI/MI). Using this classification scheme, you can determine if students are reading for meaning, if they are using syntax to guess at the word, or if they are focusing on the word level of

---

Box 5.1

"I never said 'Actors are cattle,' " Alfred Hitchcock was fond of remarking. "What I said was: _____(1)_____ should be treated like _____(2)_____."

This was part of _____(3)_____ image that the film _____(4)_____ nurtured for half a _____(5)_____. He delighted in presenting _____(6)_____ to the public as _____(7)_____, if not outrageous, a _____(8)_____ provocateur.

This side of _____(9)_____ career began early. As _____(10)_____ rising young film director _____(11)_____ London during the 1920s, _____(12)_____ became noted for his _____(13)_____ jokes. Somehow he managed to place a workhorse in the dressing room of Gerald Du Maurier while the famed actor was performing on stage.

* * * * * * *

1. actors	7. irreverent
2. cattle	8. master
3. the	9. his
4. maker	10. a
5. century	11. in
6. himself	12. he
	13. practical

Table 5.1

Text	Student	CW	SYN	SC/MI	SI/MI
Actors	They		X		
cattle	cattle	X			
the	the	X			
maker	producer		X		
century	decade			X	
himself	actors			X	
irreverent	- - - - - -				X
master	very				X

analysis and not using the context to determine the meaning or the part of speech of the missing word. Table 5.1 contains a sample coding sheet for this type of analysis.

This technique also allows you to obtain percentages in each of the four categories and then develop a profile for each student, much in the same spirit as the profile on the Reading Miscue Inventory, which we will discuss later in the chapter.

Maze Technique

The maze technique is a modification of the cloze procedure. Instead of leaving a blank space in place of a deleted word, three alternatives are presented to students. To develop a maze test, use the following process:

1. Choose material that students have not read. The material should be between 250 and 300 words.
2. Leave the first sentence intact. Starting with the second sentence, delete every fifth word. Do not delete any words in the final sentence.
3. Substitute three alternative words for each deletion: (a) the correct word, (b) an incorrect word that is syntactically acceptable but semantically unacceptable, and (c) an incorrect word that is syntactically and semantically unacceptable.
4. Administer the maze test as you would the cloze test.
5. Count the number of correct responses.
6. Determine a student's comprehension score by dividing the total number of deleted words into the number of correct responses made.
7. Interpret student' scores using the following criteria:
   85%–100% = Independent Level
   60%–84% = Instructional Level
   0%–59% = Frustration Level

Guthrie (1973; Guthrie, SeiFert, Burnham & Caplan, 1974) is commonly credited with originating the maze technique; however he validated it with primary school children only. Further validation studies with secondary school students might yield a new set of criteria. Besides the cloze and maze techniques, group reading inventories may be used for whole-class assessment.

Group Reading Inventories

Group reading inventories (GRI) are designed to determine if students can read specific types of content area material. W.H. Miller (1978) distinguished among a number of different types of group inventories. We will consider two here.

The first type helps you determine if students can effectively use the aids found in their content-area textbooks. This type of inventory is usually given at the beginning of a course or at the beginning of a semester. To construct this type of inventory, use the textbook required for the students and then formulate about 15 questions on the use of such textbook features as the table of contents, the index, the glossary, italicized words, maps, graphs, diagrams, tables, and pictures. Questions might resemble the following:

1. According to the map on page 148, what are the states bordering Colorado?
2. According to the table of contents, where does the chapter entitled "A New Frontier" begin?
3. What are the five major subheadings within chapter 7?
4. How many appendices are in this textbook, and what is contained in each?

Students should be given as much time as they need to answer these questions.

The second type of GRI is more a test of general reading ability within a specific content area. Students are presented with a chapter or a fairly long selection from a textbook (e.g., 1,000–2,000 words). They read the selection silently and then are asked specific comprehension questions. W.H. Miller (1978) stated that the questions should cover different types of information. When we discuss teacher-made individual reading inventories in the next section of this chapter, we will consider in depth how to structure comprehension questions. For now the general rule of thumb to follow is that these comprehension questions should sample students' knowledge of different levels of meaning across different types of information.

Shepherd (1973) recommended a combined format for a GRI, one in which students are asked questions about textbook aids and text content. Shepherd's directions for a social studies GRI are presented in Box 5.2.

INDIVIDUAL READING INVENTORIES

The informal group tests, discussed in the previous section, can be administered to an entire group of students. They provide general information about how effective each student's reading is relative to specific content areas. In general,

---

Box 5.2   *Social Studies—Group Reading Inventory*

Directions for the diagnostic survey test are based on a social studies textbook.

  I. Use between 26–30 questions.
 II. Write questions to measure the following reading skills shown below:
     A. Using parts of the book (5 questions)
     B. Using resource (library) materials (4 questions)
     C. Using maps, pictures, charts, etc.
     D. Vocabulary (3 questions)
     E. Noting the main idea (3 questions)
     F. Noting pertinent supporting details (3 questions)
     G. Drawing conclusions (3 questions)
     H. Noting the organization of the material (1 question)
III. Choose a reading selection of not more than 3–4 pages.
IV. Have questions of skills D through H—vocabulary, main ideas, details, conclusions, and organization—based on the reading selection.
 V. In administering the reading inventory:
     A. Explain to the pupils the purpose of the test and the reading skills the test is designed to measure. As the test is given, let the students know the skill being measured.
     B. Read each question twice.
     C. Write the page reference of each question on the blackboard as the question is read if the student is to refer to the text.
VI. A student is considered to be deficient in any way if he gets more than one question in any of the skills wrong.

Note. Adapted from *Comprehensive High School Reading Methods*, Third Edition (p. 271–272) by D. Sheperd, 1973, Columbus, OH: Charles E. Merrill. Copyright 1982 by Charles E. Merrill Publishing Co. Reprinted by permission.

---

though, informal group tests do not provide detailed information about specific reading skills. That is, they won't provide you with much information about students' performance on specific skills within your model of reading, whether it be top-down, bottom-up, or another one. For this level of detail one must usually resort to the use of an IRI.

Howards (1980) stated that *IRI* is a generic term for nonstandardized, non-criterion-referenced measures of reading performance. Because IRIs are generally administered to individual students rather than to a group, some theorists have referred to them as *individual reading inventories* (W.H. Miller, 1978). In this section we will first consider commercially prepared IRIs. We will then consider teacher-made IRIs.

Commercially Prepared IRIs

Two commonly used commercially prepared IRIs are the Analytical Reading Inventory by Woods and Moe (1981) and the Classroom Reading Inventory by Silvaroli (1982). The Analytical Reading Inventory contains reading passages up through grade 9; the Classroom Reading Inventory contains passages up through grade 8. An IRI developed specifically for use at the secondary level is the Advanced Reading Inventory by Johns (1981). It contains reading passages that range from grade 7 through college.

The administration of a commercially prepared IRI is fairly simple. Commonly, students begin by reading orally a graded word list. That is, students are provided with lists of words like that in Box 5.3.

An IRI usually has as many word lists, as it does reading passages. Each list contains words that get progressively more difficult. Students continue reading until they make a certain number of errors. Performance on the graded word lists is then used to place students in the graded reading passages.

The word list section of an IRI can be used to obtain information about a student's sight vocabulary and word-recognition strategies. Words that students recognize immediately are probably in their sight-word vocabularies. From a production-theory point of view, this is declarative knowledge used in word identification. If a student does not recognize a word immediately, you can try to determine what word identification strategy the student is using by observing him or her trying to figure out the word. For example, you might notice that the student tries to decode the word letter by letter. This would indicate that he or she is not using an efficient word-identification strategy (e.g., the recognition of spelling patterns). Or you might notice that the student looks for affixes only at the beginnings of words or only at the ends of words. Conversely you might find that the student looks for spelling patterns anywhere within a word.

Box 5.3

————	1. pig	————	21. bed
————	2. it	————	22. call
————	3. big	————	23. time
————	4. milk	————	24. sleep
————	5. dog	————	25. mouse
————	6. grass	————	26. morning
————	7. are	————	27. see
————	8. day	————	28. children
————	9. ran	————	29. play
————	10. all	————	30. around
————	11. father	————	31. tree
————	12. door	————	32. another
————	13. like	————	33. over
————	14. bat	————	34. cry
————	15. eat	————	35. bird
————	16. good	————	36. dinner
————	17. girl	————	37. chair
————	18. name	————	38. rain
————	19. from	————	39. live
————	20. that	————	40. peep

Figure 5.3

1	was	saw	(error)
2	day	+	
3	three	DK (don't know)	(error)
4	farming	+	

Note. From *Classroom Reading Inventory*, 5E (p. 7) by N.J. Silvaroli, 1982, Dubuque, IA: Wm. C. Brown. Copyright 1969, 1973, 1982 by William C. Brown. All rights reserved. Reprinted by permission.

Both Silvaroli and Johns recommended that, when marking a student's performance on the graded word lists, you record (a) correct responses, (b) mispronunciations or miscues, and (c) words the student does not attempt to pronounce. Figure 5.3 contains a sample of Silvaroli's recommended recording procedure.

Silvaroli's DK (don't know) category can provide information as valuable as a student's attempt to recognize unfamiliar words. If a student does not attempt to decode unknown words, it might be an indication that the student is not comfortable with, or has no word-identification strategies for words not recognized by sight. This occurs if the student has been taught only declarative information (e.g., letter/sound relationships, phonics rules) and not strategies relative to word identification.

Another possibility you should be sensitive to when administering the word lists on an IRI is that of a student's being a "word caller." A word caller is a student who is very proficient at figuring out words that are not in her or his sight vocabulary; so proficient that the word caller can pronounce words for which he or she does not know the meaning. Such students are commonly the product of overemphasis on word identification strategies. That is, within the reading instruction they have received, so much attention has been paid to word-identification strategies that the students have come to think of reading as pronouncing words rather than obtaining meaning from what is read.

Word callers generally try to figure out all words on a list. They systematically attack words, sometimes even those they know by sight. A simple technique for identifying word callers is to have students use a few of the words on the graded word list in a sentence or to have them tell you the meanings of a few of the words on the list.

Once the word lists are completed in an IRI, a student is placed in the oral passages on the basis of how well he or she performed on the word lists. As students read the passages orally, the examiner marks (on a separate examiner's page) the types of miscues the student makes. Johns suggested identifying four main errors and four additional errors. They are reported in Figure 5.4.

Although the various types of miscues are considered equal within most IRIs, we believe it is not the quantity but the types of miscues that are important.

Figure 5.4 A Suggested Method for Recording a Student's Oral Reading Miscues. *Note.* From *Advanced Reading Inventory: Grade Seven Through College* (p. 20) by J.L. Johns, 1981, Dubuque, IA. All rights reserved. Copyright 1981 by Wm. C. Brown. Reprinted by permission.

Substitions

the

His hands were slender; he walked in a fashion that . . .

Omissions

. . . the praying mantis is (absolutely) harmless to man.

Insertions

of

On a brilliant day in May, in the year ˅1868 . . .

Repetitions

1. Correcting a miscue

Ⓒ *secure*

He had taken \serene possession of the softest . . .

2. Unsuccessful attempt at correction

ⓊⒸ *2. stride*
1. str —

. . . left him less jaded than his tranquil\stroll . . .

Additional Markings

1. Partial words

physio-

His physiognomy would have sufficiently indicated . . .

2. Phonic attempt

ēmulated

. . . and his male subjects emulated the fashion.

3. Dialect

Ⓓ *burnin*

. . . for ancient man's custom of burning hair clippings . . .

4. Intonation

˅

What is a praying mantis?

We made this point in our discussion of naturalistic assessment. The seminal research on miscue types has been reported in an edited volume by P.D. Allen and Watson (1976). Most of that research was done in conjunction with the development of the Reading Miscue Inventory (RMI), which we will discuss in depth later in this chapter. Although we will review various miscue types in that discussion, here we will consider some common interpretations of miscues.

Perhaps the most widely known practitioner in the instructional interpretation of different miscue types is Ekwall (Ekwall, 1977; Ekwall & Shanker, 1983). He identified a number of oral reading errors. In Table 5.2 we summarize nine of his miscue types.

Ekwall's interpretation is mostly from a skills approach. In fact, if you are using a bottom-up model, his instructional recommendations for each miscue type are as good as you will find anywhere.

Basically, a skills approach would interpret each miscue as poor performance in a particular skill. That is, each miscue would be considered the negative counterpart of a particular competency. Hence, for Ekwall, and others who use a skills approach, each miscue type is considered to be a discrete area to be reinforced separately. However, using other models of reading (e.g., top-down, interactive, or production-theory), the miscue types take on different meanings. Some are even an indication of good reading habits. In Table 5.3 we offer a reinterpretation of the nine oral reading errors from the perspective of the other models.

In addition to miscues you should also be attentive to some general characteristics of how the student approaches the reading of a passage. This can provide you with valuable information about how the student processes information. Use of a predominately top-down or interactive strategy would be manifest in a number of ways. Before beginning to read, the student might pause

Table 5.2

MISCUE TYPE	*RECOGNIZED BY*
1. Word-by-word reading	Student pauses after each word; reading does not flow.
2. Incorrect phrasing	Student fails to pause at punctuation marks, particularly commas and periods.
3. Poor pronunciation	Student fails to pronounce word correctly.
4. Omissions	Student omits entire words or phrases.
5. Repetitions	Student rereads words or phrases.
6. Inversions or reversals	Student reads words from right to left instead of left to right (e.g. *was* for *saw*); student reverses two or more words (e.g. *the boy hit the ball* instead of *the ball hit the boy*).
7. Insertions	Student adds words or phrases not present in the text.
8. Substitutions	Student substitutes one word for another.
9. Guesses at words	Student makes wild guesses at unknown word.

Table 5.3

MISCUE TYPE	INTERPRETATION
1. Word-by-word reading	Possible lack of top-down strategies; not processing information from the schema level down.
2. Incorrect phrasing	Lack of declarative knowledge of the syntax of English and/or the written symbols for syntactic boundaries. Lack of emphasis on top-down strategies.
3. Poor pronunciation	Lack of declarative knowledge of letter/sound relationships or meaningful word parts. Lack of phonemic analysis or word identification strategies.
4. Omissions	Strong top-down approach to reading; skips words not necessary for comprehension. Poor word recognition strategies; skips words not immediately recognized.
5. Repetitions	Awareness and use of syntactic analysis; goes back to natural syntactic boundaries after pausing to decode unknown word.
6. Inversions and reversals	Possible perceptual problems (e.g. failure to develop left-to-right eye movement). Overemphasis on top-down processing, lack of attention to lower levels of processing.
7. Insertions	Strong top-down approach to reading; inserts words to create coherence in text.
8. Substitutions	If the substitution makes sense, indicates strong top-down approach and poor word level analysis strategies; if substitution does not make sense, indicates poor top-down strategies and poor bottom-up strategies.
9. Guesses at word	Poor top-down and bottom-up strategies.

and skim the material to obtain a general idea of its content. When reading, the student might substitute words that make sense within the passage but have little relationship with the letters on the page. Recall from chapter 4 that this was one of the characteristics K. Goodman (1967) noted as a trait of good readers. When a student is processing information from the schema level down, she or he is not as concerned with decoding individual words as with making sense of what is read. A bottom-up approach would be evidenced by overattention to individual words. When the student encountered a passage with words she or he did not know, reading would be laborious and slow. The student would probably try to decode each unknown word rather than make a calculated guess and then move on.

Working from a bottom-up approach, the student would be more likely to doggedly read through an entire passage, even though it made no sense; however, a student using a top-down or interactive approach would be more likely to stop somewhere in the passage and state that he or she did not understand the material.

After a student has completed reading a passage orally, she or he answers comprehension questions about the passage. Figure 5.5 contains a passage from the Classroom Reading Inventory. Note that the comprehension questions are coded *F*, *I*, and *V*. *F* stands for factual questions, *I* stands for inferential questions, and *V* stands for vocabulary questions. These are the most common categories of questions found in IRIs, although some provide more questions, with a wider variety of types. For example, the Analytical Reading Inventory has about 10 questions per passage that fall into six categories:

M: Main idea
F: Fact
V: Vocabulary
I: Inference
S: Sequence
E: Experience/evaluation

One important feature to consider about comprehension questions is whether or not partial credit can be given for answers. Unless precisely structured, most comprehension questions are not dichotomous (either right or wrong). There can be shades of correctness in an answer. Some IRIs provide for the assignment of partial credit (e.g., The Classroom Reading Inventory); others do not (e.g., The Analytical Reading Inventory).

Some IRIs make provisions for measuring a student's reading rate or have such subtests as spelling and word-recognition inventories. One of the more thorough comparisons of the different IRIs was conducted by Jongsma and Jongsma (1981). They reviewed the eleven IRI's listed next on a number of dimensions.

Analytical Reading Inventory (ARI) by Mary I. Woods and Alden J. Moe. Columbus, OH: Charles E. Merrill, 1981.

Basic Reading Inventory (BRI) by Jerry L. Johns. Dubuque, IA: Kendall/Hunt, 1978.

Classroom Reading Inventory (CRI) 3rd ed., by Nicholas J. Silvaroli. Dubuque, IA: Wm. C. Brown, 1979.

The Contemporary Classroom Reading Inventory (CCRI) by Lee A. Rinsky and Esta de Fossard. Dubuque, IA: Gorsuch Scarisbrick, 1980.

Diagnostic Reading Inventory (DRI)(2nd ed.), by H. Donald Jacobs and Lyndon W. Searfoss. Dubuque, IA: Kendall/Hunt, 1979.

Diagnostic Reading Scales (DRS) 3rd ed., by George D. Spache. Monterey, CA: CTB/McGraw-Hill, 1981.

Edwards' Reading Test (ERT) by Peter Edwards. Exeter, NH: Heinemann, 1980.

Ekwall Reading Inventory (ERI) by Eldon E. Ekwall. Boston, MA: Allyn and Bacon, 1979.

Informal Reading Assessment (IRA) by Paul C. Burns and Betty D. Roe. Chicago, IL: Rand McNally, 1980.

Figure 5.5 *Note.* From *Classroom Reading Inventory*, 5E (p. 96) by N.J. Silvaroli, 1982,
Dubuque, IA: Wm. C. Brown. Copyright 1982 by Wm. C. Brown. All rights reserved. Reprinted by permission.

Name _____ W.P.M.
$$\frac{}{\sqrt{8880}}$$

Form B Part 2/*Level 8* (48 words)

Motivation Read to find the author's attitude regarding the behavior of pitchers
during a professional baseball game.

So Throw the Ball

Comprehension Check

One day recently when my wife turned on our television set to a Yankee-White Sox game, I noticed a phenomenon that intrigued me greatly. I happened to have the New York Times on my lap. When the catcher threw the ball back to Jim Brosnan, the Sox pitcher, I discovered that I could safely look away from the television screen, read a couple of paragraphs in the Times, and still revert my eyes in time for the pitch.

Subsequently I have begun timing baseball games with a stopwatch. I can only conclude that the modern pitcher hates to pitch. He cannot bear the thought of throwing the ball toward the plate. His ingenuity at postponing the fateful moment is uncanny. In the fastest game I have observed recently, the pitchers on the two teams held the ball for a total of one hour, eight minutes, and thirty seconds!

(F) 1. ___ Name the teams mentioned in the story?
(Yankees and White Sox)

(F) 2. ___ What paper was the man reading?
(New York Times)

(I) 3. ___ How did the author feel about the pitcher holding the ball so long?
(He felt it was unnecessary.)

(V) 4. ___ What does ingenious mean?
(Clever, original, smart, etc.)

(V) 5. ___ What does revert mean?
(To go back, return, etc.)

Scoring Guide Eighth

WR Errors		COMP Errors	
IND	3	IND	0–1
INST	7–8	INST	1½–2
FRUST	15	FRUST	2½+

Standard Reading Inventory (SRI) by Robert A. McCracken. Klamath Falls, OR: Klamath Printing Co., 1966.

Sucher-Allred Reading Placement Inventory (SARPI) by Floyd Sucher and Ruel A. Allred. Oklahoma City, OK: Economy, 1973.

Their comparative analysis is reported in Table 5.4.

According to most IRIs, one of the main uses of reading passages is to calculate a student's reading level. (We introduced the concept of reading level in our discussion of the cloze technique). Commonly, IRIs define reading levels in the following ways:

1. *The independent level.* This is the level at which students can read with no more than one uncorrected miscue in each 100 words (99%) and with at least 90% comprehension. At the independent level, the student's reading is fluent and expressive, with accurate observation of punctuation, and the student recognizes the print with confidence.

2. *The instructional level.* This is the level at which the student can read with no more than five uncorrected miscues in 100 words (95%) and with at least 75% comprehension. At the instructional level, the student's reading is generally expressive, although he or she might read more slowly than at the independent level.

3. *The frustration level.* This is the level beyond which reading has little meaning. Miscues exceed 10% (less than 90%) with comprehension at about 50%. At this level, the student exhibits obvious frustration because material is too difficult.

4. *Listening level.* This level is the one at which the student can comprehend 75% of the material read aloud by the examiner. This level purports to provide an estimate of the student's reading potential.

The first three reading levels (independent, instructional, and frustration) and the criteria for establishing the levels have generally been attributed to Betts (Beldin, 1970; Pikulski, 1974). However, Powell (1970) and Powell and Dunkeld (1971) have questioned the validity of the commonly used cutoff criteria, particularly at the instructional level.

Although they can be used as tools in planning instruction, we recommend that you interpret reading levels cautiously. As evidenced by the previous discussion, we believe that an IRI can provide far more useful diagnostic information than the somewhat artificial levels of reading.

Virtually all IRIs provide summary sheets that allow you to aggregate a student's performance both qualitatively and quantitatively. For example, Figure 5.6 contains a summary sheet from the Analytical Reading Inventory.

This summary sheet illustrates the fact that most IRIs are set up to be interpreted from a skills (bottom-up) perspective. John Stone's frustration level is grade four, his instructional level is between the second and third grade, and his independent level is the first grade. These scores indicate that John can be instructed with materials that are one to two grades below his chronological age, and, when reading for pleasure, John should choose books on about the first-

Table 5.4

FEATURES	ARI	BRI	CRI	CCRI	DRI	DRS	ERI	ERT	IRA	SARPI	SRI
Contents											
No. of forms	3	3	3	3	1	2	4	2	4	1	2
Range of passages	P-9	PP-8	PP-6	P-9	1-8	1-8	PP-9	6-13 yrs.	PP-12	P-9	PP-7
Graded word lists	P-6	PP-8	PP-6	P-7	1-8	1-6	PP-9	6-13 yrs.	PP-12	P-9	PP-7
Separate student passages	Yes	Yes	Yes	Yes	Yes	Yes	Yes	Yes	Yes	Yes	Yes
Student summary sheet	Yes	Yes	Yes	Yes	Yes	Yes	Yes	Yes	Yes	Yes	Yes
Class summary sheet	Yes	Yes	No	No	No	No	No	No	No	Yes	No
Pictures/illustrations	No	No	Yes	Yes	No	No	No	No	No	No	No
Motivation/purpose statement for each passage	Yes	No	Yes	Yes	Yes	No	No	No	Yes	Yes	Yes
Supplementary features[1]	B	B	ST	B, ST	ST	CL, ST	ST	B, ST	B	TT	CL, RS
Passages											
Length (words)	50–339	50–100	24–174	47–316	224–361	29–221	31–202	25–100	61–217	51–191	47–151
Content[2]	N, E	N, E	N, E	N, E	N	N, E	N, E	N, E	N, E	N, E	N, E
Readability estimates given	Yes	Yes	No	Yes	No	No	No	No	No	Yes	No
Readability formulas used[3]	HJ, SP	DC, FR, SP	DC, FL, SP	BG, DC, FR, HJ, SP	NI	DC, SP	DC, HJ	E, SM	FR, SP	DC, SP	DC, SP
Same format student/teacher copies	No	Yes	No	No	No	No	No	Yes	No	No	Yes
Questions											
No. per passages	PP-2.6 3-9.8 3-9.8	PP-4 P-8:10	5	P-1:5 2:6 3:7 4-9:8	1-3:12 4-8:20	1-2:7 3-8:8	PP.5 1-9:10	4-10	PP-2.8 3-12:10	5	PP.5 P-7:13-15
Types of questions[4]	L, I, CE, MI, V	L, CE, MI, V	L, I, V	CE, MI, S, V	L, I, CE, V	NI	L, I, V	NI	L, I, CE, MI, S, V	L, I, CE, MI, V	L, I, V
Suggested answers given	Yes	Yes	Yes	Yes	No	Yes	Yes	Yes	Yes	Yes	Yes

Table 5.4 (continued)

FEATURES	ARI	BRI	CRI	CCRI	DRI	DRS	ERI	ERT	IRA	SARPI	SRI
Administering											
Require											
Oral	Yes	Yes	Yes	Yes	Yes	Yes	Yes	Yes	Yes	Yes	Yes
Silent	Optional	Optional	Optional	NI	Yes	Yes	Yes	Yes	Optional	No	Yes
Listening comprehension	Yes	Optional	Optional	Optional	Yes	Yes	Optional	Yes	Optional	No	Optional
Directions given for Starting/stopping	Yes	Yes	Yes	Yes	Yes	Yes	Yes	Yes	Yes	Yes	Yes
Marking miscues/errors	Yes	Yes	Yes	Yes	Yes	Yes	Yes	Yes	Yes	Yes	Yes
Aid given in oral reading	Yes	No	Yes	Yes	Yes	Yes	Yes	Yes	Yes	Yes	Yes
Probing of comprehension recommended	NI	Yes	NI	Yes	No	Yes	Yes	NI	Yes	NI	Yes
Timing of rate	NI	Optional	Optional	NI	NI	Yes	NI	Yes	Optional	NI	Yes
Scoring											
Types of miscues/errors counted[5]	A, I, I/R, O, R, S	"Sig. Miscues"	A, I, O, R, S	A, I, I/R, M, O, R, S	A, I, O, S	A, I, I/R, M, O, R, S	A, I, I/R, M, O, R, S	I, O, S	A, I, I/R, M, O, R, S	A, I, M, O, R, S	A, I, M, O, P, R, S, SC
Partial credit for Comprehension questions	NI	Yes	Yes	Yes	No	Yes	Yes	Yes	NI	Yes	Yes
Criteria for levels independent WR	99/more	99/more	NI	97/more	98/more	NI	99/more	95/more	99/more	97/more	
Comp.	90/more	90/more	95/more	80/more	90/more	60/more	90/more	70/more	90/more	80/more	NI
Instructional WR	95/more	95/more		92/more	92/more	NI	95/more	90/more	85–95/more	92/more	

	1	2	3	4	5	6	7	8	9	10	11
Comp. Frustrational	NI	60/more	75/more	70/more	60/more	60/more	60/more	60/more	75/more	75/more	75/more
WR	NI	92/less	90/less	90/less	90/less		90/less	91/less	NI	90/less	90/less
Comp.	NI	60/less	50/less	70/less	50/less	NI	50/less	60/less		50/less	50/less
Listening comprehension	40 unaided 70 aided	NI	75/more	70/more	70/more	60/more	60/more	60–75/more	75/more	75/more	75/more
Interpreting											
Suggestions for diagnostic interpretation	Yes	No	Yes	Yes	No	Yes	Yes	Yes	Yes	Yes	No
Sample cases demonstrated	No	Yes	Yes	No	Yes	No	Yes	Yes	Yes	Yes	No
Teaching suggestions offered	No	No	No	No	No	No	No	No	No	Yes	No
Guidance for handling discrepancies in performance	Yes	Yes	Yes	No	Yes	Yes	Yes	Yes	Yes	Yes	Yes

Key:
NI = Not Indicated

[1] Supplementary Features: B, Bibliographies; CL, Checklists; CS, Case Studies; RS, Rating Scales; ST, Additional Student Tests; TT, Teacher Test.

[2] Content: N, Narration; E, Exposition.

[3] Readability Formulas: BG, Botel-Granowsky; DC, Dale-Chall; E, Edwards; FL, Flesch; FR, Fry; HJ, Harris-Jacobsen; SM, SMOG; SP, Spache.

[4] Types of Questions: CE, Critical-Evaluative; I, Interpretive-Inferential; L, Literal-Factual; MI, Main Ideas; S, Sequence; V, Vocabulary.

[5] Types of Miscues/Errors: A, Aid; I, Insertions; I/R, Inversions/Reversals; M, Mispronunciations; O, Omissions; P, Punctuation; R, Repetitions; S, Substitutions; SC, Self-Corrections.

STUDENT RECORD SUMMARY SHEET

Form A

Student _John Stone_   Grade _4_   Sex _M_   Age _9-10_
                                                      yrs. mos.

School _Merrill Elementary_ Administered by _M. L. Woods_   Date _4-28-80_

Grade	Word Lists	Graded Passages			Estimated Levels	
	% of words	WR	Comp.	Listen.		
Primer	100 %					
1	100 %	-1 Ind.	-0 Ind.			Grade
2	100%	-3 Inst.	-2 Inst.		Independent	1
3	95 %	-7 Inst.	-3 Inst.	Inst.	Instructional	2-3
4	60 %	-11 Inst.	-5 Frust.	Inst.	Frustration	4
5		-18 Frust	-6 Frust.	Inst.	Listening	5
6				Frust.		
7						
8						
9						

Check consistent oral reading difficulties:

____ word-by-word reading
____ omissions
_✓_ substitutions ← (makes numerous word guesses)
____ corrections
____ repetitions
____ reversals
_✓_ inattention to punctuation
____ word inserts
____ requests word help

Check consistent word recognition difficulties:

____ single consonants
____ consonant clusters
_✓_ long vowels ⎫ medial
_✓_ short vowels ⎰
____ vowel digraphs
____ diphthongs
____ syllabication
_✓_ use of context (must strengthen)
____ basic sight
_✓_ grade level sight

Check consistent comprehension difficulties:

_✓_ main idea
____ factual
_✓_ terminology
_✓_ cause and effect
____ inferential
____ drawing conclusions
_✓_ independent recall

Identifying special reading strengths:

John displays skill in the use of initial consonants and some blends. He also uses configuration clues as a word recognition strategy. His listening capacity is above both his grade level and instructional level. He displays some use of context clues and recalls factual information more readily than other types of comprehension information.

Figure 5.6 STUDENT RECORD SUMMARY SHEET. *Note.* From *Analytical Reading Inventory* Third Edition (p. 75) by M.I. Woods and A.I. Moe, 1981, Columbus, OH: Charles E. Merrill. Copyright 1985 by Charles E. Merrill Publishing Co. Reprinted by permission.

grade level. The summary sheet also highlights the types of word-recognition errors that John makes. John makes many substitutions and does not pay attention to punctuation. Particularly, he has problems with long and short vowels. This provides a great deal of information if you wish to heavily emphasize word identification. As far as types of comprehension questions missed, John has problems with main idea, terminology, and cause and effect.

Teacher-made IRIs

Some reading teachers would rather develop their own IRIs than use commercially prepared ones. The advantage to developing your own IRI is that you can use reading material students will actually encounter in class. You can also tailor the inventory to highlight the specific components of your model of reading. The disadvantage to preparing your own IRIs is that it is very time consuming. You have to select passages and make sure they are suitable for the students you wish to test. Also, developing comprehension questions can be an arduous task. Following is a series of steps for developing your own IRI.

Step 1. Select a list of words that can be used to assess a student's sight vocabulary level and her or his word recognition strategies. You may choose to use a graded word list already developed (see chapter 8 for discussion of various word lists), or you can select words from the basal series you are using. At each level, pick a random 20 words for the word-recognition list. These words should be typed by level on a sheet of paper for your use and placed individually on index cards for the student's use.

Step 2. Select two passages of approximately 100–200 words for each grade level you want to include in your IRI. Two passages at each grade level will allow you to develop different forms of your IRI.

It is important to select passages that will interest students, regardless of age. You might have an 8-year-old who reads three age levels above his or her chronological age and a 14-year-old who reads three age levels below his or her chronological age. If a student's interest in the content of the material is high, a more accurate and complete diagnosis is likely.

Another consideration when selecting reading passages is their level of difficulty. The most commonly used formulas for determining the readability of a passage seem to be the Dale-Chall, Flesch, Fry, and Raygor. A number of years ago, Dale and Chall (1958) compared many of the reading formulas. Virtually all of them rely on two variables to determine readability: the ratio of short to long words in a passage and the ratio of short to long sentences in a passage. In other words, most readability formulas operate on the assumption that short words are easier to read than long words and short sentences are easier than long sentences. More recent research indicates that this is too simplistic a view of readability. For example, L.A. Smith (1976) found that, when material is familiar to students, they can read very long, complex, syntactic structures.

Figure 5.7

Directions: Count out three 100-word passages at the beginning, middle, and end of a selection or book. Count proper nouns, but not numerals.

1. Count sentences in each passage, estimating to the nearest tenth.
2. Count words with six or more letters.
3. Average the sentence length and word lenght over three samples and plot the average on the graph.

RAYGOR READABILITY ESTIMATE

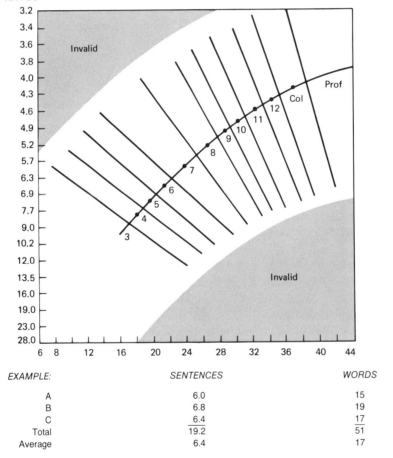

EXAMPLE:	SENTENCES	WORDS
A	6.0	15
B	6.8	19
C	6.4	17
Total	19.2	51
Average	6.4	17

Note mark on graph: Grade level is about 5.

Note. From "A concurrent validity study of the Raygor Readability Estimate" Scott Baldwin and Rhonda Kaufman, 1979, *Journal of Reading 23*, pp. 48–153. This graph is not copyrighted. It may be reproduced. Copies can also be obtained from Dr. Alton L. Raygor, University of Minnesota, 192 Pillsbury Drive S.E., Minneapolis, Minnesota 55455.

We suggest you determine the readability of your passages by the combined use of a reading formula and field testing. That is, use a formula to obtain initial grade-level estimates for your passages. Then administer the passages to selected students. Ideally, try to administer the passages to students at different grade levels. If you can't do this, administer the passages to students at a single grade level whom you know have differing levels of reading ability. Ask students comprehension questions, or ask them to retell the information in the passage. Then adjust the grade levels of your passages on the basis of the feedback from students. The Raygor readability formula is presented in Figure 5.7. We suggest that you also consider some of the other formulas mentioned previously.

Step 3. Develop comprehension questions for each of the passages. This is the most difficult part in the development of an IRI. Depending on the length of the passage, you should develop from 5 to 10 questions. As we saw in the discussion of commercially prepared IRIs, most inventories contain different levels of questions. Three levels commonly used in the development of teacher-made IRIs are literal, interpretive, and applied. Literal questions are textbound. That is, the answer can be found directly in the text. The second level of questioning, the interpretive level, begins to move away from the text and becomes reader based. This level is often called *reading between the lines*, because the reader has to combine information and make inferences. Depending on the question asked, the answer might be found directly in the text by combining pieces of information to make a generalization, or the answer might draw on the reader's knowledge of the subject, with little information actually coming from the text. The third level of questioning, called the *applied level*, requires the reader to use information in the text to express opinions and to form new ideas. This level is also very reader based.

Another way of developing comprehension questions for an IRI is to write questions that directly reflect elements of the reading model you subscribe to. For example, at a very general level, this means that you would write questions relating to the word, discourse, and schema levels of analysis. Questions written at the word level would test students' knowledge of specific concepts within the passage. Questions written at the discourse level would determine whether students could recognize basic relationships among ideas, larger patterns of ideas, and superstructures for entire passages. Questions written at the schema level would require students to fill in all the nontextbound information the reader must have to understand the passage. In chapters 9, 10, and 11 we will provide specific examples of such questioning techniques.

Regardless of which scheme you use, make sure to include in your IRI questions at all levels. It is best to write the reader-based questions first because they are the most difficult. Then write the text-based questions. Most teacher-made IRIs have a preponderance of text-based questions.

There is one other important point that we should note about writing questions. When writing, make sure that your questions are passage dependent. That is, students should have to read the passage to answer the questions. Tuiman (1976) and Hanna and Oaster (1978–79) found that subjects could answer questions to many reading passages without reading the passages. These researchers labeled such questions *passage independent*. Although we have seen that background knowledge plays an important function in the reading process, you want to ask passage-dependent questions so that you can assess students' strengths and weaknesses in reading, not their prior knowledge.

Step 4. Develop response sheets for use while administering the IRI. You need response sheets on which to record students' errors made during the administration of the IRI. These response sheets may have various formats, from a one-page sheet with blanks for recording errors to copies of each page of the inventory, on which you mark oral reading errors. Your response sheets should include the following information:

1. Student's name
2. Your name and date of administration
3. Levels of IRI passages used
4. Responses to the comprehension questions
5. Summary of word recognition and comprehension
6. Special notes

Step 5. Type the passages the student will read. You will need to type the passages for the students on a separate sheet of paper or on index cards. We recommend that you use primary type and double-spaced lines. This way the student will not be hampered by type that is too small to read.

The administration and the interpretation of the teacher-made IRI are the same as for commercially prepared IRIs. Administer the word list to assess a student's sight vocabulary and word-recognition skills. Have students read the passages orally and answer the comprehension question. Identify miscues as students read and interpret them along with students' answers to the questions. Finally, interpret all the information in light of your model of reading.

THE READING MISCUE INVENTORY

As alluded to previously, the Reading Miscue Inventory (Y.M. Goodman & Burke, 1972) is one of the, if not the, most sophisticated tools for analyzing a student's oral reading. Because of this we have chosen to consider it a special type of informal test. The RMI is an outgrowth of research studies conducted by Kenneth and Yetta Goodman at Wayne State University in the 1960s. The authors of the RMI, Yetta Goodman and Carolyn Burke, provided four basic assumptions for the development of this instrument, as follows:

1. All readers bring an oral language system to the reading process.
2. All readers bring the sum total of their past experiences to the reading process.

3. Reading materials represent the language patterns and past experiences of the author.
4. Reading is an active process, which involves constant interaction between the reader and the test. (pp. 10–15)

We will discuss the RMI in some detail because of its sophistication. Even though most classroom teachers will never use it, an understanding of the RMI can provide valuable insights into oral reading errors, insights that can be used with an IRI or even casual observation of students' oral reading.

The first step in administering the RMI is to select a passage that is of interest to the student. Y.M. Goodman and Burke (1972) provided the following guidelines:

> The selection must be difficult enough for the student so that reading miscues will be made, but not so difficult that he will be unable to continue independently. It is helpful to have two or three selections of different difficulty levels available for use. A good rule of thumb is to choose the initial selection from material one grade level above that which is usually assigned the student in class. (p. 20)

A detailed work sheet of the material is then prepared, with each line number and page number identified. The student reads from the original material; the examiner uses the work sheet. The student reads for 15 to 20 minutes, while the examiner tape-records the session. The examiner is not allowed to provide any assistance to the student during the testing time. While the student is reading, the examiner records errors or miscues on the work sheet.

Only five types of miscues are recorded: substitutions, omissions, insertions, reversals, and repetitions. However, these miscues are broken down into fine detail. For example, repetition miscues are divided into four subcategories:

A. *Correcting a miscue:* The reader makes a mistake and then backs up to correct it.
B. *Abandoning a correct form:* The reader says a word correctly but then repeats the word incorrectly.
C. *Unsuccessfully attempting to correct:* The reader makes a mistake and then tries to correct it but is unsuccessful.
D. *Anticipating difficulty with a subsequent word:* The reader repeats a word or phrase because he or she sees an upcoming word that is difficult.

When the student has finished reading, she or he is asked to retell the information in as much detail as possible. The examiner is free to ask probing questions of the student during the retelling phase. The examiner should take notes on the student's retelling and tape-record it for future analysis.

Once the session is over, the teacher plays the tape recording of the session, checking to see if miscues were correctly identified and the student's retelling accurately represented. The miscues are then analyzed in detail. This analysis begins with the asking of nine questions about each miscue:

Sample: Mike's Complete Coding Sheet

READING MISCUE INVENTORY

Miscue Number	Reader	Text	DIALECT 1	INTONATION 2	GRAPHIC SIMILARITY 3 Y	P	N
01-1	Knew	Know			✓		
03-2	the	a					✓
04-3	seven	Sven			✓		
05-4	—	olsen			—	—	—
05-5	went	wanted			✓		
06-6	never	ever	Y		✓		
06-7	•	—		Y	—	—	—
08-8	—	Claribel			—	—	—
10-9	music	musical			✓		
14-10	heard	had			✓		
15-11	Clardo	Claribel			✓		
16-12	—	small			—	—	—
16-13	care	canary				✓	
18-14	and	at				✓	
19-15	have stayed	stay			—	—	—
21-16	had	—			—	—	—
01-17	carrot	canary				✓	
04-18	$ cainery	candry			✓		
05-19	it done	done it			—	—	—
01-20	Steve's	Sven's			✓		
02-21	—	a			—	—	—
05-22	—	space			—	—	—
06-23	could not	couldn't			—	—	—
06-24	rules	rule			✓		
07-25	put	but			✓		
		COLUMN TOTAL			11	3	1
		PERCENTAGE			73	20	7
		QUESTION TOTAL					15

Figure 5.8 READING MISCUE INVENTORY CODING SHEET

CODING SHEET

SOUND SIMILARITY 4			GRAMMATICAL FUNCTION 5			CORRECTION 6	GRAMMATICAL ACCEPTABILITY 7	SEMANTIC ACCEPTABILITY 8	MEANING CHANGE 9	COMPREHENSION			GRAMMATICAL RELATIONSHIPS			
Y	P	N	Y	P	N					No Loss	Partial Loss	Loss	Strength	Partial Strength	Weakness	Overcorrection
✓			✓			N	Y	Y	P		✓		✓			
✓			✓			N	Y	Y	P		✓		✓			
✓	✓				✓	N	P	P	Y			✓			✓	
						N	P	P	Y			✓			✓	
✓			✓			Y	P	N	Y	✓			✓			
✓			✓			Y	Y	Y	N	✓						✓
						N	P	P	P		✓				✓	
						N	N	N	Y			✓			✓	
✓			✓			N	Y	Y	P		✓		✓			
✓			✓			N	Y	P	Y			✓		✓		
	✓		✓			P	Y	N	N	✓	✓			✓		
						N	P	P	P	✓						
	✓				✓	P	N	N	Y			✓			✓	
		✓				P	P	P	Y			✓			✓	
						N	Y	Y	N	✓			✓			
						N	Y	P	N	✓					✓	
	✓		✓			N	Y	P	Y			✓			✓	
✓			✓			N	Y	N	Y			✓			✓	
						Y	Y	P	Y	✓			✓			
	✓		✓			N	Y	Y	N	✓			✓			
						N	Y	Y	Y		✓		✓			
						N	Y	Y	N	✓			✓			
						Y	Y	Y	N	✓						✓
✓			✓			N	Y	Y	N	✓			✓			
	✓				✓	Y	N	Y	Y	✓			✓			

SS-Y	SS-P	SS-N	GF-Y	GF-P	GF-N											
9	**5**	**1**	**11**	**2**	**2**	**COLUMN TOTAL**				10	7	8	11	5	7	2
60	33	7	73	13	13	**PERCENTAGE**				42	28	32	44	20	28	8
	15			15		**PATTERN TOTAL**					25			25		

The Reading Miscue Inventory (p. 82–83) by Y.M. Goodman & C.L. Burke, 1972. New York: Macmillan. Copyright 1972 by C.L. Burke and Y.M. Goodman. Reprinted by permission.

1. *Dialect.* Is a dialect variation involved in the miscue?
2. *Intonation.* Is a shift in intonation involved in the miscue?
3. *Graphic Similarity.* How much does the miscue look like what was expected?
4. *Sound Similarity.* How much does the miscue sound like what was expected?
5. *Grammatical Function.* Is the grammatical function of the miscue the same as the grammatical function of the word in the text?
6. *Correction.* Is the miscue corrected?
7. *Grammatical Acceptability.* Does the miscue occur in a structure that is grammatically acceptable?
8. *Semantic Acceptability.* Does the miscue occur in a structure that is semantically acceptable?
9. *Meaning Change.* Does the miscue result in a change of meaning? (Y.M. Goodman & Burke, 1972, pp. 49–50).

As mentioned previously, these questions were developed after extensive research. In its early stages of development, the RMI asked as many as 17 questions of each miscue, each question with a number of subquestions (see P.D. Allen & Watson, 1976). However, research indicated that the nine questions provided all necessary information with which to make interpretations about a student's reading performance. As the questions are asked for each miscue, the answers are recorded on an RMI coding sheet. Figure 5.8 contains a sample coding sheet.

Table 5.5 Patterns of Comprehension

NO LOSS		*PARTIAL LOSS*		*LOSS*
Columns $6+8+9$	*Columns* $6+8+9$	*Columns* $6+8+9$	*Columns* $6+8+9$	*Columns* $6+8+9$
Y+Y+N	Y+P+N	N+P+P	P+N+P	N+N+P
Y+P+P	Y+N+N	N+Y+P	P+P+P	N+N+Y
Y+P+Y	N+N+N	P+Y+N	P+Y+P	N+P+Y
Y+N+Y	Y+Y+P	P+Y+Y	P+P+N	P+N+Y
N+Y+N	Y+N+P	N+Y+Y	P+N+N	P+P+Y
N+P+N	Y+Y+Y			

Patterns of Grammatical Relationships

STRENGTH	*PARTIAL STRENGTH*	*WEAKNESS*	*OVERCORRECTION*
Columns $6+7+8$	*Columns* $6+7+8$	*Columns* $6+7+8$	*Columns* $6+7+8$
Y+N+N	N+Y+N	N+N+N	Y+Y+Y
Y+P+N	N+Y+P	N+P+N	P+Y+Y
Y+Y+N	P+Y+N	N+P+P	
Y+P+P	P+Y+P	P+N+N	
Y+Y+P		P+P+N	
N+Y+Y		P+P+P	

From *The Reading Miscue Inventory* (p. 128) by Y.M. Goodman and C.L. Burke, 1972, New York: Macmillan. Copyright 1972 by C.L. Burke and Y.M. Goodman. Reprinted by permission.

Meaningful patterns are then identified within the list of miscues. Specifically the examiner tries to identify: (a) the extent to which the miscues interfered with the student's comprehension, (b) the extent to which the student used the letter-sound relationships in a word even when he or she did not know the word, and (c) the extent to which the miscues represented the same syntactic function and made sense within the context of the surrounding words. The identification of patterns within the miscues is not a subjective process. Rather, the inventory authors provide "pattern charts" like those in Table 5.5. Once miscue patterns are identified, they are recorded on a Reader Profile, an example of which is presented in Figure 5.9.

The graph at the upper right-hand corner of the profile with the shaded areas labeled *no loss*, *partial loss*, and *loss* represents the extent to which the student's miscues affect comprehension. This is directly interpretable in terms of a model of reading. More specifically, it provides you with information as to how efficient the student's schema-level processing is. If a student is processing information from the top down, then she or he is constantly trying to maximize meaning. Errors or miscues that are made tend to be logical within the general domain of the story.

The chart labeled *Grammatical Relationships* in Figure 5.9 provides information about the student's performance at the syntactic and discourse levels of analysis. The subheading entitled *function* relates to syntax. High scores on the *identical* column indicate that the student is using the syntactic cues in the language to help determine unknown words. The subheading labeled *relationships* in the grammatical relationships chart deals with the semantic acceptability of the miscue at the local level, the level of information immediately surrounding the miscue. A high score in the *strength* column within the relationships section indicates that a student is using his or her knowledge of discourse structures to identify unknown words.

Finally, the chart labeled *Sound/Graphic Relationships* provides information about the student's performance at the phonemic and perhaps letter-recognition levels of analysis. The *Graphic* section of that chart identifies the extent to which the student uses the letter cues in attacking a difficult word; the *Sound* section of the chart indicates the extent to which the student's miscues contained the correct sounds for the actual words in the text.

While identifying meaningful patterns in miscues, the examiner also notes any repeated miscues at the bottom of the Reader Profile. Finally, the teacher evaluates the student's retelling. The RMI provides a scoring system for story and informational material. That scoring system is presented in Table 5.6.

We believe this to be the weakest part of the RMI. Although the system presented in Table 5.6 does provide guidance for the teacher when analyzing the content of the retelling, it does not reflect the current knowledge base we have about the information in different types of discourse. In chapter 9 we will discuss in depth the types of information you would expect students to remember from different types of discourse. Briefly, though, for story (narrative) material,

READING MISCUE INVENTORY

Selection *Space Pet*
School

Date
Class

Reader *Mike*
Teacher

COMPREHENSION PATTERN

Percent of relationships of No
Comprehension Loss to Partial
Comprehension Loss to
Comprehension Loss

**Reader's Use of
Reading Strategies:**

Highly Effective	☐
Moderately Effective	☐
Some Effective	☐
Ineffective	☐

SOUND/GRAPHIC RELATIONSHIPS

Graphic			Sound		
High	Some	None	High	Some	None

Repeated and Multiple Miscues

Reader	Text	Frequency of Miscue Occurrence	Frequency of Text Item Occurrence	Occurrence of Correction
seven	sven	1	7	0
Steve	sven	7	7	0
—	Claribel	1	10	8
Clardo	Claribel	1	10	8
claredo	Claribel	1	10	8
Claribul	Claribel	3	10	8
Claribil	Claribel	3	10	8
care	canary	1	6	0
carrot	canary	3	6	0
$ cainery	canary	3	6	0
cannery	canary	1	6	0

Figure 5.9 READING MISCUE INVENTORY READER PROFILE. *Note.* From *The Reading Miscue Inventory* (p. 90–91) by Y.M. Goodman and C.L. Burke, 1972, New York: Macmillan. Copyright 1972 by C.L. Burke and Y.M. Goodman. Reprinted by permission.

READER PROFILE

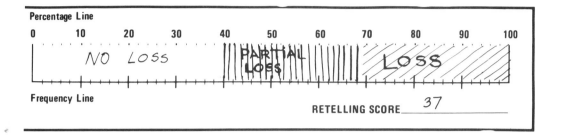

Percentage Line

0	10	20	30	40	50	60	70	80	90	100

NO LOSS   PARTIAL LOSS   LOSS

Frequency Line

RETELLING SCORE ___37___

GRAMMATICAL RELATIONSHIPS

Function			Relationships			
Identical	Indeterminate	different	Strength	Partial Strength	Weakness	Overcorrection
100	100	100	100	100	100	100
90	90	90	90	90	90	90
80	80	80	80	80	80	80
70	70	70	70	70	70	70
60	60	60	60	60	60	60
50	50	50	50	50	50	50
40	40	40	40	40	40	40
30	30	30	30	30	30	30
20	20	20	20	20	20	20

Reader	Text	Frequency of Miscue Occurrence	Frequency of Text Item Occurrence	Occurrence of Correction
$canries	canary	1	6	0

Table 5.6 Point Distribution for Retelling Formats

STORY MATERIAL	MAXIMUM POINTS	INFORMATIONAL MATERIAL	MAXIMUM POINTS
Character Analysis:			
Recall	15	Specifics	40
Development	15	Generalizations	30
Events	30	Major Concepts	30
Plot	20		
Theme	20		

From *The Reading Miscue Inventory* (p. 24) by Y.M. Goodman and C.L. Burke, 1972, New York: Macmillan. Copyright 1972 by C.L. Burke and Y.M. Goodman. Reprint by permission.

you should expect students to remember such elements as

1. Setting: time, place, and context of the story
2. Initiating event: something that causes the main character to respond in some manner
3. Reaction of the characters to the initiating event
4. Overt action or actions carried out to attain some goal
5. Attainment of the goal
6. Characters' reaction to attaiment of the goal

For informative (expository) material, you would expect students to remember such information as

1. The characteristics of any major concepts presented
2. Any major generalizations and their examples
3. Any processes described
4. Major cause-effect relationships
5. Any comparisons that were made
6. Major claims and their supporting arguments

Again, for a detailed discussion of these types of information, we refer you to chapter 9. These organizational structures can be used to probe a student's retelling to obtain a very accurate view of her or his overall comprehension of the passage.

As this discussion has indicated, the RMI can be a very effective tool in the hands of a skilled diagnostician. However, it requires a great deal of practice and a specific view of reading. As K. Goodman (1973) suggested, use of miscue analysis as a diagnostic tool is dependent on the teacher's moving to a view of reading as a primarily top-down, meaning-getting, language process.

As alluded to previously, many classroom teachers and some clinicians

Table 5.7

Word in Text	Word as Stated by Student	1. Core list grade level of word in text	2. Semantic acceptability of stated word (H-M-L)	3. Syntactic acceptability of stated word (H-M-L)	4. Sound-symbol acceptability of stated word (H-M-L)
1. coat	boat	1	L	H	M
2. apple	waffle	1	L	H	M
3. battle	war	3	H	H	L
4.					
5.					
6.					

find the RMI too complex or too time consuming to use. Some of them develop their own modified versions of it. As an illustration, consider the example in Table 5.7.

When you use a modified miscue, you do not look at miscues the student has corrected. If the miscue is corrected, there is no loss of comprehension. Similarly, you do not have to code all of the different types of miscues. We recommend that you code substitutions and insertions and possible omissions but exclude reversals and repetitions. The reason is that substitutions, insertions, and omissions provide the most information about the student's process of reading. Also, when using a modified RMI, you don't need to ask all nine questions. Rather you should select three or four that provide you with the most meaningful information based on your beliefs about reading. For example, in Table 5.7 four categories are used. Categories 2, 3, and 4 analyze the miscue's semantic, syntactic, and sound-symbol acceptability. Respectively, they are similar to questions 8 and 7 and the combination of 3 and 4 in the RMI. Category 1 in Table 5.7 gets at the level of sight vocabulary for the student (something not included in the RMI). If the student has miscues on words that come from a core vocabulary list, it is probably an indication that he or she does not have an adequate store of immediately recognizable basic words.

This illustrates the fact that, by combining some of the features of the RMI with aspects of other assessment techniques, you can develop a very personalized and highly useful informal assessment scheme.

SUMMARY

In this chapter we have presented informal assessment techniques. Informal techniques can be used by the classroom teacher or the reading specialist. We first discussed simple observation and interview techniques under the general heading of *naturalistic assessment*, "kid watching" in its most basic form. We then discussed a number of informal group tests. These included the cloze procedure, the maze procedure, and group reading inventories. These techniques can be used with materials students actually encounter in class and can be administered to large groups of students. Informal reading inventories, on the other hand, are administered individually to students. However, they can yield a great deal of information about the strategies a student uses while reading. We discussed commercially prepared and teacher-made IRIs. Finally we considered the Reading Miscue Inventory, the most sophisticated informal assessment tool. The technique allows you to determine the extent to which a student reads for meaning, using the semantic, syntactic, and grapho-phonic cuing systems of language.

6

FORMAL ASSESSMENT

In the last chapter, we presented a number of ways that a classroom teacher or a reading specialist can assess students' reading abilities through informal measures. In this chapter, we will present methods for assessing reading ability using standardized measures. Although many critics of standardized tests assert that they do not accurately assess reading ability, we believe it is possible to gain reliable information if these tests are interpreted properly. The advantage of a standardized test over an informal test is that you can compare your students' performance with that of other students across the nation from the same age group and you can compare your students' performance to some preestablished criterion.

In this chapter, we will discuss (a) norm-referenced tests, (b) criterion-referenced tests, (c) methods of probing tests, (d) technical characteristics of tests, and (e) criteria for selecting tests.

NORM-REFERENCED TESTS

Standardized tests are usually grouped into two broad categories: norm-referenced and criterion-referenced. Norm-referenced tests are used to compare individual performance to that of a norm group, which presumably represents an appropriate larger population. Many children across the country take norm-referenced tests each year in the form of achievement tests such as the California Achievement Test, the Iowa Test of Basic Skills, or the Comprehensive Test of Basic Skills.

One of the most important qualities of a norm-referenced test is its norms. Before using a norm-referenced test you should carefully study the test manual, paying special attention to the following factors:

1. *Age of the sample*. You will want to make sure that the norming sample represents the age group you are testing. Most reading tests cover two or three age levels, and those levels should be represented in the norming sample.
2. *Grade level of the sample*. Some tests give the age levels and grade levels of the sample population. As with the age of the sample, you will want to make sure that the sample grade level represents the grade level you are testing.
3. *Sex of the sample*. The percentage of males and females taking the test should be approximately equal.
4. *Socioeconomic status of the sample*. The sample population should represent a variety of social classes.
5. *Ethnicity of the sample*. The norming sample should include a mixture of races and cultures. Hispanics will soon become the largest minority in this country. If you have Hispanic students or other minorities in your class, you should find a test that was normed on a sample including Hispanics and the other minority groups.
6. *Date the sample was tested*. This is a crucial aspect when considering a norm-referenced test. If a test was normed 20 or 30 years ago, you can be sure that the norming sample is not representative of today's population. Ideally, you want to find a test that was normed fairly recently. However, a recent copyright date on a test does not necessarily mean that the test was recently normed. Mehrens and Lehmann (1980) warned that "the recency of norm groups on a published test can not be judged by the copyright date of the test manual. Any change in the test manual allows the publisher to revise the copyright date of the manual although the later date may not be an indication of the recency of the norms" (p. 87).
7. *Sample size*. In general, the more subjects in the norming population, the better. Salvia and Ysseldyke (1981) recommended that a norming population have a sample of at least 100 subjects. Realistically, a sample population should have more than 100 subjects, and, if the test covers a few grade levels, the subject pool should include 100 people at each level.

Survey Tests

Norm-referenced tests can be divided into two categories: survey tests and diagnostic tests. Survey tests are used for screening; they do not yield specific information about a reader's strengths and weaknesses in a given reading skill. Instead they measure more general reading ability.

Some survey tests are meant to be administered to groups of students; some are meant to be administered individually to students. We recommend that you use a group survey test. For example, the Gates-MacGinite Reading Tests is a group survey test, as are the reading tests from achievement batteries, such as the California Achievement Test. Many teachers assume that an individual test is always superior to a group test. However, given the purpose of a survey test, there is no need for it to be individual. According to W.H. Miller (1978), the major purpose for giving a survey test is "to determine the general reading achievement of all of the students in a class and to locate those students who need to have their reading competencies assessed by [further diagnostic techniques]" (p. 82).

Survey tests, then, are useful as a general measure of reading ability and are not intended to identify specific skill weaknesses. Hence, no matter what model of reading you ascribe to (e.g., skills approach, top-down) a survey test is a useful screening device.

In general, standardized survey tests are quite easy to administer. They do not require a trained examiner and can be administered in a short period of time. Commonly, students answer questions using a separate answer sheet. This is either scored by hand or sent back to the testing company and machine scored. The results are then translated into grade equivalency scores, percentile ranks, or stanines (we will discuss these scores in depth in a subsequent section of this chapter) and used to determine whether students are to be considered developmental, corrective, or remedial readers.

Recall from chapter 1 that students who learn to read successfully with a minimal amount of instruction are considered developmental. They generally score at or above grade level on a survey test or are at the 50th percentile or higher for their grade level. Corrective readers generally score one year or less below their grade or are slightly below the 50th percentile for their grade level. Their reading problems are regarded as being correctable in a regular classroom setting. Remedial readers have more serious problems and generally score two or more years below grade level or at the low end of the percentile distribution on a survey test. Both corrective and remedial readers generally require more testing.

At the elementary level, classroom teachers usually administer survey tests. At the secondary level, the guidance department is sometimes responsible for all testing. If you administer a survey test, study the manual carefully. It will provide very detailed instructions, which will add to the test reliability. For example, each student will need a pencil with an eraser. The room should be quiet and free from distraction. As much as possible you should try to lower the anxiety level of students, because high anxiety produces artificially low scores.

An important distinction to make about survey tests is the variables they use to measure overall reading ability. For example, the reading section of the Wide Range Achievement Test (WRAT) measures reading ability by testing only word recognition and pronunciation skills. Given our assertions in chapters 2, 3, and 4 that reading includes many levels of analysis, these tests might not be representative of overall reading performance. However, the Gates-MacGinite Reading Tests measure vocabulary in isolation, reading comprehension, and reading rate. These seem much more representative of general reading competence.

Diagnostic Tests

If you have students in a reading class whom you want to test further after you have administered a survey test, the next step is to administer a diagnostic test. Diagnostic tests are designed to assess specific reading skills so that you can pinpoint strengths and weaknesses for instructional purposes. Diagnostic tests take a much longer time to administer than survey tests, commonly as long as 2 to 3 hours. As is the case with survey tests, there are group diagnostic tests and individual diagnostic tests.

Group diagnostic tests are similar in format to survey tests but include more subtests. The subtests can be used to develop a profile of a student's competencies. For example, the Stanford Diagnostic Reading Test (SDRT) (Karlsen, Madden, & Gardner, 1976), which many reading teachers use, assesses a number of skill areas. There are four different levels with two forms at each level:

Red Level (grades 1.6–3.5) Auditory vocabulary, auditory discrimination, phonetic analysis, word reading, and reading comprehension

Green Level (grades 2.6–5.5) Auditory vocabulary, auditory discrimination, phonetic analysis, structural analysis, and reading comprehension

Brown Level (grades 4.6–9.5) Auditory vocabulary, reading comprehension, phonetic analysis, structural analysis, and reading rate

Blue Level (grades 9–13) Reading comprehension, word meaning, word parts, phonetic analysis, structural analysis, fast reading, skimming and scanning

The materials for each level include test booklets, a manual for interpreting and administering, and an Instructional Placement Report.

The SDRT is meant to be interpreted from a skills perspective. In fact, the test authors clearly articulate their model in the test manual.

> In the early stages of learning to read, pupils generally translate, or decode, the printed word into the spoken word; then, as they mature and develop a fair degree of competency in decoding, attention is given to building vocabulary, improving comprehension, and finally, to increasing reading speed. It is this philosophy of the nature of the reading process that has guided the authors in the development of the SDRT series. (Manual for Administering and Interpreting, p. 5)

The overall philosophy of the SDRT series, then, is to concentrate first on the "bottom" skills discussed in chapters 3 and 4 and to then gradually shift the emphasis to the "top" skills. To illustrate how the SDRT can be interpreted from the perspective of some of the other models, we will consider in depth the subtests of the Red Level. We should note here that the examples we use are not actually from the SDRT; they are simply *like* the items on it. In keeping with the overall scheme, the Red Level emphasizes decoding skills and excludes reading rate. Figure 6.1 illustrates the relationship of the subtests to the SDRT model.

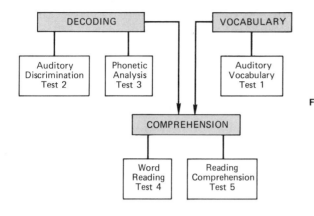

In the Auditory Vocabulary subtest, the meaning of a word is described to students. They must then select the picture that represents the word. For example, students might be asked, which picture shows an animal? They are presented with options like the following:

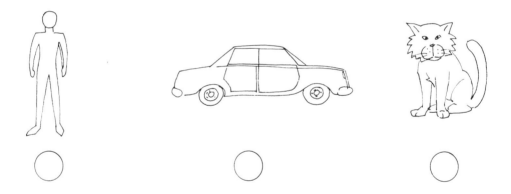

This subtest is best interpreted as a measure of what many reading teachers call *listening vocabulary*—those words the student understands when heard. Most theorists agree that a word must be in a student's listening vocabulary before it can become a part of his or her sight vocabulary. Hence, the Auditory Vocabulary subtest of the SDRT can be viewed as a measure of declarative knowledge necessary for word recognition.

Test 2, Auditory Discrimination, is a measure of students' ability to hear similarities and differences among the sounds in words. In chapter 3 we discussed the fact that this *phonetic hearing* is considered a prerequisite for the phonemic analysis level of the reading process. From a production-theory perspective, it is declarative knowledge necessary for effective use of sounding and blending strategies. To assess auditory discrimination ability, students are presented with pairs of words dictated by the teacher and then asked questions about the sounds in those words, for example,

> Do *step* and *line* begin with the same sound?
> Do *gone* and *home* end with the same sound?

Test 3 is entitled Phonetic Analysis and is concerned with relationships between letters and sounds. Students are presented with a word and then asked to identify letters that begin or end the word. For example,

> Here you see a picture of a car. Mark the space next to the letters that tell the beginning sounds of *car*.
> Here you see a picture of a dog. Mark the space next to the letters that tell the beginning sounds of *dog*.

At the lower levels (e.g., Red, Green), the phonetic analysis tests measure only letter-sound relationships, declarative knowledge necessary for the use of sounding and blending strategies. At the upper levels, the phonetic analysis subtests include spelling patterns. Recall that in chapters 2 and 3 we discussed the fact that these are considered declarative knowledge used in word-recognition strategies within the production-theory approach.

In Test 4, Word Reading, students are presented with pictures and asked to find the word that goes with the picture. For example, students might be shown a picture of a cake and given three word choices: *boat, book, cake*. Students are allowed to progress at their own rate through the items of this test. Consequently, it is impossible to tell whether they recognize the words by sight or use word-recognition strategies to decode words they do not recognize immediately.

The final test of the SDRT, Test 5, is entitled Reading Comprehension. At the higher level, students are presented with passages they read silently. They then answer questions about those passages. At the lower levels, students read a sentence or two and are required to select a picture that best represents the meaning of a sentence. For example, Figure 6.2 contains the type of comprehension item you might find at the lower levels.

In general, this is a fairly straightforward measure of comprehension; however, the validity of each item depends on the extent to which the picture represents the meaning conveyed in the sentence. That is, the way the information is pictured in the item must accurately represent the question being asked. We are not suggesting that picture comprehension items on the SDRT are invalid, only that, when pictures are used to test comprehension, the teacher should be aware of the increased possibility of student confusion.

As indicated, the SDRT provides useful information that is primarily declarative in nature. If you use a strict skills approach, each score can be interpreted as an explicit strength or weakness and instructional activities pre-

Figure 6.2 Which glass has fallen over?

scribed. However, if you use top-down, interactive, or production-theory models, the SDRT does not provide much information about the reading strategies a student is using. Most reading teachers rely on individual diagnostic tests to analyze reading strategies.

Two popular individual diagnostic tests are the Spache Diagnostic Reading Scales (Spache, 1981) and the Durrell Analysis of Reading Difficulty (Durrell & Catterson, 1980). As is the case with most individual diagnostic tests, both of these are very similar to the IRIs discussed in chapter 5. The main difference is that standardized individual diagnostic tests provide norms for interpretation. We will briefly consider the Spache and then the Durrell.

The Spache Diagnostic Reading Scales can be used with most students in grades 1 through 6 and with remedial students in junior and senior high school. The test consists of an Examiner's Manual, an Examiner's Record Booklet, and a reusable Test Book. The Test Book contains three word-recognition lists, 22 reading passages, and eight supplementary phonics tests.

As is the case with an IRI, a student keeps reading the word lists orally until she or he makes a specific number of errors. Again the word lists are used to obtain information about a pupil's word analysis skills and to determine the level at which she or he should be introduced to the reading passages. As an aid to interpreting student miscues on the word lists (and during oral reading), the test manual suggests that errors should be classified as to whether the student

> Spells out the unknown word letter by letter
> Uses some phonic method (e.g. sounds initial letter and fuses it with rest of word)
> Identifies spelling patterns within the word

Once the word list section of the test is completed, the student begins reading, using the reading passages. These range in difficulty from the mid first-grade reading level through the eighth-grade reading level. The first few passages are narrative in nature. The rest reflect different discourse types (e.g., descriptive, expository) from different content areas. The student begins by reading each passage orally. After completing this, the student answers questions about the passage.

The student's performance on the word list and oral reading sections of the test is also used to determine his or her instructional and independent levels of reading, as is the case with an IRI. As defined by the Examiner's Manual of the Spache Scales, the instructional level is the reading level at which instruction can be carried on. This is the point at which the student has no undue difficulty reading the words of the material. The independent level identifies the grade level of recreational and supplementary reading materials at which the student can read silently with adequate comprehension. If the test administrator so desires, the passages can be read silently to the student and a potential level identified. According to the Examiner's Manual, the potential level represents the level to which a pupil's reading might be raised through remedial or classroom training.

The Spache Scales also contain eight supplementary phonics tests:

Test 1:   Consonant Sounds
Test 2:   Vowel Sounds
Test 3:   Consonant Blends
Test 4:   Common Syllables or Phonograms
Test 5:   Blending
Test 6:   Letter Sounds
Test 7:   Initial Consonant Sounds
Test 8:   Auditory Discrimination

Tests 1, 2, 3, 6, and 7 are best interpreted as measures of declarative knowledge that might be used in a phonemic analysis strategy. Test 4 is primarily a measure of phonogram knowledge. A student might use this declarative knowledge for word recognition. Test 8 assesses a student's ability to discriminate among the different sounds (phonemes) in the English language. The remaining subtest, Blending, is the only one that directly assesses procedural knowledge. In this case it is the process of phonemic analysis. Students are presented with sets of nonsense syllables and asked to combine or blend them into a word. Box 6.1 contains examples of the types of nonsense words encountered in Test 5.

The Durrell Analysis of Reading Difficulty is also a commonly used

---

Box 6.1   Examples: re – ter   con – ett

fl – ide	fr – est – ed	ch – ell – er
br – opp	ch – ay – tore	gr – ill – on
st – on – ite	shat – ed	tr – ell – ent
sp – ick – ful		

individual diagnostic test. It is very similar to the Spache Scale. For example, it is most appropriate for students from the first through the sixth grades. There are a number of oral reading passages from which oral reading errors are analyzed. The student then reads selected passages silently. However, instead of being asked predesigned questions about each passage, a student is asked to tell everything she or he remembers, much like the retelling technique used in the RMI. This is a much better method of assessing overall comprehension. As mentioned in chapter 5, many of the predesigned questions on standardized tests are written in such a way that a student could possibly answer them correctly without reading the passage. The "retelling" technique can also provide information about a student's use of discourse-level information. For example, if the passage contained some obvious pattern of information (e.g., the description of a process), the student should recognize and include that organizational pattern in the retelling.

Like the Spache Scale, the Durrell Analysis of Reading Difficulties assesses listening comprehension and has a series of word lists and tests that assess phonemic analysis and word-recognition variables. In addition, the Durrell contains tests for visual memory, spelling, and handwriting.

CRITERION-REFERENCED TESTS

The stated purpose of criterion-referenced tests is to determine a student's abilities in specific skill areas when compared with a set criteria rather than when compared with the performance of other students. The difference between criterion- and norm-referenced tests is described by Venezky.

> Norm-referenced and criterion-referenced tests differ both in content and utility. Writers of test items for norm-referenced tests generally do not begin with a well-defined set of performances which they intend to measure, and further, because of the need to obtain variability among individuals, they avoid items that are either too easy or too difficult, regardless of their importance for the subject matter of the test. Writers of test items for criterion-referenced tests, on the other hand, begin with a definition of desired behavior (instructional objections), from which test items are derived. Since variability across the total range of students is not an issue for criterion-referenced tests, the percentage of students who pass or fail an item does not by itself serve for selection or rejection of the item. Finally, norm-referenced tests have their main application in assessing individuals when selectivity is a factor, for example, in determining which students should be placed in a special program which can accommodate only a small number of items. Criterion-referenced tests are applicable when individuals are to be matched to instructional alternatives. (1974, pp. 12–13)

Venezky's point is that criterion-referenced tests analyze a student's strengths and weaknesses relative to a set standard; norm-referenced tests, on the other hand, compare a student's strengths and weaknesses to the performance of other students.

Much of the impetus for criterion-referenced tests came from the emphasis in the 1960s on behavioral objectives. Behavioral objectives, first popularized by Mager (1962), specify the skill to be learned, the condition under which the skill must be demonstrated, and the level at which the student must perform. For example, here is a behavioral objective for sight word performance:

> Given a list of 10 basic words, the student will correctly identify 8 when given 2 seconds to recognize each word.

Popham (1978) stated that, prior to the mid-1960s, educators were content to use general standardized tests to measure achievement, because they were unsure as to what competencies they wanted to measure in students. However, as educators became more precise in their description of student objectives, they became more dissatisfied with norm-referenced tests. This led to an emphasis on criterion-referenced tests.

Within reading education, most criterion-referenced tests are tied to reading programs that are diagnostic and prescriptive in nature. According to W.H. Miller such programs contain

> . . . a pre-assessment device to help the teacher determine a student's competency in the various reading skills which are evaluated in that program. The program then usually refers the teacher to a number of instructional reading materials at the appropriate level which will enable the student to attain mastery in the specific reading skills in which he or she has been diagnosed to be weak. Usually the diagnostic-prescriptive reading program does not contain material to provide the required instruction or practice but rather refers the teacher to the appropriate pages in basal readers, basal reader workbooks, phonics materials, programmed reading materials, or other types of supplementary materials. (1978, p. 103)

When a student has completed the prescribed material, he or she is given another criterion-referenced test to determine if the criterion level of performance has been reached. Commonly, this is called reaching the level of *mastery*. If mastery has not been attained, students are given more practice using prescribed material. If mastery has been attained, students move to another objective.

Some of the more popular criterion-referenced programs are

1. *Criterion Reading* (available from Random House)
2. *Harper and Row Classroom Management System* (available from Harper & Row, Publishers)
3. *Individualized Reading Skills Program* (available from Houghton Mifflin)
4. *Prescriptive Reading Inventory* (available from CTB/McGraw-Hill)
5. *Right-to-Read Management System* (available from Winston Press)
6. *SRA Diagnosis* (available from Science Research Associates)

The major shortcoming and criticism of criterion-referenced programs is the overwhelming number of skills that are assessed (Howards, 1980). For example, the Criterion Reading program assesses over 450 different reading skills. On the other hand, the success of criterion-referenced systems in improving student achievement is well documented (e.g., Levine, 1985). It appears that the more specific the instructional objective and the method of assessing that objective, the higher the probability of students' performing well.

A growing trend in standardized reading tests is to provide ways to interpret norm-referenced tests as criterion-referenced tests. For example, the SDRT Stanford Diagnostic Reading Test provides for this. Specifically, the manual reports Progress Indicator scores. The test designers have organized the items into clusters that purportedly represent distinct skills that are more specific than those indicated by the subtest names. The teacher determines how a student performed on the items constituting a specific skill. If a student answers a specific number of items correctly within a cluster, the test producers assert that this can be interpreted as evidence that the student has mastered the skill measured by the cluster. For example, at the Red Level of the SDRT is a cluster of eight items labeled *Consonant Sounds Represented by Consonant Clusters*. According to the manual, a student must answer six of the eight items correctly to master this skill.

Even though its intent is noteworthy, we find this practice questionable, specifically because the skills represented by the cluster were identified *post hoc*, after the fact. That is, more than likely the items were clustered on the basis of their surface similarities only and not on the basis of any organized theory of reading.

PROBING A STANDARDIZED TEST

The discussion in the previous section indicates that scores on standardized tests frequently require a great deal of interpretation, depending on the model of reading you are using and the format of the test. A growing trend within reading diagnosis is to "probe" standardized tests. For example, Michael Kibby (1985), who based much of his work on the research of Rebecca Barr, suggested that reading teachers probe standardized tests in a number of ways. Kibby stated that a reading teacher should pose specific questions about test results. We will consider a few of those questions.

Question #1. What effect did time have on the child's performance?

Kibby stated that the rationale behind this is that students should be given sufficient time to complete all sections of a standardized test unless it is a test of reading rate. In more technical terms, Kibby was suggesting that reading tests should be "power" tests rather than "speed" tests (Mehrens & Lehmann, 1980).

If you suspect that speed might be a compounding factor in students' test results, Kibby has recommended the following procedure:

1. Mark on the test or answer sheet the item last completed within the time limit.
2. Allow all students who did not finish enough time to complete the test (this can be done at a later time).
3. Correct and score the test in two ways: timed and untimed.

To illustrate, Kibby offered the example of a fifth-grade student who received a raw score of 22 and a grade-equivalent score of 3.3 on the comprehension section of the Gates-MacGinite Reading Test when it was administered in a timed fashion. However, when the student was allowed to complete the test in an untimed fashion, his raw score rose to 41 and his grade-equivalency score to 6.1.

Question #2. What effect did guessing have on the child's performance?

The effects of guessing can artificially inflate reading scores. Edward Fry (1972) warned of the effects of guessing in his discussion of the "orangutan score."

> Suppose we took an orangutan and taught him to put a pawprint in one of four squares. He could choose any square he wished. Next we placed a typical multiple-choice item in front of him with four choices. After he has read the item, he chooses one of the squares on which to place his pawprint. On the average, out of 100 items he will get 25 correct by pure chance; this raw score of 25 correct can then be translated into a grade-level score. (p. 18)

Kibby suggested using the following procedure if you suspect that guessing is a significant factor in a child's test performance:

1. Give the child a clean test booklet.
2. Begin 10 items before the point where consistent errors were made. Cover the key items (picture or word) and ask the child to read to you the one response she or he selected (you point it out to her or him).
3. If the child is unable to read a significant number of the correctly marked items, continue backward until you reach the point where she or he is able to read the responses.
4. Record all responses to these items in the student's test booklet.

Kibby warned that guessing can have a particularly heavy impact in vocabulary subtests. He gave the example of a second-grade student who received a raw score of 30 on the Metropolitan Achievement Test. However, when asked to read the test items using the procedure just described, the student received a raw score of 17.

Question #3. Is this a reliable estimate of the child's reading ability?

By this question Kibby meant: Did the testing situation affect the child's performance? He stated that students frequently perform poorly on group tests and then prove to be better readers in one-on-one oral reading situations. This is usually due to what measurement theorists call *test anxiety*. Jensen (1980) reported that test anxiety has been shown to be significantly negatively correlated with achievement scores. That is, as anxiety goes up, test scores go down. Simply put, some people react negatively to being tested and, consequently, do not perform up to their level of competence.

Kibby recommended the following procedure for retesting:

1. Give the child a clean copy of the test.
2. Ask the child to read the items aloud to you and to answer the appropriate questions. Begin at the point where the child has missed about one-half of the items. Continue until the child is unable to read and answer any further items.
3. Record the child's responses.

Question #4. Relative to the reading process, what are the underlying reasons for poor performance in any subtest area?

This question is actually a composite of three separate questions Kibby recommended:

Is low vocabulary performance due to limited word recognition ability or to limited knowledge of word meaning?
Does poor word recognition account for poor performance in silent reading?
To what extent does the child's knowledge of word meanings affect performance on comprehension?

The basic purpose of all of these questions is to hypothesize causes for poor performance in a given area, based on your particular model of the reading process. For example, if you place a great deal of emphasis on word-recognition skills, then you must be alert to the effect on other tests that poor word-recognition ability might have.

To obtain information about the underlying causes for poor subtest performance, Kibby recommended that students be asked to read test passages and questions orally while the teacher tries to analyze the student's oral reading errors in a fashion like that described in the last chapter. Here it should suffice to say that you should always be looking for explanations for a student's poor performance from the perspective of your theory of reading. In chapter 7 we will consider a way of formalizing your theory of reading.

TECHNICAL CHARACTERISTICS OF STANDARDIZED TESTS

As testing procedures become more sophisticated, so must the reading teacher's understanding of tests grow to encompass the increased complexity. Relative to standardized tests, this necessarily means a knowledge of some of the technical aspects of tests. In this section we consider some of those technical aspects. We have selected only those characteristics with a direct bearing on test interpretation.

Developmental Scores

Grade-equivalent and age-equivalent scores are both called *developmental*. They are ways that raw scores are translated into a more interpretable format. Grade equivalency scores compare a student's ability to that of students at various grade levels. If a fourth-grade student received a grade-equivalency score of 3.9 on a reading achievement test that had included third graders in its norming group, it could be interpreted that the child performed at a level that is average for children who have completed 9 months of third grade. If a fourth-grade student received a grade equivalency of 7.3 on a test that had *not* included seventh graders in the norming sample, the score would be a prediction that the student could possibly perform as well as a student in the third month of the seventh grade. This does not mean that the student should be placed in seventh-grade reading material. It simply means that he or she performed well on that particular test. The student might not score as well when faced with seventh-grade items on a seventh-grade reading test.

Grade-equivalent scores provide a reference for comparing students' reading achievement in years and months. They are not, however, directly comparable across tests or subtests but can only be compared within a given test or subtest. Grade-equivalency scores are often misinterpreted. In fact, the Delegates Assembly of the International Reading Association passed a resolution (April, 1981) enumerating the misuses of grade-equivalency scores and advocated "that those who administer standardized reading tests abandon the practice of using grade equivalents to report performance of either individuals or groups of test takers" and urged test publishers "to eliminate grade equivalents from their tests." Age-equivalency scores have the same shortcomings as grade equivalents and should be used with discretion.

Relative Scores

Relative scores more directly rank order students within their age or grade level. We will consider a number of different types of relative scores.

Percentile Ranks   Percentile ranks provide an indication of relative performance within a particular grade level or age group. A student's percentile rank can be interpreted as the percentage of students in the norm group that scored equal to or lower than that student. For example, if a student scored at the 55th percentile, this means that she or he did as well as, or better than, 55% of the students in the norm group at her or his grade level or age. Unlike grade or age equivalents, percentile scores can be compared directly across subtests or tests. A percentile of 27 means the same whether it is from a reading subtest, a math test, or a language arts test.

A scale of percentile ranks is not a scale of equal measurement units. That is, percentile ranks tend to bunch up and spread out in odd ways. As an illustration of this, consider Table 6.1, which is an adaptation of the percentile norms from a commonly used standardized test. If you study the scores in Table 6.1, you will notice that the difference in percentile rank between some raw scores is not consistent with the differences in percentile ranks between other scores. For example, the difference in percentile ranks between the raw score of 43 and the raw score of 42 is 10 percentile points; however, the difference in percentile ranks between a raw score of 32 and 33 is only 1 percentile point. In general, percentile ranks tend to bunch up in the middle and spread out at the extremes. We recommend that you interpret very high or very low percentile scores with caution.

Standard Scores   Standard scores represent the location of a student's raw score in relation to the mean or average of the norm group scores. All standard scores (stanines, Z-scores and T-scores) are based on norm groups for specific age or grade levels. Figure 6.3 compares percentiles and standard scores for a normal distribution.

Of these different standard scores, stanines are the most widely used. With most standardized reading achievement tests, the stanine is the most reliable measure of student performance. It gets its name from the fact that it is a standard score with nine equal units. The median, or middle stanine, is 5. Stanines 6, 7, 8, and 9 indicate increasingly better performance, whereas stanines 4, 3, 2, and 1 indicate decreasing performance. Stanines can be directly comparable

Table 6.1

Raw Score	Percentile Rank
48	99
47	99
46	91
45	77
44	62
43	51
42	41
41	34
40	28
39	23
38	20
37	17
36	15
35	13
34	11
33	9
32	8
.	.
.	.
.	.

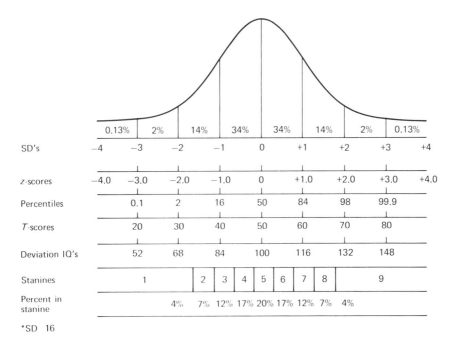

Figure 6.3 Corresponding standard scores, stanines, and percentiles in a normal distribution.

across tests and subtests and are the only scores that take into account the standard error of measurement (we will discuss this shortly).

Normal Curve Equivalents Normal curve equivalents (NCEs) deserve special attention because they are commonly used to report scores for Chapter 1 and other federal projects. Like stanines and percentiles, NCEs describe levels of achievement relative to a norm group of students at the same grade level or age and may be used to compare performance across tests and subtests. NCEs of 1, 50, and 99 correspond to percentiles of 1, 50, and 99. Unlike percentiles, however, NCEs are equal units of measure whether they are at the low, middle, or high range of the distribution. They are useful for comparing growth of students at all levels of achievement. A gain of five NCEs represents the same amount of improvement in performance for pupils at the extremes of the distribution as it does in the middle of the distribution. Figure 6.4 compares percentiles with normal curve equivalents.

Reliability

Reliability is another technical aspect of tests that is worthy of note. Reliability refers to the degree to which a measurement from a test is consistent.

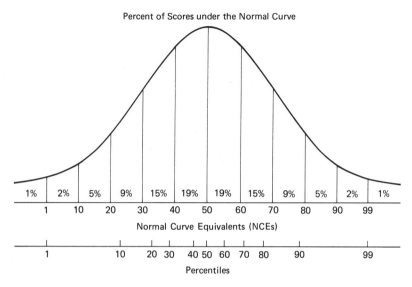

Percent of Scores under the Normal Curve

Figure 6.4 Comparison of Scales: Normal Curve Equivalents and Percentiles

Scores are consistent if they stay the same for an individual on different days or if they stay the same across different forms of the same test. The confidence you can place in a test's scores is directly proportional to its reliability.

There are a number of factors that influence a test's reliability. One is the length of the test. The longer the test, the more reliable it is. Another factor is length of time between testing. The shorter the interval between testing situations, the higher the reliability. A final factor is guessing. The more a test allows an individual to guess at answers, the less reliable the test is. This is why we stated in a previous section that retelling is a better measure of passage comprehension than answering multiple-choice items. A student can guess the correct answer to a multiple-choice item.

Reliability is expressed as a decimal, called a coefficient, ranging from .00 to 1.00. A reliability coefficient of 1.00 would mean that a test has perfect reliability. A coefficient of .00 indicates that a test has no reliability. Teachers often ask how high the reliability coefficient should be for a test before it can be considered adequate. Salvia and Ysseldyke (1981) recommended three standards or "cutoff" points for reliability coefficients. If test scores are to be reported for groups rather than individuals and are to be used for general administrative purposes, a reliability coefficient above .60 is acceptable. If test scores are to be used to make decisions about individual students, the standard should be much higher. For important educational decisions, such as placing a student in a Chapter 1 class, a reliability of .90 should be considered minimum. For more general purposes, a reliability of at least .80 is acceptable.

Validity

Validity is the extent to which a test measures what it purports to measure. A test must be reliable before it can be valid. However, a high reliability coefficient does not assure a test's validity. There are three types of validity commonly discussed in test manuals.

Content validity is a measure of whether the test items represent the content area being tested. For example, if a test purports to measure auditory discrimination, then it should include items that in fact measure auditory discrimination and not some other ability. Content validity is determined by inspecting the test items or having a group of judges sort items into categories. If the test has content validity, the categories should be consistent with the skills measured by the test.

Concurrent validity is the extent to which the test results agree with other tests that measure the same skills. If two tests purport to measure auditory discrimination, then they should correlate highly. A student taking both tests should have similar scores on both.

Predictive validity, as its name suggests, is the extent to which a test accurately indicates future behavior. For example, if a test purports to measure reading readiness, students' scores on the test should correlate highly with their future reading achievement.

Standard Error of Measurement

The standard error of measurement (SEM) is a statistic that estimates the magnitude of measurement error in a score. Because there is error in every test score, it is important to interpret a student's scores as a range of possibilities rather than as an exact measurement. For example, if the standard error of measurement for grade-equivalency scores on a reading test is 4 months, then you should assume that there is a good chance that a student's true score will be somewhere between 4 months less than and 4 months greater than the reported score. To illustrate, if a student's reported score is a grade equivalency of 6.4, then you could assume that his or her true score would be somewhere between 6.0 and 6.8.

SELECTING TESTS

Selection of formal tests is an important part of the diagnostic process. Venezky (1974) summarized the major considerations in test selection.

> There is an instructional goal—and only one goal—which may be realized or aided through assessment, and this is instructional decision making. Knowing a child's reading level or his competence in pronouncing initial consonant cluster

or his ability to select the main points of a story from four options is of little value unless these data are collected as an aid to a particular decision. Collecting periodic data on reading ability, as many school districts do today, merely for "knowing" what is happening is a monstrous waste of time and money and serves no purpose other than to create suspicion among politicians and parents (pp. 6–7).

Venezky's point is that the only reason for selecting and administering a particular test is for instructional purposes. The emphasis should be on finding out what students know and do not know and planning instruction accordingly.

In addition you will want to consider who will be tested and the level of specificity required from the test. Sometimes you will need to test a large group of students; other times you will need to test only one. Even if you are testing only a single student, you might still want to use a group test because of some specific information it contains.

When it is time to select tests, your most valuable source will be *The Eighth Mental Measurement Yearbook* (Buros, 1978) or its companion volume *Reading Tests and Reviews II* (Buros, 1975). The Buros references contain descriptions and reviews of almost all commercially published tests. Both are revised periodically, on a 6- to 10-year cycle. Kavale (1979) pointed out that test reviews can help you answer four basic questions:

1. Which tests might serve my present purpose?
2. What are the new tests in the field?
3. What is test X like?
4. What do specialists in the field have to say about test Y?

Besides Buros's yearbook and reviews, the *Standards for Educational and Psychological Tests* (1974) is also an excellent resource. This reference gives specifications for tests, manuals, and norms, as summarized next.

1. A test manual should include information on the development of the test including the rationale, procedures for writing items, and results of item analysis.
2. The scoring and interpretation procedures should be detailed as clearly as possible to the reader. Cautions against misuses of the test should be listed.
3. Comprehensive directions for administering the test should be stated so that the testing situation mirrors the conditions under which normative data were obtained.
4. Information about reliability and validity should be readily available.
5. If the test can be hand scored, the scoring procedures should be specific and clearly interpretable.
6. The norming population should be stated, including dates of norming and geographical location.
7. The norms should be available for comparisons if the test can be hand scored.

Some additional variables that should be included in your list of test selection criteria are time limits, scoring procedures, and test cost. In the day-to-day world of teaching, these can be important criteria. If a test contains valuable information but requires too much time for administration, it will dominate the interaction between you and the students. Overtesting is an easy trap to fall into, especially for zealous reading teachers eager to try out newly learned techniques. Similarly, scoring can present a problem. Some hand-scoring processes are very time consuming and difficult.

One final point should be made about test selection. If you have students from an ESL (English as a Second Language) background, this should be given strong consideration in your selection criteria. Given their limited ability to speak the English language, you do not want to test these students with a standardized reading test that was normed on a population of native English speakers. Many reading teachers have to test ESL students with standardized reading tests. Because these tests are not appropriate for ESL students, students score artificially low and are sometimes incorrectly placed in remedial settings. Students who speak English as a second language should not be tested with traditional standardized tests. Instead, diagnostic information should be obtained, using the informal assessment techniques presented in chapter 5.

SUMMARY

In this chapter, we have described formal methods of reading assessment. Standardized tests were divided into two broad categories: norm-referenced tests and criterion-referenced tests. Norm-referenced tests were further subdivided into survey and diagnostic tests. Both of these types can be administered to individual students or to groups. The purpose of survey tests is to assess overall reading ability. Survey tests are commonly used as screening devices to identify students who need further testing with a diagnostic test. Two commonly used diagnostic tests were described in some depth: the Stanford Diagnostic Reading Test (a group test) and the Spache Diagnostic Reading Scales (an individual test). Both were discussed from the perspective of the various reading models. To facilitate test interpretation, methods of probing standardized tests were discussed, along with technical characteristics of standardized tests. These characteristics included reliability, validity, standard error of measurement, and different types of scores reported in test manuals (e.g., stanines, percentiles). Finally, criteria to consider when selecting a test were discussed.

7

SYNTHESIZING AND INTEGRATING TEST DATA: AN ETHNOGRAPHIC APPROACH

In chapter 1 we stated that a basic assumption underlying this textbook is that reading diagnosis is an inexact process that utilizes many of the techniques of ethnographic research. In this chapter, we will describe some ethnographic techniques that can be used to synthesize and interpret data collected both formally and informally. Specifically, we will consider building conceptual frameworks, instrument selection, data collection, and generating and testing hypotheses.

BUILDING A CONCEPTUAL FRAMEWORK

In chapter 4 we discussed the importance of having a model for the reading process. Without a model, diagnosis can be unsystematic and ineffective. Miles and Huberman (1984) recommended that the model be represented in graphic format. They call such a graph a *conceptual framework*.

Constructing a conceptual framework takes care and thought; however, it is well worth the effort, for it provides a framework for interpretation. The first step is to identify those components you wish to include within your model. In chapter 3 we discussed six levels of analysis within reading:

1. Letter recognition
2. Phonemic analysis
3. Word identification

4. Syntactic analysis
5. Discourse-level analysis
6. Schema-level analysis

However, in chapter 4 we mentioned some other aspects of reading including attention and capacity, inferring, metacognition, and attitudes. You can include all of these components in your model or select those you feel have the most explanatory power in terms of describing students' reading performance. Some of the characteristics listed are not easily translated into instructional practices or assessment techniques. Consequently, you might not want to include them in your conceptual framework. Or you might believe that some of the characteristics listed are contained within other competencies. In the examples that follow in this chapter we will not include attention and capacity or inferring. This is because we believe they can be addressed as components of other skill areas. We will discuss how in chapters 8, 9, 10, and 11. This does not mean that you cannot or should not make them explicit components of your conceptual framework. As mentioned in chapter 4, your model should be personal to your beliefs about reading, your instructional style, and the resources available to you. A strange anomaly within reading education is that teachers with drastically different, even opposing, models of reading can produce similar results in terms of student achievement. Hence, we encourage you to select the variables in your conceptual framework on the basis of your personal experiences and beliefs, rather than on the misconception that there exists some absolute, correct model.

Once you have selected the variables in your model, you should identify the "flow of processing." At this stage, you will be selecting from various theories presented in chapter 4. For example, if you subscribe to the top-down theory of reading, you might depict the flow of processing like that in Figure 7.1a. A bottom-up theory might be portrayed by Figure 7.1b, and an interactive model like Figure 7.1c. Again, don't be overly concerned about the precision of your representation of the flow of processing. You are developing a schematic framework for the interpretation of test results and the planning of instruction. You are not trying to develop a theory of cognition.

If you decide to adopt a production-theory approach, your model will necessarily include more variables. This is because you will be identifying the declarative knowledge necessary for each level of analysis, along with the procedural information (reading strategies) appropriate to each level. In Table 4.1 in chapter 4, we identified some of this information. Put into a conceptual framework that information might resemble Figure 7.2.

At this point, a conceptual framework like that in Figure 7.2 might seem overwhelming. However, by the time you have completed chapters 8–11, you will be familiar with all the components mentioned. Hence, if you wish to use a production-theory model, the remainder of this text should provide you with the necessary background.

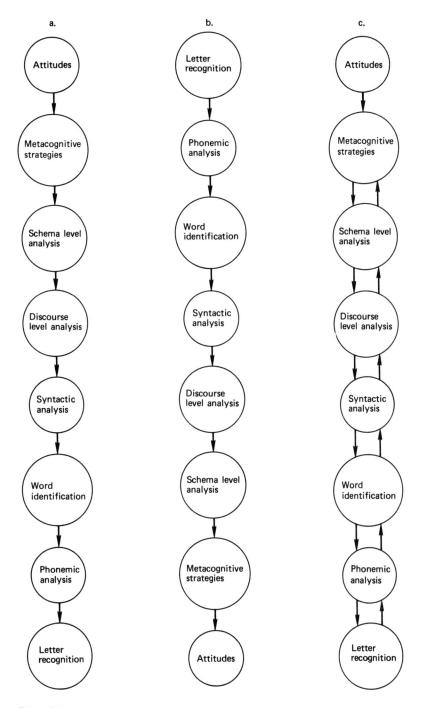

Figure 7.1

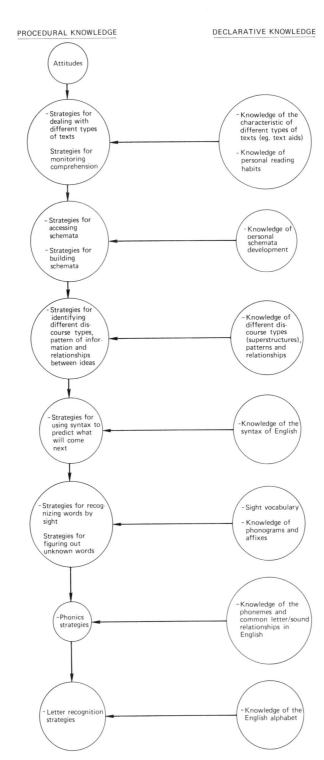

Figure 7.2

SELECTING ASSESSMENT INSTRUMENTS

One of the ways that a conceptual framework pays off immediately is that it allows you to identify those assessment instruments you will need. Specifically, you should have a way of assessing each component of your model. Unless your conceptual framework is very simple, with only a few components, you will probably need more than one test. In fact, the testing procedure of most reading teachers is best described as a patchwork of formal, informal, and teacher-made assessment techniques. We consider this very healthy. That is, we encourage you to select portions of tests to cover various components of your conceptual framework. It might be that you use no test in its entirety. Instead, you use a subtest or two from a standardized diagnostic instrument, a section from an informal inventory, and a few teacher-made tests. Some variables you might not even explicitly test for; instead you might collect data about a student's performance via observation, using the naturalistic techniques described in chapter 5. To systematize your assessment techniques, it is helpful to fill out an instrument chart like that in Table 7.1.

If you study Table 7.1, you will note that most of the assessment techniques are either teacher-made tests or observation during testing and instruction. This underscores the importance of naturalistic assessment. For many areas of your conceptual framework you will probably not find commercially prepared assessment tools. Consequently, you will need to rely on your personal observation, tests you develop yourself, or both. Again, we consider this a healthy situation. We have found that, with a little practice, teachers can develop assessment instruments that are highly sophisticated and that meet the specific needs of their models of reading much better than commercially prepared tests. These teachers began by developing one or two short and simple tests to supplement the commercially prepared tests they were using. Over time, they refined and added to their collection of teacher-made techniques until, eventually, they had a battery of assessment procedures specific to their models of reading.

DATA COLLECTION

Ethnographic inquiry is essentially an investigative process not unlike detective work (Douglas, 1976). This is a good metaphor for reading diagnosis. The reading teacher is a detective trying to piece together a riddle entitled "Why Is This Student Having Difficulty Reading?" To do this, the reading teacher collects "clues" but not all at once. A good detective might go to site A to collect clues relative to the motivation behind a crime; she or he goes to site B to collect data about the weapon used in the crime and to site C for clues about the effects of the crime. Throughout the course of the investigation, the detective might periodically return to all of these sites a number of times.

So too, the reading teacher collects information over a period of time.

Table 7.1

READING CHARACTERISTIC	ASSESSMENT TECHNIQUE
Attitudes	Teacher-made test Observation during instruction
Strategies for dealing with different types of texts	Observation and questioning during testing and instruction
Strategies for monitoring comprehension	Observation and questioning during testing and instruction
Knowledge of the characteristics of different types of texts	Teacher-made tests
Knowledge of personal reading habits	Teacher-made test
Strategies for accessing schema	Teacher-made test Observation during instruction
Strategies for building schema	Observation during instruction
Knowledge of personal schemata development	Observation during instruction
Strategies for identifying different discourse types, patterns of information, and relationships among ideas	Retelling portion of the RMI
Knowledge of the different discourse types, patterns, and superstructures	Teacher-made test
Strategies for using syntax to predict what will come next	Grammatical relationships score on RMI
Knowledge of syntax	Grammatical function section of RMI
Strategies for recognizing words by sight	Word list section of IRI
Sight-word vocabulary	Word list section of IRI Vocabulary section of SDRT
Strategies for figuring out unknown words	Oral reading passages in IRI
Knowledge of phonograms and affixes	Subtest 4 of the Spache Scales Teacher-made test
Sounding and blending strategies	Word list section of IRI Sound-graphic relationships section of RMI
Knowledge of phonemes and common letter-sound relationships	Subtests 1, 2, 3, and 7 of Spache Scales
Letter-recognition strategies	Subtest 6 of Spache Scales
Knowledge of alphabet	Subtest 6 of Spache Scales

In other words, testing is not lumped into one large block of time at the beginning of your involvement with a student. Unfortunately, this is the case with many reading teachers. They administer a group survey test to screen students and then administer the SDRT, the RMI, and a series of teacher-made tests in rapid succession to those students identified as remedial or corrective by the survey test. All too often students become "tested out" and learn to associate reading instruction with evaluation that threatens their self-concepts. It is no wonder that they don't view reading as a pleasurable experience.

The alternative is to strategically space assessment activities between instructional activities. You might begin by administering all or a portion of your primary diagnostic tool (e.g., the RMI). You would then plan instruction based on the test results. During instructional activities you would observe the student's reading performance to obtain information about those variables in your conceptual framework for which you do not have explicit tests (e.g., *strategies for monitoring comprehension* and *knowledge of personal schemata development* in Table 7.1). Not too far into instruction you might administer a section or two of the SDRT or the Spache Scales to obtain more data (clues) about other components of your model.

The assessment and instructional processes, then, are symbiotically linked. One feeds into the other. The diagnostic process is a constant interplay between assessment and instruction. Over time, your data base about a student builds, until the pieces begin to fall together and the riddle has an answer.

To facilitate the collection of data, Miles and Huberman (1984) recommended use of a *time-ordered matrix*. A time-ordered matrix is simply a structured log indicating (a) the type of data collected, (b) the date of collection, and (c) your interpretation of the information. Table 7.2 contains a few beginning entries in a sample time-ordered matrix.

The advantage of a time-ordered matrix is that it provides a quick history of your interactions with a student and the decisions based on those interactions. As was alluded to in chapter 4, this is a systematic way of ensuring accurate anecdotal records.

Table 7.2 Sample Time-Ordered Matrix

STUDENT NAME: MARCIA BAKER		GRADE 3
DATE	TYPE OF DATA	INTERPRETATION
3/5	Comprehension and word reading sections of the SDRT: second stanine in comprehension; third stanine in word reading.	Marcia's poor comprehension seems to be because of her lack of vocabulary knowledge.
3/7	Flash card game for vocabulary development. Marcia missed some very easy words.	Today seems to validate my guess that Marcia's vocabulary knowledge is very low.
3/8	Language experience story: Marcia did well.	When Marcia knows the words she is to read, she does well; vocab still seems to be the key.
3/11	Oral reading passages of the Analytic Reading Inventory: Marcia did poorly while attacking unknown words.	It also appears that Marcia has no mediated word-recognition strategies; when she encounters an unknown word she makes a wild guess.

GENERATING HYPOTHESES

As you collect data, your interpretations should gradually develop into hypotheses. As used here, a hypothesis is a statement of causality about the student's reading performance. Look back to Table 7.2, and you will find one hypothesis under the interpretation column: "Marcia's poor comprehension seems to be because of her lack of vocabulary knowledge." It is an assertion that the reading variable called vocabulary knowledge exists in a causal relationship with comprehension. In this case, poor ability in the variable called vocabulary knowledge causes poor performance in reading comprehension.

Hypotheses should always fit within the boundaries of your conceptual framework. Indeed, the reason for developing a conceptual framework is to identify those variables you will use to generate hypotheses.

Ethnographic researchers have some specific strategies for generating useful hypotheses and ensuring the validity of these hypotheses. We consider a few of those strategies next.

Looking for Converging Patterns

The most common strategy for generating hypotheses is to look for patterns of converging information. A converging pattern would include similar findings from different sources. For example, if a student scored in the second stanine for the phonetic analysis test of the SDRT, did poorly on the blending subtest of the Spache Scales, and seemed to make miscues while reading orally that had little relationship to the sound-symbol cues provided by unknown words, this would be a converging pattern indicating that the student did not know important declarative and/or procedural knowledge relative to the phonemic level of analysis.

When generating hypotheses you might first get an inkling of a causal relationship from initial testing or your initial interactions with the student. You then begin looking for converging evidence. Within ethnographic research this process is called *triangulation*.

The term *triangulation* was coined in 1965 by Webb, Campbell, Schwartz, and Sechrest. Technically, triangulation is subjecting an idea "to the onslaught of a series of imperfect measures" (p. 86). This, too, is an excellent metaphor for reading diagnosis. The formal and informal measures discussed in chapters 5 and 6 must definitely be considered imprecise when compared with measurement techniques used in the hard sciences. This does not necessarily mean that hypotheses generated using such assessment techniques will be imprecise or biased. Many other professions rely on imprecise measurement devices yet generate highly accurate hypotheses:

> Detectives, car mechanics and general practitioners all engage successfuly in establishing and corroborating findings with little elaborate instrumentation. They often use a *modus operandi* approach which consists largely of triangulating

independent indices. When the detective amasses fingerprints, hair samples, alibis, eyewitness accounts and the like, a case is being made that presumably fits one suspect far better than others. Diagnosing engine failure or chest pain follows a similar pattern. All the signs presumably point to the same conclusion. (Miles & Huberman, 1984, p. 234)

As you collect and interpret more information, your hypotheses become more reliable. No single piece of information should be considered definitive. However, many pieces of information gathered from different sources at different times can build a powerful case for a specific hypothesis.

Looking for Plausibility

Looking for plausibility is a phrase that refers to trusting your intuition about possible reading problems. Miles and Huberman (1984) stated that often during ethnographic investigations a conclusion just seems to "fit" and make good sense. This is also true in reading diagnosis. After testing a student and working with him or her for an extended period, you might develop a feeling that the problem lies in a certain area, a feeling that persists even without evidence. This is actually quite consistent with the way many scientists work: "Many scientific discoveries initially appear to their authors in this guise; the history of science is full of global, intuitive understandings that, after laborious verification, proved to be true" (Miles & Huberman, 1984, p. 217).

However, the most trustworthy intuitions come after intense interaction with a student, thorough testing and, perhaps most important, a thorough knowledge of the reading process and its related factors. The reasoning behind this assertion is contained in chapters 2, 3, and 4. Recall that we discussed the effects of prior knowledge on perception. In other words, what you know affects what you see. If a reading teacher knows a great deal about language and cognition and their relationship to reading, then she or he is able to "see" more of the possible underlying reasons for reading. Consequently, if you have studied the reading process thoroughly, then you can trust that the data you collect about a student are being processed through your knowledge base (schema) of reading. Intuitions or hunches that appear to materialize out of thin air are actually the product of rigorous processing at an unconscious level. Bertrand Russell (1971) spoke of this phenomenon as it relates to writing:

> I have found, for example, that if I have to write upon some rather difficult topic, the best plan is to think about it with great intensity—the greatest intensity of which I am capable—for a few hours or days, and at the end of that time give orders, so to speak, that the work is to proceed undergound. After months I return consciously to the topic and find that the work has been done. (p. 154)

Intuition, then, to a well-prepared reading teacher can be a valuable tool. However, Miles and Huberman made one comment about intuition worth noting: "Trust your plausibility intuitions but don't fall in love with them" (p. 217).

Looking for Spurious Relationships

One strategy used by ethnographers when generating hypotheses is to look for spurious relationships. A spurious relationship occurs when you assume that one variable has a causal effect on another, such as

when in fact a third variable is affecting the relationship between the two under study:

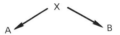

Wallis and Roberts (1956) used an example from medicine to illustrate the impact of a spurious relationship. In a medical study, researchers noticed that polio patients who traveled longer distances to a hospital were more likely to die and to die sooner than patients who traveled shorter distances. They reasoned that long travel increased the rate of polio spread, causing earlier death. Their hypothesis might be depicted in the following way:

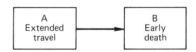

After more rigorous investigation, Walis and Roberts reasoned that a third variable was influencing both A and B. That variable was the severity of the initial attack. It seems that all severe polio attacks were brought to one hospital, regardless of how far patients had to travel. It just so happened that it was the same hospital used to conduct the study. Patients who experienced less severe attacks were taken to neighboring hospitals. Consequently, the researchers studying the problem had selected a site where virtually all patients who came from long distances had severe cases of polio. Some of those who came from shorter distances also had severe cases, but some had milder cases. The true relationship, then, among the variables in the study could have been depicted in the following way:

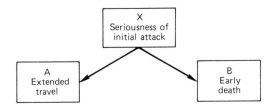

Within reading diagnosis, a spurious relationship might take the form of some variable outside of your conceptual framework exerting an influence on a student's performance. For example, a student might make a great many miscues while reading orally and exhibit poor comprehension of the material. You might logically hypothesize that the student's lack of word-recognition strategies caused poor comprehension:

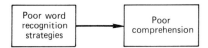

However, it might be that the student was self-conscious about reading orally. When reading silently, the student utilized various word-recognition techniques well. In this case, the variable with the spurious relationship would be embarrassment during oral reading. The relationship among the variables might be diagrammed as follows:

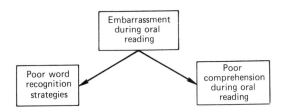

Some of the variables that commonly cause spurious relationships within reading diagnosis are

1. Extreme nervousness during testing
2. Test-wiseness (ability to perform artificially well on tests)
3. Content-specific performance (poor or good reading ability in a specific area but not in others)

Letting the Student Generate Hypotheses

A phrase commonly used within ethnography is "acquiring information from an informant" (Guba, 1981). An informant is an individual who is part of the phenomenon under investigation. Within reading diagnosis the informant is the student. What we are suggesting here is that students be invited to generate hypotheses about why they are experiencing reading problems. According to Bussis, Chittendon, and Amarel (1976), using the student as a resource is a highly useful technique, commonly overlooked in diagnosis: "The emphasis on child as resource . . . clearly contrasts with the idea of child-as-deficient, an idea that underlies many diagnostic and remedial programs" (p. 113). However, use of the child as resource (informant) is becoming widely practiced in the study of metacognitive awarenesses (Swarts, Flower & Hayes, 1984).

As it relates to generating hypotheses about reading difficulty, the process simply involves asking a student to describe why he or she is having difficulty reading. Such a conversation might take some coaxing by the teacher:

TEACHER: Carmen, tell me. Why do you think you're having problems reading?
CARMEN: I can't read good.
TEACHER: Tell me about times when it is easy for you to read.
CARMEN: When the words are little.
TEACHER: Okay, I see. When the words are little, it's easier for you to read. Now tell me what happens when you run into big words.
CARMEN: I try to figure them out, but I can't.
TEACHER: How do you try to figure them out?
CARMEN: I look at the letters.
TEACHER: What do you do when you look at the letters?
CARMEN: I try to see what they sound like, but it's hard.

In effect, what Carmen has done during this discussion is generate the hypothesis that her poor reading is due to her lack of knowledge of letter-sound relationships. She has a basic awareness that she should try to sound out unknown words but doesn't have the necessary declarative knowledge to utilize this strategy.

TESTING HYPOTHESES

Once you have generated hypotheses about a student's reading ability, the next step is to test them. To accomplish this you should turn each hypothesis into an IF/THEN statement. The IF part of the statement identifies some instructional emphasis; the THEN identifies what will happen as a result of the instructional emphasis. As an illustration, consider the following:

IF   Bob receives instruction in phonics strategies
THEN   he will be able to recognize more words while reading.

The IF part of the statement identifies what instructional steps the teacher will take; the THEN part identifies the expected behavior change on the part of the student. Box 7.1 contains some further examples of IF/THEN statements.

Box 7.1

IF	Bob receives instruction in the five basic patterns
THEN	his discourse-level analysis will improve.
IF	Kathy receives instruction in metacognitive strategies
THEN	her overall comprehension will increase.
IF	Sue receives instruction in meaningful word parts and structural analysis strategies
THEN	she will be able to decode more unknown words while reading.

The purpose of generating IF/THEN statements is to systematically test the effects of your instruction. All too often, reading teachers prescribe instruction and then never look for feedback as to whether the instruction is producing any change in the student's reading behavior. IF/THEN statements force you to predict what will occur as a result of instruction.

Once IF/THEN statements have been generated, you should begin to look for the hypothesized behavior change. That is, you should look for evidence about the THEN part of the statement. Evidence can be quantitative or non-quantitative. If you wish to take a quantitative approach, you identify some measure of the hypothesized behavior change. For example, consider the last IF/THEN statement about Sue in Box 7.1. The expected behavior change is an increase in her ability to decode unknown words while reading. A direct measure of this would be the number of unknown words Sue could correctly decode while reading orally. Consequently, once you had generated the IF/THEN statement about Sue, you would begin to keep track of the number of words she did not recognize by sight and the number of those that she correctly figured out using some word-recognition strategy. You would probably express Sue's decoding ability as a ratio:

$$\frac{\text{\# of correctly decoded words}}{\text{\# of words not identified by sight}}$$

Table 7.3 Sue's Time Ordered Matrix

DATE	TYPE OF DATA	INTERPRETATION
3/15	Oral reading of story	Sue's decoding ability seems poor. She is missing some fairly easy words to analyze structurally.
3/20	Drill with nonsense words	No sign of improvement in structural analysis.
3/21	Oral reading of story	Sue recognized some phonograms in unknown words.
3/22	Drill with nonsense words	Sue has begun to use phonograms and affixes.
3/25	Oral reading	Definite improvement now in word attack.

Over time you would expect this ratio to become larger. Sue would begin to decode more and more of the words she did not recognize by sight. This would indicate that your hypothesis was correct.

A nonquantitative approach would be one in which you simple recorded your impressions of Sue's word-recognition ability without attempting to measure it. This can be done by making systematic entries in the time-ordered matrix for Sue. Table 7.3 illustrates a possible format for these entries.

Regardless of whether you take a quantitative or a nonquantitative approach, systematic testing of your hypotheses will pay great dividends over time. You will begin to see which of your hypotheses are most accurate and which of your instructional techniques are most efficient. In addition, you will be documenting student progress. This can be a great incentive to both teacher and student.

SUMMARY

In this chapter we have presented techniques for synthesizing and integrating test data using ethnographic strategies. It was suggested that you begin by developing a conceptual framework. This is a diagram of the variables you consider important within the reading process and the flow of information among those variables. Once a conceptual framework is developed, assessment techniques can be identified for each variable within the framework. It was suggested that data on students be collected from testing and from instructional interactions with students. As soon as possible, hypotheses should be generated as to possible causes of students' reading difficulties. Techniques for generating useful hypotheses were discussed: looking for converging patterns, looking for plausibility, looking for spurious relationships, and letting students generate hypotheses. Finally, methods for testing hypotheses were described.

8

THE WORD LEVEL
AND BELOW

In this chapter we will discuss strategies and techniques for instruction at the word level and below. Recall the variables, or levels, of analysis relative to reading that were highlighted in chapters 2, 3, and 4:

> Schema-level analysis
> Discourse-level analysis
> Syntactic analysis
> Word identification
> Phonemic analysis
> Letter recognition

Here we will consider instruction to improve word identification, phonemic analysis, and letter recognition, those skills that help students recognize units of meaning up to and including single words. We will first consider each area separately and then discuss their integration. We will also consider ways of increasing students' knowledge of concepts and the words representing those concepts.

LETTER RECOGNITION

As was noted in chapter 2, a child's ability to recognize and name the letters of the alphabet is highly correlated with later reading achievement. In fact, letter knowledge is one of the best predictors of success in learning to read (Finn,

135

1985). This does not mean that knowing the letters of the alphabet will in and of itself increase reading achievement (Samuels, 1972). It does mean that the ability to name letters is essential to teaching children the "sounds letters make", a skill important for beginning reading and writing.

The process of letter recognition should be treated as an integrated whole for instructional purposes. That is, no attempt should be made to isolate the declarative knowledge from the procedural knowledge necessary to recognize letters. If, from your diagnosis, you find a child cannot recognize and name particular letters of the alphabet, there are a number of strategies and techniques that can be used.

Because we probably identify letters by feature analysis (see chapter 3), F. Smith (1982) suggested that a letter can best be learned by presenting it with other letters in pairs and groups. For example, the letter *m* can be presented along with the letters *o* and *t*. The teacher can then point out the similarities and differences among the letters. (The *m* has two humps, the *o* and *t* have none; *m* is one space high, but *t* is two, etc.). Initially you should choose letters that are very different from the target letter. As the students become more proficient at noticing differences, letters that are more similar can be used (e.g., *m*, *n*, *h*). Use of letters from a child's name adds familiarity and a personal touch to this activity. Whether working with an individual child or a small group, you can print each letter on a separate 3″ × 5″ card, select the target letter, and choose two, three, or four other letters with which to make the comparisons.

You can also help children learn letters by providing functional kinds of reading materials for them to observe and play with. For example, toothpaste boxes, cereal boxes, milk cartons, egg cartons, and soft drink cans are all usable for letter-recognition activities.

The newspaper is also a rich resource of letter-recognition activities. After a particular letter has been introduced, ask children to circle it on a newspaper page. The words in which the letters are found can be listed and read by the teacher. Those that are in the children's speaking and listening vocabularies can be put in sentences.

Another option is to have children cut out words from the newspaper that contain a particular letter and paste them on a sheet of paper. Using this activity, the children quickly become aware that any letter can be printed in many different styles. Once again, teachers and students can work together to make sentences using the words that are a part of the children's listening and speaking vocabularies.

"Concentration-type" matching games also help children learn letters. To develop concentration games, write the letters of the alphabet on 3″ × 2½″ cards, one letter per card, two cards per letter. Turn the cards upside down and put them in rows. Playing in pairs or threes, children take turns turning over any two cards, saying each letter on the card turned over. If a child matches two letters, he may keep those cards.

With young students, it's better to play with 8–10 letters (16–20 cards) at first. As children become more proficient at the game, more cards can be added. It is best to start by using all capital letters and then progress to matching capitals with corresponding lowercase letters (Ekwall & Shanker, 1983).

A less structured but effective technique is to point out as often as possible various letters in children's names that are found in books and on signs, notes, posters, labels, and charts. Reading alphabet books to children will also help with letter recognition, as will teaching the alphabet song and having children point to the letters as they are sung (Ekwall & Shanker, 1983).

PHONEMIC ANALYSIS

As described in chapter 3, phonemic analysis is the act of translating letters into speech sounds. The process of teaching the declarative knowledge of phonemic analysis is commonly called *phonics*, or instruction in the relationship between letters and speech sounds. However, when we use the term *phonics* in this text we also mean teaching students how to use their knowledge of letter-sound relationships to figure out words not recognized by sight.

How important is phonics instruction in learning to read? We believe that phonics is but one strategy children can use if they do not know a word by sight, and it should be used in combination with other strategies. We agree with the authors of *Becoming a Nation of Readers* (R.C. Anderson, Hiebert, Scott & Wilkinson, 1985), who stated that the goal of phonics is not to have children be able to state a series of rules, but to help them realize that there are relationships between letters and sounds and that these relationships can be used to figure out unknown words.

We strongly believe that phonics should be taught not in isolation, but through context whenever possible. This makes sense if you consider the idea that the sound or sounds a letter makes are partially determined by the other letters in a word (F. Smith, 1982). The strategies presented here will emphasize learning sounds in context and/or learning sounds in isolation and putting them back into context.

The question frequently arises within reading education as to which letter sounds should be taught first. Ekwall and Shanker (1983), noted that "most reading experts recommend teaching the consonant sounds before the vowels" (p. 180). Johnson and Pearson (1984) agreed that consonant sounds are more important to teach. Consonant differences are a primary way we distinguish one word from another. You can illustrate this to yourself by trying to read the following sentences:

1. Th__ d__g w__s d__gg__ng __p __ b__n__.
2. __e___o __e__ a__ i__e ___ea__ __u___ea.

The first sentence, with vowels removed ("The dog was digging up a bone"), is far easier to read than the sentence with the consonants removed ("Let's go get an ice cream sundae").

If, from your diagnosis, you conclude that a student is deficient in certain letter-sound relationships, specific contextual strategies and techniques can be used.

Recent research by Ehri, Deffner, and Wilce (1984) has shown that children more efficiently learn to associate letters with their sounds if they are taught the associations from a picture whose shape includes the letter. For example, the letter *f* drawn as the stem of a flower or the letter *b* drawn as a boot were shown to be more effective than a picture that started with an *f* or *b* or than teaching the sounds with no picture accompaniment.

A useful technique is to make 3″ × 5″ or 4″ × 6″ cards with the letter integrated within a picture on one side of the card and the word the picture represents on the other side. For example, the sound of *f* would be represented by and *f*lower. Students can work in pairs or small groups with the cards, playing concentration or path games (discussed later in this chapter) with them. Some of the letters and pictures used in the research are presented in Figure 8.1.

Johnson and Pearson (1984) suggested a "letter of the week" activity in which the students are asked to gather as many objects as possible beginning with a particular letter. The names of the objects can be listed on a chart, their beginning sounds can be compared and discussed, and the names can be used in oral and written sentences.

A common distinction made within phonics instruction is between synthetic approaches (also known as explicit) and analytic approaches (also known as implicit). In synthetic phonics a child is taught the sounds of the letters and then how to blend those sounds into words. The emphasis is on going from parts to wholes. In analytic phonics the child is exposed to a number of sight words. She or he is asked to read these words and listen for the sounds the words have in common. If the sounds follow a pattern, or rule, the teacher guides the students into discovering the rule. This method of teaching phonics moves from whole to part.

In keeping with our philosophy that phonics should be taught through context, we recommend the analytic strategy for teaching letter-sound relationships advocated by Johnson and Pearson (1984). If you find, for example, that a child does not know the sound that corresponds to the beginning sound of *k*, the following technique can be used:

1. List known sight words on the board that begin with *k*.
2. Ask the students to read each word aloud, listening for the beginning sound.
3. Ask students what the words have in common. Students should notice that the words all begin with *k* and have the sound that *k* makes at the beginning of a word.
4. Ask the students to tell you other words that have this same sound at the beginning. If words that begin with the letter *c* are given, list these separately and discuss the fact that one sound of *c* is like the sound of *k*.
5. Ask students to read the list again and discuss the meanings of the words.

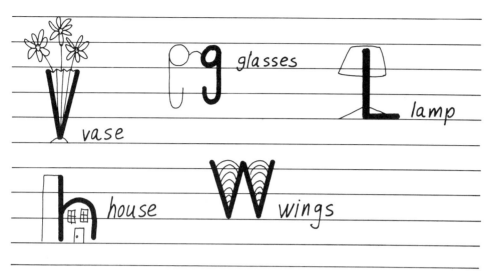

Figure 8.1

> 6. Together, you and the students make up oral and written sentences that contain the words.

Another way to teach letter-sound relationships is through the use of word families. A word family is a group of words all of which are basically the same except for the initial letter or letters. For example, *ball, fall, call,* and *hall* represent a word family. Teaching words in families began with the linguistic approach to reading, which was based on the work of such linguists as Fries (1955) and Bloomfield and Barnhart (1961). They argued that the English language is basically phonemically regular and that children can learn to read easily once they discern this regularity.

Classroom teachers can use the word-family approach by selecting a phonogram such as *all*, putting different consonants and blends in front of it (ball, call, fall, hall, mall, tall, small, etc.), and helping children pronounce the words by modeling how the sounds would be combined to form new words. These new words can be written on the board or on a chart and then put into oral and written sentences. As children become more proficient at this, the teacher can select a word family and ask the students to think of, pronounce, and write the new words created by adding consonants, blends, or digraphs to it.

Teachers can also write word families on flash cards, one family per card. Consonants, blends, and diagraphs can be written on additional flash cards. Children can work in pairs or groups to match the beginning sounds through the *ake* family, for example, you might use the following cards:

Children would line up beginning sounds or blends with *ake*. If the combined cards made a real word, the children would write it. To put the word back into context, discussion of the word, along with using it in oral and written sentences, should follow. For a comprehensive list of word families, you should consult *The Reading Teacher's Book of Lists* (Fry, Polk, & Fountoubidis, 1984).

The language experience approach (LEA) to teaching reading noted earlier is another commonly used approach to teaching letter-sound relationships. This approach, based on the work of R.V. Allen (1976), Stauffer (1970), and Hall (1965), uses a child's experiences, thoughts, and language to produce reading material. Nessell and Jones (1981) noted that the procedure is based on two assumptions: (a) A child's interests and life experiences are of great personal value and are highly meaningful, and (b) learning to read is easier and more enjoyable when reading materials match the language and speaking vocabularies of the reader. There are generally two parts to the LEA: taking dictation and follow-up or reinforcement activities.

Generally, the dictation part of the LEA follows two steps: preparing the child or children for dictation by providing an experience that can be discussed, and giving dictation. (For a complete treatment of the LEA, see Nessell and Jones, 1981.)

The follow-up or reinforcement part of the LEA also consists of two main steps: rereading the story and skill development. Any letter sound relationship skill can be taught during the skill-development phase of the LEA. For example, in the dictated story in the following box, the teacher decided to work with the sound of *w*. After reading and rereading the story to the children, reading the story with the children, and asking various children to read the story by themselves, she asked them to point to words that began with the sound of *w*. These words were listed separately, discussed, and written by the students. New words beginning with the same sound were added to the list as the children thought of them.

Windows

We made windows out of paper. We looked through our windows to see things. We saw a bird with a worm and some children walking. We saw a man and a lady driving. We saw our principal. His name is Mr. Warner. We want to make more windows.

The same inductive strategy for teaching phonics discussed on page 138 can be used with language-experience stories, only the sight words used come from the language-experience stories. For example, when teaching the sound of *w*, you would list the words from the story that begin with that letter. You would then ask the children to read each word, listening for the beginning sound. After eliciting from the children that the words all begin with the sound of *w*, you would ask them to tell you other words that begin with this sound. These would be listed and their meanings discussed. You and the children might then make up sentences for *w* words that are not from the story and write the sentences from the story for the remaining words. For a wealth of other follow-up and skill-reinforcement activities using the LEA, see Garton, Schoenfeider, and Skriba (1979) and Garman (1978).

The cloze procedure discussed in chapter 5 as an informal diagnostic procedure can also be used to teach and reinforce letter-sound relationships. When using cloze as a teaching technique for phonics, Bortnick and Lopardo (1973) have suggested that cloze passages be prepared with deleted words containing certain letter-sound relationships. For example, to emphasize blends, you could find or write a 50–150 word passage and delete all words containing blends. A sample passage might look like that in Box 8.1.

Box 8.1

As we walked along the city _____, we saw many interesting things. _____ were blooming everywhere and the _____ were full of _____ leaves. It was a beautiful _____ day.

Read the passage to the students and ask them to fill in the deleted words so that the passage makes sense. When they have completed the passage, list the words the students have used and have a discussion in which you attempt to guide the children to an awareness that the deleted words all contain a particular letter-sound correspondence or follow a specific pattern. With younger students, you can read the story orally and ask them to tell you what words would make sense. If the children tell you words that make sense but do not begin with blends, list them in a separate column and draw the children into a discussion of how these words are different from those that begin with blends.

Whatever strategy is used to teach letter-sound relationships, it is important to remember that the final test of whether a child has mastered phonics as a skill is if he or she can read, in context, words that contain that sound. We believe that there is no substitute for allowing children to read for sustained amounts of time from self-selected materials. As noted in *Becoming a Nation of Readers* (R.C. Andersen et al., 1985), "once the basic relationships have been taught, the best way to get children to refine and extend their knowledge of letter-sound correspondences is through repeated opportunities to read" (p. 58).

WORD IDENTIFICATION

Instructional strategies to improve word identification are usually categorized into two broad areas: immediate word identification and mediated word identification. *Immediate word identification* refers to the ability to recognize words by sight (F. Smith, 1982). Strategies a child uses when she or he doesn't recognize a word by sight are called *mediated word recognition*. Phonics, as described in the previous section, is usually considered one of the mediated-word-recognition strategies. That is, within reading instruction, practitioners usually don't make the distinction between phonemic analysis and other word-identification strategies (e.g., the recognition of spelling patterns). Instead, practitioners usually follow the scheme represented in Figure 8.2.

In this section we will discuss techniques for improving immediate word recognition and mediated word recognition, although we will not include a discussion of phonics in the later, given that it was covered under phonemic analysis. In actual practice it probably does not matter whether you have a separate level of analysis entitled *phonemic analysis* so long as you attend to the issue of phonics as part of your diagnosis and instruction.

Immediate Word Recognition (Sight Vocabulary)

Words recognized instantly by a reader are commonly called *sight words*. From a production-theory perspective, the use of sight words is not a reading strategy (procedural knowledge). Rather it is declarative information used when word recognition is almost instantaneous. People who take a bottom-up approach, on the other hand, consider the use of sight words a skill and devote a great deal of time to its development. Those who take top-down and interactive approaches also recognize the importance of sight-word recognition but do not believe that sight words should be taught as an isolated skill. Relative to the top-down versus bottom-up controversy regarding sight words, we take a compromise position; we believe sight words should be overtly taught, but, as much as is possible, instruction should not focus on teaching sight words in isolation.

Regardless of your theoretical position, it is difficult to ignore the research indicating the importance of sight-word knowledge. Johnson and Pearson (1984) cited research indicating that the ability to recognize words rapidly is essential to comprehension. LaBerge and Samuels (1974) used the term *automaticity* to describe the fluent reader's ability to recognize words immediately. They asserted that readers who are capable of automatic word recognition are free to focus their attention on higher levels of processing (e.g., discourse and schema levels of analysis), whereas those who must attend to individual words have no capacity left for these higher levels of analysis (see the discussion in

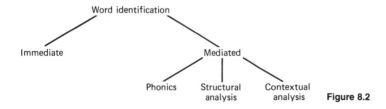

Figure 8.2

chapter 4 on attention and capacity). Finally Burns, Roe, and Ross (1984) listed a number of more practical reasons why the development of sight vocabulary is important to reading:

> Many words commonly found in print can't be "sounded out" (e.g., *the*, *know*). Learning a number of words by sight provides students with immediate success at reading and, consequently, helps develop a positive attitude toward reading. After children have built up a limited sight vocabulary the teacher can begin phonics instruction using an analytic approach.

One fact that significantly eases the task of teaching sight words is that there are a relatively small number of words that account for a large percentage of the words students encounter when they read. Ekwall and Shanker (1983) examined research studies to determine the percentage of total running words in reading materials composed of different words. Their findings, which are reported in Table 8.1, indicate that teaching only 200 common sight words will enable a child to recognize 66% to 70% of the words he or she encounters in print. These words, known as *high-frequency words*, are the most important ones for children to learn by sight.

There are a number of basic sight-word lists available for teachers' use. Probably the most well-known of these is the Dolch list (1936), composed of 220 words. Other basic lists include the 300-word Fry list (1980); the Harris-Jacobson list (1973), containing 333 words; and Johnson's Basic Vocabulary list (1974). Johnson's first- and second-grade lists are reported in Tables 8.2 and 8.3 respectively.

Some teachers prefer to create their own basic word lists. Culver (1982) recomended that school districts develop a locally relevant word list by examining levels at which words are introduced in the basal series used in the district. This

Table 8.1 The Percentage of Total Running Words in Reading Materials Composed of Different Words.

NUMBER OF DIFFERENT WORDS	% OF TOTAL RUNNING WORDS[1]
3	8–12%
10	20–25
100	60–65
200	66–70
500	75–80
1000	83–85
1500	87–88
2000	89–90
3000	91–92
5000	92.5–93.5

[1]The total running words are all the words that appear in one section.

Table 8.2

JOHNSON'S FIRST-GRADE WORDS

---

a	day	I	off	table
above	days	if	old	than
across	did	I'm	one	that
after	didn't	in	open	the
again	do	into	or	then
air	don't	is	out	there
all	door	it	over	these
am	down	its		they
American		it's	past	think
and	end		play	this
are		just	point	those
art	feet		put	three
as	find	keep		time
ask	first	kind	really	to
at	five		red	today
	for	let	right	too
back	four	like	room	took
be		little	run	top
before	gave	look		two
behind	get	love	said	
big	girl		saw	under
black	give	make	school	up
book	go	making	see	
boy	God	man	seen	very
but	going	may	she	
	gone	me	short	want
came	good	men	six	wanted
can	got	miss	so	was
car		money	some	way
children	had	more	something	we
come	hand	most	soon	well
could	hard	mother	still	went
	has	Mr.		what
	have	must		when
	he	my		where
	help			which
	her	name		who
	here	never		why
	high	new		will
	him	night		with
	his	no		work
	home	not		
	house	now		year
	how			years
				yet
				you
				your

From *Teaching Reading Vocabulary* (p. 15) by Dale D. Johnson and P. David Pearson, 1984. Copyright 1978 by Holt, Rinehart & Winston. Reprinted by permission.

Table 8.3

JOHNSON'S SECOND-GRADE WORDS				
able	different	last	real	water
about	does	leave	road	were
almost	done	left		west
alone		light		while
already	each	long	same	whole
always	early		say	whose
America	enough		says	wife
an	even	made	set	women
another	ever	many	should	world
any	every	mean	show	would
around	eyes	might	small	
away		morning	sometimes	
	face	Mrs.	sound	
because	far	much	started	
been	feel	music	street	
believe	found		sure	
best	from	need		
better	front	next	take	
between	full	nothing	tell	
board		number	their	
both	great		them	
brought	group	of	thing	
by		office	things	
	hands	on	thought	
called	having	only	through	
change	head	other	together	
church	heard	our	told	
city		outside	town	
close	idea	own	turn	
company		part	until	
cut	knew	party	us	
	know	people	use	
		place	used	
		plan		
		present		

From *Teaching Reading Vocabulary* (p. 16) by Dale D. Johnson and P. David Pearson, 1984. Copyright 1978 by Holt, Rinehart & Winston. Reprinted by permission.

enables teachers to use words that children will be exposed to locally rather than words found on lists determined on a nationwide basis (Ekwall & Shanker, 1983).

  Whatever list you decide to use, it is important that words be taught in context as much as possible. As noted in *Becoming a Nation of Readers* (R.C. Andersen et al., 1985), studies by Meyer and Schraneveldt, and Zola have shown that "a meaningful context speeds word identification" (p. 11).

  Johnson and Pearson (1984) recommended a five-step plan for teaching sight vocabulary. The students first see the word in its written form, either on the chalkboard, on a flash card, or on a piece of paper. As the children look at the word, it should be said orally. If the word can be related to a picture (e.g., *children*, *house*, *car*), the picture should be shown at this time. Next, the word is discussed in a way that relates to the children's interests, experiences, and environment. That is, the teacher should try to relate the word to what the students already know. The word is then used by the children in phrases or sentences. These should be written on the board and discussed.

The next step involves having the children define the word, if possible. Finally, children should practice writing the word in isolation and in context. Personal word books, or dictionaries, of new words can be kept.

Using games to teach sight words can be effective and motivating (Ekwall & Shanker, 1983). One type of sight-word recognition game is the path game. A sample path game is illustrated in Figure 8.3. This game can be constructed and used in a variety of ways. If a "blank" path game is made on a piece of tagboard and then laminated, you can write in the words you want to reinforce with the children. To play the game, the children roll a die and move along the board, landing on words. They then say the word and use it in a sentence.

Another option in making a path game is to write the words to be reinforced on cards, which the children take turns drawing. At the bottom of each card is a number. If a child can read the word and use it in a sentence, she or he may move the number of spaces along the path indicated by the number on the card.

We believe that it is very important for the children to say the word and use it in a sentence, no matter what kind of game is used. We also believe that the best way to reinforce sight vocabulary is through many meaningful reading experiences. For a wealth of ideas on make-it-yourself games to reinforce sight-word identification, see Burns, et al. (1984).

Neurological Impress (Heckelman, 1969) is another way to build and reinforce a child's sight vocabulary. Although this technique was originally designed

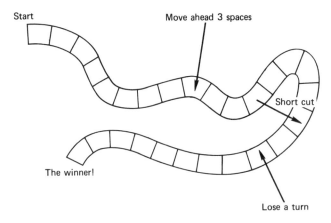

Start

Move ahead 3 spaces

Short cut

The winner!

Lose a turn   **Figure 8.3**

to improve reading fluency, we have also found it helpful in building a sight vocabulary, because a child simultaneously sees, hears, and "feels" each word. Using this method, the child selects reading material that is, preferably, at his or her instructional level. The teacher and child sit side by side. Both read orally in unison as the teacher moves a finger or the child's finger under the line of print. Each word is said as it is being pointed to.

An alternative to unison reading is echo reading, in which the teacher reads a sentence, pointing to each word as she or he says it. The teacher then moves a finger or the child's finger under the words in the sentence a second time. This time the child "echoes" what the teacher has read. If a child doesn't know a word or forgets one, the teacher simply says it, and the child keeps reading.

The key to learning new vocabulary through Neurological Impress is consistency. It must be used 5 to 10 minutes a day, 4 to 5 days a week. If scheduling is a problem, teachers can teach parent volunteers or older students to use Impress.

Repeated Readings (Samuels, 1979) is a technique that can also be used to build a sight vocabulary. As with Neurological Impress, it was orginally designed to improve fluency. The procedure is actually quite simple. A student rereads a short, meaningful passage several times until a satisfactory level of fluency is reached. Then the procedure is repeated with a new passage.

To begin, let the student choose an easy story of interest. Mark off short sections of 50–200 words from the story. Then have the student read a section aloud and record his or her reading rate and the number of word recognition errors. Next, have the student return to his or her desk and practice the passage. Finally, have the student return and reread the passage aloud until a predetermined criterion for fluency is reached.

Generally, you will find that, as reading speed increases, word-recognition errors decrease. Also, the initial speed of each new selection should be faster than the previous speed.

The LEA was described previously as a way to reinforce phonics skills. It is also an excellent way to build and reinforce a child's sight vocabulary. After a child has dictated a story and you have read it to her or him several times, ask the child to read it back to you. In the next day or so, ask her or him to underline or circle any known words. Most children will be able to remember a few words from the story; others will remember many. Words that have been underlined can then be isolated by using a "word bank" card. Each word the child can read in isolation is written on a card and becomes part of the child's word bank. Many vocabulary reinforcement activities can be used with word bank cards. Children can write sentences and stories using them, make up rhyming words, use them in games, read them to each other, and find the same words in other reading material.

When using a story that has been dictated by a group of students, the procedure varies somewhat. After several readings of the story by teacher and students, the teacher makes a copy of the story for each child in the group. In the next day or two, the teacher asks the children to work individually to circle words they know. Words that are known become part of a child's word bank.

Mediated Word Identification

Recall that *mediated word identification* refers to strategies that students use when they don't know a word immediately by sight (Smith, 1982). Johnson and Pearson (1984) believed, and we concur, that three types of mediated word-identification skills need to be taught: phonic analysis, structural analysis, and contextual analysis. Again, phonic analysis (phonics) was discussed previously in this chapter in the section on phonemic analysis. In this section we discuss structural analysis and contextual analysis.

Structural Analysis Structural analysis, also knows as *morphemic analysis*, is a method of word identification in which the reader learns an unfamiliar word by looking for smaller meaningful parts within the word. As an example, a child might figure out the word *enjoyable* by recognizing the more familiar root word *joy* or the suffix *able*.

In chapter 3 we discussed the various types of meaningful word parts (e.g., affixes, morphographs, and phonograms). When reading educators talk of meaningful word parts, they are usually referring to affixes (prefixes and suffixes), spelling patterns, morphographs, phonograms, word roots, plural endings (-s, -es), verb tenses (-ed, -ing, -s), possessives, compound words, and contractions. The use of any of these elements to identify an unknown word is called *structural analysis*. Next, a number of ways to reinforce structural analysis are briefly described.

CLOZE One way that teachers can help students learn the strategy of structural analysis is through the cloze procedure. A teacher can create short cloze passages, leaving off parts of words such as plural endings or verb tenses. Students are to read the passage and fill in the word part so that the passage makes sense. An example of such a procedure using plurals is illustrated in Box 8.2.

Box 8.2

He really wants to bake some cook_____ to bring to all the part_____ he will be attending. His mom will get angry, however, if he mess_____ up the kitchen or breaks any dish_____.

An example of a cloze passage utilizing verb tenses is found in Box 8.3.

Box 8.3

As she walk_____ along the street, she look_____ at the store windows. She was wish_____ for some of the toys she saw in the window of the toy store.

An alternative to deleting only portions of words is to delete the entire word that contains the target word part. A passage can be written deleting all words containing prefixes, or compound words, or contractions. After the students have filled in the words, a discussion should ensue. You can list the words the students have used and lead them to the realization that each deletion has a common characteristic.

FINDING WORDS IN PARAGRAPHS AND STORIES   Another way to help children become aware of the importance of word parts is to have them underline or circle words in a story or paragraph that contain particular word parts. This activity helps students acquire the declarative information necessary for structural analysis but does not reinforce the strategy itself. As an illustration of the activity, consider the paragraph below:

> I told her how disappointed I was that she didn't reread the story. It was so unfair, since everyone else did.

Ask the children to go through and circle the words with prefixes. When the activity is completed, the words can be listed on the board and discussed. Students can then write their own sentences or paragraphs, using the words in a way that shows they understand the meanings of the prefixes.

MATCHING ACTIVITIES   Matching activities are another way of reinforcing structural analysis skills. List words and/or meaningful word parts in two columns. Ask the students to draw lines between the correct words or parts and to rewrite the new words in the third column. Use compound words, prefixes, suffixes, word endings, or any other structural analysis components. A matchup for compound words might look like this:

A	B	C
foot	noon	_____
after	light	_____
head	ball	_____

For suffixes:

A	B	C
nice	dom	_____
employ	est	_____
free	ment	_____

For prefixes:

A	B	C
un	view	_____
sub	marine	_____
re	happy	_____

For contractions:

A	B	C
let	am	_____
is	not	_____
I	us	_____

The new words the students write should be used in oral and written sentences.

CONCENTRATION GAMES   Concentration games are a good way to have students match word parts. Using cards approximately 3″ × 2½,″ write the word parts you wish to reinforce, one word part per card. For prefixes, you might make an equal number of root-word cards and prefix cards:

For contractions you might write the contraction on one card and the words the contraction is made from on another card:

For possessive words, write phrases such as *the dog belonging to Bill* on one card and *Bill's dog* on another card.

All cards are spread out upside down on the floor or table. Playing in groups of two or three, students take turns turning over any two cards. If a match is found, the student uses the new word (or phrase) in a sentence and keeps the cards. All words a student keeps are later written in sentences.

USING THE NEWSPAPER   The newspaper can also be used to teach and reinforce declarative information necessary for structural analysis skills. Children can find and circle words with prefixes, suffixes, contractions, compound words, verb tenses, and so on. These words can then be listed by the teacher, discussed, and used in oral and written sentences. For a number of ideas on using the newspaper to teach and reinforce reading skills, see *Teaching Reading Skills Through the Newspaper* (Cheyney, 1984).

IDENTIFICATION BY ANALOGY   The final type of structural analysis strategy we will consider is identification by analogy. Some reading textbooks classify this as a phonics strategy. We classify it as a structural analysis strategy because it makes use of spelling patterns, phonograms, and morphographs. Identification by analogy is the comparing of parts of the unknown word to parts of known words. For instance, the pronunciation of the word *bane* might be worked out by knowing how to pronounce the word *vane*.

F. Smith (1982) defined identification by analogy as "looking for clues to a word's pronunication and meaning from words that look the same" (p. 146). One might figure out how to pronounce the word *medicinal*, and also discover its meaning, by comparing it to the word *medicine*.

You can help students identify words through analogy by showing them how to look for and focus on similarities in words. A student who cannot pronounce *slant* can be shown the words *ant* and *can't* as clues.

Contextual Analysis Contextual analysis, more commonly known as the *use of context clues*, is the use of surrounding words in a sentence or paragraph to help determine an unknown word. Here we will stress the semantic rather than syntactic aspects of contextual analysis. We will consider syntax in chapter 9, when we discuss the syntactic level of analysis.

Although some children intuitively understand context clues, most children, especially beginning readers, have to be taught how to use them (Ekwall & Shanker, 1983). There are various types of context clues, including the following:

1. *Description clues.* A description of the word might be used. This description is often in a phrase set off by commas.
   Example: The *general*, a great leader, was worried about the battle.
2. *Comparison/contrast clues.* A comparison or contrast of the unknown word to a known word might be used.
   Example: He was *upset* instead of happy about winning the election.
3. *Experience or familiar expressions clues.* A child's background of experience or knowledge of familiar expressions might help determine the unknown word.
   Example: She was as *quiet* as a mouse.
4. *Synonym clues.* A word with a similar meaning might be used.
   Example: Todd's *automobile* was one of the nicest cars on the block.
5. *Example clues.* An example is given to provide the needed clues for identification.
   Example: Cliff is extremely competitive. For example, he will bet on almost anything.
6. *Definition clues.* A word might be directly defined in context.
   Example: A *noun* is a person, place, or thing.

To reinforce the use of context clues, a teacher must provide opportunities and activities that encourage children to examine the context in order to guess at unfamiliar words (Johnson & Pearson, 1984). A number of such activities are described next.

CLOZE   Cloze-type activities are especially useful when teaching context clues. One activity for beginning readers is to read a sentence with a word left out. Children are asked to suggest words that would make sense, based on the surrounding context (see Box 8.4). Any appropriate contribution should be accepted. The teacher should also ask the students to explain why a particular word would be appropriate.

Box 8.4

A _____ was running away. We sat down to _____. _____ is going home now. I want to _____. We _____ down the street.

A variation of this strategy is to write a sentence and provide multiple-choice answers for the deleted words. Students are asked to select the appropriate word, tell why it was chosen, and give reasons why the other words are not appropriate. Sentences such as the following can be used:

Nancy _____ the dress.
(ate, wore, talked)
She has a big red _____.
(moon, kite, tree)
It's time to _____.
(eat, lunch, book)

OPIN   Opin is another variation on the use of cloze (Vacca, 1981). Opin stands for *opinion* and is play on the term *cloze*. It works like this: (a) The teacher provides four or five sentences, each with a word deleted. (b) Working alone, a student fills in a word that makes sense. (c) Students meet in small groups to discuss their choices. The objective for a student is to convince the rest of the group that his or her word is the best one for the sentence. The group must come to a consensus on the most appropriate word for the sentence. (d) The small groups meet again in a large group and share their group word for each sentence. The teacher lists words provided by each group and discusses the appropriateness of each with the students. (e) The large group selects the most appropriate word for the sentence.

With older students, teachers can introduce the various kinds of context clues, providing sample sentences with each type. The target word should be highlighted in some way. Together, teacher and students should read the sentences and underline the word or phrase that helps identify the meaning of the target word. Students should then use the new word, orally or in writing, in a sentence that connects the word with some aspect of their lives (McNeil, 1984).

A CONTEXTUAL ANALYSIS PROCESS   Readance, Bean, and Baldwin (1981) suggested a five-step procedure for helping students understand context clues. The first step is to identify the word or words that might present problems for students or that are central to understanding important concepts they will encounter in reading. For example, in a unit on World War II sea battles, the word *dreadnought* might present a problem.

The second step is to write a sentence for the word(s), using appropriate context clues, or to use the sentences in the text in which the word is found. A sentence for *dreadnought* might be. "The dreadnought was chasing the smaller ship in hopes of beginning a battle."

Next, the teacher should present the word(s) to the students in isolation and ask them to provide the meanings. The answers are written on the chalkboard. All answers should be accepted, but students should be asked to come to a consensus about what they think the best meaning is and why.

Then the teacher presents each word in the sentence(s) developed in the second step. Students should again be asked to provide a meaning for the unfamiliar word and to give a rationale for it. Finally, a student volunteer can look up the word in the dictionary to verify the guesses offered by the class.

A Strategy for Mediated Word Identification

The most effective way to reinforce mediated word identification is to provide students with a strategy that incorporates the three mediated word identification techniques: phonics, structural analysis, and contextual analysis. This, of course, is in keeping with the production-theory model, which emphasizes the importance of procedural knowledge—process or strategy knowledge.

Next is described a general strategy for mediated word identification. When a child encounters an unrecognized word during oral or silent reading she or he should

1. Skip the word and read to the end of the sentence.
2. Go back to the word and ask "What word would make sense here (context) that has this word part (structural analysis) and begins with this letter or letters (phonics)?"
3. If unable to determine the unknown word, reread the previous sentence or continue reading the next sentence and try Steps 1 and 2 again.
4. If still unable to recognize the word, identify a word that would make sense and continue reading.

The intent of this process is for students to be aware of words they do not recognize and to make an initial guess at them by using context as the primary source of information. However, structural analysis and phonics are also used as secondary strategies. If this technique does not cue the student as to the identity of the word, more information to use for contextual analysis is gathered by reading further. Structural analysis and phonics are also reapplied. If the word remains unrecognized, a logical substitute is provided to aid comprehension, and reading is continued.

TEACHING WORD MEANINGS

Use of word identification strategies over time has the effect of increasing a student's "meaning vocabulary"—those words he or she knows the meanings of (Pearson, 1985). Many theorists within reading make a distinction between two types or levels of meaning vocabulary. Vacca (1981) called these levels simple and complex. At the simple level of meaning vocabulary, children generally know a word's definition. The complex level of development involves what Beck (1984) called owning a word and Pearson (1985) called "knowing a word in its fullest sense" (p. 729). As an example, being able to recite that *duralumin* means a strong, lightweight alloy of aluminum is knowledge of the word at the simple level. Such knowledge does not indicate that a pupil really knows what the word means. Nagy (1985) warned that it takes far more than this simple or superficial knowledge of words to make a difference in reading comprehension.

Pearson (1985) noted that several studies have shown the advantage of a more complex, concept-development approach to teaching vocabulary over the more conventional ones of defining words and using them in sentences. In this section we will discuss ways of deepening students' understanding of word meanings.

Semantic Mapping

Semantic mapping develops meaning vocabulary by showing, in categories, how a given word relates to other words. As Johnson (1983) noted, "seeing 'old' words in a new light and seeing the relationships among words are the desirable and inevitable outcomes of semantic mapping." Here is a description of semantic mapping:

1. Select a word that is important to the understanding of a story to be read or that is determined by class interest or need.
2. Write the word on the chalkboard.
3. Ask the students to write as many words as they can that relate to the target word and categorize them. With younger students who could have problems writing, you might have to provide "think time" for them to come up with related words.
4. Ask students to share words from their lists while you write them on the board in categories. These words should be arranged in a "map" format similar to Figure 8.4. Note that the target word is in the center of the map with the categories emanating from it. You should feel free to add words to categories, especially if that category is essential to the understanding of a reading selection. Be aware that some words could fit in more than one category and some students might disagree on the placement of a word.
5. Ask students to give each category a name. In the semantic map shown in Figure 8.4 the categories might be sizes of trees, colors, kinds, parts of trees, things made of trees, and so on.
6. Discussion, both during the construction of the map and after its completion, is

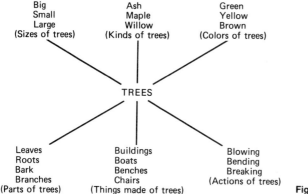

Big
Small
Large
(Sizes of trees)

Ash
Maple
Willow
(Kinds of trees)

Green
Yellow
Brown
(Colors of trees)

TREES

Leaves
Roots
Bark
Branches
(Parts of trees)

Buildings
Boats
Benches
Chairs
(Things made of trees)

Blowing
Bending
Breaking
(Actions of trees)

Figure 8.4

perhaps the most important part of the activity. It is during this discussion that you help students see both the old words in a new way and the relationships among words and terms.

7. If you use this activity as a prereading technique to develop a word necessary to the understanding of a story, it might be necessary to focus on a particular category or two and discuss how they relate to the upcoming story.

Semantic Feature Analysis

Semantic feature analysis is a strategy that uses a child's prior knowledge and the way it is organized to develop vocabulary in a logical and sensible way (Johnson & Pearson, 1984). Besides helping children see the uniqueness of a word, it also helps children understand that the term *synonym* means words are somewhat the same in meaning but not exactly the same. Students see how words can be related yet remain unique. The following steps are used with semantic feature analysis:

1. Select a category (pets)
2. List, in a column, words within the category (dogs, cats, birds). (See Table 8.4.)
3. In a row across the top of the grid (see example), list some features shared by some of the words (*furry, bark, four legs*).
4. Put pluses or minuses beside each word under each feature. A plus indicates that a word usually has a given feature.
5. Ask students to help you add additional words and features and complete the expanded matrix with pluses and minuses.
6. As a group, discuss the words and their features. This is essential to the success of this activity.

Help children discover that no two words have the same pattern of pluses and minuses and, therefore, no two words are exactly the same.

Table 8.4

TOPIC: PETS	furry	bark	four legs	eats lettuce	lives in trees
dogs	+	+	+	−	−
cats	+	−	+	−	−
birds	−	−	−	−	+
gerbils	+	−	+	+	−

As children become better at distinguishing features, a numerical system can be used in place of the pluses and minuses. Johnson (1983) suggested using 0 (none), 1 (few or some), 2 (most or much), and 3 (all).

Semantic feature analysis can be used with preschoolers as well as college students. It works as well with content-specific vocabulary words as it does in building a general vocabulary (Johnson & Pearson, 1984). To illustrate its use with content-area vocabulary, assume that a geography class is beginning a unit of study on physical features of European countries. The countries can be listed down the left column of the grid, and physical features can be written across the top (see Table 8.5). Students can fill in pluses or minuses or even a question mark if they are unsure of an answer. A question mark can be changed to a plus or minus when the unit has been completed. As the unit progresses, new countries and features can be added to the grid.

Cluster Approaches

One way to enhance word meaning is to teach words together that share a common conceptual basis (McNeil, 1984). Marzano (1984) noted that research indicates that presenting vocabulary in semantically related clusters can improve students' vocabulary knowledge and reading comprehension. A cluster is a group of related words, not necessarily synonyms. Rather, they are words that share some common basis. For example, here is a cluster of related verbs:

hold   wring
catch   clench

Table 8.5

	mountains	desert	land-locked	ocean border
Spain	+	?	—	+
Portugal	−	—	—	+
Germany	+	—	—	−
France	+	—	—	+
England	+	—	—	+
Switzerland	+	—	+	−

squeeze   hug
grab   wrap
grip   cling
clutch   embrace
clasp

Marzano organized the 7,300 words found in elementary school text-books into 61 instructional clusters. The first 15 clusters account for over 50% of the words found in elementary school textbooks; the first 25 clusters account for over 75% of the words found in elementary school texts. The names of those clusters, along with some sample concepts, are presented in Table 8.6. Marzano suggested that teachers introduce two or three clusters at a time to students as general categories about which they will be learning new words. For each category, *anchor words* should be identified for students—words that are familiar to the students and are representative of the other words in the cluster. These anchor concepts, along with the cluster names, should be kept in individual student notebooks. As vocabulary words are introduced, students describe, don't define, the new words as they relate to the anchor words and others within the cluster. Students are continuously integrating new words into their meaning vocabularies by relating them to words they already know (the anchor concepts). For a complete listing of the 7,300 words in their clusters, see Marzano (1985).

Marzano's approach is similar in many respects to a hierarchical approach. There are instances when a teacher can help students learn a new word by relating it to a hierarchy of related concepts (McNeil, 1984). Some of the concepts should be more abstract (superordinate) than the new word, some should be subordinate, and others should be of equal importance (coordinate) to the target word.

The Frayer Model for developing vocabulary is based on a hierarchial approach. As McNeil (1984) noted, "the model offers a systematic procedure for conceptualizing words" (p. 107). The following steps are included in the model (McNeil, 1984):

1. Discriminate the relevant qualities common to all instances of the concept. The relevant attribute of *globe* is *spherical*.
2. Discriminate the relevant from the irrelevant properties of the concept. *Large*, *medium*, or *small* are irrelevant properties of *globe*.
3. Provide an example of the concept such as a classroom globe.
4. Provide a nonexample of the concept such as a nonspherical chart.
5. Relate the concept to a subordinate concept. A subordinate concept for *globe* is *ball*
6. Relate the concept to a superordinate term. *Global* is superordinate to *globe*
7. Relate the concept to a coordinate term. A coordinate term for *globe* is *map*.

If a concept cannot be defined by its relevant attributes, steps 1 and 2 are omitted, and a synonym and an antonym are used in their places (McNeil,

Table 8.6 Superclusters Identified in Elementary Textbooks

SUPERCLUSTERS, EXAMPLES OF CONSTITUENT WORDS, AND DESCRIPTIONS	NUMBER OF WORDS IN SUPERCLUSTER	CUMULATIVE NUMBER OF WORDS
1. Occupations: career, manager, mayor, coach, businessman, printer, publisher.	364	364
2. Types of motion: action, stillness, begin, end, chase, toss, pull, plunge, shrink	321	685
3. Size/quantity: tiny, large, amount, many, monstrous, one, two	310	995
4. Animals: pet, dog, snake, fish, spider, bird	289	1284
5. Feelings/emotions: feeling, terror, shame, anger, sad, happy, love, excitement	282	1566
6. Food types/meal types (names for various food types and situations involving eating): food, supper, meal, cookie, meat, vegetables, butter, cook	263	1829
7. Time (names for various points and periods of time and words indicating various time relationships between ideas): lifetime, noon, season, month, today, earlier, now, afterward	251	2080
8. Machines/engines/tools: equipment, engine, oven, hammer, axe, spoon	244	2324
9. Types of people (names for various types or categories of people that are not job-related): person, woman, boy, neighbor, dweller, hero, enemy, mother, dad	237	2561
10. Communication (names for various types of communications and actions involving communications): explain, talk, suggest, question, command, vow, complain	235	2796
11. Transportation: car, plane, jeep, boat, bicycle, ship	205	3001
12. Mental actions/thinking: wonder, plan, search, solve, teach, select, wisdom, belief	193	3194
13. Nonemotional human traits (general, nonphysical traits of people): nice, lazy, sure, patient, stubborn, humorous, heroic	175	3369
14. Location/direction: here, back, end, to, inside, on, under, close	172	3541
15. Literature/writing: story, novel, poem, music, telegram, pen, write	171	3712
16. Water/liquids (names for different types of liquids and bodies of water): rain, dew, silt, river, stream, snow, ice	164	3876
17. Clothing: suit, shirt, cap, boots, shawl, pants, belt, coat	161	4037
18. Places where people live/dwell: city, town, neighborhood, country, state	154	4191

Table 8.6 Superclusters (continued)

SUPERCLUSTERS, EXAMPLES OF CONSTITUENT WORDS, AND DESCRIPTIONS	NUMBER OF WORDS IN SUPERCLUSTER	CUMULATIVE NUMBER OF WORDS
19. Noises/sounds: noise, clatter, quiet, peep, moo	143	4334
20. Land/terrain (names for general categories of land or terrain): land, territory, valley, mountain, field, planet	142	4476
21. Dwellings/shelters (names for various types of dwellings/places of buisness): building, motel, home, store, school, hospital, station	141	4617
22. Materials (names for materials used to make things): canvas, metal, wood, lumber, steel	140	4757
23. The human body: body, hips, head, hair, mouth, eye	128	4885
24. Vegetation: shrub, tree, bush, branch, grass, spruce	116	5001
25. Groups of things (general names for groups and organizations): group, network, gang, committee, conference, club	116	5117
26. Value/correctness: true, false, important, worthless	108	5225
27. Similarity/dissimilarity (names indicating how similar or different things are and the sameness or difference between ideas): like, equal, different, and, moreover, but, contrariwise	108	5333
28. Money/finance: fortune, money, cash, rich, poor	102	5435
29. Soil/metal/rock: ground, sand, stone, iron, metal	102	5537
30. Rooms/furnishings/parts of dwellings: kitchen, basement, table, chair, chimney, wall	97	5634
31. Attitudinals (words indicating the speaker/writer's attitude about what is being said or written): frankly, fortunately, evidently, truthfully	96	5730
32. Shapes/dimensions: shape, round, curve, straight, long, level	90	5820
33. Destructive/helpful actions: hurt, break, help, cure, crash	87	5907
34. Sports/recreation: game, contest, football, play, racket	80	5987
35. Language (names for different aspects of written and oral language): grammar, sentence, phrase, alphabet, syllable	80	6067
36. Ownership/possession: have, own, keep, win, escape, flee	68	6135

Table 8.6 Superclusters (continued)

SUPERCLUSTERS, EXAMPLES OF CONSTITUENT WORDS, AND DESCRIPTIONS	NUMBER OF WORDS IN SUPERCLUSTER	CUMULATIVE NUMBER OF WORDS
37. Disease/health: illness, health, pain, ache, well, sick	68	6203
38. Light (names for light/darkness and things associated with them): sunshine, shade, candle, spark, clarity	68	6271
39. Causality: cause, reason, result, because, hence, therefore	59	6330
40. Weather: climate, weather, sunny, storm, foggy	55	6385
41. Cleanliness/uncleanliness: clean, dirty, soap, brush	53	6438
42. Popularity/knownness: familiar, common, unknown, secret	52	6490
43. Physical traits of people: strong, slender, neat, fat	51	6541
44. Touching/grabbing actions: feel, stroke, grab, clench	50	6591
45. Pronouns (personal, possessive, relative, interrogative, indefinite pronouns): you, your, someone	50	6641
46. Contractions: can't, I've, they'll, it's, I'd, we're	49	6690
47. Entertainment/the arts: movie, concert, play, sculpture, performance	48	6738
48. Walking/running actions: run, jog, crawl, leap, hop	46	6784
49. Mathematics (names for various branches of mathematics, operations, and quantities): geometry, minimum, formula, addition	46	6830
50. Auxiliary/helping verbs (forms of to be, modals, primary and semiauxiliaries): are, do, have, will, is going to	46	6876
51. Events (names for general and specific types of events): occasion, event, holiday, festival, ceremony	44	6920
52. Temperature/fire: cold, heat, fire, ash, smoke	40	6960
53. Images/perceptions: image, representation, look, glance, perception	39	6999
54. Life/survival: survive, mature, live, death	38	7037
55. Conformity/complexity: unique, distinct, simple, complex	34	7071
56. Difficulty/danger: easy, difficult, safe, perilous	30	7101
57. Texture/durability: hard, soft, flimsy, durable	30	7131
58. Color: red, blue, yellow	29	7160
59. Chemicals: oxygen, nitrate, boron, acid	28	7188
60. Facial expressions/actions: smile, frown, smell, breathe	21	7209
61. Particles of matter: atom, ion, electricity	21	7230

From A cluster approach to vocabulary instruction. A new direction from the research literature, *Reading Teacher* *38* pp. 170–172. Copyright 1984 by the International Reading Association. Reprinted by permission.

1984). For the concept *beautiful*, the synonym *lovely* might be used at Step 1 and the antonym *ugly* might be used at Step 2.

Using Guided Imagery

All of the techniques discussed thus far rely on linguistic information for learning a new word. However, some theorists stress the "imagery" nature of vocabulary (e.g., Paivio, 1983; Richardson, 1983). By imagery we mean more than just "pictures in the mind." Mental images include the tactile, auditory, emotional, and visual aspects of perception (Sheikh, 1983). For example, when you ride on a roller coaster, you store in your long-term memory all the sensations (sounds, feel, emotions) associated with the ride, as well as mental pictures of the ride. Those theorists who stress the imagery aspect of vocabulary knowledge claim that students must have primary experiences with concepts. These primary experiences are stored as images and then become the basis for vocabulary development. This, of course, is consistent with developmental models of concept attainment (e.g., Piaget).

A developmental model would suggest a sequence in the acquisition of new vocabulary words. For example, students should first have experiences that create images. They should then be given a label for those experiences. They might then be asked to describe what they know about the label. Over time, this description would become more and more precise, until it finally evolved into what we might call a technically accurate definition. This developmental process can be stated as a four-step instructional sequence:

Step 1: Provide primary experiences in the vocabulary word that develop the imagery characteristics of the word (e.g., visual, tactile, auditory, emotional).

Step 2: Provide students with the label (word) to represent the experiences.

Step 3: Require students to describe the new concept in their own words.

Step 4: Over time, have students sharpen their description of the vocabulary word until it evolves into a technically accurate definition.

The stumbling block in this sequence would appear to be Step 1. How can you provide primary experience for all concepts you wish to teach? If you wish to teach the concept of *parachuting* to young students, do you take them up in an airplane and give them direct experiences? Of course the answer is no. Step 1 need not be a stumbling block because primary experiences do not have to be direct. Imagery characteristics can be developed by "guided imagery," that is, imagining what an experience is like. In effect, this is the way we obtain primary experiences about most of our concepts. Few people have parachuted from an airplane. However, most people have jumped from a limited height, felt a strong wind rushing against them, and stood at a great height. They then put the remembrance of these experiences together to form their concept of parachuting, even though they have never directly experienced it.

Guided imagery is a way of artificially creating primary experiences for concepts within a classroom setting. The technique has a rich theoretical and research basis. Guided imagery has long been used in psychotherapy under the name of *oneirotherapy*. It has been shown to be basic to most memory techniques (Bellezza, 1981; Paivio, 1983) and is one of the most powerful techniques currently in use in sports training (Suinn, 1983). Also, many of the learning techniques purporting to integrate left-, and right-brain functions (e.g. Hart, 1983; Zdenek, 1983) are basically adapations of guided imagery (see chapter 4 for a discussion of right-brain–left-brain techniques).

When you use guided imagery, have students relax (closing their eyes helps) and then try to remember or simply imagine experiences that relate to the new vocabulary word. Modeling also helps here. That is, describe to students some of the images you are having as a way of stimulating their thinking. Students should feel free to create whatever images best represent the new concept to them. If they have had no direct experiences related to the new concept, have them recall a movie or television program that illustrated the new concept.

Once students have a firm grounding in the imagery characteristics of the new concept, they can then proceed to Steps 2, 3, and 4. It is important to remember that, at first, students' descriptions of the new concept (Step 3) will be fuzzy. However, if you systematically have students revise their descriptions of the concepts (Step 4), over time, they will approach technically accurate definitions.

Using Word Meanings to Make Assocations

Nagy (1985) stated that, in order for students to be able to use the meanings of a word to facilitate comprehension, instruction should include activities in which students are asked to use the meanings of the words to generate associations.

Some of the instructional techniques used by Beck, Perfetti, and McKeown (1982) are specifically designed to do this. For example, after being introduced to the vocabulary words for the week, the student can be provided with a word-association activity. To illustrate, assume that some of the words for the week are *virtuoso, philanthropist, novice, hermit,* and *accomplice.* Students might be asked to choose the word that goes best with *crook* and to justify their answers.

Another activity might involve affective associations. When the teacher reads the vocabulary words, students are asked to respond with *yea* or *boo* depending on how they feel about the word.

A third activity is to provide a multiple-choice test in which the choices are not definitions but involve making inferences ("Would an *accomplice* be more likely to (a) squeal to the police in return for not having to go to jail? (b) rob a bank himself? (c) enjoy babysitting?") Students must justify their choices.

A final activity attempts to encourage students to think about vocabulary words in new ways by asking questions that probe relationships among words ("Could an accomplice be a novice?" "Would a hermit be an accomplice?").

Learning Vocabulary Through Reading

Recent research suggests that many children learn the meanings of words incidentally through wide reading. Nagy and Anderson (1984) estimated that the average child learns about 3,000 words a year between grades 3 and 12, and the average high school senior has a vocabulary of around 40,000 words. Because even the most effective vocabulary instruction is extremely time consuming, they suggest that vocabulary can be developed best by providing a moderate amount of time for students to read during the school day. Students should be provided with many different kinds of reading material in a classroom. Maps, charts, graphs, brochures, menus, newspapers, magazines, trade books, and catalogs are but a few of the materials that should be made available. Along with Nagy (1985), we believe that a combination of direct vocabulary instruction and moderate amounts of long-term sustained silent reading optimizes the growth of children's word meaning vocabulary.

SUMMARY

In this chapter we have presented instructional techniques for the letter-recognition, phonemic analysis, and word-identification levels of reading. Letter-recognition strategies included use of commonly encountered functional words and concentration games. Techniques for teaching phonemic analysis, or phonics, included word families, language experience, and the cloze process. The teaching of word identification was divided into sight vocabulary techniques (immediate word recognition) and the mediated word-recognition strategies of structural analysis and contextual analysis. An integrated mediated word-identification strategy was presented that combines characteristics of phonemic and word-level analyses. Finally, different strategies for teaching word meanings were considered.

SYNTACTIC
AND DISCOURSE-LEVEL
ANALYSIS

Above the level of recognizing words, students must recognize the syntactic structures and discourse structures of material they read. In this chapter, we will consider both these levels of analysis. As in preceding chapters, we will try to consider declarative and procedural aspects of these types of analysis. However, within the area of syntax, this distinction is not as clean as it is within other areas. This is because syntactic analysis, for the most part, occurs automatically, probably unconsciously, to the reader. Our knowledge of syntax comes from years of practice and repetition in hearing and speaking the language. In our discussion of syntax we will present techniques that augment that gradual buildup of knowledge, both declarative and procedural, relative to syntax. These procedures are more holistic than some of those described for the other levels of analysis.

SYNTACTIC ANALYSIS

As noted in chapter 2, syntax is the way words fit together in sentences. We all have an intuitive knowledge of syntax. For example, we can tell that "the big brown dog ran away" sounds right but that "ran the away dog brown big" does not. It is this intuitive knowledge, or internalized set of rules, of syntax that provides us with much of the information we need to construct meaning from text.

In this section we will consider ways of increasing students' general syntactic ability and ways of remediating problems with specific aspects of syntax.

Oral Language Development

Language ability plays an important role in the development of reading, and, even though most children intuitively know the way words are put together in sentences, oral language activities strengthen and expand this knowledge. Exposing children to many different kinds of oral language facilitates the development of syntax. There are a number of useful classroom activities that do this.

Reading Aloud   Reading aloud to children is one of the best ways to develop oral language; research shows that reading aloud to children has a significant effect on their language growth (Durkin, 1966).

Norton (1980) listed a number of benefits of reading aloud. Not only do children learn that literature is a source of pleasure, but they also develop an appreciation for literature that they themselves cannot yet read. In addition, reading aloud to children improves their overall reading achievement. Norton (1980) reported a study by Cohen (1968) that showed "that seven-year-olds who were read to twenty minutes a day gained significantly in vocabulary and comprehension scores" (p. 330).

Reading aloud also motivates students to read for themselves. Children who cannot yet read are commonly motivated to learn as a result of their desire to emulate their peers and teacher.

Similarly, reading aloud provides children with a good role model. They hear the teacher read with intonation and correct phrasing, and they begin to transfer this behavior to their own silent reading experiences.

DiStefano et al. (1984) listed an additional benefit from reading aloud to children: enhancement of writing ability. Through hearing good literature, children become aware of how writers begin and end a story and how they develop tone, mood setting, plot, and character. Good literature provides children with models of writing that they can later use in their own writing.

Finally, reading aloud to children helps them learn the distinction between oral language and the language found in books. Because of the different social registers (see chapter 2), the syntactic structure found in texts usually differs from what the child is accustomed to hearing. This is particularly true for students from nonnative-English-speaking backgrounds. Reading aloud from a variety of materials provides exposure to the many different kinds of syntactic structures that a child will encounter in her or his own reading.

What kinds of books should teachers read to students? Norton (1980) believed that teachers should choose books containing quality literature and "challenge children to grow in new appreciation and new interests" (p. 331). She also suggested that teachers should keep in mind such factors as the children's ages, interests, attention spans, and previous experiences with literature when choosing a book.

DiStefano et al., (1984) stated that it is important to read with expression and enthusiasm, maintain some eye contact with students, and enunciate clearly. Questions can be asked at the beginning of a story that will help children make predictions. Questions and discussion can also occur during the story, to help keep children's interest and enthusiasm alive. For an excellent source of books to read aloud to students, see *The Read Aloud Handbook* by Jim Trelease (1982).

It is important to note here that a teacher should read from a variety of materials, not just from library books. Reading aloud from newspapers, magazines, brochures, letters, and menus helps children become aware of, and accustomed to, the many kinds of syntactic structures they will encounter in print.

Predictable Books   Providing children with predictable books or "patterned books" is an excellent way to help them develop their oral language. Rhodes (1981) defined predictable books as those in which the language flows naturally, those with which the students can quickly predict what the author is going to say and how he or she is going to say it, and those in which the vocabulary and content reflect what the children know about their language and their world. She noted that predictable books contain one or more of the following characteristics: (a) repetitive patterns (same words, phrases, or sentences used over and over again); (b) familiar concepts; (c) good match of text and illustrations; (d) rhyme; (e) rhythm of the language, including stories set to music; (f) cumulative patterns (a new incident or character added in each verse); (g) familiarity of the story or story line (e.g., fairy tales); and (h) familiar sequences, such as numbers, days, or months.

You can read predictable books to students, ask them to join in and read along with you, and pause in selected places to allow them to predict upcoming words or phrases. Students can use the patterns found in predictable books to create their own materials. See Rhodes (1981) for an extensive bibliography of predictable books that can be used with children.

Many predictable books have accompanying tapes. You can purchase a variety of commercially prepared books and tapes or make your own. After children have listened to a tape a number of times, reread the story with them and then ask them to read it to you.

Rhymes, poems, and songs are another type of predictable material. Learning and reciting rhymes, poems, and songs expands a child's experience with syntax. Often the words and phrases used in these forms of literature do not match the way children naturally speak. Knowledge of how rhymes, poems, and songs are written helps sharpen children's oral language development and prediction abilities.

Language Experience   In chapter 8 we discussed how the LEA can be used to teach the skills associated with beginning reading. It is also one of the best ways to develop children's oral language. Gillet and Gentry (1983) described a four-step LEA activity designed to provide exposure to and experience with Standard English syntax while maintaining the integrity of a child's native dialect even if it is nonstandard. Here is a summary of that four-step process.

Step 1: Take dictation, using the children's natural language. Have the children practice reading the story until they can read it fluently.

Step 2: Prepare an account of the same experience written in Standard English. Incorporate as many words as possible from the original story, but use the sentence structure, patterns of organization, and words with which you want the children to become familiar. Introduce the story to the children, read it aloud several times, and invite the children to join in. Have a discussion, with students comparing the two versions of the story.

Step 3: Ask children to rewrite sections from the original story, making the sentences longer and the language more elaborate. Write a new story, using the revised sentences.

Step 4: Once the new story written by the children can be read fluently, use simple sentences from any of the three stories (children's original, teacher's Standard English version, and children's revision) to demonstrate how sentences can be generated by the addition and subtraction of different words. This activity provides children with opportunities to invent new, more elaborate sentences while modeling standard sentence structures and grammatical patterns.

Using Writing for Syntactic Development

In chapter 2 we discussed Chomsky's (1965) theory that there are two levels of syntax: surface structure and deep structure. Surface structure is the syntactic form the sentence takes; deep structure is tied more to meaning. That is, it is at the level of deep structure that syntax conveys meaning. Some reading theorists (e.g., McNeil, 1984) have translated Chomsky's theory into the assertion that comprehension involves the translation of surface structures to deep structures. When there is a close match between surface structure and deep structure ("The dog ate the meat"), little translation is required. Other sentences ("Because Mary decided to stay up later than usual, she had time to finish washing the dishes") require "special operations" (McNeil, 1984, p. 115) on the reader's part to make the transition from surface to deep structure.

McNeil (1984) noted that students have more problems with sentences that use the passive voice ("He was given the book by John") than the active voice ("John gave him the book"). They also have problems with sentences that

1. Use the passive voice
2. Contain relative clauses ("The woman saw the man who robbed the store")
3. Reverse the true order of events ("Before I ate, I took a walk")
4. Contain conflicts in semantic structure ("He didn't say he couldn't go")

5. Include anaphoric relationships ("John went to the store and *he* bought potatoes")
6. Contain certain kinds of punctuation (semicolon, colon, comma, dashes, ellipses, and parentheses)
7. Use figurative language (metaphors, similes, and so on)

We will briefly consider each type of problematic syntactic structure.

Passive Voice Pearson and Johnson (1978) referred to the ability to recognize the equivalence in meaning between two or more sentences as *paraphrasing*. To help students paraphrase active and passive voice sentences, try giving them a standard sentence in the active voice along with two or three syntactically related sentences, one of which is in the passive voice. Ask them to select the sentence that best paraphrases the target sentence or is the equivalent in meaning of the target sentence. An example is presented in Box 9.1.

Box 9.1

Target Sentence: Sally read the book.

1. The book was read by Sally.
2. Sally was read by the book.
3. Sally was read the book by.

When using this kind of activity, McNeil (1984) suggested that students be taught to ask the key question of "Who is the recipient of the action?" when selecting the paraphrased sentence. He also suggested giving students simple sentences written in the active voice to rewrite in passive form.

A variation of this activity is to give students a set of three sentences and ask them to select the one that does not mean the same as the other (Pearson & Johnson, 1978). You might want to use sentences like these:

1. Mary was asked to play by the boy.
2. The boy asked Mary to play.
3. Mary asked the boy to play.

Relative Clauses Students will better comprehend sentences with relative clauses (a subordinate clause embedded in the main clause) if you give them complex sentences and ask them to identify the embedded sentences. In the sample sentence, "The woman saw the man who robbed the store," the two sentences would be "The woman saw the man" and "The man robbed the store." After students become proficient at identifying embedded sentences, ask them to write their own sentences with relative clauses and then give them to other students to rewrite. You can also help students look for these kinds of sentences in the material they read. These sentences can be listed, discussed, and rewritten.

Reverse Order of Events   Sentences that reverse the order of events often pose comprehension problems for students. A student's natural expectation, especially a younger child's, is that the sentence will list events in the order of their occurrence. The reversal of such events means that a student has to make a mental transformation. For example, "I watched television after I took a bath" means that the bath came first. Pearson and Johnson (1978) suggested a number of activities to help students with reversed time relations, among them:

1. Give a sentence (e.g. "She watched television before she took the dog for a walk") and ask students specific questions such as "What happened first, watching television or taking the dog for a walk?" "What happened second, watching television or taking the dog for a walk?" "Did watching television happen before the dog was walked?" "Did walking the dog happen before she watched television?"

2. Place scrambled events in order. List five events in random order and assign each a letter: A, B, C, D, E. Then give the students a set of choices from which they are to select the choice that lists the events in correct order:
   1. B C A D E
   2. D E C A B
   3. A C B D E

3. Place cartoon frames in order. Cut out and laminate cartoon frames from the newspaper. Ask students to place them in their original order. Ask questions such as "What happened before . . . ?" "What happened after . . . ?" "What happened first . . . or . . . ?"

Conflicts in Semantic Structure   McNeil (1984) suggested that sentence containing conflicts in semantic structure often mix something negative with something positive. In the sample sentence, "He didn't say he couldn't go," the reader must transform the clauses into a positive format and then apply the negative meanings. To help students comprehend these kinds of sentences, provide sentences with conflicting semantic structures and ask students to transform them. Try having them write the positive interpretation over the negative interpretation, for example,

> She is organized.
> She's not disorganized.
> There is someone here who is not able to do this.
> There is no one here who is able to do this.
> Do ask me to do it if he does want to.
> Don't ask me to do it if he doesn't want to.

Anaphoric Relationships   Anaphora is the use of one word as a substitute for a preceding word or group of words. For example, in the sentence "The boy cried. He was hungry," *he* has an anaphoric relationship with *boy* because *he* refers to *boy*.

McNeil (1984) identified several kinds of anaphoric relationships:

1. Pronouns are usually used as substitutes for nouns or groups of nouns.
2. A pro-verb makes reference to a preceding verb. ("Jan ate the grits. She didn't want to do it.").
3. A pro-sentence is a group of words that substitute for previous sentences. ("The car won't start and breakfast was cold. *This* started Bob's day off poorly.")
4. Invisible anaphora occurs when there is no explicit "pro-form," but context implies the existence of a word, phrase, or clause. As an illustration, consider the following: "Is Marcia going to go?" asked Yvonne. "I don't know," answered Kathy. Here there is an invisible anaphoric reference to the clause "if Marcia is going to go." That is, the reader assumes that Kathy is saying "I don't know if Marcia is going to go."

There are a number of instructional activities that can be used to reinforce recognition of anaphoric relationships. One is to construct a list of sentences or a paragraph with numbers placed over various forms of anaphora (see Box 9.2). Students must write the same number over the antecedent for each anaphora.

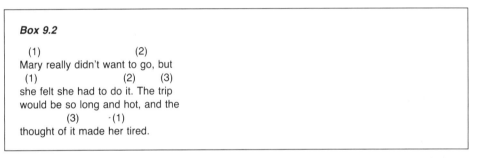

Box 9.2

```
  (1)                    (2)
Mary really didn't want to go, but
 (1)              (2)       (3)
she felt she had to do it. The trip
would be so long and hot, and the
            (3)        ·(1)
thought of it made her tired.
```

A variation of this activity is to ask students to circle the anaphoras and draw arrows to their matching antecedents (see Box 9.3).

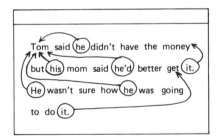

Box 9.3

Another activity is to construct sentences or a paragraph with all antecedents rewritten in place of their anaphoras. Students then rewrite the sentences or paragraph, using correct anaphoras (See Box 9.4).

With all of these activities, discussion is imperative. The teacher should guide students to an understanding of the function of anaphoras.

McNeil (1984) suggested a related activity to increase students' awareness

---

Box 9.4

Billy and Steve went to the fair.
Billy and Steve had such a great time.
Billy and Steve rode on the rides and ate hot dogs as they rode on the rides.
Billy and Steve also had Billy and Steve's picture taken. After a long day, Billy and Steve decided to head for home.

---

of the use of anaphora. Take a selection with which students are familiar and ask them to circle or underline all words that substitute for other words. Once these replacement words have been identified, work with students to name the different types of anaphoras.

Punctuation   The way in which a sentence is punctuated often gives clues to its deep structure. Most children are familiar with the meaning that capitals and periods convey but do not understand the inherent meanings of colons, semicolons, commas, ellipses, parentheses, and dashes.

The best way to teach the meanings of these clues is through the contexts of reading and writing (McNeil, 1984). You might find several examples in basals and library books of the kinds of punctuation clues you want to teach and present these examples to students. Guide them to inductively state the meaning behind the use of the clue by observing its use in writing. Students should then generate their own sentences using the punctuation clue you have been studying.

Figurative Language   Language is used figuratively when "what is said is different from what is meant" (Ortony, 1984). As an example, consider the expression, "It's raining cats and dogs." We do not take this expression at face value but have learned to interpret it to mean that it is raining very hard. Sentences using figurative language, especially metaphors and similes, often cause problems for students. Similes make comparisons using the words *as* or *like* ("She's as happy as a clam."), whereas metaphors make comparisons without the use of these words ("He is a holy terror."). These kinds of sentences require interpretation of the literal words. However, some students might not have the background experience to make the interpretation. To illustrate, consider the sentences "She's as quiet as a mouse." A child must know that mice are generally quiet so they won't be noticed. The interpretation of "His eyes were as big as saucers" would require a child to know that saucers are round and usually large.

McNeil (1984) suggested that you can introduce the concept of figurative language by asking students to match a literal meaning with a figurative expression. Sentences such as these can be used:

LITERAL	*FIGURATIVE*
Her eyes sparkled.	Her eyes were like diamonds. Her eyes were like roses. Her eyes were like baskets.
Timmy gets into everything.	Timmy is like a book on a shelf. Timmy is like a whirlwind. Timmy is like a picture on a wall.

You can also ask students to change literal sentences into sentences with figurative language and vice versa.

Looking for examples of figurative language in students' reading materials, presenting these to students, and having students describe their meanings is also helpful. Once students become familiar with figurative language, you can ask them to find and share examples from their own reading. A bulletin board can display these examples. You might also ask students to draw pictures to illustrate them.

DISCOURSE-LEVEL ANALYSIS

As was discussed in chapter 3, discourse-level processing refers to the recognition of the format and organization of a paragraph or an entire passage rather than of a single sentence. We also mentioned in chapter 3 that there are three levels of discourse-level structures: simple relationships between ideas, basic patterns among ideas, and superstructures. Although we will present techniques for each of these levels, the distinctions are somewhat artificial. That is, there is a great deal of overlap among levels. Instructional activities that facilitate the use of information at one level also improve the use of information at another. However, the three levels do have distinct enough characteristics to justify considering them separately.

Teaching Simple Relationships

As described in chapter 3, propositions or statements are tied together by relationships. Reading teachers are commonly concerned with *cue words* or *linguistic connectives*, used to signal the relationships. For example, McNeil (1984) offered the following list of linguistic connectives for some basic relationships:

CAUSE-AND-EFFECT RELATIONSHIPS	CONCLUSIONS OR SUMMARIES	IDEAS LINKED TO TIME
because	consequently	when
so	therefore	until
since	thus	meanwhile
if	hence	before
as	accordingly	always
for		following
		finally
		during
		initially
		after

These connectives convey a great deal of meaning within discourse. Change the connective, and you have changed the meaning. As an illustration, consider the following sentences:

He called out to me when I left.
after
before
and
but

It's five o'clock and I will go.
but
so

The linguistic connective used in each sentence changes the meaning of the sentence, sometimes slightly, other times significantly.

We suggest that linguistic connectives be approached as declarative knowledge necessary for discourse-level analysis. That is, a knowledge of basic relationships does not usually involve any strategies for reading. However, a knowledge of basic relationships does provide the necessary information for the discourse analysis strategies used at the higher levels.

We mentioned in chapter 3 that theorists and researchers have identified many different types of basic relationships (e.g., Halliday & Hasan, 1976; Meyer, 1975; Pitkin, 1977). These systems are meant for research and are far too complex for instructional purposes. Here we will present a system of basic relationships drawn from the research literature but specifically designed for reading instruction (Marzano & Dole, 1985).

The basic relationships between ideas can be categorized into four groups: addition, contrast, time, and cause. At a very simple level these relationships can be described in the following way:

Addition: One idea is stated as similar to or "going with" another idea in some way (He is tall and he is handsome.).

Contrast: One statement does not go with another statement in some way (He is tall but he is not a good basketball player).

Cause: One statement is the cause or condition for another statement (He went home because she went home.)

Time: One statement is stated as occurring before, during or after another statement (She left before he left).

However, each type of basic relationship can be subdivided into more specific types of relationships:

ADDITION:

1. Equality:
   He is tall and he is handsome.
2. Restatement:
   I am tired. In fact, I am exhausted.
3. Example:
   He does many things well. For example, he is excellent at cards.
4. Summation:
   He does many things well.
   He cooks.
   He sews.
   In all he is an excellent homemaker.

CONTRAST:

1. Antithesis:
   I will be there, but I won't be happy.
2. Alternative:
   Either it will rain or it will snow.
3. Comparison:
   Bill is tall. In comparison his brother is short.
4. Concession:
   I don't like violence. Nonetheless, I'll meet you at the fights.

CAUSE:

1. Direct Cause:
   He won the race by maintaining his concentration.
2. Result:
   Bill went home. Consequently the party ended.
3. Reason:
   He went to the store because he needed food.
4. Inference:
   Mary is going on a long trip. In that case, she should plan well.
5. Condition:
   Unless you stop, I will leave.

Table 9.1

	TIME
1. Subsequent Action:	Afterward, next, since, then, after that, later, in the end, shortly, subsequently, so far, as yet, before, until, finally
2. Prior Action:	After, earlier, initially, in the beginning, originally, at first, previously, beforehand, formerly, before that, before now, until then, up to now, by now, by then
3. Concurrent Action:	Simultaneously, while, meanwhile, meantime, at this point, at the same time

	CAUSE
1. Direct Cause:	By
2. Result:	Consequently, hence, now, so, therefore, thus, as a consequence, for all that, as a result, whereupon, accordingly, the result was, this is the reason why
3. Reason:	Because, because of, in that, so that, since, so on account of, for the fact that
4. Inference:	Else, otherwise, in that case, then
5. Condition:	Now that, providing that, supposing that, considering that, granted that, admitting that, assuming that, presuming that, seeing that, unless . . . then, as long as, in so far as, if, where . . . there, when . . . then, no sooner . . . .

	ADDITION
1. Equality:	And, moreover, equally, too, besides, furthermore, what is more, likewise, similarly, as well, in addition, besides, at the same time
2. Restatement:	Indeed, actually, in actual fact, in fact, namely, that is, that is to say, another way of saying this
3. Example:	For example, first, second, third, one, two, three . . . , for a start, to begin with, next, then, finally, last but not least, for one thing, for another thing, another example would be
4. Summation:	Altogether, over all, then, thus, in all, therefore, all in all, in conclusion, in sum, in a word, in brief, briefly, in short, to sum up, to summarize

	CONTRAST
1. Antitheses:	But, yet, or rather, what is better, what is worse, contrariwise, conversely, oppositely, on the contrary, else, otherwise, on the other hand
2. Alternative:	Alternatively, either . . . or, neither . . . nor, rather than, sooner than
3. Comparison:	In comparison, in contrast, like
4. Concession:	However, anyhow, besides, else, nevertheless, nonetheless, only, still, though, in any case, in any event, for all that, in spite of that, all the same, anyway, though, at any rate, in any case, regardless of this

TIME:

  1. Subsequent Action:
     They went to the game. (Afterward) they went to the dance.
  2. Prior Action:
     They went to the dance (after) they went to the game.
  3. Concurrent Action:
     Bill thought about Mary (while) Mary thought about Bill.

Note that we have circled some words and phrases in these examples. As mentioned previously, these are the linguistic signals, or connectives, that indicate the presence of a relationship between ideas. Table 9.1 contains a detailed list of the linguistic connectives for each of the relationships.

   There are a number of ways to teach and reinforce these connectives. Marzano and Dole (1985) recommended the use of relationship diagrams. Diagrams of time and cause relationships are called TICA diagrams. A TICA diagram can be represented as

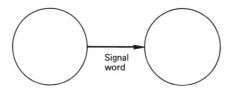

A clause or statement can be placed in each circle, with the arrow indicating that one proposition took place after another.

Sentence 1.   Marilyn sat down, turned on the light, and then opened the book.

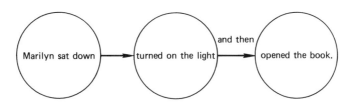

Sentence 2.   First, I got up. Next, I got dressed. Then, I ate breakfast.

With causal relationships, time is a factor. However, beyond that there is a further relationship between the statements. One event is the cause of another event. As an illustration, consider the following:

> *Sentence 3.*   Alcohol can lead to many crimes because it reduces or eliminates self-control.

This sentence can be diagramed similarly to Sentences 1 and 2 because it is time related. We used a double line, however, to indicate the cause-and-effect relationship and the time relationship.

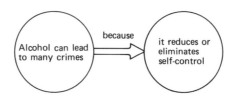

Teachers can extract paragraphs from content-area texts and have students diagram sentences using a TICA diagram. This procedure can help teachers discover if students understand the

Significance of the signal words
Organization of text
Time and sequence versus cause-and-effect relationships

Diagrams of addition and contrast relationships are called ADCON diagrams. ADCON diagrams use the mathematical symbols = and ≠ to indicate addition and contrast respectively.

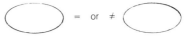

For example, consider the following sentences:

> *Sentence 4.*   I will be home early. Actually, I'll be home by 10:00.
> *Sentence 5.*   He is tall; in fact, he is a giant.

Both sentences contain propositions joined by addition relationships. They can be diagramed as follows:

Likewise, contrast can be diagramed:

Note that TICA and ADCON diagrams are similar in intent to the arrow-drawing techniques suggested for anaphora (see Box 9.3). In fact, anaphora is another way that propositions are linked together to create cohesion and coherence within discourse. When all relationships are considered (addition, contrast, time, cause, and anaphora), the ties among ideas can be identified and "mapped" with these diagramming procedures.

For primary school students, diagraming provides a vivid visual representation of the meaning of these relationships. However it can also be used in the upper grades. For example, T. H. Anderson (1978) recommended that mapping the basic relationships among ideas is a useful outlining technique for students studying content-area material.

There are a number of other ways of reinforcing a knowledge of basic relationships. For example, the cloze procedure can be used to teach signal words. Find paragraphs that use linguistic connectives. Retype the paragraphs, deleting all connecting words. Then ask students to fill in words that make sense. Discuss the answers with students and lead them to an awareness of the different categories of relationships.

Sentence combining is another useful activity for teaching basic relationships. Sentence combining is the process of taking short sentences and combining them into more complex sentences by changing, deleting, or adding words. Although this technique was originally designed to improve written composition, research has shown that it also improves reading comprehension (Finn, 1985).

Sentence combining can be cued or uncued (DiStefano et al., 1984). Cued sentence combining gives students specific words to use when putting two or more sentences together. As an illustration, consider Box 9.5.

Box 9.5

I went to the store (because)
I was hungry =
I went to the store because I was hungry.

I went to the store (because)
I was hungry (and)
I wanted cookies =
I went to the store because I was hungry
and I wanted cookies.

When using cued sentence combining activities, the position, capitalization, and punctuation of the cued word indicates its meaning. For example, consider the following set of sentences:

The party was over (Because)
The kids went home.
The party was over.
The kids went home (because)

The first set of sentences would be combined to read "Because the party was over, the kids went home," whereas the second set would read "The party was over because the kids went home."

Uncued sentence combining involves giving students a set of two or more sentences and letting them use their intuitive language ability to generate a new sentence. As an illustration, try combining the following sentences:

The dog was brown.
The dog was tired.
The dog was hungry.
The dog ate his bone.

One possible combination is

The tired brown dog was hungry so he ate the bone.

Another combination is

Because he was hungry, the tired, brown dog ate the bone.

Uncued sentence combining allows for great divergence in students' answers. It creates opportunities for discussions about the nature and form of different types of relationships between ideas.

Another version of sentence combining is to choose a sentence from a basal reader or library book and ask students to reduce it to a series of short sentences (Klein, 1984). For example, "The brown striped pony ate the hay because he was hungry" might be reduced to the following sentences:

The pony was brown.
The pony was striped.
The pony was hungry.
The pony ate the hay.

Sentence combining is a very powerful and flexible instructional technique. For a complete description of sentence combining activities, see O'Hare (1973) and Strong (1973).

Basic Patterns Among Ideas

As mentioned previously, the simple relationships are the declarative knowledge that can be used in more advanced discourse analysis strategies. One advanced strategy is pattern recognition. Patterns are large organizational frameworks. Whereas a simple relationship joins two ideas together, a pattern might unify 10 ideas. For example, when you read a page in a textbook, you look for the overall pattern of the information. It might be that the page is actually about some major generalization, or it might describe a series of events that happened in a set order. These are both examples of organizational patterns. If we miss the overall organization of a piece of information we might be able to understand bits and pieces of it, but we will not understand the information as a unified whole (Meyer, 1975).

Unfortunately most textbooks are not written in a format that makes these organizational patterns obvious to students (Pearson, 1981). Similarly, information presented orally in content-area classrooms is not organized into salient patterns. For the most part, then, the burden is on the student to create some type of organizational pattern for information read or heard. In fact, studies indicate that better students look for or create patterns as a basic comprehension strategy; less successful learners do not appear to have this metacognitive awareness. Fortunately, current research indicates that students can be taught organizational patterns and how to use them as a basic technique for understanding material they read (Leslie & Jett-Simpson, 1983; B. Taylor & Samuels, 1983).

Marzano and Dole (1985) have suggested five basic pattern types as a beginning point for teaching organizational structures. We will consider those five pattern types and then discuss strategies for using them for discourse-level analysis.

Concept patterns. Concept patterns are those in which the characteristics of a single concept are described. As an illustration, consider the following paragraph:

> My car is the nicest on the block. It is painted powder blue with white trim. It has whitewall tires and a 409 engine. It does the quarter mile in 9.7 seconds.

Here the information in the paragraph is about the concept "my car." Concept patterns usually tie information together via anaphoras. Their purpose is to describe the characteristics of a concept. For example, after reading this passage, we know the following characteristics about the concept "my car":

> It is the nicest car on the block.
> It is painted powder blue.
> It has white trim.

It has whitewall tires.
It has a 409 engine.
It does the quarter mile in 9.7 seconds.

Concept patterns are usually about persons, places, and things.

Generalization patterns. Generalization patterns contain a generalization and a list of examples of that generalization. The propositions within a generalization pattern are linked by the different types of addition relationships described in the previous section.

a. At times life gets difficult.
b. Finances become a problem.
c. A period of poor health might develop.
d. Family problems can crop up.
e. Work might become dull and boring.

Here, *b*, *c*, *d*, and *e* are examples of the generalization in *a*. As a set they have an example relationship with *a*:

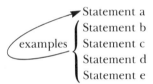

At first glance a generalization pattern might look the same as a concept pattern. Actually they are very similar in that both patterns contain information that describes something. However, concept patterns describe a single concept; generalization patterns describe an entire statement or proposition. In the sample sentences, the information in sentences *b–e* is not about any one concept in statement *a* (i.e., The information is not about *life* or *difficult*). It is about the entire statement, "At times life gets difficult." A generalization pattern contains a generalization with examples; a concept pattern contains a concept with characteristics.

In many cases a generalization pattern contains a summary statement at the end.

a. At times life gets difficult.
b. Finances become a problem.
c. A period of poor health might develop.
d. Family problems can crop up.
e. Work might become dull and boring.
f. In short, life is hard.

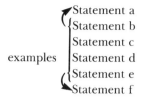

examples — Statement a / Statement b / Statement c / Statement d / Statement e / Statement f

Similarity-Dissimilarity Patterns. Similarity patterns (also known as *comparison patterns*) are those in which the underlying theme is that a group of ideas are similar.

a. The two fighters were very similar.
b. The first fighter entered the ring with a great deal of bravado.
c. Similarly, the second fighter brought with him a large entourage of admirers.
d. The first one wore a brightly colored robe.
e. The other one wore a black satin robe.
f. The first fighter used fancy footwork and quick jabs.
g. Similarly, the second one relied on cunning and speed.
h. The first one scored many points for style.
i. The second fighter was equally adept at scoring.

Here the basic organizational pattern is sets of adjacent similar statements. The predominant relationship connecting propositions is addition.

Statement c is likened to b.
Statement e is likened to d.
Statement g is likened to f.
Statement i is likened to h.

Dissimilarity patterns (also known as *contrast patterns*) are those in which the unifying theme is that ideas are different.

a. The two fighters were very different.
b. The first one entered with a great deal of bravado.
c. In contrast, the other entered with little fanfare.
d. The first one wore a brightly colored robe.
e. The other wore black.
f. The first fighter used fancy footwork and quick jabs.
g. In comparison, the quiet one protected himself and waited for an opening.
h. The first one scored many points for style.
i. The quiet one won by a knockout.

The predominate relationship connecting statements with dissimilarity patterns is contrast. Adjacent statements are dissimilar.

Statement c is contrasted with b.
Statement e is contrasted with d.
Statement g is contrasted with f.
Statement i is contrasted with h.

Sequence Patterns. Sequence patterns (also called *time-order patterns*) use repeated time relationships as the basic link among statements.

a. I have a regular routine in the morning.
b. First, I brush my teeth.
c. Then, I get dressed.
d. Next, I eat breakfast.
e. Finally, I go to school.

Here the relationship among *b*, *c*, *d*, and *e* might be diagramed in the following way:

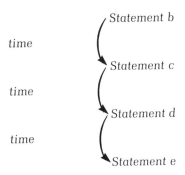

It is important to note that sequence patterns must involve true time relationships. Consider the following:

Bill does many things well.
First, he plays basketball like a pro.
Second, he is good in school.
Next, he is excellent at cards.
Finally, he plays the piano well.

Here we have the use of some signal words that might appear as though they represent a sequence. In fact, they introduce a set of statements that have an example relationship with the first statement. This is quite common. To qualify as a sequence pattern, the statements must represent an ordered set of events.

Process Patterns. Process patterns (also known as *simple listing patterns*) are sets of ordered events that produce a specific result.

a. First, get out the pots and pans.
b. Then, mix in the sugar, eggs, and flour.
c. Then, put the mix in the oven.
d. Twenty minutes later you have a cake.

As is the case with sequence patterns, process patterns use time as the predominant relationship.

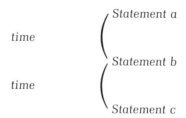

However, inherent in a process pattern is the assumption that a set of statements has a causal relationship with a single statement.

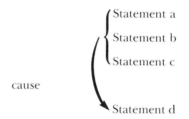

Before students can use patterns as tools to improve reading comprehension, they must first be taught the patterns as a form of declarative information. However, if anaphora and the four basic relationships have been taught to students, patterns are a logical extension. For example, concept patterns use anaphoras to link information to a specific concept. Generalization patterns use example relationships to explicate a specific statement. Similarity and dissimilarity patterns use addition and contrast relationships respectively. Sequence patterns use time relationships; process patterns use time and cause.

To teach pattern types you can use many of the diagraming techniques described in the section on relationships, or you can use the procedure suggested by Readence et al., (1981), which includes the following four steps:

Modeling. Demonstrate the use of organizational patterns before you expect students to use them. Use passages drawn from student textbooks. As you point out a particular pattern, it is essential to discuss *why* it is a certain type and *how* that pattern type is organized. Any signal words should also be pointed out and discussed.

Recognition.   Next, walk students through a passage with very obvious patterns. Ask questions that focus their attention on the text structure. Start with patterns that span only a few sentences and then move on to paragraphs and longer passages. Essential to this step is the students' verbalization of the specific elements of the pattern being studied.

Practice.   Once students have gained some expertise in perceiving patterns of organization, provide guided practice. One way to do this is to provide a cloze-type practice with the signal words deleted. After the students have completed the exercise, discuss the patterns they saw in the passage.

Production.   The final step is to have the students write passages using the various patterns. Writing is a valuable reinforcement tool for discourse-level analysis. As part of a writing assignment, ask students to use a particular pattern and the signal words associated with it.

Once students have a working knowledge of patterns, have them use the patterns to organize information they read or hear. As an illustration, consider the passage in Box 9.6.

One obvious pattern in Box 9.6 is a concept pattern about Roady Roadrunner

Roady Roadrunner

> Lived in the high desert
> Lived in a prickly bush house by the side of the road
> Every morning ran out to meet Yoshi
> Had strong legs for running
> Had a strong tail

> The tail

> Stayed out straight behind him when he ran
> Would stand up straight when he stopped running
> Was like a brake
> Helped Roady make quick stops

Roady Roadrunner

> Sang a song like a cuckoo
> Was a member of the cuckoo family

Notice that, embedded in the concept pattern about Roady, is a concept pattern about Roady's tail.

Another obvious pattern is sequence, or the listing of the events as they happened to Yoshi and Roady on a particular morning.

Box 9.6

Roady Roadrunner lived in the high desert. His house was a prickly bush by the side of the road. Yoshi lived in the high desert too. Every morning on her way to school Yoshi passed Roady's house, and he always ran out of the bush to greet her.

Roady had strong legs for running, and a long strong tail. The tail stayed out straight behind him when he ran. When he stopped running, his tail would stand straight up. It was like a brake. It helped Roady to make a quick stop.

One morning when Roady ran to meet Yoshi, he sang a strange song. It sounded a little like a cuckoo, because Roady belonged to the cuckoo family. He sang the song, and then he cocked his head.

Yoshi stood and looked at him. "If I could run as fast as you run," she said, "I could be on time for school. I am late every day."

Roady ran ahead of Yoshi and made a quick stop at the fork in the road. He braked his run with his strong tail. Then he stood there, waiting for Yoshi.

At the fork one road went on in a straight line to the school. It was the best way to go. It was the shorter way.

Yoshi did not go the shorter way. On that road a big black dog lived. He barked at her. He was very strong, and one day he had pushed her down. She was afraid of him.

The other road was longer. Yoshi went that way to school. She hurried. Sometimes she ran. But she was always late for school because that way took longer.

Her teacher, Mr. Pine, always looked upset when she came in late. Today he said, "Yoshi, you are late again! Please promise to be on time tomorrow. Why is it that you are always late?"

Yoshi stood with her head down and could not answer. If she told about the dog, the children would laugh at her. . . .

Note. From *How Is It Nowadays* (pp. 57–62) by Theodore Clymer, et al., 1976 Lexington, MA: Ginn. Copyright 1976 by Ginn and Co.

Roady ran to meet Yoshi.
He sang a strange song.
Yoshi stood and looked at him and said: "If I could . . ."
Roady ran ahead of Yoshi.

. . . .
Yoshi stood with her head down and could not answer.

There is a very important point to be gleaned from this illustration: *No one pattern exclusively fits the passage*! This means that two different readers might see two different patterns in the same information. As simplistic as this awareness is, it can be a tremendous insight to students. The knowledge that there is no single correct interpretation of information can be a very enlightening piece of information. It is information that good readers operate from. That is, a good reader is confident that his or her organization of information is a useful one.

Poor readers believe that there is a single correct way of organizing information and are not very confident that theirs is it!

This illustration also has implications for teachers, not only reading teachers but also content teachers. Basically, the implication is that teachers should act as guides in helping students see the various ways of organizing information. Rather than as static data to be learned as presented by the teacher or the textbook, content should be viewed as fluid information that can be arranged in many ways to best fit the prior knowledge of the student.

In addition to identifying obvious patterns, students can be asked to identify implied patterns. For example, as the story continues, Yoshi sees Roady being brave as he faces a rattlesnake. She uses Roady's example to be brave herself. Students might be asked to interpret this story as a process pattern—the process of Yoshi learning bravery.

Superstructures

Superstructures are the largest organizational structures within discourse. As mentioned in chapter 3, we might liken them to patterns of patterns. Whereas a basic pattern will organize a few paragraphs or even a few pages of information, a superstructure will organize an entire book. In the early grades, students most commonly read narrative information, that is stories. As students progress through the grades, the emphasis changes to expository material (e.g., science and social studies textbooks). Narrative and expository material, then, are the two main types of information students encounter in school. In this section we will consider superstructures for both types. We consider narration first.

Narrative Superstructures   To describe the various components of narratives, many researchers have proposed story grammars. Among the more widely used story grammars are those by Mandler and Johnson (1977), Rumelhart (1975), and Stein and Glenn (1979). Stein and Glenn's story grammar includes the following elements, as outlined by M. W. Olson (1984):

1. *Setting*: Introduction of the main characters and information about the time, place, and context in which the story occurred
2. *Episode*:
    a. Initiating event (sets the story in motion, causing the main character to respond in some manner)
    b. Internal response (reaction of the characters to the initiating event; it results in some feeling, thought or goal that initiates action)
    c. Attempt (overt action or series of actions carried out in order to attain a goal)
    d. Consequence (event or action, marking the attainment or nonattainment of the goal)
    e. Reaction (expression of the protagonist's feelings about the outcome of the action or its consequences) (p. 460)

Most students, even young children if they have been read to, have a basic understanding of the structure of stories. This internalized superstructure greatly influences what they recall from a story (McNeil, 1984). Whaley (1981) found that children expect stories to conform to a story grammar, and they use this knowledge as a strategy to help fill in missing parts of stories. Baker and Stein (1981) found that children use knowledge of story structure to recall and understand a story's events.

These findings suggest that teachers should reinforce children's knowledge of story structure. One way to do this is to ask students questions about stories based on story grammars. McNeil (1984) stated that teachers should ask questions based on the organization of events and ideas of central importance to the story, and Pearson (1985) suggested that the flow of a story serves as the most important criterion for question selection or creation. That is, questions should be asked about "problems, goals, attempts to solve problems, characters' reactions, resolution, and theme (or moral)," (p. 727).

Sadow (1982) offered five generic questions that can be asked of younger students about stories. These questions, based on Rumelhart's simple story grammar, are

1. Where and when did the events in the story take place and who was involved with them? (Setting)
2. What started the chain of events in the story? (Initiating Event)
3. What was the main character's reaction to the event? (Internal response)
4. What did the main character do about it? (Attempt)
5. What happened as a result of what the main character did? (Consequence)

Although Rumelhart's grammar does not include the final element found in Stein and Glenn's grammar, reaction, a question based on this element could be

6. How did the main character feel about what she or he did or about what happened?

Sadow (1982) suggested that teachers should not use these questions to test comprehension after reading. Instead, children should be taught to use them as prereading "frames" to guide their reading. For example, prior to reading the story *Ira Sleeps Over* (Waber, 1975), the teacher would present students with the following questions as a frame for organizing the information in a story:

1. Who is Ira? Where does he live? (Setting)
2. Where was Ira going that night and what was he going to do there? (Initiating event)
3. How did Ira feel about going to bed without his teddy bear? (Internal Response)

Box 9.7

Frame 1

Story summary with one character included

Our story is about _____. _____ is an important character in our story. _____ tried to _____. The story ends when _____ _____.

Frame 2

Important idea or plot

In this story the problem starts when _____ _____. After that, _____. Next, _____. Then, _____. The problem is finally solved when _____. The story ends _____.

Frame 3

Setting

The story takes place _____. I know this because the author uses the words "_____." Other clues that show when the story takes place are _____ _____.

Frame 4

Character analysis

_____ is an important character in our story. _____ is important because _____. Once he/she _____. Another time, _____. I think that _____ is _____.
                                                    (character's name)   (character trait)
because _____.

Frame 5

Character comparison

_____ and _____ are two characters in our story. _____ is _____ while
                     (character's name)   (trait)
_____ is _____. For instance, _____
       (other character)   (trait)
tries to _____

and _____ tries to _____ _____ learns a lesson when _____ _____.

4. What did he decide to do about his teddy bear? (Action)
5. What did his parents do when he went home? (Consequence)
6. How did he feel once he had his own teddy bear? (Reaction)

Fowler (1982) described a "macro-cloze" technique for reinforcing story structure called "story frames." Fowler stated that these are sequences of spaces "hooked together by key language elements" (p. 176). Box 9.7 contains five frames presented in a macro-cloze format.

Fowler suggested that, after reading a story with students, you should give them one of the story frames. Students should then discuss possible responses to the first line of the frame. Possible answers to each of the subsequent lines of the frame should then be discussed, with the teacher helping students relate the different lines to each other.

Semantic webbing is still another way to enhance story structure. Similar to semantic mapping (see chapter 8), semantic webbing is a way for students to visually organize the structure of information (Freedman & Reynolds, 1980).

The semantic-webbing model incorporates four components: the core question, web strands, strand supports, and strand ties. The core question chosen by the teacher is the focus of the web. Web strands are the answers students give to the core question. Strand supports are facts, inferences, and generalizations that students take from the story to support the web strands. Finally, strand ties are the relationships of strands to each other.

There are a few basic steps to the semantic webbing process (Freedman & Reynolds, 1980):

1. Formulate a core question for the web strand and depict it as the center of the web.
2. Elicit from student possible answers to the core question and depict these as web strands.
3. Build support for web strands and relate the strand supports to the strands.
4. Guide students in relating the strands.

To utilize semantic webbing to teach story grammar, create a core question that involves one of the elements of story structure. For example, the core question could be "What is the setting of the story?" or "Who are the main characters of the story?"

Students' responses to these questions then become the web strands. For example, if we use the question "What is the setting of the story?" for *The Three Bears* (North, 1983), the resulting web strands might resemble those shown in the diagram below:

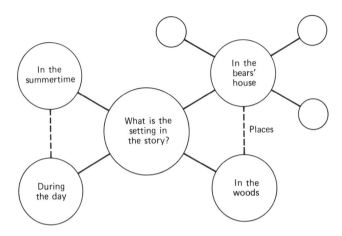

Strand supports (facts, inferences, and generalizations from the story that support web strands) are then generated for each web strand. The supports for the strand "in the bears' house" might resemble those in the next diagram.

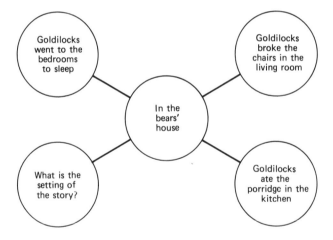

The elicitation of strand supports usually requires that the teacher ask such leading questions as "Why can we say that part of the story took place in the bears' house?" or "What happened in the story that would tell us that the bears' house is part of the setting?"

After completing strand supports for each web strand, the students should be asked to tie the strands together in some way. The teacher's role here is to help students determine how web strands can be related. Using our example, the teacher might ask "Do any parts of the setting go together?" or "How are parts of the setting alike?" Through discussion, the teacher can help students see that "In the bears' house" and "In the woods" might go together because they are places, and "In the summertime" and "During the day" might be related because they are aspects of time.

Once students have determined relationships between web strands, dotted lines can be drawn between them. The strand ties for *The Three Bears* might resemble those in the diagram.

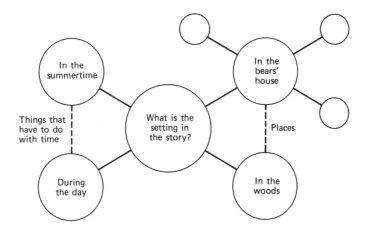

Although we focused on the use of semantic webbing to teach story grammar, Freedman and Reynolds (1980) listed a number of reading-thinking strategies that can be enhanced with this activity:

Getting the main idea
Drawing conclusions
Making generalizations
Using context clues for meaning
Predicting events
Identifying author's purpose
Identifying author's point of view
Recognizing major characters
Story setting
Story theme
Recognizing and evaluating author's use of:
    Alliteration
    Jargon
    Humor and puns
    Dialect

Each of these can be formulated into a core question for which students provide answers that become the web strands.

Expository Superstructures As can be inferred from the previous section, narrative superstructures have been thoroughly studied and many teaching techniques developed that utilize them. However, although expository material has been studied, teaching techniques for such superstructures are not as well developed. One of the problems with identifying superstructures for expository material is that it commonly has no obvious end point, as does narration. Whereas a story will come to an explicit conclusion, expository information is more open ended. We might say that some expository material is made of patterns connected in a serial fashion (e.g., those patterns described in the previous section). For example, the first part of a chapter in a science text might contain a concept pattern about some scientific term. The chapter might then shift to a description of some scientific process. A generalization might then be stated, with supporting examples. The instructional implication is that students can be asked to identify strings of patterns in expository material. Box 9.8 represents a visual schematic for how the superstructure of a selection of expository material might be represented.

Box 9.8

Concept Pattern

_____
_____
_____

Generalization Pattern

_____
_____
_____

Concept Pattern

_____
_____
_____

Process Pattern

_____
_____
_____

Concept Pattern

_____
_____
_____

A number of formal superstructures have been developed for expository material, although they are not commonly used in reading education. Drawing from tagmemic descriptions of language, Young and Becker (1980) stated that many expository works follow the superstructure *topic, restriction,* and *illustration.* A topic (T) is a very general statement of the information to be discussed. The restriction (R) limits that information in some way. The illustration(s) (I) exemplifies the restriction. Box 9.9 illustrates a T-R-I superstructure.

Box 9.9

(T)	The 1945 Cardinals were the best baseball team ever.
(R)	Their pitching staff was excellent.
(I)	Cliff Nolte was 20-2 for the season.
(I)	Mark Phillips was 24-3.
(R)	Their hitters were also excellent.
(I)	Bob Ewy batted. . . .

Boast (1974) identified definition as a basic type of expository superstructure. Definition superstructures contain the following elements:

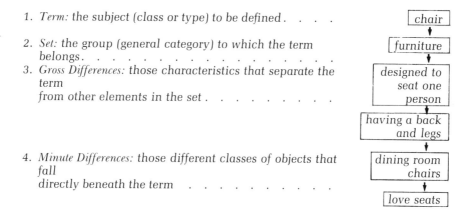

1. *Term: the subject (class or type) to be defined .   .   .   .*
2. *Set: the group (general category) to which the term belongs. . . . .*
3. *Gross Differences: those characteristics that separate the term from other elements in the set . . . .*
4. *Minute Differences: those different classes of objects that fall directly beneath the term . . . .*

Van Dijk (1980) identified argumentation as another form of expository superstructure. Drawing on the work of the logician and philosopher Stephen Toulmin (1969), van Dijk explained that an argumentation superstructure is composed of the following elements:

1. Evidence that leads to a claim . . . .

Last night the streets were filled with violence

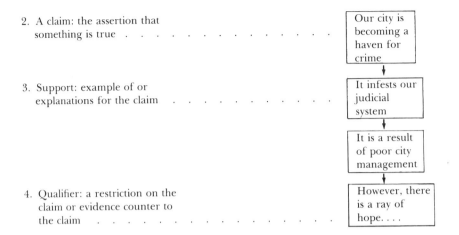

2. A claim: the assertion that
   something is true . . . .

> Our city is becoming a haven for crime

3. Support: example of or
   explanations for the claim . . . .

> It infests our judicial system

> It is a result of poor city management

4. Qualifier: a restriction on the
   claim or evidence counter to
   the claim . . . .

> However, there is a ray of hope. . . .

Finally D'Angelo (1980) identified comparison and contrast as another type of expository superstructure. Within comparison and contrast, the characteristics of two subjects are listed. That listing might take the form presented in Box 9.10a or that in Box 9.10b.

Note that D'Angelo's comparison-contrast superstructure is similar to what we called similarity-dissimilarity patterns in the previous section. The difference is one of scope. Similarity-dissimilarity patterns might be a paragraph or two within a text; a comparison-contrast superstructure would provide the framework for the total text.

We have identified five superstructures that can be used to describe expository material: (a) serial patterns, (b) T-R-I structures, (c) definition structures, (d) argumentation structures, and (e) comparison-contrast structures. These superstructures can be used in the same way as story grammars to provide students with strategies for reading, understanding, and organizing the information in expository material. First students must be taught the superstructures as declarative information. To do this, provide students with very clear examples or models of the various superstructures. Then have them write their own examples of the superstructures until they have a clear understanding of them.

Because expository superstructures are more complex than story grammars, and not as common to students, you should introduce them gradually to students. We suggest you begin with serial patterns because they are a natural extension of basic patterns. Next introduce the T-R-I superstructure, because it is a very general superstructure. Finally, introduce definition, argumentation, and comparison-contrast as very specific types of expository superstructures.

Once thoroughly known as declarative information, the superstructures can be powerful reading tools. Following the suggestions by Sadow (1982) for story grammars, you can ask generic questions for each type of expository superstructure, for example,

---

Box 9.10

a

Introduction

Characteristic 1
    Subject 1
    Subject 2

Characteristic 2
    Subject 1
    Subject 2

Characteristic 3
    Subject 1
    Subject 2

Characteristic 4 . . .
    Subject 1
    Subject 2

Conclusion (summary)

b

Introduction

Subject 1
    Characteristic 1
    Characteristic 2
    Characteristic 3
    Characteristic 4 . . .

Subject 2
    Characteristic 1
    Characteristic 2
    Characteristic 3
    Characteristic 4 . . .

Conclusion (summary)

---

1. *Serial Pattern Structures:*
   a. Are there any concepts described in the passage? How are they described?
   b. Are there any generalizations made? What are the generalizations and their examples?
   c. Is there a sequence of events described? What are they?
   d. Is there a process described? What are the parts of the process, and what do they produce or cause?
   e. Are two concepts described that are similar or different? How are they similar? How are they different?

2. *T-R-I Structures:*
   a. What is the topic or most general statement in the information?
   b. How is the topic limited or restricted?
   c. What are the examples or explanations used within the restricted topic?

3. *Definition Structures:*
   a. What is the term that is defined?
   b. What general class or category of terms does it belong to?
   c. What are some characteristics that separate it from other things within its class?
   d. What are some examples of the term?

4. *Argumentation Structures:*
   a. What is the basic claim or assertion?
   b. What evidence led the author to make this claim initially?
   c. What are some examples of the claim or evidence that the claim is true?
   d. What are some reasons given for the existence of the claim?
   e. Are there any qualifications put on the claim or statements that are contrary to the claim?

5. *Comparison-Contrast Structures:*
   a. What are the two elements compared and contrasted?
   b. What are the characteristics of the first element?
   c. What are the characteristics of the second element?
   d. Which characteristics are similar, and which are different?

Frames can also be developed for expository superstructures similar to the story grammar frames described by Fowler (1982). Box 9.11 contains a sample frame for the T-R-I superstructure.

Box 9.11

The most general statement in the passage is _____.
A limitation put on this topic is _____. Some examples within the limitation include:

_____

_____

_____

Another limitation on the topic is _____. Some examples within that limitation are:

_____

_____

_____

Teaching students superstructures for narrative and expository material is a very sophisticated reading instructional activity. It can be difficult, and it certainly takes time and practice. However, the rewards can be great. Armed with strategies for identifying superstructures, students can better read and understand even the most complex content-area material.

SUMMARY

In this chapter we presented instructional techniques for the syntactic and discourse levels of analysis. Two basic classes of techniques were presented for syntactic analysis: oral language development and use of writing. Oral language techniques involved reading aloud to students and using predictable books. Written language techniques included sentence combining and working with specific syntactic structures (e.g., passive voice, anaphora). Three levels of discourse structures were considered for discourse-level analysis. Simple relationships were presented as declarative information necessary for higher levels of analysis. Basic patterns were discussed in terms of their use as discourse-analysis strategies. Finally, superstructures were considered for narrative and expository information, and related strategies were described.

10

SCHEMA ANALYSIS INFERENCE AND METACOGNITION

In this chapter we will discuss techniques for improving students' use of schemata when they read. We saw in previous chapters that this represents a high level of analysis. Top-down and interactive models of reading assert that comprehension begins with schema-level analysis. We will also consider techniques for improving inference and metacognitive awareness about reading. Inference is the identification of information that is implied. As mentioned in chapter 4, it is fundamental to almost all aspects of reading. Metacognition is consciousness of and control over your thinking processes as you read. Again, as mentioned in chapter 4, it is one of the most exciting and promising new areas of reading research. We begin with schema-level analysis.

IMPROVING SCHEMA ANALYSIS

It is our schemata that contain the "old information" we use to interact with "new information" as we read (R. C. Anderson & Pearson, 1984). Pearson and Spiro (1982) stated that there are several schema-related reasons why we might not comprehend as we read; we might not have the schema available to help us understand or we might have the schema available but fail to access it. To illustrate this, reconsider the paragraph that was first presented in chapter 4.

> The procedure is actually quite simple. First, you arrange things into different groups. Of course, one pile may be sufficient depending on how much there is

to do. If you have to go somewhere else due to lack of facilities, that is the next step; otherwise you are pretty well set. It is important not to overdo things. That is, it is better to do too few things at once than too many. In the short run, this may not seem important but complications can easily arise. A mistake can be expensive as well. At first, the whole procedure will seem complicated. Soon, however, it will become just another facet of life. It is difficult to foresee any end to the necessity for this task in the immediate future, but then, one never can tell. After the procedure is completed, one arranges the materials into different groups again. Then they can be put into their appropriate places. Eventually they will be used once more, and the whole cycle will then have to be repeated. However, that is part of life (Bransford & Johnson, 1973)

Recall that at first this passage made no overall sense. You could recognize letters (letter recognition), letter-sound relationships (phonemic analysis), words (word identification), sentences and clauses (syntactic analysis), and even some generalizations with examples and concepts with characteristics (discourse-level analysis). However, the information did not "fit" with anything you already knew. This is because an appropriate schema for the information had not been accessed and brought into the comprehension process. However, when you were given a title for the passage ("Washing Clothes" or "Doing the Laundry"), the information made sense all of a sudden. This is because you had a schema for washing clothes. It simply had not been accessed previously. If you had no schema for doing laundry, the passage would have remained uncomprehensible.

What can be learned from this demonstration is that some students might already possess background knowledge (schemata) about information to be read but might not know how to access it or even that they should. Other students might not have the necessary schema for the upcoming information. Teachers need to find out what students already know, help them build a conceptual background if they do not have the necessary knowledge, or help them call up the appropriate schema if they possess it. The instructional techniques presented in this section will enable you to do this. We should note at the outset that improving students' schema-level analysis necessitates emphasis on strategies. That is, there is very little new declarative information that must be taught students at this level. Your focus is on teaching students strategies they can use for schema activation.

Building Bridges

The way we learn is by relating new information and experiences to what we already know. When reading, the building of bridges between the known and the unknown involves making predictions, or guesses, about what will come next on the basis of what we already know. Prediction-related instructional activities are essential to activating schema.

One way to build background for story comprehension using prediction is to ask a set of questions that require students to tell what they would do in a situation similar to the one found in the story and to then make predictions about what the main character(s) will do on the basis of their own experiences (Hansen, 1981). After reading the story, the students discuss how their predictions compared with what the character(s) really did. Hansen and Pearson (1980) found that this kind of prereading questioning promoted comprehension of literal ideas as well as of implied ideas. It also helped students process the text at a deeper level. The following questioning process is recommended:

1. Read the story.
2. Select two or three key points that are important to the understanding of the story: the protagonist's goal; an important action, event, or feeling; etc.
3. Develop two sets of questions: (a) a set that asks students what they would do if they found themselves in a situation similar to that in the story and (b) a set of questions that asks them to predict what they think the protagonist will do in the situation. For example, using the story *Ira Sleeps Over* (Waber, 1975), you might ask students questions to find out what they would do in a similar situation: "Did you ever have a teddy bear you slept with at night? What did you do with the teddy bear when you went to stay overnight with a friend?" "Did you want to take it or were you afraid to?" You might then ask the following questions to get students to predict what they think Ira will do:
"Ira, the main character in our story, sleeps with his teddy bear every night. He is invited to a friend's house to stay overnight. Do you think he will bring his teddy bear with him?" "Why or why not?"
4. Have the students read the text or text segment.
5. Ask students to compare their own hypothesized behaviors and their predictions of the character's behavior with the character's actual actions.
6. Check their comprehension of other elements of the story.

Pearson (1982) suggested a general guide for question development before, during, and after the reading of a story. He recommended that lessons begin with questions that focus student attention on appropriate background experiences. Next allow students to use background knowledge to predict what might happen in the story. Then establish a purpose for reading. Many times, the prediction strategy automatically takes care of purpose setting, but, if not, set fairly general purposes.

During guided reading, ask questions that cover the important elements in a story much like those we discussed in chapter 9 for narrative and expository superstructures. Immediately following reading, return to the purpose-setting question(s) and discuss them.

Finally, Pearson suggested a discussion of the story in which you ask students to retell the story, taking them beyond the literal level by asking them to compare this story to their own experiences or by asking them to predict how the characters might react in a new situation.

Semantic Mapping

Semantic mapping is another way to build appropriate background or activate students' schemata. We discussed semantic mapping in chapter 8 as a technique for developing and enhancing students' vocabulary. The steps involved in constructing a semantic map to build schema are basically the same as those used to develop vocabulary.

When using semantic maps to develop background for a story, it is important to focus on one or two of the categories mapped from the central word. The ones you choose to focus on should contain words most related to the upcoming story. As an example, refer back to the semantic map shown in Figure 8.4. If you used this map as a prereading strategy to develop schema for *The Giving Tree* (Silverstein, 1964), you might focus on the categories *things made of trees* and *parts of trees* because these are important to the story. You would ask students to think of other words and phrases that fit in these categories and offer some words and phrases yourself. You might then tie these categories into the theme of the story in the following way: "We now have a map about 'trees' and have listed words in many categories. The story you are going to read today tells about the ways a tree can give to people. What categories on our map have words that might tell about this?"

Reciprocal Questioning

Reciprocal Questioning or Request (Manzo, 1969) is a technique that can be used to help students' formulate their own questions about the material they are reading, develop an active attitude toward reading, and develop independent comprehension abilities (Moore, Readence, & Rickelman, 1982). It involves students and teacher reading parts of the text and taking turns asking and answering questions about the material. It utilizes the following components (Manzo, 1970):

1. Both teacher and student have a copy of the selection to be read. The teacher states the purpose of the lesson.
2. The teacher guides the student through the first paragraph of the selection, using the following steps:
   a. The student and teacher both silently read the first sentence of the selection. The student asks the teacher as many questions as she or he wants about that sentence. The student is told to ask the kinds of questions the teacher might ask in the way the teacher might ask them.
   b. The teacher answers the question(s) asked by the student as much as she or he is able.
   c. The teacher asks as many questions as are needed to add to the student's understanding of the selection.
   d. While questioning the student, the teacher periodically asks her or him to verify responses by reading a word or phrase. If a student feels she or he cannot answer a question, she or he should explain why.

    e. The pattern continues through the first paragraph, with the teacher drawing on information in previous sentences to ask new questions and form predictions for reading the remainder of the selection.

3. Throughout the procedure, the teacher positively reinforces student questions that imitate the teacher's questioning behavior. Reinforcement can be direct (e.g., "That's a good question") or indirect (e.g., responding more fully to those questions the teacher wants to reinforce).

Although Manzo first designed Request to be used in one-to-one situations with remedial readers, we have successfully used this strategy with small groups of students at all ability levels. A good way to introduce this procedure to groups of students is to make a transparency of the first page of a basal story or a chapter in a textbook. Project the transparency, covering all but the first sentence, and then begin the procedure.

Active Comprehension

Singer (1978) believed students should be taught to formulate their own questions before they read. Using the process termed *active comprehension*, the teacher asks questions to elicit questions about the upcoming reading. As an illustration, first read the paragraph in Box 10.1.

Box 10.1   *Today's Stone Age Elephant Hunters*
           B. F. Beebe

Some pigmies of the western Congo use a system of concealing their scent when hunting elephants. Few of these little jungle dwellers hunt elephants but those that do have chosen about the most dangerous way to secure food in today's world.

Hunting is done by a single man using a spear with a large metal spearhead and thick shaft. After taking the trail behind an elephant herd the hunter pauses frequently to coat his skin with fresh elephant droppings for several days until he has lost all human scent.

Closing on the herd the pigmy selects his prey, usually a young adult. He watches this animal until he is aware of its distinctive habits—how often it dozes, eats, turns, wanders out of the herd and other individual behavior.

Then he moves toward his huge prey, usually at midday when the herd is dozing while standing. The little hunter moves silently between the elephant's legs, braces himself and drives the spear up into the stomach area for several feet. The elephant snaps to alertness, screaming and trying to reach his diminutive attacker. Many pigmy hunters have lost their lives at this moment, but if the little hunter is fast enough he pulls out the spear to facilitate bleeding and ducks for safety.

Death does not come for several days and the hunter must follow his wounded prey until it stops. When the elephant falls the pigmy cuts off the tail as proof of his kill and sets off for his village which may be several days away by now.

Note. From *African Elephants* (pp. 91–97) by B.F. Beebe (1968), New York: David McKay. Copyright 1968 by B. F. Beebe. Reprinted by permission.

A lesson using active comprehension might proceed in the following way:

TEACHER:	Look at the title. What questions could you ask from the title alone?
STUDENT:	What does the Stone Age have to do with today? Why do hunters want elephants? How are elephants hunted today? How were elephants hunted in the Stone Age?
TEACHER:	Let's read the first paragraph. What would you like to know about pigmies and the Western Congo?
STUDENT:	What are pigmies? Why are they little? Where is the Western Congo? Why do pigmies live there? Do pigmies live anywhere else? What's the weather like in the Western Congo?
TEACHER:	Is there anything you want to know about the phrase "concealing their scent"?
STUDENT:	How do pigmies conceal their scent? Why do pigmies conceal their scent? Is concealing their scent dangerous? (At this point, the teacher might ask a question that gets students to focus on the upcoming portion of the selection).
TEACHER:	What would you like to know about the most dangerous way to hunt elephants?
STUDENT:	Why is it so dangerous? What do the pigmies do that makes it so dangerous? Would it be dangerous for someone other than a pigmy? Do pigmies die when they hunt elephants?

The process of active comprehension can also be used with pictures. A kindergarten or first-grade teacher might display a picture about a story and ask the children what they would like to know about it. For example, with a picture showing a boy with a baseball bat standing by a broken window, students might ask questions such as "Did the boy break the window?" "Did he break the window with a baseball?" "Will the boy run away?" "Will he get in trouble?" The teacher can ask the children to predict what they think the answers are and read the story to find out what happened.

McNeil (1984) mentioned that pupil-initiated questions reflect students' prior knowledge and cognitive development. Some students ask questions that concern details, whereas others ask those that deal with the main idea or theme. Teachers can use this information as informal diagnostic data.

DR-TA

The Directed Reading-Thinking Activity, or DR-TA (Stauffer, 1969), is another technique that can be used to get students to ask their own questions and make predictions about what they will be reading. There are two basic parts to the DR-TA: directing the reading-thinking process and developing skills. During the first part, the teacher divides the reading selection into segments and guides the children through each segment using a three-step process of *predict*, *read*, and *prove*.

For example, while using the first segment of a story, you might direct the students to read the title or look at the pictures on the first page, then ask questions such as "What do you think a story with this title might be about?" "What do you think might happen in the story?" After students had made their predictions, you would encourage them to select the predictions they think are most likely to occur.

Students then read the segment of the story silently to check their predictions. After the segment has been read, you would guide students through the *prove* step by having them evaluate their predictions by answering such questions as "Were you correct?" or "What do you think now?" At this point, students would go back to the reading material and orally read words, phrases, and sentences that proved a prediction correct or incorrect. A new predict-read-prove cycle would then begin with the next segment of the reading material.

Part two of the DR-TA, fundamental skill training, begins after the students have read the selection. As Tierney, Readence, and Disher (1980) noted, this phase involves reexamining the story for the purpose of developing systematically the students' reading-thinking abilities and other reading-related skills. Skills reinforced during this phase might include concept development, semantic analysis, and development and reinforcement of any of the skills suggested in the teacher's edition of a basal textbook.

Stauffer (1970) suggested that the reading material used with the DR-TA be well-written, interesting, and at the students' instructional level. He also suggested that students be taught strategies for dealing with unknown words encountered during the *read* step. We suggest that you teach students the integrated mediated word-identification strategy described in chapter 8.

PReP and ARC

There are a number of strategies to activate students' schemata that are particularly useful with expository material. Among these are PReP and ARC.

Pre Reading Plan, or PReP, is a three-step procedure that teachers can use to help students access prior knowledge and elaborate on and evaluate this knowledge (Langer, 1982). The assessment aspect of PReP helps the teacher (a) determine the prior knowledge a student possesses about the topic to be studied and how this knowledge is organized; (b) become aware of the language a student uses to express knowledge about the topic; and (c) judge how much additional background information must be taught before the student can successfully learn from the text.

The instructional aspect of the PReP begins with the selection of a key word, phrase, or picture to stimulate discussion about a key concept in a text. For example, in a unit dealing with the Civil War, you might select the word *slavery*. Instruction occurs in three phases (Langer, 1982):

1. *Initial Associations with the Concept.* During this phase the teacher asks the students to describe anything that comes to mind when they hear the word or phrase. As students provide words and ideas, the teacher writes them on the board.
2. *Reflections on Initial Associations.* During this phase students are asked to tell what made them think of the responses they made in phase 1. This allows students to become aware of the associations they have made, become aware of other students' associations, and evaluate the usefulness of these ideas.
3. *Reformulation of Knowledge.* After each student has had the opportunity to tell what triggered his or her response, the teacher asks "Based on our discussion, do you have any new ideas about . . . ?" Students then describe any associations that have been elaborated or changed as a result of the discussion.

Based on the levels of response in phases 1 and 3, teachers can evaluate students' prior knowledge about a topic. If a student has a great deal of prior knowledge, responses generally take the form of superordinate concepts, definitions, or analogies. If the student has a moderate amount of prior knowledge about the topic, responses usually take the form of examples, attributes, and defining characteristics. If a student has little prior knowledge about the topic, responses generally focus on prefixes, suffixes, or root words; words that sound like the stimulus word; or firsthand experiences that are not relevant to the topic.

Many students show an increase in their level of knowledge between phases 1 and 3, because they have had the opportunity to refine and elaborate their initial associations through class discussion. Students who respond at the little-prior-knowledge level during phase 3 might require further direct instruction on specific concepts before reading. Students whose responses are at the moderate level during phase 3 could be ready to read the text but should be closely monitored by the teacher in the event that concept elaboration becomes necessary. Finally students whose responses fall into the great-deal-of-knowledge category are probably ready to read the text with adequate comprehension.

ARC is an acronym for Anticipation, Realization, and Contemplation (Estes, 1984). The process begins with the teacher asking students to list everything they know about a topic before reading. These words, phrases, and statements are written as a class list. This is called the "Anticipation" phase. During reading students engage in "Realization," or the recognition of the validity or nonvalidity of what they listed during Anticipation. During "Contemplation," students return to the list to confirm, disconfirm, revise, and add to the information.

We have used a variation of the strategy with primary-grade students and students in college courses. Before students begin a unit or chapter, make a chart with the following headings. (Use a large piece of butcher paper with younger students or a sheet of notebook paper with older students.)

WHAT WE THINK WE KNOW	WHAT WE WANT TO KNOW	WHAT WE FOUND OUT

Ask students to tell you what they think they know about a topic and write this under the first heading. Next, ask students to tell you what they *want* to know about the topic and record this under the second heading. Finally, after the unit of study is completed, fill in the third section of the chart. Begin this part of the activity by returning to the *What We Think We Know* column and reviewing what has been listed. Through class discussion, lead students to determine if any of the original statements are incorrect. Cross out any untrue statements and rewrite any correct statements under *What We Found Out.*

Move on to the *What We Want to Know* section. Review each of the questions that have been listed. Those that were answered during the unit should be written under *What We Found Out*. Those that were not answered can be researched by interested students. Finally, any new facts or pieces of information learned during the unit but not yet recorded are listed under *What We Found Out.*

Prediction Guides

Nichols (1983) suggested a number of formal and informal instructional activities to help students activate prior knowledge and make predictions.

One activity is the Prediction Guide. Much like an Anticipation Guide (Herber, 1978), a formal prediction guide is "designed to enhance comprehension by encouraging students to make predictions about concepts to be covered in the text (Moore et al., 1982). To construct a prediction guide, list correct and incorrect statements related to the unit of study and ask students to identify those they think will be validated through the reading. After reading or listening to the material, students are asked to check those statements they now believe to be correct. By responding to such a guide, students become motivated to accept, reject, or modify their prior knowledge on the basis of the new information they obtain while reading (Moore et al., 1982). A generic model of a prediction guide is presented in Box 10.2.

Box 10.2 *Prediction Guide*

Directions: In the first column, check those statements you think are true concerning _____. After you have read the selection, go back and place a check next to the statements that you have found to be true.

(1)   (2)

          1.

          2.

          3.

          4.   (teacher writes

          5.   statements here)

          6.

          7.

Note. From "Using Prediction to Increase Content Area Interest and Understanding." J. N. Nichols, 1983, *Journal of Reading*, 27 p. 220. Copyright 1983 by International Reading Association. Adapted by permission.

For a less structured activity to activate schema and make predictions, Nichols (1983) suggested that the teacher write the first sentence or major heading of a chapter on the board and then ask students to develop 5 to 10 questions they predict will be answered in the chapter. They then read to determine which of their questions were actually answered. Nichols also suggested an adaptation of Fowler's story frames (see chapter 9) to help students develop prediction strategies. After reading the title or opening paragraph of a chapter, students complete framed paragraphs such as those in Box 10.3. When prediction frames are being used with students, we suggest you implement the same instructional sequence as that described in chapter 9 for superstructure frames.

Box 10.3

From the title/paragraph, I predict that this chapter will be about _____ .
I think this because _____
_____ .
After looking over this chapter, I think the major figure(s) will be _____ .
Some major events might include _____ .
Some important dates appear to be _____ .

Finally, Wood and Robinson (1983) have designed a strategy that uses important vocabulary in a story as a basis for prediction. The VLP Strategy (Vocabulary, Oral Language, Prediction) also provides a means for preteaching vocabulary using oral language activities that reinforce each word's structural and semantic characteristics.

The strategy has seven basic steps, four involving vocabulary development, one dealing with oral language development, and two involving prediction. The steps are as follows:

VOCABULARY:

1. Examine the selection to be read and determine which words are important and which might cause students difficulty.
2. Note the skill to be emphasized in the unit (e.g., long vowels) and determine other previously taught skills that might need review. Think of ways these skills can be associated with the vocabulary words.
3. Put the words on separate flash cards, indicating in one corner the page on which the word appears. This page number allows teachers to emphasize only the words from the pages to be covered during a given class period.
4. Place the cards on a table in front of the students and explain that they will see these words in the reading selection. Then explain that the object is to point to the word that answers the question or fills in the blank.

LANGUAGE:

5. Begin the oral language activities by asking questions about the structural and conceptual elements of each word. In addition to any skill areas emphasized in the instructional unit, ask questions in the following areas:

   Synonyms: Which word means the same as . . . ? What is another name for . . . ?

   Antonyms: Which word means the opposite of . . . ?

   Categorization: Group all words that have something to do with. . . . What label can we give to these three words?

   Homonyms: What is another way of spelling . . . ?

   Context: People in some parts of our country and in other countries speak a different . . . than we do.

   Dictionary usage: Using your dictionaries, find the definition of . . . that fits this sentence.

   Parts of speech: Which words show action? Which words name something?

   Structural analysis: In which words do you find the same sound for *a* as in play? Which words end like . . . ?

PREDICTION:

6. Once the students understand the vocabulary, ask them to use the words to predict what the story might be about, or, if part of the story has already been covered, to anticipate what might happen next.

   Characterization: Which words probably tell you about the main character?

   Setting: Which words tell where she or he lives?

Mood or feeling: Do any words tell you about the mood of the story?

Reality/fantasy: Do you think the story will be fantasy or a realistic story? Use the words to support your answer.

Events/outcome: Which words give clues about the events in the story?

7. These predictions can be recorded on the board to be confirmed, rejected, or modified during the reading, to correspond with the actual selection.

Summarizing

Whereas most of the techniques mentioned thus far in this chapter help students activate schema, the summarization of information is a way of developing schema. The composing of summaries is a complex task and requires considerable skill (Baker & Brown, 1984). Most teachers find it difficult to teach students how to summarize. However, with the systematic instruction, students can learn how to write effective summaries. For example, Brown and Day (1983) identified five operations involved in summarizing:

1. *Delete trivial material* (material that is unnecessary to understanding).
2. *Delete redundancy* (material that is important but mentioned more than once).
3. *Substitute superordinate terms for lists of items or actions* (*flowers* can be substituted for *daisies*, *roses*, *snapdragons*, and *persimmons*; "Sally went to the grocery store" can be substituted for "Sally left her house," "Sally got in her car," "Sally drove to the store," "Sally got out of her car" and "Sally went into the store."
4. *Select a topic sentence* (usually the author's summary of the paragraph).
5. *Invent your own topic sentence* if one is missing.

Brown and Day (1983) found that even young children were able to use the first two deletion rules with a high degree of accuracy, showing that they understood the basic concept behind summarization—deleting unnecessary material.

Even older students, however, had difficulty with the invention rule, which requires that students add information rather than just delete, select, or manipulate sentences (Baker & Brown, 1984).

The rules for summarization can be taught, however. Baker and Brown described a procedure used by Day (1980). Junior college students of all ability levels were given various colored pencils and told to delete redundant information in red, trivial information in blue. They were also instructed to write in superordinate terms for lists of events or items, to underline any topic sentences in the passage, and to write in topic sentences if needed. Day found dramatic improvements in students' abilities to summarize, after many examples using this technique and some practice. Some students needed only to be trained in learning the rules, whereas others needed additional training in how to check and monitor themselves after completing each rule.

McNeil (1984) cited a similar study (McNeil & Donant, 1982) in which fifth graders were retaught to apply the summarization rules. These authors suggested beginning with material that is two grade levels lower than the reading level of the students. Students can be taught to invent topic sentences by listening to passages from selections in science, social studies, and literature, offering ideas about what the topic sentence might be and discussing these responses.

McNeil also offered an interesting format for checking summary writing. The checklist shown in Box 10.4 can be used with students of all ability levels, using terminology that students can readily understand. Notice that a summary of summaries is written for all summary statements. This is an excellent way to write a summary of several pages of text.

Box 10.4

Directions: For each paragraph that is read, check any rules that were used to write your summary sentence. Then combine your summary statements into one summary.

Rules Applied   Summary Sentences

1. Deleted unnecessary material.   _____ 1.
2. Deleted redundancies.   _____ 2.
3. Substituted superordinate term for list.   _____ 3.
4. Substituted superordinate term for a number of _____ 4.
   actions.
5. Selected a topic sentence.   _____ 5.
6. Invented a topic sentence.   _____ 6.
                                                   Summary of Summaries

---

Note: From *Reading Comprehension*: *New Directions for Classroom Practice* (p. 151) J. D. McNeil (1984) Glenview, Il: Scott, Foresman. Copyright 1984 by Scott Foresman & Company. Reprinted by permission.

We suggest that you start with the first two rules when working with students. Provide appropriate paragraphs, and, as a group, work to delete trivial material and redundant information. After students have become proficient at doing this individually, move to the third rule. Provide paragraphs that contain sentences that can be replaced by a superordinate term or sentence. As a group, work to replace the sentences, and continue until students become proficient at doing this on their own. You might then begin to work on paragraphs, as a group, using the first three rules, and so on.

INFERENCE

In chapter 4 we discussed the importance and the role of inference in the reading process. Inference is a fundamental part of all thought processes. Although many of the instructional activities already discussed in this chapter and in chapters 8 and 9 require students to use inference, here we will consider some activities that have inference as their sole purpose. We will discuss three types of inference strategies: inferring characteristics, inferring causes and consequences, and inferring events.

Inferring Characteristics

In chapter 9 we discussed concept patterns. We saw that they are organizational structures that describe the characteristics of concepts. Recall that we operationally defined a concept as a word that represents a set of organized experiences (see the discussion in chapter 8 on teaching word meanings.) Virtually every time you read a word that represents an animate creature (e.g., person or animal), place, or thing, the socially accepted, cumulative set of experiences represented by the word is either brought to your consciousness or is available to your consciousness. For example, when you read the passage in chapter 9 about the little girl named Yoshi, all of the characteristics you know about little girls were available to you. The author of the passage did not have to describe the way little girls commonly act, how they look, and other girlish attributes. You already knew these characteristics as part of your knowledge of the concept *little girls*.

The reading teacher can use this basic principle of cognition to structure questions so as to stimulate inference. Specifically, the teacher can select important creatures, places, and things mentioned in a story or textbook and ask students to infer unstated characteristics about those creatures, places, and things. To facilitate this activity it is useful to know the common types of characteristics associated with animate creatures, places, and things. Those common characteristics are

1. *Animate creatures (e.g., dog, person):*
   a. Physical dimensions.
      Dog: four-legged, furry . . .
      Person: two-legged, not furry . . .
   b. Emotional and psychological state, of being.
      Dog: friendly, vicious . . .
      Person: happy, sad . . .
   c. Habitual actions
      Dog: chases cars, chews on bones . . .
      Person: has a job, lives in a family . . .
   d. Out-of-the ordinary actions.
      Dog: A particular dog saved someone's life . . .
      Person: A particular person saved someone's life . . .
2. *Places (e.g., Denver):*
   a. Location: in Colorado
   b. Size, shape, terrain:
      Colorado is a moderately large state that has a square shape. It is mountainous, but it also has flatlands.
   c. Events that habitually occur there:
      Colorado has a lot of snow in the winter but very little rain in the other seasons.
   d. Out-of-the ordinary events or other characteristics.
      Colorado has one of the highest elevations of any state in the union.

3. *Things (e.g., the Empire State Building):*
   a. Physical dimensions:
      Over 100 stories high.
      Has an antenna on top
   b. Location:
      In Manhattan, New York
   c. Customary use:
      Office building
      A place where tourists go
   d. Out-of-the ordinary use or other characteristics:
      Once was the tallest building in the world

These "frames" can be used as a way of structuring questions for concepts found in reading material. For example, using the story about Yoshi and the roadrunner, the following questions about Yoshi could be asked, using the animate-creature frame:

> What did Yoshi look like?
>
> How tall do you think she was?
>
> How did she dress?
>
> What type of personality did she have? Was she a happy child? Sad? Shy?
>
> What are some things you think Yoshi might have normally done on the way to school?
>
> What are some things Yoshi did that were very different from what you or other children normally do?

As students respond to these questions, you should encourage them to explain why their inferences make sense. There are no correct or incorrect answers to questions such as those above, only answers that are logical to some and not logical to others. If a student can explain her or his reasoning behind an answer, it should be accepted and reinforced.

Inferring Causes and Consequences

Inferring causes and consequences appears to be a basic human drive. Johnson-Laird (1983) identified causation as one of the basic "conceptual primitives that . . . build up more complex concepts out of underlying primitives" (p. 413). That is, we attempt to infer causes about our own and others' behavior and subsequent behaviors and attitudes. This natural tendency can be translated into questioning techniques. Specifically, you might select statements from reading material and ask students to elaborate on the causes and consequences of those statements. For example, you might select one of the sentences in the story about Yoshi and the roadrunner (e.g., "He always ran out of the bush to greet her.") and ask students

Why do you think Roady ran out to meet Yoshi each day?

Describe what you think might have happened to start this morning routine?

Imagine some of the things that might happen in the future because of this routine?

What do you think would happen if Yoshi stopped passing Roady's house on the way to school?

Again, students should be asked to explain and defend their answers.

Inferring Events

In chapter 4, in the discussion of inference, we considered van Dijk's (1980) hypothesis that we organize some types of information as facts. A fact contains

1. An event
2. Participants in the event
3. The goal of the event
4. Time and duration of the event
5. Location of the event

This knowledge structure can be used to help students elaborate on information presented in reading material. The first step in the process is to look for explicit or implied events. Events are commonly represented by a single word. For example, the words *wedding*, *expedition*, *conversation*, and *breakfast* are all labels for events. The next step is to have students identify the unstated

1. Participants in the event
2. Goals of or reason for the event
3. Time and duration of the event
4. Location of the event

For example, assume that, in the story about Roady and Yoshi, there was some mention of a carnival. You might use the following questions to help students elaborate on the event, the carnival:

Tell me who usually goes to the carnivals.

When do they take place? What time of year? How long do they last?

Why do you think people put on carnivals? Why do people go to carnivals?

Where are carnivals held? Describe their common locations.

A General Procedure for Teaching Inference

Davis (1978) has suggested a procedure that can be used to teach any of the three types of inference strategies:

1. Select a paragraph in which the author has implied an idea. Read the paragraph with the students. State the inference and the supporting contextual clues. Provide as much guidance as necessary.
2. Using a second paragraph that all students have read, state the inference and ask students to supply the contextual clues that support the inference.
3. Using a third paragraph that all have read, state the contextual clues and ask students to supply the inference.
4. Using a fourth paragraph, ask students to state the inference and the supporting contextual clues.

Notice that, with this procedure, the teacher gradually releases responsibility for task completion. In Step 1, the teacher provides a model by stating the inference and the supporting clues; by Step 4 the student is practicing the procedure independently. Davis (1978) cautioned that this procedure must be repeated many times before students are able to independently use the skill.

METACOGNITION

The ability to monitor or judge the quality of one's thinking is known as metacognition. As mentioned in chapter 4, various theorists have identified different types, or categories, of metacognitive abilities. For example, McNeil (1984) described three kinds of metacognitive processes: self-knowledge, task knowledge, and self-monitoring.

Fitzgerald (1983) listed four aspects of metacognition: (a) knowing when you know (and when you don't know), (b) knowing *what* it is that you know in order to comprehend, (c) knowing what it is that you *need* to know in order to comprehend, and (d) knowing the usefulness of intervention strategies when you know you don't understand.

Many poor readers are not aware of their failure to comprehend. Other poor readers know they don't understand but do not know what to do to help themselves. In this section, we will discuss a number of instructional activities that can be used to help students develop their metacognitive skills. As with schema techniques, metacognitive skills are primarily strategy oriented.

Thinking Aloud

Davey (1983) suggested a procedure that demonstrates to learners that reading should make sense and that readers should use intervention strategies when reading doesn't make sense. This procedure, called a *Think Aloud*, involves students listening to teachers verbalize their own thoughts while reading orally. According to Davey, poor readers commonly do not

1. Form good hypotheses about the text's meaning before they begin to read
2. Spontaneously organize information into mental images while they read
3. Effectively use their prior knowledge about the topic

4. Monitor how well they are comprehending as they go along
5. Use fix-up strategies when they encounter a comprehension problem.

To reinforce these strategies with poor readers, Davey recommended the following Think Aloud procedure:

1. Select or develop a passage to read aloud that contains points of difficulty, contradictions, ambiguities, or unknown words.
2. Ask students to read silently as you read the passage aloud and to note how you orally think through trouble spots. Examples of points to make during think alouds include:
   a. *Making predictions.* "From the title I think this will be about . . . ." "I bet this passage is going to tell how to . . . ." "In this next part, I think we'll find out how . . ."
   b. *Describing the pictures you are forming in your head about the information.* "I have a picture of this scene in my head and this is what it looks like . . ."
   c. *Developing analogies.* (Show how to link prior knowledge with new information in the text. This is called the *like a* step). "This reminds me of the time I . . . ." "This is like what happened when . . ."
   d. *Identifying confusing points.* (Show how you monitor comprehension) "This doesn't make sense." "This is not what I had expected."
   e. *Demonstrating fix-up strategies.* (Show how you try to make sense of the passage) "I'd better reread." "I'll just read ahead and see if I can get some more information." "Let me think about this a minute." "Maybe the author meant . . . ." "I'd better change my picture of the story."
3. After you complete the oral reading and the Think Aloud, encourage students to add their thoughts to yours.
4. After several modeling experiences, have students work with partners to practice thinking aloud.
5. Encourage students to practice the strategies silently. Have students use a check-list like that in Box 10.5 to stimulate student involvement and verify that readers are using the procedure.
6. Provide practice with Think Alouds, using daily school material and tasks.

Box 10.5   *Self-evaluation of Think Alouds*

While I was reading how did I do? (Put an X in the appropriate column)

	Not very much	A little bit	Much of the time	All of the time
Made predictions				
Formed pictures				
Used *like a*				
Found problems				
Used fix-ups				

Note. From "Think Aloud: Modeling the Cognitive Processes of Reading Comprehension" by B. Davey, 1983, *Journal of Reading, 37* p. 46. Copyright 1983 by International Reading Association. Reprinted by permission.

Reader Selected Miscues

Reader Selected Miscues (Watson, 1978) is a strategy that students can use during silent reading to monitor their own understanding of what they have read. Before students read silently, give them several 2″ × 8″ bookmarks. As they read they should place markers in their books at troublesome points and keep reading. At the end of the reading period, each student selects three miscues, or deviations from the text, that caused him or her the most trouble in terms of lost meaning and disrupted language flow.

Students then write each sentence containing the selected miscue on a marker and underline the trouble spots. They also write their names, book titles, and page numbers on the markers before turning them into the teacher. After collecting miscues from students, the teacher categorizes them according to similarity (unknown names, foreign words, dialect variations, use of context, etc.). The teacher then engages students who have similar problems in group discussion about their problems and their strategies for solving those reading problems. For example, students who have problems pronouncing names might identify the strategy of substituting a nickname, a letter, or a known name for the unknown name and then continuing on with their reading.

Watson (1978) listed several advantages of allowing readers to select their own miscues. Interaction between reader and text is enhanced because readers are encouraged to keep reading. The reader has autonomy in selecting and rejecting material. Even if a number of miscues have been made, the reader, not the teacher, decides if the miscues cause significant loss of comprehension. Finally, readers become actively involved in the meaning-seeking process by constantly matching up text information with the information in their own heads. They do this by insisting that what they read makes sense.

QARS

QARS, or Question-Answer Relationships (Raphael, 1982), is a technique that focuses students' attention on how they should vary their strategies for answering questions about text. It is based on a taxonomy developed by Pearson and Johnson (1978) that proposes a three-way relationship among the question, the text, and the prior knowledge of the student. The QARS technique teaches students this relationship and three strategies they can use to find the information needed to answer specific questions.

The questions used in QARS are given three labels: Right There, Think and Search, and On My Own. With Right There questions (those asking for details that require an answer explicit in the passage), students are taught the strategy of finding the words used to create the question and looking at other words right there in the same sentence to find the answer.

Think and Search questions require students to look at more than one sentence or paragraph in the text to find the answer, and On My Own questions require students to look into their own schemata to find the answer. As an illustration, consider the following paragraph:

> John was so hungry he decided to make a sandwich to eat. He went to the kitchen but found out he was out of bread. He decided to borrow two slices from his neighbor.

A Right There question might be "Why did John decide to make a sandwich?" because the words used to form the question are found right there in the same sentence. A Think and Search question might be "What did John do when he found out he was out of bread?" because more than one sentence is required to find the answer. An On My Own question might be "What do you think John will do if his neighbor isn't home?"

To teach QARS, Raphael (1982) put forth four principles of instruction that should be integrated into the lessons: (a) give immediate feedback, (b) progress from shorter to longer texts, (c) guide students from group to independent activities, and (d) provide transition from the easier task of recognizing an answer to the more difficult task of creating a response from more than one source of information.

Raphael also suggested that QARS be taught in four lessons. In the first lesson, the QARS concept and terminology are introduced to students. The lesson progresses in three phases, each requiring a different 2- or 3-sentence passage with one question from each QARS category. In the first phase, give students the passage to read along with the questions, their answers, and the identified QARS. Discuss why the questions and answers are Right There, Think and Search, and On My Own.

During phase two, give the students the passage to read, followed by questions and their answers. Students should identify the QARS for each and justify their answers. Discuss the answers as a group. By phase three, students should be able to read the passage, decide on the QARS, and answer the questions in writing. Once again, discuss the answers as a group, asking students to justify their answers.

During lesson two, introduce passages of 75–100 words with up to five questions per passage. One question must be from each QARS category. Students complete the first passage as a group and then work through the rest of the passages on their own. When all students have completed the passage, questions should be discussed as a group.

In the third lesson, introduce a story about the length of a basal story, divided into four parts, each followed by six questions, two in each QARS category. After a brief review using the first part of the story, students work independently on the last three sections and then correct as a group.

The fourth lesson introduces material used in typical classrooms, such as basal stories or a chapter in a content-area text. Present the material as a single unit accompanied by six questions from each QARS category. Students read the unit and respond to the questions by identifying the QARS and providing the answer.

QARS provide readers with a systematic means of approaching question answering (Raphael, 1982). With systematic and direct instruction, students of all abilities and all grade levels should be better able to comprehend new text and monitor their own comprehension (Pearson, 1985).

Reciprocal Teaching

Reciprocal Teaching was developed by Palincsar and Brown (1984) to help remedial junior high school students. The procedure was designed to foster students' comprehension of content-area materials and to improve their comprehension monitoring. To implement the activity, the teacher meets with a small group of 5 to 15 students and models four strategies to be used on paragraphs or small segments of text (Pearson, 1985). The first task is to summarize the paragraph or text segment in a single sentence. Next, a question or two is asked. Clarification of confusing parts of the text (if any) follows. The final task is to predict what the next paragraph or segment will be about.

At first, the students' role is to comment on the summary and the quality of the questions and to answer the questions and help clarify unclear parts of the text. After observing a significant amount of modeling by the teacher, the students take the role of teacher. As Pearson (1985) noted, "Whoever plays the teacher must generate the summary, ask a few questions, lead a discussion of unclear words or parts, and predict the next subtopic. Whoever is playing student must help revise the summary, answer the questions (or suggest alternative questions), clarify unclear parts, and concur (or disagree with) the prediction" (p. 733).

Once the teacher has turned over the teaching to the students, she or he should take a regular turn as teacher, provide feedback about the summaries and questions, encourage students in the role of teacher, and keep the students on task.

Palincsar and Brown (1984) found dramatic student gains in comprehension with the use of Reciprocal Teaching. Student scores on daily independent exercises went from less than 40% to 80%, and gains in social studies and science classwork moved from the 20th to the 60th or 70th percentile.

Coding

J. Smith and Dauer (1984) designed a strategy to help students monitor their comprehension while reading content-area materials. Students use a teacher-determined code to record their cognitive and affective responses to assigned material. The specific code is determined by a number of factors: the responses the teacher wants to elicit from students, the characteristics of the assigned material, and the teacher's curriculum objectives.

For example, a code for a social studies textbook might be A (Agree), B (Bored), C (Confused), D (Disagree), M (Main Idea). Science teachers might use the following code: C (Clear), D (Difficult), I (Important), S (Surprising), and so on.

Students are given the code before they read. They then monitor their responses as they read and record responses on strips of paper they affix to the margins of the pages they are reading.

Postreading discussion using the students' responses is imperative to the success of the strategy. As students discuss confusing or difficult sections of text, teachers can determine what concepts need to be clarified and teach or remind students to use specific strategies that might lead to better comprehension.

Several assumptions underlie the use of this strategy (Smith & Dauer, 1984):

1. The particular code assigned by a teacher will direct students' thinking according to the purposes for reading considered important by the teacher.
2. Students will be aware of what they do and do not understand about a selection while they are reading and perhaps take any needed corrective action.
3. Coding while reading aids motivation and deters wandering of the mind.
4. Students' responses can serve as diagnostic information for structuring upcoming reading assignments and for teaching reading skills in conjunction with content.
5. Postreading discussion highlights effective strategies.

Smith and Dauer (1984) stressed that students need to be introduced to the process carefully, because most students are not used to monitoring their comprehension with a code. You might try making a transparency of an excerpt from a text you want to use and modeling the process by incorporating portions of the Think Aloud technique discussed earlier. After modeling the process with one excerpt, have the students try the code with a second excerpt and discuss the results.

Informal Strategies

Fitzgerald (1983) offered a number of informal strategies to use when helping students develop metacognitive strategies. One such activity is to have students rate their confidence in what they've read. Give students a passage that is difficult to understand and ask comprehension questions of varying levels of difficulty. Ask them to write their answers and then rate how sure they are of their answers by assigning a number from 1 (*not sure*) to 5 (*very sure*). Answers and ratings are then discussed. You should then lead the students to an understanding that a low rating doesn't mean failure. It simply means that more information is needed; more importantly, it shows that the student is aware of what he or she knows and doesn't know.

Rating the adequacy of instructions is another coding activity. Students rate the adequacy of a set of incomplete or misleading instructions on a scale from 1 (*very bad*) to 5 (*really good*). Then they rewrite the instructions so students their own age can understand them. Suggested materials include incomplete card game instructions, poorly written recipes, and directions for putting together a model or toy.

Teaching metacognitive strategies is one of the most impactful instructional activities you can perform. The research clearly indicates that good readers use these strategies, and poor readers do not. It also indicates that poor readers can be overtly taught these strategies with some spectacular results. We strongly recommend thoughtful and systematic integration of metacognitive strategies into your instruction.

SUMMARY

In this chapter, techniques for developing schema-level analysis were discussed along with techniques for improving inference and metacognition. All of these areas are primarily procedural in nature. That is, little new declarative information must be taught to students. Instead the emphasis is on building strategies. Schema-level strategies included semantic mapping, reciprocal questioning, DR-TA, PReP, and ARC. In general, these strategies rely on prediction as a way of activating schemata. Inference was divided into three major areas: characteristics, events, and causes and consequences. The process for reinforcing each of these areas is to develop questions requiring students to go beyond what is provided in the text. Metacognitive strategies included thinking aloud, reciprocal teaching, reader selected miscues, and QARS. These strategies sensitize students to when they are not comprehending and provide them with techniques for adjusting their reading.

11

READING AND THINKING SKILLS

As you might have inferred from the preceding chapters, reading is more than just one of the many skills a student learns in school. Reading is more of a fundamental cognitive ability that is the underpinning of many school-related tasks. We might say that the teacher of reading is a teacher of thinking, one who provides students with the basic cognitive skills necessary for success in society. This emphasis on teaching thinking is a growing national concern, sparked by an awareness that American education appears to be successful at teaching basic skills but lacking in ability to reinforce more complex or higher order thinking skills. For example, the Education Commission of the States (1982), in a report entitled *The Information Society: Are High School Graduates Ready?*, stated

> Survey results indicate that today's minimum skills are demonstrated successfully by a majority of students. Higher order skills, however, are achieved only by a minority of 17-year-olds. If this trend continues, as many as two million students may graduate in 1990 without the skills necessary for employment in tomorrow's market place. (p. 12)

In this chapter we will treat some of those competencies considered necessary thinking skills for the Information Age. Here we will focus on many of those general characteristics alluded to in chapter 1 that form the framework within which reading occurs. Some of these areas are not commonly mentioned in reading textbooks. However, we consider them vital to the process of reading instruction.

We will deal with seven areas: (a) critical thinking, (b) evaluation of value, (c) analogical reasoning, (d) wordless thinking, (e) memory frameworks, (f) general metacognition, and (g) attitude monitoring.

CRITICAL THINKING

Critical thinking has received a great deal of national attention in recent years. According to Richard Paul, the massive 19-campus California state university system equates critical thinking with

> . . .an understanding of the relationship of language to logic leading to the ability to analyze, criticize and advocate ideas, to reason inductively and deductively and to reach factual or judgmental conclusions based on sound inferences drawn from unambiguous statements of knowledge or belief. (1984, p. 5)

The importance of critical thinking to reading is fairly obvious: Students need to be able to think critically about the information they read. They need to know when they can consider information reliable versus when they should question its validity.

There are some programs within education that attempt to teach critical thinking as formal logic—how to determine the validity of syllogisms, how to analyze propositions with ordinal relationships. Here we take a much more applied approach. We define critical thinking as the ability to determine if a piece of information that you read about or hear about needs backing or proof, and, if so, how valid the backing or proof is. This definition of critical thinking is based on the work in logic of Toulmin (Toulmin, 1969; Toulmin, Rieke, & Janik, 1979).

Students can be taught a fairly straightforward process for critically thinking according to this definition. That process contains five steps.

Step 1:   Identify an unusual claim. A claim is a statement of fact. Almost all statements are claims in one way or another. An unusual claim is one that is not self-evident or one you weren't aware of before. For example, "The sky is sometimes blue" is self-evident. However, the claim that "From an aerodynamic perspective, bees should not be able to fly" is not self-evident.

Step 2:   Determine if the claim is in the domain of common knowledge. That is, determine whether the claim is considered common knowledge. If it is, then it requires no backing or proof.

Step 3:   If the claim is not considered common knowledge, is proof presented for it? If no proof is presented, the claim is unsubstantiated.

Step 4:   If proof is presented, how reliable is it?

Step 5:   If the proof is unreliable, the claim is unsubstantiated; if the proof is reliable, the claim is substantiated.

This process is represented diagramatically in Figure 11.1.

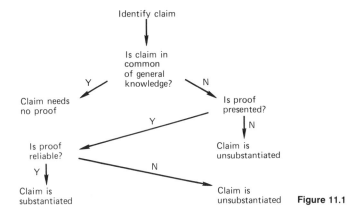

Figure 11.1

The key component of the process is Step 4—determining the reliability of the proof or backing for a claim. There are some common ways in which proof can be unreliable. We will consider three such ways.

Oversimplification of Cause As an illustration of this type of unreliable backing, consider the following:

> The primary cause of World War I was the unrest of the working classes in Europe.

This statement is not totally incorrect. There is some truth to the assertion that the unrest of the working classes in Europe added to the outbreak of World War I. However, it was not the primary cause of World War I; it was not even one of the more important causes. Here the author has taken a very complex set of causal relationships (e.g., the relationship of World War I to its many causes) and oversimplified them.

Overgeneralization Overgeneralization occurs when a generalization is made that far exceeds the facts accompanying it. As an illustration, consider the following:

1. The situation couldn't have been worse.
2. The team's best pitcher quit in the middle of the game.
3. The new uniforms were lost on the way to the game.
4. The team's leading hitter was injured in the first inning of play.

Here Statement *1* is an overgeneralization of the facts presented in the rest of the statements. Things could have been worse (e.g., all the players could have quit). Although these sentences are obviously contrived to illustrate a point, overgeneralizations are usually found in everyday speech, in media reports, and even in textbooks.

Use of Informal Fallacies   According to Lipman (1985), the backing for a claim can contain informal fallacies. Common informal fallacies include ambiguities, vagueness, and part-whole and whole-part errors. Ambiguities exist when a word is used that can have more than one meaning. As an illustration, consider the following examples of ambiguity offered by Lipman, Sharp, and Oscanyan (1979, p.87):

> My brother has some white mice but he doesn't care for them.
> Girls alone are not permitted in the pool.

Lipman stated that certain types of ambiguities must be tolerated in social interaction. Sometimes ambiguities even serve a useful purpose. For example, in poetic writing, ambiguities are very valuable because they add to the richness and suggestiveness of the work.

Vague words lack clean cutoff points. That is, they suggest some definite quantity or value but offer no precise description. Again Lipman, Sharp, Oscanyan (1979, p. 89) offered some examples.

> Is it cold today?
> Do you feel well?

Lipman stated that students should be able to recognize such words and be able to distinguish contexts in which vague words are unsuitable from those in which they are acceptable.

Part-whole and whole-part errors occur when you assume that, if a part of a whole has a specific feature, then the whole must have the feature (part-whole error) or when you assume that, if the whole has the feature, then all the parts must have the feature (whole-part error). Here are examples of these two type of errors:

> Mary's face is beautiful; therefore she must have a beautiful nose (whole-part error).
> My car has the best tires made; therefore it is one of the best cars made (part-whole error).

Reinforcing Critical Thinking

The purpose of providing reinforcement activities in critical thinking is to have students use the critical-thinking process when they hear or read information. Basically, any time information is presented as fact (e.g., in a news report, in a textbook, in a lecture), students should use critical thinking. This means that they should mentally ask such questions as

> Are there statements being made that are out of the realm of common knowledge?

Is there proof or backing for these claims?

Does the proof or backing contain any of the common sources of unreliability (e.g., oversimplification of causal relationships, overgeneralizing, use of informal fallacies?)

The best reinforcement activity is to have students look for unsubstantiated claims in material they read and hear. To this end, students can be given assignments like the following:

1. Watch for and identify at least one unsubstantiated claim in a newscast. Describe the type of unreliability in the proof or backing.
2. Identify an unsubstantiated claim in the newspaper. Describe how the claim should have been substantiated.
3. Identify an unsubstantiated claim you have recently made. Describe the type of error you made and how you could correct it.

In addition to assignments such as these, students can be given formal exercises in which they are asked to identify specific types of errors. Box 11.1 illustrates such an exercise.

Box 11.1

Directions: Describe the type of error in each statement below:

1. If the shell is part of the nut and the nut is part of my lunch, I will have to eat the shell as part of my lunch.
2. The picnic was ruined because Bill came.
3. Mary is the most talented girl in school. She is an athlete. She is pretty and she is nice.
4. Is Fred bald?
5. Mike broke his father's will.

EVALUATION OF VALUE

Closely related to critical thinking is a process we are calling evaluation of value, which starts with the determination of whether information is good, bad, or neutral, on some internalized scale. Consider the following two statements:

1. Wood is used to build houses.
2. The Russians pulled out of the 1984 Olympic games.

Most people consider the information in Statement *1* neutral; however, many Americans consider the information in Statement *2* negative. You can usually tell if you value something by the emotional reaction it elicits. To understand this we must expand on our model of the mind. We have already established that long-term memory contains information stored as concepts and propositions. Imagine, now, that most of those concepts and propositions have a value weight attached as an additional piece of information. For ease of discussion assume these value weights are *good*, *bad*, or *neutral*. We attach these weights on the basis of some set of assumptions or beliefs. For example, assume that you have attached the value *bad* to the concept *Denver Broncos*. That value might have been assigned on the basis of the following assumptions:

> Professional football teams should win at least 75% of their games.
> The Denver broncos do not win 75% of their games.

However, under another set of assumptions, the concept *Denver Broncos* might be given a different value weight:

> Professional football teams should generate revenue and provide diversion for their fans.

The purpose of the evaluation of value process is to identify the value weight placed on certain information, identify the assumptions upon which the value weight was assigned, and identify a set of assumptions that would yield a different value weight. The process might be outlined in the following way:

1. Identify whether a concept is considered good, bad, or neutral.
2. Identify the assumptions underlying the assignment of value.
3. Identify another set of assumptions that would render a different value for the information.

An outcome of the evaluation of value process is that students recognize the subjectivity of their own value systems. This is consistent with Paul's (1984) conception of *dialectic thinking*, which he asserted is one of the primary thinking skills of the future. He stated that

> Children can learn to consider it natural that people differ in their beliefs and points of view, and they can learn to grasp this not as a quaint peculiarity of people but as a tool for learning. They can learn how to learn from others, even from their objectives, contrary perceptions and differing ways of thinking. (p. 12)

ANALOGICAL REASONING

P. Alexander (1984) stated that few intellectual skills are as pervasive or as essential to one's existence as the ability to reason analogically. According to Reese Jenkins (in *Personal Report*, 1985), historian and director of the Edison papers at Rutgers University, Edison's genius was based on his ability to think analogously, to use as a stepping-stone any resemblance that might exist between an active invention and one as yet unborn. For instance, when writing about the kinetoscope, a forerunner of the motion picture, Edison is quoted as saying

> I am experimenting upon an instrument which does for the eye what the phonograph does for the ear. . . . The invention consists in photographing continuously a series of pictures in a continuous spiral on a cylinder or plate in the same manner as sound is recorded on the phonograph.

Broadly defined, analogical reasoning occurs when "unfamiliar stimuli are introduced with some reference to the more familiar" (P. Alexander, 1984, p. 192). In a very broad sense, teachers are using analogies when they preface a new lesson with a review of known, related knowledge (Hayes & Tierney, 1982). At a more specific level, analogical reasoning refers to a particular type of reasoning problem of the form A:B::C:D. According to Sternberg (1977), the process of analogical reasoning contains four components: encoding, inferring, mapping, and applying. Encoding is the identification of the attributes or characteristics of the concepts within the analogy. Inferring is the identification of the rule that relates adjacent concepts. For example, in the analogy *feather: bird :: leaf: tree*, the relationship between adjacent concepts is part to whole. Mapping is the identification of the relationship between nonadjacent terms. For example, in the analogy just given, *feather* and *leaf* are parts; *bird* and *tree* are wholes. Applying refers to identifying the missing component in an analogy of the form *feather: bird::———: tree*.

Sternberg's components can be translated into a fairly straightforward procedure for solving problems of analogy:

1. Identify characteristics of the concepts in the first set of concepts and possible relationships between these concepts.
2. Identify which concept in the first set is most closely related to the element in the second set.
3. Identify what is missing in the second set.

Students usually benefit if the teacher reviews with them the different types of relationships that can exist among concepts in an analogy problem. According to Lewis and Green (1982), there are a few basic types of relationships commonly found in analogy problems in IQ tests, some of which are listed next.

1. *Similar Concepts*: Adjacent concepts are synonyms or similar in meaning. e.g., jump: leap:: shout: _____
   a. whisper
   b. argue
   *c. scream
2. *Dissimilar Concepts*: Adjacent concepts are antonyms or dissimilar in meaning. e.g., this: that:: go: _____
   a. proceed
   b. run
   *c. come

3. *Class Membership*: Adjacent concepts belong to the same class or category.

 e.g., elephant: lion:: blue: _____
 a. bird
 *b. pink
 c. mood

4. *Class Name and Class Member*: One element in a set is a class name, the other is a member of the class.

 e.g., fork: utensil:: bee: _____
 a. flower
 b. spring
 *c. insect

5. *Part to Whole*: One element in a set is a part of the other element in the set.

 e.g., wheel: car:: heel: _____
 a. sidewalk
 *b. leg
 c. show

6. *Change*: One element in a set turns into the other element.

 e.g., plant: seed:: _____ : butterfly
 a. pollen
 b. wings
 *c. caterpillar

7. *Function*: One element in a set performs a function on or for another:

 e.g., tutor: student:: _____ : driver
 a. golf
 b. speed
 *c. car

8. *Quantity/Size*: The two elements in the set are comparable in terms of quantity or size.

 e.g., valley: hole:: _____ : tiger
 a. jungle
 b. housecat
 c. lion

There are a number of ways that students can be given reinforcement in analogical reasoning. Students can be presented with analogics from published materials, a teacher can develop analogy problems, and students can develop analogies. This last activity is the one most directly related to reading. For example, using the story of Roady Roadrunner and Yoshi, a student might create the following analogy problem:

 tail: Roady:: _____ : car

When students develop their own analogies, they should be able to explain the types of relationships that exist among component elements. At first they should be encouraged to use the eight basic relationships just described. Over time they should be encouraged to create their own relationships.

WORDLESS THINKING

Lewis and Greene (1982) reported that Einstein was capable of conceptualizing such complex physical relationships as the theory of relativity because he had developed his powers of concentration and imagination to such a high degree. He had disciplined himself to engage in a type of wordless thought that resembled a highly structured daydream. He is reported to have said, "When I examined myself and my methods of thought I came to the conclusion that the gift of fantasy has meant more to me than my talent for absorbing positive knowledge" (Lewis & Greene, 1982, p. 24).

Apparently Einstein had perfected this technique of wordless thought to such a high level that he preferred to perform experiments "in his mind." Lewis and Greene referred to these as "thought experiments." About Einstein's thought experiments they wrote

> In the early 1900's Einstein performed a thought experiment that was to shake the world of physics to its foundations. He had begun to realize that Newton's theory of gravitation, until then the unchallenged dogma, was seriously flawed. To explore the concept he pictured himself as the passenger in an elevator hurtling through the farthest reaches of space at a speed faster than light. He then visualized a slot opening on one side of the elevator cage so that a beam of light was projected onto the opposite wall. This enabled him to realize that if the elevator were moving with sufficient velocity, it would travel a finite distance in the time required for the beam to pass across the cage so that an observer in the cage would see the light beam as curved. (1982, p. 245)

A representation of this thought experiment is presented in Figure 11.2.

Students can be taught to value and use their wordless thought. Lewis and Greene (1982) recommended the following process:

1. Have students learn how to attain a state of relaxation. They should loosen any tight clothing, sit in relaxed positions, and keep their breathing regular and shallow.
2. Next students should open their minds to images of all kinds. At first they should make no attempt to exert any control over their images. However, they should attempt to create detail in their images; they should see shapes and details in color and enhance the images by adding sounds and scents.
3. Once they have obtained a basic ability to create images, students should practice "holding" a particular image for an extended period. At first this will be very difficult, because the mind will want to jump to associated images.
4. Step 3 should be continued until students have a sense of control over their ability to image things.

Wordless thinking can be used in many ways. One way is as an attention-focusing tool. If students are particularly unattentive and lethargic, they can be guided through the process as a way of generating energy and gaining control

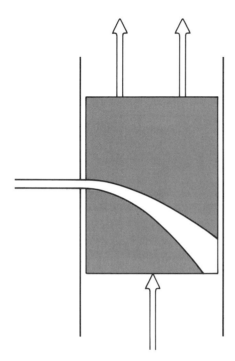

Figure 11.2

over their attention. Wordless thinking can also be used as a prereading activity. Before students read a selection, they can go through the process and imagine what might be in the material they are about to read. Finally, wordless thinking can be used as a problem-solving technique. When faced with a problem, students can vividly imagine the elements of the problem. Often possible solutions, will "pop into consciousness" somewhere during the process.

MEMORY FRAMEWORKS

One way that you can dramatically illustrate to students the power of their minds is to teach them some simple memory frameworks. Memory frameworks create easily retrieved cues with which information is associated. When students retrieve the cues, they also retrieve the information associated with the cues. A good metaphor to describe memory frameworks is that they create mental "slots" into which students deposit information via guided imagery.

One of the simplest memory frameworks to teach students is the rhyming pegword method (Miller, Galanter, & Pribram, 1960), with which they first memorize the following jingle: "One is a bun; two is a shoe; three is a tree; four is a door; five is a hive; six is sticks; seven is heaven; eight is a gate; nine is a line; ten is a hen."

If a student wanted to deposit information into one of the slots, he or she would use guided imagery to make the association between the pegword and the information. As an illustration, assume that a student wanted to put the following information about Roady Roadrunner in slot 1:

Lived in the high desert
Lived in a prickly bush house by the side of the road
Ran out to meet Yoshi every morning
Had strong legs and a strong tail
Sang a song like a cuckoo
Was a member of the cuckoo family

The student would form visual images of this information and include the "bun" in the visualization; for example, the student might visualize the high desert in an enormous hot-dog bun. The student would then put the prickly bush into the image along with Roady running out to meet Yoshi in the morning, and so on. The student would also say the information in her or his "mind's ear": "Let's see, Roady lived in the high desert. He lived in a prickly bush by the side of the road and every morning. . . ." When the student wanted to retrieve the information (e.g., for a test), she or he would simply say the jingle, which would remind her or him that the pegword for slot 1 is the bun. This cue would then call up the visual images of Roady in the giant bun, which would cue the remaining information.

Lindsay and Norman (1977) discussed another memory framework, which they called the *method of places*; it is technically termed the *method of loci* (Ross & Lawrence, 1968). According to Lindsay and Norman, with this method you memorize some geographic locations and then use them as the slots into which you deposit information. Often, familiar places are used as frameworks, for instance, the floor plans of buildings, the paths students take to class, or the inside of living quarters. Lindsay and Norman illustrated the method of places by using the following shopping list:

bread
eggs
butter
salami
corn
lettuce
soap
jelly
chicken
coffee

These 10 items are the information to be memorized. The familiar places, or slots, are places that lie along the path one of the authors took every day when going to the university where he taught. A fanciful figure of such a path is shown in Figure 11.3.

To memorize the list of 10 grocery items, one must associate each one with some spot along the path. Lindsay and Norman described the visualization in the following way:

1. A very large loaf of bread is blocking the front door (the bread is bigger than the door).
2. The sailboat on the beach is filled with eggs.
3. The railroad train is carrying a stick of butter.
4. The street of the town is covered with slices of salami.
5. The sand on the beach is made up of kernels of corn.
6. Giant heads of lettuce are rolling down the hill.
7. The trees are all standing in deep pools of soap suds, only the very tops are visible.
8. There is a big pool of strawberry jelly on the golf course.
9. Chickens are sitting in the gliders, acting as pilots.
10. A huge coffee pot is hanging over the Psychology Building at the university, pouring coffee into the building. (pp. 360–361)

A representation of those visualizations is presented in Figure 11.4.

Using guided imagery, more abstract and complex information than a grocery list can be deposited in each slot along the path. For example, the information about Roady is similar to that which a student might want to remember for a test.

Memory frameworks are very useful study tools and illustrate to students the power of their minds. Unfortunately many classroom teachers never utilize them because of the unwarranted educational stigma attached to rote learning. Certainly, having students memorize information verbatim via rehearsal (repetition) is not a useful educational practice. However, here we are suggesting that students be taught to identify important information in material they read and to then store that information efficiently, using memory frameworks.

A GENERAL METACOGNITIVE STRATEGY

In chapter 4 we introduced the concept of metacognition, describing it as the awareness of one's own cognitive performance and the use of that awareness to alter behavior. In chapter 10 we presented some metacognitive strategies specific

Figure 11.3

Note. From *Human Information Processing* (p. 360) by P.H. Lindsay and D.A. Norman (1977) New York: Academic Press. Copyright 1977 by Harcourt Brace Jovanovich Inc. Reprinted by permission.

Figure 11.4

to reading (e.g., Palincsar and Brown's Reciprocal Teaching). Here we consider a more generalized strategy, one that can be used in almost any situation:

1. Before performing a task, relax for a moment and then try to focus all of your attention on what you are about to do.
2. Set a specific goal or goals for the task.
3. Begin the task.
4. While performing the task, notice what you are thinking. If you get stuck, try talking to yourself.
5. Monitor your activity to see how well things are going. Make corrections or adjustments if you think they are necessary.
6. When you have completed the task, review how it went. Identify those things that worked well and those things that did not.

The overall intent of Step 1 is to help students realize that attention requires a decision on their part and that, in certain situations, attending requires that you "bracket" certain ideas. J. B. Goodman (1977), working with small children who exhibited a high level of impulsivity in their inability to focus on a single stimulus, found that they could be made aware that they had voluntary control of what they attended to and could be trained to attend more directly for longer periods of time. With very young students, training takes the form of having them focus their attention on some distinct stimulus (e.g., a picture or an object in the room) and become aware of what the characteristics of attending are. Students commonly find that, when they attend, they adopt a certain body position and have certain sensations of energy. With older students, this exercise can be coupled with discussion about their responsibility or decision-making ability in the attention process and the need to "bracket" certain thoughts.

Bracketing is a concept with philosophical roots. The working principle behind bracketing is that sometimes it is beneficial to put certain ideas on the back burner and think about them at a later date. This is a skill that has reportedly been used by many of the great minds of civilization (e.g., Bertrand Russell, 1971). In a classroom situation bracketing can be used to set aside important thoughts that are unrelated to the topic of instruction. For example, in carrying out Step 1, a student in a reading class might become aware that he or she is thinking about the quiz in the upcoming math class and not about the reading lesson. Although the math quiz is certainly important, thinking about it during reading does little for the student's performance in reading or math. Hence the student would bracket his or her thoughts about the math quiz and return attention to them after the reading lesson.

Step 2 deals with setting explicit goals. It has been shown that training students to set explicit goals increases performance (Brophy, 1982). Performance is increased even more if students are taught to set goals that are slightly beyond what they think they can do. As it translates to instruction, this step implies that students should be constantly encouraged to keep pushing the limits of their expectations about themselves.

In Step 3 students simply engage in the task. If they have gone through Steps 1 and 2, they should experience a high level of energy and involvement.

At the core of Step 4 is thinking aloud. Recall that in chapter 10 we introduced Thinking Aloud as a metacognitive strategy for reading. Technically, thinking aloud is called *verbal mediation*, which is simply talking to oneself about the thinking one is doing. Apparently the very act of expressing one's thoughts makes them more controllable. In Step 4 students are encouraged to think aloud so that they can see the decisions they are making as they try to accomplish a goal.

Step 5 is meant to help students monitor their performance in a task. Research indicates that students taught to monitor their performance show significant gains in performance (Sagotsky, Patterson, & Lepper, 1978). Verbal mediation can also be used in Step 5. That is, students can be encouraged to talk to themselves about how well the task is going. This might take the form of self-instructions. Meichenbaum and Goodman (1971) used this technique with cognitively impulsive students. They found that it helped them make necessary corrections when solving problems.

Finally, in Step 6 students evaluate their performance. This provides closure for the task and facilitates learning from experience.

General metacognitive strategies such as the one just discussed communicate a very powerful message to students, namely, that they are responsible for their involvement in the learning process. About this, Baird and White (1982) have stated that only minor improvements will be made in learning outcomes unless there is a fundamental shift from teacher to student responsibility for learning. McCombs (1984) reported that strategies such as the one presented here have the potential to unlock doors to those who will otherwise always be limited by what others teach them.

ATTITUDE MONITORING

The final thinking skill we will consider is attitude monitoring. In chapter 4 we discussed the importance of attitudes and their relationship to motivation. Here we will consider some basic attitudes that relate to success in and outside of school. Specifically we will consider three types, or categories, of attitudes.

General Attitudes About Work

What makes some people more efficient at performing tasks (school-related or otherwise) than others? Current research is beginning to provide answers to this question. For example, in the area of problem solving, Whimbey (1980) found that good problem solvers exhibited the following characteristics: (a) faith in persistent, systematic analysis of problems; (b) concern for accuracy; (c) the patience to employ a step-by-step process; (d) avoidance of wild guessing;

and (e) determination to become actively involved with the problem. These attitudes represent high-level controlling principles possessed by successful people. Similar findings to Whimbey's have been reported by Sternberg (1984) and Larkin (1981). If we combine the research, three basic attitudes emerge:

1. Willingness to be actively involved in a task
2. Commitment to persistence
3. Sensitivity to feedback

Individuals who are highly efficient at accomplishing tasks operate from these principles. They have an ability to get deeply involved in, in fact, dive into, tasks; they have a strong commitment to precision and accuracy in whatever they do; and they are sensitive to how well the task is going, making corrections or trying something different if necessary.

Attitudes that Stimulate Exploration

Some theorists believe that, at an unconscious level, human beings refrain from engaging in learning that threatens their fundamental beliefs. For example, Abraham Maslow. (1968) points out that humans are culturally taught not to trust themselves or the inherent order of life. This is consistent with some of the findings of Harter and Connell (1981) discussed in chapter 4. Specifically, Harter fund that a key factor in motivation to complete a task is the student's trust that the task is "knowable." It appears, then, that two controlling principles relevant to academic success might be

1. Belief that life is trustable (that is, circumstances do not automatically work against the accomplishment of a goal).
2. Belief that an individual will generally make decisions supportive of her or his well-being (trust in one's decisions).

Research indicates that individuals who operate from these controlling principles are willing to be engaged in a wider range of behaviors than those who operate from their negative counterpart (i.e., life is not trustable; individual decisions are not trustable). It has been found that willingness to engage in many and varied activities is a major factor in problem solving (Whimbey, 1980), creativity (Perkins, 1984), and productivity (Fromm, 1968).

Attitudes that Broaden Perception

One of the more powerful recent scientific realizations has been that perception is fundamentally subjective in nature. That is, we perceive only what we expect to perceive. In chapter 4 we discussed Frank Smith's assertion that we have in our heads a theory of what the world is like. This theory is the basis of all our perceptions, our understanding of the world. It is the root of all learning and the source of all hopes, fears, motives, expectations, and reasoning.

In isolation this assertion implies a deterministic view of human cognition. If we perceive only what we expect to perceive, we are tantamount to being stuck in a perceptual "programming loop." However, along with science's realization that perception is subjective (driven by schemata that create perceptual expectations) is the parallel hypothesis that human beings have the power to shift paradigms at will. That is, we can choose to see things in different ways. This concept of voluntary paradigm shifting has affected a wide range of human endeavors, from theory and practice in research theory (Schwartz & Ogilvy, 1979; Skrtic, 1983) to economic theory (Henderson, 1984/1985) to human productivity (Bodek, 1984/1985). Another way of saying this is that individuals who know that their perceptions are subjective and can voluntarily shift those perceptions have a very powerful tool that can be used for school-related and non-school-related tasks. We might say, then, that two attitudes that exert a high level of control over cognition and behavior are

1. Belief that perceptions are subjective and are generated from a specific point of view.
2. Belief that one's point of view is controllable and a willingness to change a given point of view.

Exploring Attitudes with Students

How do you introduce these attitudes to students and provide a way for students to acquire them *if they so choose*? The first step is to make students aware of basic attitudes. This can be done via discussion, and via reading books, short stories, and plays that seem to emphasize these principles. For example, Carol Snyder's *Memo: To Myself When I Have a Teenage Daughter* (1983) is about a 13-year-old girl named Karen who isn't ready for love affairs but is going through those painful formative years convinced that her mother doesn't understand her. However, her mother gives her a diary that she began when she was 13. This totally shifts Karen's perception of her mother. Suddenly, Mom becomes a human being. This dramatic turnaround in Karen's perceptions of her mother can be used to introduce the concept that perceptions emanate from specific points of view. Change the point of view and you change the perceptions.

Another technique for introducing basic attitudes is the use of a discovery approach. For example, you might ask students to select people they know and admire and try to discover how those individuals think. What basic attitudes do they possess that makes them who they are?

Once the attitudes have been introduced and discussed, the next step is to help students identify their own thinking relative to the attitudes. Which attitudes do they already operate from? How do these attitudes affect their lives? This might be done in an experimental fashion. Students can be asked to keep a journal for a few days. Every time they become aware of one of the attitudes in their own lives, they can record their thoughts and describe how the attitude shapes their behavior.

Finally students can experiment with adding new attitudes to their lives. That is, if they feel that they do not use a particular attitude in their lives and would like to do so, they might try to introduce the attitude into their behavior, using guided imagery and affirmations. Students can visualize themselves operating from a particular attitude. That is, students might spend time each day picturing themselves trusting in life, feeling how they might feel if they generally trusted their decisions and believed that life would support them in their efforts. At the same time they might use some affirmations. An affirmation would be a positive statement on the student's part about the attitude. For example, students might practice saying the following affirmations along with their visualizations:

> I can trust that, when I try to do something, things will generally go well.
> I can trust my own decisions. I know what is good for me.

We should caution the reader here, that the whole area of intervening to change attitudes is highly experimental and sometimes controversial. Research does support the importance of attitudes in general behavior and the fact that attitudes can be changed by conscious effort. However, the overall effect of such change and its duration is not known. The area is a new one, to say the least, within education. Yet it offers some exciting possibilities. We recommend you explore the area as a teacher and pass on this same sense of exploration to your students. Certainly no specific attitude should be prescribed for a student. However, we believe that students should be encouraged to examine their stances relative to the attitudes described above and to experiment with consciously adding positive attitudes to their behavior and controlling negative ones.

SUMMARY

In this chapter we have presented some skill areas not commonly considered part of reading instruction yet important to reading and other academic and nonacademic tasks. These areas were (a) critical thinking, (b) evaluation of value, (c) analogical reasoning, (d) wordless thinking, (e) memory frameworks, (f) general metacognitive work strategies, and (g) monitoring attitudes. Critical thinking involves analyzing the need for backing or proof of information. It is a useful process for critiquing the validity of information read or heard. Evaluation of value is the process of identifying one's value judgments about a topic and recognizing other possible judgments about the topic. Analogical reasoning involves solving specific types of problems, which requires identifying how sets of concepts are related. Wordless thinking refers to the cultivation of one's imagination. Memory frameworks are techniques for storing information in a fashion that makes it easy to retrieve. General metacognitive strategies are those that facilitate effective performance on tasks of any type. Finally, attitudes are those basic beliefs that control general behavior. Techniques were presented for integrating these areas into the reading classroom and using them to improve general reasoning ability.

12

EFFECTIVE READING INSTRUCTION: MANAGEMENT AND INSTRUCTION IN THE REGULAR CLASSROOM

Diagnosis is an essential element of all effective classroom reading instruction, not just a strategy to be used with students who are experiencing difficulty. Possession of the skills and knowledge to diagnose and remediate students' needs, however, is not enough to insure a successful classroom reading program. A well-managed classroom and sound principles of instruction enable the teacher to utilize those diagnostic and remediation capabilities by establishing an environment that is conducive to fostering reading achievement. Without such elements, even the most well prepared teachers are likely to find their skills unused and their efforts frustrated. Rosenshine and Stevens (1984) have estimated that approximately 15% of the variation in students' reading achievement can be attributed to factors that relate to the general skill and effectiveness of the teacher. Clearly, the research on classroom management and instruction has enormous relevance for classroom and remedial reading teachers.

In this chapter we will review the research on effective management and instruction and translate theory into practice. Specifically, we will consider strategies for managing the regular classroom and techniques for making reading instruction as effective as possible. We will pay special consideration to grouping techniques within the regular classroom, because grouping has historically been one of the primary tools of the reading teacher. Finally, we will consider record keeping as an aid to management and instruction.

Recent years have seen a dramatic increase in the number and quality of studies attempting to identify characteristics of effective instruction associated with increased student achievement. Those characteristics that have been identified can be categorized as interventions of effective schooling and indicators of effective schools. Table 12.1 lists the major indicators and interventions identified from the research. The *indicators* column in Table 12.1 lists those characteristics that commonly signal instructional effectiveness. In other words, if instruction is effective, these characteristics tend to look a certain way. The *interventions* column in Table 12.1 lists those characteristics that tend to affect the indicators. This is why we have drawn arrows from the interventions to the indicators. The research suggests that what you do relative to scheduling and planning affects allocated time; what you do relative to your rules and procedures affects instructional time, and so on. Also note the arrows connecting the indicators. They signal a loose system of interdependency. That is, the level of successfully engaged time presupposes a certain level of engaged time, which presupposes a certain level of instructional time, and so forth. We will first consider those characteristics called *indicators* and then consider those characteristics called *interventions*.

INDICATORS OF EFFECTIVE INSTRUCTION

As shown in Table 12.1, all of the indicators of effective instruction relate to the use of time. We have divided time usage into four categories: (a) allocated time, (b) instructional time, (c) engaged time, and (d) successfully engaged time.

Table 12.1

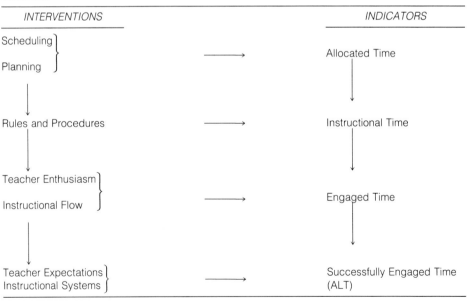

Allocated Time

One of the most well publicized findings on effective instruction is that time is used differently from teacher to teacher, school to school, and even district to district. Aspects of time usage that are relatively stable are days spent in school and hours spent during the school day, primarily because state laws dictate both. The number of days scheduled for school across the United States ranges from 175 to 184 for an average of 179 (Karweit, 1983). Time spent in school, although a stable characteristic, exhibits more variation than days in school. In an early study, Reuter (1963) found that the length of the elementary school day varied from 4 to 6 hours. The Beginning Teacher Evaluation Study (BTES) (Fisher et al., 1978) found that second graders are in school 5½ hours, whereas fifth graders are in school 6 hours. Harnischfeger and Wiley (1978) found that the length of the school day within the same district could vary as much as 45 minutes.

Within the school day, time can be divided into two major segments: time scheduled for instruction and time not scheduled for instruction (e.g., lunch, recess, breaks between classes). The time scheduled for instruction is commonly referred to as *allocated time*. The BTES suggests that, of a typical 6-hour day, 4 hours are scheduled for instruction.

The amount of time allocated for instruction in a particular curriculum area increases the likelihood of student achievement in that subject. Interestingly, within the time allocated for instruction, there is a great deal of variation in how teachers assign time for various subjects, particularly at the elementary level. For example, Berliner (1984) found that

> While observing fifth grade teachers it was noticed that one teacher could find only 68 minutes a day of instruction in reading and language arts, while another teacher was able to find 137 minutes a day. At the second grade level one teacher allocated 47 minutes a day for reading and language arts, another teacher managed to find 118 minutes a day or 2½ more times per day to teach reading and language arts. (p. 54)

Instructional Time

Allocated time can be divided into two basic categories: instructional time and noninstructional time. Here we refer to instruction in a very broad sense. Instruction time would encompass such teacher activities as presenting a lesson, giving a test, reviewing homework, and monitoring students as they work independently. Noninstructional time includes such activities as collecting and passing out papers, attending to outside interruptions, making a transition from one activity to another, and disciplining students.

Although both instructional and noninstructional activities are necessary for effective instruction, in general, the more a teacher is aware of maximizing instructional time, the more opportunity students have to learn and the more likelihood there is that student achievement will increase.

Research indicates that there is great variation in the amount of instructional time available in a school day. Conant (1973) reported that only 31% of the school day is used for instruction. Park (1976) reported that between 21% and 69% of the school day was used for instruction in the classes he observed. In a study of over 600 classes, Marzano and Riley (1984) found that, on the average, 66% of the school day was devoted to instructional time.

Engaged Time

Within the time that instruction is occurring, students are either engaged in instructional activities or not engaged. When engaged, students are actively involved in relevant, meaningful learning tasks. When students are not engaged, they are involved in activities such as making transitions to new activities, waiting for help, socializing, or daydreaming. The amount of time students are engaged in academic work has been shown to be significantly related to reading achievement, as measured by a standardized test. This is particularly true for lower ability students. As an illustration, consider Table 12.2, with information from a 3-year study by Rossmiller (1982). The data indicate that, for the students in the lower quartile, engagement accounts for more of the variance in achievement than in the other three quartiles. A possible explanation for this is that students who are experiencing difficulty with a task (e.g., reading) must concentrate more attention on the task than students who have a higher level of mastery of the task. This explanation is consistent with J. R. Anderson's (1983) assertion that, when a process is being learned, a great deal of overt attention must be paid it by the learner. When a task has been mastered, a high level of attention to it is not necessary.

Table 12.2	Variance Accounted for by Engaged Time		
GRADE 2 ACADEMIC YEAR	*LOWEST 25% IN READING ABILITY*	*MIDDLE 50% IN READING ABILITY*	*HIGHEST 25% IN READING ABILITY*
3rd Grade 1979–1980	55%	8%	14%
4th Grade 1980–1981	27%	6%	4%
5th Grade 1981–1982	73%	16%	16%

Note. From "The Half-Full Glass: A Review of Research on Teaching" (p. 58) by D.C. Berliner, in *Using What We Know About Teaching* by P.L Hosford (Ed.) (1984) Alexandria, VA: Association for Supervision and Curriculum Development. Copyright 1984 by Association for Supervision and Curriculum Development. Adapted by permission.

Successfully Engaged Time

The BTES provided the initial link between student success in academic tasks and student achievement. As reported by Berliner (1984), for younger students and for the academically less able, almost errorless performance is recommended as a way of increasing student achievement. In other words the reading tasks prescribed for students should be of such a nature that students with lower ability can experience almost total success. Rosenshine (1983), in a major review of studies on teaching, recommended that, during the initial phases of learning and during recitation or small group work, success rate in reading should be about 70% to 80%. When students are engaged in independent activities or working on homework, their success rate should approach 100%. Relative to this issue Brophy commented

> . . . bear in mind that we are talking about independent seatwork and homework assignments that students must be able to progress through on their own. These assignments demand application of hierarchically organized knowledge and skills that must be not merely learned but mastered to the point of overlearning if they are going to be retained and applied to still more complex material. Confusion about what to do or lack of even a single important concept or skill will frustrate students' progress, and lead to both management and instructional problems for teachers. Yet this happens frequently. Observational studies suggest that, to the extent that students are given inappropriate tasks, the tasks are much more likely to be too difficult than too easy. (1983, p. 271)

Unfortunately, high success rates are not the norm in many classrooms. Fisher et al. (1980) reported that, in the classes they observed, students' success rates were as low as 0% for 14% of the time they were working on academic tasks.

The amount of time that students are engaged *and* experiencing high success rates has been labeled Academic Learning Time (ALT). The practical importance of ALT was dramatically illustrated by Berliner (1984). Consider an imaginary student, Christine, whose reading score in October is at the 50th percentile on some standardized test of reading. If Christine receives 23 minutes per day of ALT in reading, she will again score at the 50th percentile in December. Now consider another student, Todd, who also begins at the 50th percentile in October. However, Todd receives only 4 minutes of ALT per day. When tested in December, Todd will have dropped from the 50th percentile to the 39th percentile. However, if Todd had received 53 minutes of ALT per day, he would have been expected to score at the 60th percentile in December.

At first glance this scenario might seem unrealistic. How could one student receive 4 minutes of ALT per day and another 53 minutes? Again Berliner (1984) illustrated. Given that ALT is also a function of allocated time, instructional time, and engaged time, large variations in ALT are quite possible. If 50 minutes of reading instruction are allocated to a student who is engaged only

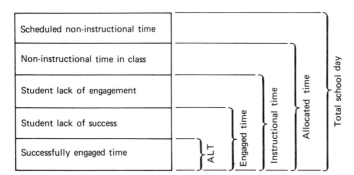

Figure 12.1

one-third of the time, and only one-fourth of that student's reading time is at a high level of success, the student will experience only about 4 minutes of ALT. Similarly, if 100 minutes per day are allocated to reading instruction for a student who is successfully engaged 80% of the time, and two-thirds of that time is at a high level of success, the student will experience about 53 minutes of ALT per day. Figure 12.1 illustrates the interrelationships among allocated time, instructional time, engaged time, and academic learning time.

INTERVENTIONS

As was mentioned previously, each of the indicators listed in Table 12.1 is affected by certain characteristics that we have chosen to call *interventions*—things you can do to control performance on the indicators. In this section we consider those interventions and specific ways they can be implemented in your classroom.

Interventions Affecting Allocated Time

Allocated time is affected by scheduling and planning. Most teachers have little control over scheduling practices within a school. However, they do have a great deal of control over what is taught within the time scheduled for instruction. In fact, teachers appear to have so much control that it can easily lead to abuse. For example, Fisher et al. (1978) reported that one elementary school teacher who was observed for over 90 days taught nothing about fractions, despite the fact that the topic was mandated by the state to be taught at that grade level. When asked about this, the teacher responded "I don't like fractions."

We saw in the previous section that there can be a tremendous variance in the amount of time teachers spend on reading instruction. Similarly, within reading instruction there is a great deal of variation in what teachers emphasize. For example, Berliner (1979), in his discussion of a study by Dishaw (1978), reported those variations listed in Table 12.3 in time allocated for various reading activities in four different classrooms.

Table 12.3   Time Spent in Content Area of Reading and Related Variables for Students in 4 Fifth-Grade Classes

CONTENT AREAS AND RELATED VARIABLES	*(TIME IN MINUTES)*			
	Class 1	*Class 3*	*Class 11*	*Class 25*
Content Areas of the Curriculum				
Word Structure				
Root words and affixes	250	112	126	103
Syllables	67	60	102	212
Word Meaning				
Synonyms	95	152	10	119
Pronoun reference	0	0	0	56
Other word meaning	558	949	1,042	615
Comprehension				
Verbatim (no rephrasing)	206	329	188	325
Translation (paraphrase)	122	151	1,649	383
Inference synthesis	235	252	1,432	306
Identifying main items	153	243	943	326
Evaluation of fact and opinion	5	0	66	56
Other comprehension	196	325	1,368	239
Reading Practice				
Oral reading	604	63	885	305
Silent reading	1,083	724	956	3,640
Reading in content areas	505	256	400	284
Related Reading				
Spelling	694	847	664	1,415
Grammar	242	183	859	413
Creative writing	56	343	98	573
Study skills	472	669	270	171
Other	207	687	1,317	426
Related Variables				
Total time in minutes	5,749	6,344	12,383	9,965

Note. From "Tempus Educare" (p. 128) by D.C. Berliner, in *Research on Teaching* by P.L. Paterson and H.J. Walberg (Eds.) (1979) Berkeley, CA: McCutchan. Copyright 1979 by McCutchan Publishing Corp. Reprinted by permission.

A teacher controls what is emphasized in the classroom via planning. Mintz (1979) reported that, although teachers are heavily involved in planning at the beginning of the academic year or at the beginning of a new course, once they have reached some basic decisions about their students, planning subsides. Shavelson and Stern (1981) reported that effective planning includes considerations about allocated time for specific activities, sequencing of activities, flow of activities, and use of appropriate content and materials during the lesson. Ineffective planning is commonly characterized by overreliance on the activities and materials provided in the textbook (e.g., basal reader).

In short, the effective reading teacher should devote a substantial amount of time and energy to planning and use good judgment in allocating time and identifying instructional activities and materials for students. If done conscientiously, planning can insure an adequate amount of allocated time for effective reading instruction.

Interventions Affecting Instructional Time

The amount of instructional time a teacher has available is primarily a function of the rules and procedures in the classroom. Recall from the first section of this chapter that instructional time is what is left when you subtract time spent in noninstructional classroom activities from allocated time. Noninstructional classroom activities include

> Beginning managerial activities (e.g., passing out materials, taking roll)
> Ending managerial activities (e.g., collecting materials)
> Transition between instructional activities

Evertson, Emmer, Clements, Sanford, and Worsham (1984) defined rules and procedures as "stated expectations regarding behavior" (p. 19). Rules identify general standards of behavior. For example, the rule "Keep your hands to yourself" covers a large set of behaviors. Procedures are applied to more specific behaviors; also, they usually refer to accomplishing something rather than prohibiting something. For example, you might establish a set of procedures for entering and exiting the classroom, distributing and passing in textbooks. The more clearly your rules and procedures are stated and the more systematically they are reinforced, the more instructional time will be available to you.

Elementary school teachers are usually more conscientious about establishing explicit rules and procedures for classroom conduct. This is not to say that secondary teachers do not have rules and procedures. It is to say that they are resistant to defining them at the level of specificity that is commonly found in elementary classrooms. Yet research has consistently shown that careful attention to explicit rules and procedures affects student engagement at all levels (L. Anderson, Evertson, & Emmer, 1980; Emmer, Evertson, & Anderson, 1980).

Some of the commonly found rules at the elementary level include

> *Rule 1:* Be polite and helpful.
> *Rule 2:* Respect other people's property.
> *Rule 3:* Don't interrupt the teacher or other students when they are speaking.
> *Rule 4:* Do not hit, shove, or hurt others.
> *Rule 5:* Obey all school rules.
> (Evertson et al., 1984, p. 22)

Rules commonly found in secondary schools include

Rule 1: Bring all needed materials to class.
Rule 2: Be in your seat and ready to work when the bell rings.
Rule 3: Respect and be polite to all people.
Rule 4: Do not talk or leave your desk when someone else is talking.
Rule 5: Respect other people's property.
Rule 6: Obey all school rules.
(Emmer, et al., 1984, p. 22–23)

As simple and straightforward as these rules might sound, they are incredibly powerful if they are explicitly stated and reinforced. Unfortunately, although most teachers would assert that they reinforce all these rules in their classrooms, there is a great deal of variation among teachers in the extent to which they actually implement them. The same is true for procedures. Procedures at the elementary level commonly cover the following topics:

I.   Room Use
    A.   Teacher's desk and storage areas
    B.   Student desks and storage areas
    C.   Storage for common materials
    D.   Drinking fountains, sink, pencil sharpener
    E.   Bathrooms
    F.   Center, station, or equipment areas
II. Seatwork and Teacher-led Instruction
    A.   Student attention during presentations
    B.   Student participation
    C.   Talk among students
    D.   Obtaining help
    E.   Out-of-seat procedures during seatwork
    F.   When seatwork has been completed
III. Transitions Into and out of the Room
    A.   Beginning the school day
    B.   Leaving the room
    C.   Returning to the room
    D.   Ending the day
IV. Procedures During Reading
    A.   Getting the class ready
    B.   Student movement
    C.   Expected behavior in the group
    D.   Expected behavior of students out of group
V.   General Procedures
    A.   Distributing materials
    B.   Interruptions
    C.   Bathrooms
    D.   Library, resource room, school office
    E.   Cafeteria
    F.   Playground
    G.   Fire and disaster drills
    H.   Classroom helpers
       (Evertson et al., 1984, p. 32)

At the secondary level, procedures are usually developed for the following areas:

I. General Procedures
    A. Beginning-of-period
        1. Attendance check
        2. Previously absent
        3. Tardy students
        4. Expected student behavior
    B. Out-of-room policies
    C. Materials and equipment
        1. Pencil sharpener
        2. Other room equipment
        3. Student contact with teacher's desk, storage, other materials
    D. Ending the period
II. Seatwork and Instruction Procedures
    A. Student attention
    B. Student participation
    C. Seatwork procedures
        1. Talk among students
        2. Obtaining help
        3. Out-of-seat
        4. When seatwork has been completed
III. Student Group Work
    A. Use of materials and supplies
    B. Assignment of students to groups
    C. Student participation and behavior
IV. Miscellaneous
    A. Behavior during interruptions
    B. Special equipment
    C. Fire and disaster drills
    D. Split lunch period
        (Emmer et al., 1984, p. 34)

In summary, instructional time can be maximized by firmly establishing, communicating, practicing, and enforcing classroom rules and procedures.

Interventions Affecting Engaged Time

Teachers help students stay engaged by monitoring the flow of instruction and by the enthusiasm with which they approach instruction. Flow of instruction is primarily a function of pace. Good teachers appear to be constantly aware of the pace of teaching and learning within the class and adjust to the natural ebb and flow of interaction (Brophy, 1982). Effective teachers ignore minor interruptions, so as not to interrupt instructional flow (Kounin, 1970). When an effective teacher notices an inattentive student she or he moves nearer to the student, uses eye contact when possible, and/or directs a comment or question to the student as a cue that she or he is not being attentive and that such behavior is not acceptable. Effective teachers also use presentation and questioning techniques to keep students alert and accountable. These include looking around the class before calling on someone to recite; keeping students in suspense as to who will be called on next; calling on all students frequently; interspersing choral responses with individual responses; suggesting challenges by declaring that the next question will be a difficult one; calling on students to comment upon or correct each other's answers. The gist of the way effective teachers monitor and control flow of instruction is keeping students attentive to content presentation because something new or exciting might happen at any time and keeping students accountable for learning by making them aware that they might be called on at any time (Kounin, 1970). Underlying this energetic monitoring of instruction is a basic enthusiasm for teaching.

According to Bettencourt, Gillett, Gall, and Hull (1983), teacher enthusiasm is one of the most important variables relative to keeping students attentive. Similarly, Hamachek (1975) stated that "you and I both know from personal experience that a teacher's enthusiasm or lack of it can have a lot to do with making or breaking a class" (p. 17). Gage (1979) suggested that enthusiasm might be an effective teaching characteristic that is generalizable across curriculum, content, and grade levels.

In the past, enthusiasm has been vaguely defined with references to such global concepts as dynamism and stimulus variation (Bettencourt et al., 1983). Recently, M. L. Collins (1978), who based her operational definition of enthusiasm on a review of the literature by Rosenshine (1970), identified eight indicators of high teaching enthusiasm. As reported by Bettencourt those characteristics are

1. Rapid, uplifting, varied vocal delivery
2. Dancing wide-open eyes
3. Frequent demonstrative gestures
4. Varied dramatic body movements
5. Varied emotional facial expressions
6. Selection of varied words, especially adjectives
7. Ready, animated acceptance of ideas and feelings
8. Exuberant overall energy.

M. L. Collins (1978) found that teacher behavior could be changed relative to these eight characteristics. That is, teachers who exhibited low enthusiasm could be taught to model enthusiastic behavior. An odd thing happened when teachers did this. When they attempted to model enthusiastic behavior, their enthusiasm actually increased. This brings to mind an old saying used in the theater: "Fake it 'til you make it." In other words a teacher can monitor his or her behaviors and attempt to emphasize those that communicate enthusiasm. If past research is correct, this should have the effect of actually increasing the teacher's level of enthusiasm. It should also have the effect of keeping student engagement high. Bettencourt et al. (1983) found that enthusiastic behavior on the part of the teacher not only affected student engagement but also was related to increased student achievement. These findings were consistent with those reported by Land (1980) and Wycoff (1973).

A logical question here is Why should teacher enthusiasm have an effect on student engagement? One explanation is that the eight characteristics listed provide a strong set of stimuli that draws the student away from other stimuli in the classroom, including their own ruminations (Bettencourt et al., 1983). This assertion is supported by research on attention, which suggests that stimulus characteristics of intensity, contrast, and movement are the critical attributes of attention-getting behavior (Hilgard, Atkinson, & Atkinson 1975).

Another explanation is that enthusiastic behavior is a form of communication from teacher to student. H. Smith (1979) has reported that body movements, gestures, and facial expressions are interpreted by students as messages that signal whether they are expected to stay on task or not. Similarly, Bettencourt et al. (1983) found that "teachers' expressions of enthusiasm convey the message that they are eager for students to learn and will persist in helping them" (p. 446).

Interventions Affecting Student Success

Before discussing those interventions that affect student success, we should first reiterate that student success refers to how successful students are at the tasks presented to them in class. For a reading class, such tasks would consist of those activities you require of students to teach, reinforce, and evaluate their reading. As listed in Table 12.1, students' success is primarily a function of teachers' expectations and the use of a strong instructional system. We will consider each area briefly.

One dominant theme in the literature on effective teaching is the importance of teachers' expectations. Most teachers have strong beliefs about the different levels of ability of their students and act differentially toward students on the basis of these expectations. This seems quite logical because students have differing abilities and should be treated differently because of these abilities. Unfortunately many of our judgments about students are incorrect.

Tom Good (1981), one of the leading educational researchers in the area of the effects of teachers' expectations on students' achievement, believes that teachers' expectations create a framework that gradually molds students. Good's model is:

1. The teacher expects specific behaviors and achievement from particular students.
2. Because of these varied expectations, the teacher behaves differently toward different students.
3. This treatment communicates to the students what behaviors and achievement the teacher expects from them and affects their self-concepts, achievement motivation, and levels of aspiration.

4. If this treatment is consistent over time, and if the students do not resist or change it in some way, it will shape their achievement and behavior. High-expectation students will be led to achieve at high levels, whereas the achievement of low-expectation students will decline.

5. With time, students' achievement and behavior will conform more and more closely to the behavior originally expected of them.

Good also believes that many of the expectations of teachers come from inaccurate sources. Among those factors that seem to foster inaccurate perceptions of students' abilities are socioeconomic status, race, sex, behavior, appearance, and labeling. Teachers tend to expect less from children of low socioeconomic or minority status, children who are less well behaved in class, and children who are poorly or sloppily dressed. Lower expectations are also held of students who are tracked, or placed, in the lower instructional groups. Interestingly, teachers also expect less from elementary school boys (slower maturation) and from older girls (sex role discrimination).

As a result of inaccurate judgments about students, teachers treat students for whom they have low expectations in ways that can be considered discriminatory. For example, in contrast with their treatment of high-achieving students, teachers tend to call on low-achieving students less often and wait less time for them to answer questions. When these low-achieving students do respond, teachers praise them less frequently after successful responses, praise them more for marginal or inadequate responses, and provide less accurate and less detailed feedback. In general, teachers demand less work and effort from low-achieving students than from high-achieving students.

It is commonly believed that a student's performance in reading in the early grades sets the stage for future expectations the student has for herself or himself and teachers have for the student. Consequently the reading teacher should be particularly aware of strategies for creating high expectations.

The first step is to alleviate the influence of negative expectations developed from external sources. Useful strategies include the following:

Refrain from making judgments about student ability on the basis of previous years' reports, grades, or unsubstantiated information.

List students and indicate those you expect to do well and those you expect to do poorly. Look for patterns evolving from race, ethnicity, or socioeconomic status.

Teach all the students in the class. Teachers who help all students succeed communicate expectations that all students can learn.

Avoid using reading ability as the only predictor of school success.

Group students by different methods for different activities. Though ability grouping is appropriate for some learning tasks, avoid using ability groups exclusively. Grouping students in varied ways helps break up the expectations set up by ability groups (see next section of this chapter).

The next step is to indirectly communicate high expectations, via the following activities:

Make a conscious effort to call on all students.

Be sure students get the help they need, even those who do not ask for it.

Allow adequate response time for each student (at least 5 seconds after asking a question).

Delve for answers by rephrasing questions, giving clues, or providing more information.

Give low achievers opportunity to practice their thinking skills on higher level questions.

Offer positive reactions to student answers, either affirmative or corrective.

Make praise specific and sincere.

Look at students when they are speaking, and listen to what they say.

Be sensitive to students' emotional needs.

Show respect for students; model the courtesy they expect in return.

Express interest in the lives and experiences of all students.

Finally, try to influence students' expectations of themselves in the following ways:

Learn what students expect from you and from school in general.

Use questionnaires and interviews to discover what students expect.

Take seriously the power to influence students' expectations of themselves and their classmates. Offhand remarks teachers make about one student to another can be damaging.

Understand that students' expectations are formed early in their school careers.

Even with high expectations, a teacher must have a strong instructional system from which to operate. If you observed good teachers and poor teachers and compared what they did, you would notice some distinct differences. One thing that would be immediately evident is that good teachers appear to be more systematic in what they do than poor teachers. There is a sense of order, a sense that they are operating from a framework (Brophy, 1982; Good, Grouws, & Ebmeier, 1983). Recent years have seen a number of theory-based "instructional frameworks," or models of good instruction (Fisher, et al., 1980; Good et al., 1983; Hunter, 1984; Pearson, 1985; Rosenshine, 1983). These models contain many common themes, among them diagnosis; clear, explicit instruction; modeling or demonstration; and the gradual shift of responsibility from teacher to student. The following generic model integrates many aspects of other models of instruction and provides a basic framework for instruction:

1. *Task Focus.* Get the students set to work in the most interesting way possible. Then tell them the purpose of the lesson. Make sure they know what the desired outcome is. Exhibit examples of acceptable and unacceptable finished work. In other words, the students should know what they're supposed to learn.

2. *Lesson Presentation.* Present new concepts or skills to the students. During the lesson, interact constantly with students. Treat material in various ways. Model skills and provide information in several different modes or styles (e.g., orally and in writing) explain strategies for accomplishing tasks (such as strategies for memorizing), and present methods for checking accuracy.

3. *Guided Practice.* Students engage in guided practice. During this phase, monitor and give continual, content-specific feedback to students. Check or monitor success. If students are not successful, try alternative methods. Provide enough time for each child to be successful.

4. *Independent Practice.* Once you believe that students understand what has been taught, allow time for them to work alone. High rates of success should be characteristic of this phase of instruction. Practice is both "massed" and "spaced." In other words, students experience an intensive period of practice immediately following instruction. Additional practice and reviews occur at regular intervals: the next day before the next class session begins (this has been found particularly helpful in mathematics), once a week, and at appropriate intervals thereafter.

The following additional techniques should also be used:

Proceed in small steps at a brisk pace.

Give detailed instructions and explanations.

Supply many examples.

Ask many questions and provide ample practice.

Check for understanding.

Provide feedback and correction, especially in the early stages of learning new material.

Divide independent assignments into understandable steps.

Monitor frequently during independent activities.

Allow practice until students achieve a high success rate and become quick, confident, and firm in their answers.

GROUPING STRATEGIES

One of the major concerns of teaching reading in the classroom is how to group students. Generally a teacher groups to counteract the inherent problems of dealing with 25–35 students with very different backgrounds and abilities. As Dallman stated,

> At the first-grade level, the range of achievement in a class can be expected to be two or more years.
> At the fourth-grade level, the range of achievement in a class may be four years or more.
> At the sixth-grade level, the range of achievement in a class may be six years or more. (1982, p. 386)

Grouping students on some dimension seems to be consistent with many of the assertions in the beginning of this chapter about the need for appropriate instructional materials, high engagement, and high success rate. In a summary of the research on grouping since 1973, Rosenshine and Stevens (1984) reviewed over 20 configurations of individual, small-group, and large-group instruction. They concluded that "without exception, the studies support group instruction" (p. 748). They pointed out that, although many educators propose individualized instruction as the optimal organizational plan for addressing children's needs, individualized instruction is often inaccurately equated with one-to-one instruction. Rosenshine and Stevens stated that, during individualized instruction, the majority of the time students work on their own without interaction with the teacher. With classes of 20–25 students, one-on-one instruction between a teacher and a student would result in 3 minutes of instruction per hour per student. They concluded that "students show both more engagement and higher achievement gain when they are placed in groups for instruction. Students are less engaged when they are working alone and achieve less in classrooms where there is a strong emphasis on independent work" (p. 752).

In an effort to get school off to a quick, well-structured start, many teachers diagnose and group students within the first few days of the new school year. However, decisions made at this time could prove to be quite problematic. *First*, it is not unusual for students to exhibit some reading-achievement loss during the summer months that is quickly regained once they are reintroduced to school. *Second*, the adjustments to new schools, teachers, friends, responsibilities, and schedules that mark the beginning of a new school year are often difficult. Consequently, it frequently takes a short time for students to feel comfortable and to begin to perform up to their abilities. It is important then, for teachers to take some time, perhaps 2 or 3 weeks, to gather information about their students before making instructional decisions. Even then, all grouping decisions should be open to change and continual review, and this flexibility should be communicated to students and parents. Unfortunately, as currently practiced, grouping is not very flexible. As reviewed by Hiebert (1983), the research indicates that, once students are grouped for instruction, few, if any, changes are made in group membership after the first month of school. If we are to break with this age-old, lock-step tradition, grouping must be dynamic. No single organizational scheme, group size, or technique is inherently better than another. There are a number of different grouping patterns that might meet the needs of your particular classroom. Among those that have been applied at both the elementary and the secondary levels are ability groups, skills groups, interest groups, research and special project groups, peer tutoring, and cooperative-learning teams. We will briefly consider each type.

Ability Groups

When we think of classroom reading instruction, the picture most often envisioned is one of small groups of children of similar ability working together. Usually the groups represent high, middle, and low ability. In fact most teachers in the United States still conduct much of their reading instruction using this organizational scheme.

On the surface, ability groups seem to make sense, especially in light of what we know about the need to meet specific needs of individual students. When students are instructed in smaller, homogeneous groups, it appears more likely that (a) teachers are able to provide appropriate reading instruction and assignments that insure a high success rate, (b) teachers provide more explicit instruction and feedback to students, and (c) students are more focused and engaged in the tasks before them. However, there is a major flaw in the reasoning underlying ability grouping—the groups are not homogeneous.

Within an ability group you will probably find a range of backgrounds, interests, learning rates, learning strategies, and abilities. Even if we could limit the range of achievement in an ability group (which is virtually impossible), we would still be unable to control those many other factors that influence students' learning (e.g., attitudes, metacognitive awarenesses). Therefore, one of the potential problems of ability grouping is the tendency to forget that important differences exist within "homogeneous" groups as well as between them.

In addition, there is evidence to suggest that tracking (assigning students of similar ability to the same classroom) and ability grouping might actually be harmful to some students. In a meta-analysis of 52 studies of homogeneous grouping, Kulik and Kulik (1982) found that ability grouping is often beneficial for high-ability students but not for low-ability students. Similarly, in a review of 217 studies of ability grouping, Persell (1977) concluded that there was a slight improvement in achievement of high-ability groups, but that gain was negated by the substantial losses by middle and low-ability groups. Further, after reviewing earlier research on grouping, Glass and Smith (1977) stated that "research shows homogeneous versus heterogeneous grouping not to be an important variable *in itself*. Only as ability grouping relates to or potentiates other changes in instructional activities is it a circumstance worth noting" (p. 38). In fact, more recent research has revealed that there *are* substantial changes in instructional activities across ability-level groups. There are significant differences in students' behavior and in the way teachers instruct and respond to low- and high-ability grouped students. The following differences were summarized from a large body of research (Hiebert, 1983; Peterson, Wilkinson, & Hallinan, 1984).

1. Low-ability groups spent more time on decoding tasks, whereas high-ability groups spent more time on meaning-related tasks.
2. Low-ability groups spent more time off task for administrative and disciplinary reasons and were less attentive to learning tasks than were high-ability groups.
3. Low-ability groups spent more time reading orally, and teachers were more apt to interrupt poor readers who made oral reading errors, regardless of the semantic appropriateness. The cues teachers offered poor readers tended to be graphophonic.
   Good readers spent less time orally and more time reading silently, were inter-

rupted less often and were offered syntactic and semantic cues when cues were suggested. Because they spent more time in oral reading, which is slower than silent reading, low-ability groups read many fewer words (one-third to one-half fewer) than high-ability students.

4. There was a marked difference in the social status and self-concept of students in high- and low-ability groups. Low-ability students were less popular with their peers and had more negative feelings toward reading and their reading group.

Even though there is negative evidence about ability grouping, both Good and Marshall (1984) and Peterson et al. (1984) argue that it would be premature to suggest that ability grouping be discontinued.

> Too much heterogeneity may create instructional problems, and there are probably limits on the amount of class heterogeneity that a teacher can reasonably handle. . . . In practice, the most prevalent problem is that ability-group membership lines are too tightly drawn. Lows in general need more opportunity to learn with highs" (p. 31).

The following suggestions by Peterson et al. (1984) are meant to alleviate many of the negative effects of ability grouping:

1. Students should be reassigned to different tracks or ability group levels if their rate of learning warrants it. Students' rates of learning change, and teachers need to be sensitive and responsive to these changes and become more flexible in grouping.
2. When teachers use tracking or ability grouping for instruction, they should make every effort to insure that the quality of instruction is constant across levels. For low-ability groups, teachers should consider limiting the size of the group, lengthening instructional time, changing the discipline or reward systems, and using alternative teaching strategies.
3. Student characteristics must be taken into account in assigning students to peer work groups. Teachers should focus on the learning process as well as its end goal. Cooperative learning and peer tutoring could diminish negative competition and increase the self-esteem, status, and participation of low-achieving students.
4. Assigning labels to students based on their track or ability group is inappropriate. Labeling can result in a self-filling prophecy that will impact on students, teachers, and parents.
5. Teachers need to be aware of the unintended consequences of tracking and ability grouping. Ability grouping can influence educational and career opportunities and self-esteem.

In summary, although ability grouping is the most common organizational pattern, it has a strong potential for creating negative effects in students. However, many of these effects can be minimized by carefully monitoring responses to, and interactions with, low-ability students and using alternative grouping strategies.

Special-Skills Groups

One alternative to ability groups is special-skills groups. Special-skills groups are formed when students have a common need for instruction in a particular skill. For example, several students in the class might need instruction on metacognitive awarenesses. These children would be grouped for one or more lessons. Another example might feature a number of students who are having difficulty identifying specific superstructures. Although these children might be reading at a variety of reading levels, they would be brought together for specific instruction on superstructures and their uses. The teacher would present examples of different superstructures and then model strategies for using this knowledge. Students would then be provided with guided practice on some common material and, finally, given independent practice using materials at their respective levels.

This type of grouping enables the teacher to maximize instructional time by limiting the number of times a given lesson needs to be taught. It also provides opportunities for children to learn in heterogeneous ability groups and to observe models of how good readers learn. Equally important, it breaks the social, psychological, and academic stigmata of ability grouping.

Interest Groups

Interest groups are formed by students who have a shared interest or concern. For example, a number of students might be interested in dinosaurs or motorcycles or mystery stories. The reading material for these students might consist of trade books at a variety of reading levels centered around a particular theme or a single story from the basal reader, or multiple copies of the book with similar or differentiated assignments for the students. Often interest groups prepare presentations for the entire class. These presentations give the groups an opportunity to share and to obtain feedback on their work. The groups are also a vehicle for expanding other students' interests. Other techniques for enriching and expanding students' interests include book talks, bulletin boards, selection and summarization of a "book of the week" or "book of the month," displays of a variety of books, and talks from guest authors, illustrators, and librarians.

The concept of multi-ability interest groups is a realistic classroom option, because students can often read at a higher level than is typical for them, if they are reading about a topic that is especially interesting to them (R. C. Anderson et al., 1985). For example, in a study by Asher (1980), students who indicated high interest in a passage demonstrated greater comprehension than when they indicated low interest in the material. This makes theoretical sense. Students who are interested in a particular topic will usually have more knowledge about the topic (better developed schemata relative to the topic) and are consequently better able to process the information from the top down. Additionally, children are more likely to remain on task and involved in learning if they are interested in the subject matter, as noted by Good and Brophy (1978); "Our interest, our drive to learn, helps us to focus attention and persist in learning even complex material if we want to do so" (p. 344).

To identify student interests, a number of inventories have been developed that can be administered to an entire class. We presented and discussed one of them in chapter 5. Box 12.1 contains another interest inventory, developed by Curry (1980, p. 232). This type of inventory can be completed independently by students or read aloud by the teacher when using it with younger or severely reading-disabled students.

Box 12.1   *Interest Inventory*

Name _____ Date _____

1. My favorite animal is _____ because _____.
2. My favorite color is _____.
3. The best book I ever read is _____.
4. My brothers and sisters _____.
5. My favorite sport is _____.
6. When I have free time, I _____.
7. My favorite television program is _____.
8. The movie I enjoyed most is _____.
9. The day of the week I like most is _____ because _____.
10. The person I admire most is _____ because _____.
11. Reading is _____.
12. I like to read stories about _____.
13. The subject in school I like best is _____.
14. The subject in school I don't like is _____.
15. When it rains, I _____.
16. My hobbies are _____.
17. I am going to be a _____ when I grow up because _____.
18. Poetry makes me _____.
19. I wish my teacher would _____.
20. My parents _____.
21. Libraries are _____.
22. If I had three wishes, they would be
    1. _____.
    2. _____.
    3. _____.
23. My favorite food is _____.
24. I'd like to visit _____ because _____.
25. If I could be anywhere in the world right now I would be in _____
    because _____.
26. If I could do anything I wanted to do I would _____.

Note: From "How Am I Doing? Assessing the Components of a Managed Curriculum" (p. 232) by J.F. Curry, in *Making Reading Possible Through Effective Classroom Management* by D. Lapp (Ed.) (1980) Newark, DE: International Reading Association. Copyright 1980 by International Reading Association. Reprinted by permission.

Research and Special-Project Groups

Sometimes you will want students to work together to investigate a particular topic. These "research groups" should consist of students of varying ability levels working collectively to explore a topic or answer specific questions about that topic. Children should have access to a variety of resources written at appropriate reading levels, so each one can experience success and contribute meaningfully to the group project.

One way to organize research or special-project groups is to use thematic units. A thematic unit is a broad topic that can be studied from many dimensions. Hagerty (1985) listed the following steps for developing a thematic unit:

1. Select a topic or theme.
2. List possible subtopics (What concepts do I want students to learn? What ideas might be investigated around this theme?).
3. Add more specific topics around each subtopic as needed.
4. Consider various subject areas for integration and various multilevel resources for students to use.
5. Develop learning activities to address the subtopics.

Figure 12.2 contains a schematic for a first-grade thematic unit on light and

Figure 12.2 Light and Shadows*

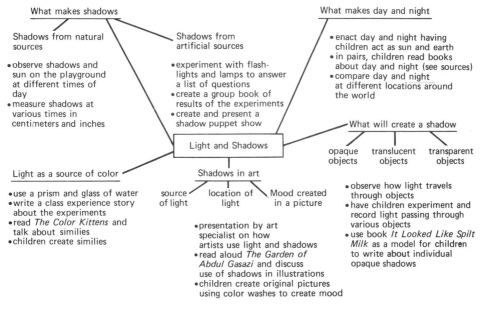

Reprinted by permission of Betty Timson, School District #12, Denver, Colorado

shadows that takes a slightly different approach to developing subunits for investigation.

One of the more demanding characteristics of thematic units is that they require a teacher to identify many resource materials for students. For example, here is a list of possible reference materials for the unit on light and shadows:

A. Tradebooks

  1. Nonfiction: Easy

    Branley, F. *Light and Darkness*
    Bulla, C. *What Makes a Shadow*
    De Regniers, B. *The Shadow Book*
    Goor, R. *Shadows Here, There, and Everywhere*
    Pine, T. *Light All Around*
    Podendorf, I. *Color*
    Reit, S. *Adventures With Colors*
    Schneider, H. *Science Fun with a Flashlight*

  2. Nonfiction: Read Aloud and Reference

    Adler, I. *Shadows*
    Arbuthnot, M. *Time for Poetry*
    Dunn, J. *Things*
    Feravolo, K. *Junior Science Book of Light*
    Highland, H. *Light and Color*
    Kettelkump, L. *Shadows*
    Mayno, N. *Pictures Without a Camera*
    Munch, T. *What Is Light?*
    Paschel, H. *The First Book of Color*
    Simon, H. *The Magic of Color*
    Suid, M. *Painting With the Sun*
    Watson, P. *Light Fantastic*

  3. Fiction

    Brooks, R. *Annie's Rainbow*
    Brown, M. *The Color Kittens*
    Brown, M. *Goodnight Moon*
    Brown, R. *A Dark Dark Tale*
    Charlip, R. *Mother Mother*
    Crews, D. *Light*
    Dragonwagon, C. *When Light Turns Into Night*
    Freeman, D. *A Rainbow of My Own*
    Galdone, P. *Henny Penny*
    Heide, F. *That's What Friends Are For*
    Hirsh, M. *How the World Got Its Color*
    Hoban, R. *Save My Place*
    Horowitz, E. *When the Sky Is Like Lace*
    Hutchins, P. *Good-night, Owl*
    Jacobs, L. *Good Night, Mr. Beetle*
    Jonas, A. *Round Trip*
    Kalan, R. *Jump, Frog, Jump!*
    Keats, E. *Dreams*
    Kent, J. *The Biggest Shadow in the Zoo*
    Lionni, L. *A Color of His Own*

Lionni, L. *Little Blue and Little Red*
Mayer, M. *There's a Nightmare in My Closet*
McGovern, A. *Too Much Noise*
Preston, E. *Squawk to the Moon, Little Goose*
Provensen, A. *What Is a Color?*
Rosetti, C. *What Is Pink?*
Sendack, M. *Where the Wild Things Are*
Shaw, C. *It Looked Like Spilt Milk*
Tompert, A. *Nothing Sticks Like a Shadow*
Tresselt, A. *A Thousand Lights and Fireflies*
Udry, J. *The Moon Jumpers*
VanAllsburg, C. *The Garden of Abdul Gasazi*
Waber, B. *Ira Sleeps Over*
Wells, R. *Good Night, Fred*
Weston, M. *Peony's Rainbow*
Wood, A. *The Napping House*
Zolotow, C. *Sleepy Book*

B. Textbooks

American Book Company. Level 1. *Science: Building Ideas*, pp. 50–72.

Harper & Row. Level 1. *The Young Scientist: Observing His World*, pp. 109–23.

McGraw-Hill. ESS. *Light and Shadows.*

Charles E. Merrill. Level 2. *Accent on Science*, pp. 119–35.

William H. Sadlier. *Ventures in Science* (Level Yellow), pp. 34–40.

Silver Burdett. Level 1. *Science: Understanding Our Environment.*

C. Films (available from SEMBCS Film Library)

Color for Beginners (2310)
Light and What It Does (2344)
Observing and Describing (2756)
Sun (0522)

D. Film Loops

Experiments with Shadows

E. Kits

Light and Shadows (ESS Kit)

F. People

Art Specialist (school volunteer mother, art appreciation program)

In reality, although thematic units are discussed under Research and Special-Project Groups, this conceptual structure can employ a variety of organizational patterns: ability groups, interest groups, specific skills groups, cooperative learning, peer tutoring, and so on. The teacher has enormous flexibility in terms of topics, time, grouping, and materials.

Peer and Cross-Age Tutoring

Peer and cross-age tutoring involve students of the same or different ages acting as tutors for other students. The purpose of this type of organizational strategy is to provide needed extra help to students without putting a drain on the time and energy of the teacher. Reviews by Otto, Wolf, and Eldridge (1984), of studies in peer, cross-age, and adult tutoring indicated that there is a positive effect on the academic performance of both the tutor and the tutees as a result of interaction.

In an interesting study of Cloward (1967) 10th- and 11th-grade remedial reading students more than two years below the norm in reading tutored 4th- and 5th-grade students who were having difficulty reading. After 26 weeks of tutoring, for 4 hours per week, the tutees gained an average of 6 months, and the tutors gained 3.4 grades in reaching achievement, both exceeding the gains of the control groups. This study not only demonstrates the growth of all participants in a tutoring program, but also suggests potential benefits for tutors who, themselves, are experiencing reading difficulty.

A somewhat different structure for peer tutoring has been described in a study by A. R. Allen and Boraks (1978). They investigated the differences between an adult-child tutoring program and what they called a "reciprocal peer tutoring" (RPT) program. In the RPT program students were trained in tutoring behaviors and paired with students of the same age and ability level. They then systematically alternated tutor and tutee roles for different lessons. The adult-child program consisted of college students tutoring one or both of the paired children. After 12 weeks of tutoring, twice each week for 50 minutes, results indicated greater gains in reading achievement for the reciprocal peer tutoring program in both urban and suburban schools. This study further supports the finding of academic gains for tutors and tutees and also supports the concept that all students can effectively function in both roles.

Student tutoring can take various formats within the classroom. For example, Hiebert (1980) described a developmental sequence for the type and amount of responsibility involved in peer tutoring. At the most basic level, *pair activities* are those in which children work on a project as a twosome; at the next level is *parallel activities*, in which groups of children work on common tasks independently but at a central location so that opportunities to share and ask questions of each other are supported. Peers as *resource helpers* marks the next level. At this level students are instructed to seek help from peers rather than from the teacher when they meet with learning difficulties. This minimizes wasted learning time that often characterizes independent classroom activities. Hiebert's final level of peer-directed learning involves students' assuming responsibility for teaching specific content to an individual or a small group of children or collaborating with a small group to complete a project without teacher supervision. This final level is similar to most other tutoring programs in which students are actually responsible for teaching other students (A. R. Allen & Boraks, 1978; Cloward, 1967; Duff & Swick, 1974; Richardson & Havlicek, 1975).

Although student tutoring is a very attractive organizational scheme, the key for the classroom teacher is to be able to implement and manage it effectively.

Hiebert's continuum (1980) would suggest that you should begin slowly, simply allowing your students and yourself an opportunity to become accustomed to this new way of interacting. Good and Brophy (1978) suggested the following practical guideline to creating and implementing peer-learning opportunities:

1. As the classroom teacher, you should establish an atmosphere that supports the belief that "we all learn from one another." Let students know that it is important to do the best job they can and to continually progress.

2. With input from your students, set up a clear step-by-step plan for peer tutoring. Define the times, places, and expected behaviors for tutoring or helping one another. If specific assignments are to be completed, specify the directions, procedures, and outcomes. Model the tutoring behaviors you expect and have students discuss and practice these behaviors for a while before releasing responsibility to them.

3. Provide opportunities for all class members to be both tutors and tutees. Slower students can be tutors for younger children or can help peers practice spelling words or math facts. This reinforces the notion that we all need help at various times and can learn from each other.

4. When using peer tutors within a single classroom, allow students to work together for a couple of weeks to ensure continuity, but then change assignments to include different combinations of children or different structures such as small-group work or teams.

5. Communicate to parents the goals and procedures of your tutoring program.

There are some clear advantages to a classroom peer tutoring program:

1. The most obvious and research-backed advantage is the reinforcement and growth of academic skills for both tutor and tutee.

2. When teachers use tutors to support the instructional program, there is, in effect, a reduction of class size that enables the teacher to work more closely with fewer students.

3. This method of learning encourages students to adopt a mode of cooperative learning and sharing, thereby creating classroom unity and positive interaction. Students develop appreciation of themselves and others as teachers and learners and, through the sharing process, they learn a great deal about interpersonal relationships.

4. Both participants have an opportunity to experience success and a chance to enhance self-esteem and attitudes toward school and reading.

Cooperative Learning Teams

Cooperative learning refers to a number of instructional and organizational techniques in which students of mixed ability levels work together in small groups toward a common goal. The key to cooperative learning is that the success of each student contributes to the success of the other students in the group. Student teams promote an all-for-one, one-for-all attitude in which teammates support, encourage, and help one another and receive awards or recognition based on group, rather than individual, performance.

Although the concept of cooperative learning has been in existence since the 1920s, classroom application and research began in 1970 with a number of educational researchers at Johns Hopkins University, the University of California at Santa Cruz, the University of Minnesota, and the University of Tel Aviv (Israel). The most well documented team-learning strategy is the student team-learning program at Johns Hopkins. This program consists of four specific cooperative learning methods (Student Teams-Achievement Divisions [STAD]; Teams-Games-Tournaments [TGT]; Jigsaw II; Team Assisted Individualization [TAI], which have been used extensively in a variety of grade levels and content areas.

These four methods have been evaluated in terms of student achievement, intergroup relations, mainstreaming, and self-esteem. As summarized by Slavin (1982), 23 studies measuring student achievement resulted in 17 significant positive student achievement gains for cooperative learning methods, with no results favoring control groups. In terms of intergroup relations, research indicates that students involved in cooperative learning express greater liking for their classmates and, in many cases, students' choices of friends showed more cross-ethnic selections. Students involved in equal-status interactions and cooperative learning evidently learn to like each other. Finally, studies have revealed that students involved in team learning have exhibited improvements in self-esteem. Students report that they experience more affection for others; others feel liked by classmates and more successful in their work.

A detailed description of all four student team-learning strategies was presented by Slavin (1980, 1982). Here is one of those strategies—TGT:

Step 1: Take your grade book and divide the class into four groups: one-fourth in a "high group," one-fourth in a "low group," and the remaining students into medium-high and medium-low groups. Ideally, you'd create four groups of four each. Since most classes are larger than that, you can double the number of groups by creating two groups at each ability level.

Step 2: Now assign students from each of these groups into teams. Each team gets one high student, one low student, and one from each of the two middle groups. As you make these assignments, juggle distributions so each team is representative of the race and sex composition of the class. If the number of students isn't divisible by four, the remaining students can be organized in 1 to 3 five-member teams.

Step 3: Prepare your lesson and introduce it to the children. Usually, but not always, teachers divide their instruction into week-long units, introducing a new unit each Monday and holding the "tournament" on Friday. On the first day, lay out the content to be covered in as clear a fashion as possible; tell them what you expect them to know by Friday. Also tell them what resource materials they need to learn the content—you may schedule a lecture during the week, tell them what pages in their text to cover and/or give them a list of resources they can get from the media center or library.

Step 4: During the period assigned to the subject each day, teams are on their own to cover the material. This is where the peer-tutoring goes on because once they understand the idea (and it probably will take one round before it is completely clear) students will want their teams to do as well as possible and, consequently, will help each other. In fact, you will find students who haven't participated all year will join in. You will also discover that you wind up doing a lot less teaching. About the middle of the week, give each team some sample items from the test and let them decide how well they're doing. This will function as a self-diagnostic procedure for the students.

Step 5: On Friday, or the last day of the unit, assign students to "Tournament Tables." Assignments to these tables are made so that only high-ability students are assigned to table 1 and medium students to table 2, medium-low students to table 3, and low-ability students to table 4. (Double the number of tables if necessary.) Thus students are competing with others of approximately equal ability. Consequently the low students as well as the high students have an equal chance of taking home winning points to their team. Children soon sense the fairness in this situation.

Step 6: Students then compete to see who can correctly answer the largest number of questions over the content. You should develop the questions just as you would any objective test with multiple-choice items, etc. Provide each tournament table with a copy of the test and an answer-key kept face-down on the table except when used to check an answer. Each table must also have a deck of cards numbered 1 through the number of items on the test. The decks are shuffled. Each student draws one card to decide who starts; the student with the winning hand starts by becoming "the first reader." Before starting, the cards are replaced in the deck and shuffled. Then the "first reader" draws the top card. The number on the card determines the question on the test he or she will try to answer. The "first reader" reads the question and gives his/her best answer. Before checking to see whether the answer is correct, the player to the left of the reader (the "first challenger") has a chance to challenge the answer. If this second player thinks another answer is better, he or she simply says "I challenge, I think the correct answer is . . . ." The third and subsequent players can challenge in turn. But they can only challenge with an answer that has not been given. Once the challenges are completed, the "second challenger" checks the answer sheet and reads the answer out loud. Whoever is right gets to keep the card representing the question number. If any challenger is wrong, he/she must put a card previously won (if any) back in the deck. Thus there is little risk to the child who has won nothing. If no one is right, the card is returned to the bottom of the deck.

For the next round the game moves to the left—the first challenger becoming the first reader and the second challenger becoming the first challenger. The game goes on either until all questions have been answered correctly or a pre-set time limit has been reached.

Step 7: Give each table a simple score sheet indicating the number of questions each student got right. You can then calculate the scores for each of the original teams. . . . Usually these tournaments go on for several weeks (after about six weeks new teams should be created to avoid the development of cliques) and the excitement grows just as it would in any competitive sport. (Mid-continent Regional Educational Laboratory, 1981)

Jigsaw II incorporates the concept of team learning and a more direct application of peer tutoring by having cross-ability team members read a common piece (book, chapter, story, etc.) and then assigning each member a section or topic on which to become an expert. Experts from all teams meet to study their topic and then return to their teams to teach their teammates and prepare for a quiz. The quiz covers the entire selection studied. Team scores are based on individual improvement scores, and rewards are in the form of a newsletter of recognition on a bulletin board.

Cooperative learning seems to be one of the more powerful new instructional techniques, its advantages including the following:

1. Research indicates that it is effective in raising achievement, promoting inter-group relations and acceptance of ethnically different and mainstreamed students, and fostering self-esteem.
2. It can be used at almost any grade level K through 12, with almost any content area.
3. It is inexpensive, easy to use, and enjoyed by students and teachers.
4. There is an increase in student responsibility for learning and the application of peer tutoring.
5. Once established, it reduces teacher instructional time and allows teachers to work with individual students or specific groups.
6. It offers an alternative to grouping patterns that place together children of similar ethnic background or ability.

As noted earlier, there is no magic formula for the types of groups or numbers of children in each that will insure a successful reading program. Once students are comfortable working in various types of groups, it becomes easier to implement flexible grouping and to have several types of groups functioning concurrently.

RECORD KEEPING

The final area we will consider in our discussion of management and instruction techniques in the regular classroom is record keeping. Most teachers consider record keeping one of their least favorite tasks. They seem to feel that, with such precious little time available for instruction, they cannot justify taking time to keep records. However, record keeping is a critical component of effective reading instruction. Good record keeping actually saves time, for it allows you to identify instructional techniques that work and those that do not work, and it facilitates grouping.

The first type of record that should be kept has already been discussed in chapter 7; it is the time-ordered matrix. Recall that a time-ordered matrix should be kept on individual students who are considered corrective or remedial. It contains both quantitative and qualitative information about a student entered over time as you interact with the student. (See Tables 7.2 and 7.3 for examples of time-ordered matrices.) In addition to a time-ordered matrix, there are some other very useful types of records that can be kept. The Class Data Summary Sheet is depicted in Table 12.4. Whereas you would fill out a time-ordered matrix for only remedial and corrective students, a Class Data Summary Sheet would contain information on all students.

The advantage of this type of record is that it enables you to simultaneously consider all students in your class on a number of dimensions. With it, various instructional grouping patterns can be considered realistically. Although you probably will not use this type of record keeping on a daily basis, it should be referred to throughout the year and updated at least every 9 weeks.

On a daily basis, information needs to be easy to use, convenient and useful to plan and teach. One way to facilitate this is to have each student keep a folder of her or his reading work. These folders should be stored in a central area at the end of each day, so you can review selected files regularly. In these folders, students can keep work sheets, individual reading records, projects in progress, and other reading-related work. Such a system provides a way to collect tangible evidence of a child's work with which to evaluate your hypotheses (see chapter 7). It also provides valuable samples to share with parents.

Another useful procedure is to have students keep anecdotal records of their own learning, much as you would in a time-ordered matrix. A learning log, or personal journal, can be used to have students reflect upon new learning or important topics, answer specific questions about a lesson, or write about their reading attitudes, interests, or reactions to something they have read. These journals should be informal and should not be graded. Their purpose is to give students an opportunity to rethink their learning, sort out any confusion they might have, and monitor their own progress. This type of record also provides another diagnostic source for the teacher. When kept in a continuous notebook or file, the learning log provides rich longitudinal data for monitoring change and growth.

Finally, some types of information are most easily kept in a checklist format. Although this type of record doesn't provide the elaborate data of anecdotal records or learning logs, it can be a simple way to keep track of specific reading skills and objectives. For the classroom teacher, it is most convenient to use a class record sheet with students' names on one side and reading skills across the other. Table 12.5 illustrates a sample checklist. Such a checklist, although not detailed in the information it presents, allows you to determine at a glance classroom trends and possible groupings for students.

Table 12.4

Class Data Summary Sheet

STUDENT NAME	CURRENT BASAL PLACEMENT	IRI INSTRUCTIONAL LEVEL	STANDARDIZED ACHIEVEMENT TEST	INTEREST INVENTORY	DIAGNOSED READING WEAKNESSESS	READING STRENGTHS	COMMENTS
Phil	3	2	34%	Likes cars	Metacognitive strategies Mediated word-attack skills	Recognizes discourse patterns well Sight vocabulary	
Sheila	4	5	45%	Likes airplanes	Mediated word-attack strategies Letter-sound relationships	Good metacognitive strategies Sight vocabulary	
Pat	6	6	74%	Likes history	None	Good strategies all over	
Bob	6	6	85%	Likes sports	None	Good strategies all over	

Table 12.5

STUDENTS	LETTER/ SOUND RE-LATIONSHIP	MEANING-FUL WORD PARTS	MEDIATED WORD REC-OGNITION	SIGHT VO-CABULARY	SYNTACTIC ANALYSIS	PATTERNS AND SUPER-STRUC-TURES	DISCOURSE ANALYSIS	SCHEMA ANALYSIS	META-COGNITIVE STRATEGIES
Cliff	✓	✓	✓	?	✓	✓	?	?	✓
Kay	✓	—	✓	?	✓	✓	?	?	✓
Carmen	—	—	—	—	✓	✓	✓	?	?
Ashley	—	—	—	?	?	—	✓	?	?
Todd	—	—	—	—	—	—	✓	✓	✓
Lorraine	✓	✓	✓	✓	?	?	—	?	✓
Christine	✓	✓	✓	✓	✓	✓	—	—	—
Ed	—	—	—	?	✓	✓	?	✓	✓

Each of the record-keeping techniques just described contains slightly different information and serves a slightly different purpose, each summarized as follows:

1. The time-ordered matrix provides longitudinal data on individual remedial and corrective students. It is used for generating and testing instructional hypotheses.
2. The Class Data Summary sheet synthesizes general information about all students.
3. The student folder offers concrete examples of a student's classroom work.
4. Learning logs provide a record of learning from the perspective of the student.
5. Checklists constitute a quick record-keeping system to keep track of students' progress in specific reading skills.

SUMMARY

In this chapter we reviewed current research and theory relating to classroom management and instruction. Many of the characteristics of effective management and instruction were classified as *indicators*, those variables that take on certain values when management and instruction are efficient. These indicators dealt with time use. Four types of time within the school day were discussed: allocated time, instructional time, engaged time, and academic learning time. In general the more efficient management and instruction are, the more of each of these four types of time is available.

A second category of characteristics of effective management and instruction was labeled *interventions*, those characteristics that are directly controllable by the classroom teacher: scheduling practices, planning techniques, rules and procedures, teacher enthusiasm, and instructional systems.

We then discussed different techniques for grouping students. Ability grouping, although the most commonly used technique, has strong potential for negatively affecting low-ability students. Alternatives that mix students of differing ability levels are special-skills groups, interest groups, research and special-projects groups, peer and cross-age tutoring, and cooperative learning.

Finally we discussed record-keeping strategies that aid management and instruction: the time-ordered matrix, the Class Data Summary Sheet, student folders, learning logs, and checklists.

13

THE MANY ROLES OF THE READING SPECIALIST

Many reading teachers who have received formal training in diagnostic and instructional techniques and have reached a high level of proficiency in these skills suddenly find themselves in a role that contains management and supervisory functions for which they were never trained. A reading teacher might be asked to serve as the specialist for an entire school or even an entire district. Many times such positions are ill defined. That is, you have to create your own job, so to speak. In this chapter we will consider some guidelines for defining and implementing your role as a reader specialist.

DEFINING WHO YOU ARE

Within public and private education the reading specialist usually has one of three roles: remedial reading teacher, reading consultant, or resource person. We will consider each:

The Remedial Reading Teacher

The remedial reading teacher is usually viewed as a specially trained teacher who provides remediation to individuals or small groups of children identified as needing additional reading instruction. This instruction usually takes the form of a "pull-out" program, a program in which children are removed from the regular classroom.

This approach has its origin in the generalized move for remedial instruction that emerged after World War II. Later, federal funding from ESEA Title I strengthened the movement. Remedial reading teachers were to correct reading problems after they had occurred rather than to help prevent them. This type of remedial program, which is still the dominant form today, seems, on the surface, to meet the perceived needs and desires of most schools and the faculty members within those schools.

Classroom teachers usually need instructional assistance with low-achieving youngsters and prefer to have these children removed from the classroom. Teachers become used to shifting the instructional responsibility from the classroom teacher to the remedial teacher. Additionally, many classroom teachers do not have the skills or the motivation to work with students who require a great deal of additional instruction and supervision. Although there is an important benefit to delivering direct services to children, a pull-out approach has many drawbacks:

1. The primary responsibility for reading instruction for remedial readers is often transferred from the classroom teacher to the reading teacher. This usually means that children receive instruction only from the remedial teacher or that classroom instruction does not parallel the emphasis in the remedial setting.

2. The notion that reading is a separate subject is reinforced when children are continually removed from the classroom for a 30- to 45-minute reading lesson. This problem impacts on both student and teacher, because reading skills are not applied and reinforced in other subject areas.

3. The instructional focus is on correction rather than prevention. Consequently, the prognosis becomes poor for eliminating the need for remediation.

4. The number of children who benefit from a pull-out program is small. The severity of disability of remedial readers is usually great, and the duration of needed remediation is long. Not only does the remedial teacher work with few students, but he or she is usually the same teacher year after year. Many of the other pupils who might benefit from additional help never receive it.

5. Pull-out programs might not work. A review of the research on pull-out programs (Glass & Smith, 1977) found that, although approximately 84% of compensatory-education pupils receive remedial reading instruction in a pull-out setting, "the 'pull-out' procedure *per se* has no clear academic or social benefits and may, in fact, be detrimental to the pupils' progress and adjustment to school" (p. 18) The authors concluded that the pull-out procedure is used more to satisfy Title I regulations than because it produces better results or is judged by teachers to be a sensible and beneficial plan. Leinhardt and Pallay (1982) pointed out that it is not the instructional setting itself that is of primary importance, but rather what happens in that setting.

So, in essence, a remedial reading teacher who restricts her or his responsibilities to a pull-out program might not be operating in the most effective mode.

The Reading Consultant

Concern about the remedial pull-out model (Bean, 1979; Bean & Eichelberger, 1985; Bean & Wilson, 1981) has motivated some authorities to suggest that the primary role of the reading specialist should be that of a consultant (H. A. Robinson, 1967; H. A. Robinson & Rauch, 1965). A consultant is largely freed of teaching responsibilities. His or her major role is to assist by coordinating and facilitating efforts to improve the reading program. In this role the reading teacher works primarily with classroom teachers to help select and evaluate new methods and materials, to provide in-service help to keep staff up-to-date, to assist with diagnosis of pupils, and to solve reading issues with the staff and the administration. Advocates of the strict consultative role support direct teaching of students *only* for the purpose of trying out new methods and materials, demonstrating new techniques, or gathering information about particular students (H. A. Robinson, 1967).

It seems fair to say that the reading consultant can potentially have a major impact on the entire school reading program through the domino effect. One reading consultant, working with five classroom teachers, can affect 5 × 30, or 150, children of all ability levels. Additionally, the five classroom teachers, through their professional interactions with other teachers, can create a ripple effect throughout the entire school.

Compare the impact of this model with that of the pull-out model, in which the reading teacher works with approximately 20–50 students. However, although the consultative role has much greater potential for impact on a school-wide basis, it does not provide as much direct expert diagnosis and remediation as the pull-out program. It assumes that all pupils can be remediated in a classroom setting and that all teachers are willing to handle, and capable of handling, a wide range of individual reading difficulties within the typical classroom.

Reading Resource Person

Another possible role for the reading specialist is that of reading resource person (Mason & Palmatier, 1973; Otto & Smith, 1970). As noted by Otto and Smith,

> The day is gone, we hope, when the person who is most knowledgeable and enthusiastic about the teaching of reading is assigned to a room or laboratory "down the hall" to meet with specially referred or volunteer students. Specialized reading personnel who are assigned to schools should always work as resource persons for the entire school as well as with selected students. (p. 162)

The reading resource role combines aspects of both the pull-out remedial role and the consultative role. There is a growing body of evidence to support the assertion that the reading specialist should perform a dual function, working with children and working with classroom teachers consulting, modeling, assisting with diagnosis, and recommending strategies and materials (Baumann, 1984; Berliner, 1981; Hoffman & Rutherford, 1984; Samuels, 1981). Recent studies by Pikulski and Ross (1979) and Bean and Eichelberger (1985) found that reading teachers saw their responsibilities as inclusive of those associated with the remedial pull-out and consultative functions.

In addition to the model of dividing time between pull-out teacher and consultant is the model of an in-class program. In this setting, the reading specialist works with students in their regular classroom under the direction of the classroom teacher. This type of program has the advantage of providing direct services to children and, at the same time, fostering closer ties between classroom teacher and reading specialist and between classroom reading program and remedial reading program. In a review of an in-class supplemental reading program in a large school district, Bean and Eichelberger (1985) found that (a) reading specialists focused less on diagnosis and more on reinforcing skills taught in the classroom, (b) teachers and specialist supported the instructional aspect of in-class assistance rather than the consultative aspect, and (c) both types of professionals had difficulty adjusting to having two instructors in one classroom. Bean and Eichelberger concluded that, although an in-class program has great potential to impact on reading achievement, a balance between pull-out and in-class programs might be optimal, and a great deal of preparation and support are required to institute such a change.

The role of the building resource teacher, then, might best be described as somewhere along the continuum between working with students as a remedial teacher and working only with teachers as a reading consultant. In addition to the advantages of providing direct services to a limited number of students and the geometric impact of working with classroom teachers, the resource role has the benefit of establishing closer ties between classroom teacher and reading specialist, a shared responsibility for teaching and learning. This association fosters consistent, appropriate, coordinated instruction for students and reinforces the notion that reading extends for more than 40–50 minutes each day.

Clearly, schools and teachers have different needs. One role for the reading specialist might be appropriate in one school but not in another. Bean and Eichelberger (1985), Pukulski and Ross (1979), and Mangieri and Heimberger (1980) noted that reading specialists themselves stress the need for selecting the role that is appropriate to the situation and to their individual professional skill levels and styles. It therefore becomes the responsibility of the reading teacher, taking into consideration the input of administrators and classroom teachers, to determine which role best meets the needs of all concerned.

Determining Your Role

Establishing your role as reading specialist requires input from building and district administration. At the beginning of each school year, the reading specialist and the principal should outline together job responsibilities and the amount of time to be devoted to specific activities. Consider the questions presented in Table 13.1, which span the range of job responsibilities of the reading specialist. To use this checklist, you should first check those tasks you consider to be part of your job. Add any others that have not been listed or are not subsumed under an existing task. Then determine the percentage of your time that is devoted to each task.

Table 13.1 Job Responsibilities of the Reading Specialist

PERCENTAGE OF TIME SPENT	
	1. Provide remedial reading instruction for specially identified students outside their regular classroom.
	2. Assume sole responsibility for testing and placement of all new students.
	3. Provide short-term instruction for children with specific needs (e.g., discourse patterns, summarizing, mediated word recognition skills) in a miniclinic or skills group setting outside the regular classroom.
	4. Communicate with parents and teachers about the progress of students with whom you work.
	5. Provide remedial reading instruction for specially identified students within the setting of the regular classroom.
	6. Assist classroom teachers with the diagnosis and placement of students.
	7. Assist classroom teachers with ideas, materials, and strategies to use in classroom reading instruction.
	8. Team teach and plan lessons with classroom teachers.
	9. Observe students and reading lessons in the regular classroom and provide feedback to teachers.
	10. Assist teachers with evaluation of specific reading lessons, class reading program, or grade-level program.
	11. Offer opportunities for classroom teachers to observe you teach or provide class coverage while they observe colleagues.
	12. Conduct demonstration lessons in regular classrooms.
	13. Provide workshops, inservices, or short up-dates on new reading information/materials for staff.
	14. Communicate with parents about the schoolwide reading program.
	15. Organize and help implement classroom and schoolwide motivational reading projects.
	16. Supervise and train paraprofessional aides in the reading program.
	17. Assist the building principal with implementation, supervision, and evaluation of the school reading program.

If you find that the greatest amount of time is clustered around Items 1–5, your job responsibilities are skewed most heavily toward the role of remedial pull-out teacher. If most of your time is spent on Items 13–17, you are probably serving as more of a consultant to teachers and administrators and are not primarily involved in working with students. Answers that center around Items 6–12 or are spread across all tasks are indicative of a resource role that includes working with students and teachers.

One useful activity is to compare your actual response with your ideal responses and to compare both of these with the responses of your building administrator. By reviewing this information with your building administrator, you can develop a useful plan of action and a meaningful job description. Box 13.1 contains a sample job description for a reading specialist at the elementary level.

Box 13.1 _____ *ELEMENTARY SCHOOL*

40% of time—Direct service to children

a. Diagnose and prescribe for children referred to the Special Reading program.
b. Instruct children placed in the special pull-out program.
c. Diagnose children on a special-need basis.

60% of time—Resource/consultative work

a. Diagnose and prescribe for classroom reading program—IRI or other appropriate test for placement.
b. Consult with teachers in developing ideas and techniques for teaching reading by working with teachers in classroom and/or small goups.
c. Assist teachers in maximum utilization of materials.
d. Conduct staff development in reading through initiating, coordinating, or conducting inservices.
e. Assist with implementation and use of basal reading materials.
f. Assist with implementation and use of supplementary materials.
g. Serve as chairperson of the building Reading Committee.
h. Attend Special Services staffings.
i. Conduct conferences with parents and teacher concerning student or reading program.

Another useful source for exploring a variety of job responsibilities is *Guidelines for the Professional Preparation of Reading Specialists and Allied Professionals*, developed by the International Reading Association (1986). This document describes several different roles for reading teachers and outlines specific attitudes, concepts, and skills that apply to each role.

Regardless of how you define your role, you will need to consider four managerial aspects of your job: organizing, scheduling, record keeping, and communicating with others. We will consider these factors as they relate to the remedial pull-out teacher and the reading consultant. We will not discuss management from the perspective of the resource teacher because this role is a combination of the other two.

THE REMEDIAL TEACHER AS MANAGER

Pull-out remedial programs take a number of forms: (a) regularly scheduled, long-term instruction; (b) regularly scheduled, short-term, specific skill instruction; and (c) lab-type settings with regularly scheduled times for students to drop in. Except in very special situations, individual remediation is discouraged. The number of students needing remediation and the limited time available make one-to-one instruction impractical. As Pearson (1984) noted in his summary of the research, "group instruction, particularly small group instruction, is consistently associated with positive gains in achievement while individualized instruction is associated with negative or negligible gains" (p. 225). In addition, homogeneous groups of 5–8 youngsters appear to produce the greatest gains (M. L. Smith & Glass, 1979).

Regardless of the format, all pull-out programs provide direct services to students in a setting outside the regular classroom, and all of them require strong organizational skills. These skills are a central aspect of the remedial teacher's responsibilities.

Organization Guidelines

One of the first organizational tasks for a remedial pull-out teacher is to establish guidelines for entrance, exit, and referrals. Try to involve the administration and at least a representative group of teachers in the development of these guidelines, or give them an opportunity to react to your guidelines. In this way those who are affected by the program have an opportunity to express their needs, and an avenue for open communication will be established.

Some questions to consider when establishing guidelines include:

1. Whom will the remedial program serve?
   What grade levels?
   How far below grade level should students be reading to qualify?
   Will the program serve only the most severely deficient students, or will it include those who are moderately behind in their reading performance?
2. Will the program provide long-term (year, semester) remediation or short-term specific skill (miniclinic) remediation?
3. Should services be provided for students who also receive other special services (e.g., learning disabilities, speech, composition, math)?
4. What will be the procedure for referring students?
5. What will determine when students exit from the program?

Generally, remedial pull-out programs serve students in grades 1–6. At the secondary level, students are usually assigned to a regularly scheduled class. The format of the program (long-term, short-term, skills group, drop-in lab) and the type of student served (severely reading disabled, moderately disabled) also affect the entrance and exit criteria.

It is entirely possible for a remedial program to address all these needs.

For example, a remedial reading teacher might decide that 50% of the job responsibility should be allocated to working directly with students and, of that time, perhaps one-half should be spent with long-term groups, one-quarter with short-term groups, and one-quarter with specific-needs groups. Those students with severe reading problems would probably be long-term students and would be probably reading two or more years below level, as determined by formal and informal tests and classroom performance. Exit criteria for these students would depend on how far below grade they were initially, the amount and rate of gain while in the remedial program, and the support available in the regular classroom.

Children with moderate reading problems would probably be reading one to two years below grade level, as determined primarily by classroom performance. These students might remain in the remedial program 1 or 2 semesters. Exit criteria would again depend on students' initial achievement level, amount and rate of improvement, and available support within the regular classroom.

Skill groups and drop-in labs would run from a few days to a few weeks in duration. Students would be referred by classroom teachers on the basis of a specific identified need (e.g., poor use of schema-level strategies). These students would exit the remedial pull-out program when they had demonstrated an understanding of and ability to apply the specific skill.

All referrals for remedial placement, skills instruction, drop-in lab assistance, or diagnostic or placement testing should be initiated by the classroom teacher in writing. The reason for referral and any current reading information should be included in the referral. This written request provides a permanent record and increases the likelihood that the classroom teacher will give careful thought to the student's specific reading needs and not misinterpret a behavior

---

Box 13.2   *Reading Referral*

Student Information

Action Taken _____
                          (Date)

Name _____
Classroom _____
Teacher
Date _____
Reading Level: _____

_____
Signature—Reading Teacher

_____
Signature—Classroom Teacher

Reason for
Referral: _____

COMMENTS

_____
_____   (Date) _____

or motivation problem. Such diagnostic information is especially important when referring students for a short-term skills group or for assistance during the drop-in lab when in-depth testing would not be conducted.

After receiving the referral, the reading teacher should arrange to test or informally diagnose the student, to determine appropriate action, and to report briefly the findings, in writing, to the classroom teacher. The reading teacher should reserve the right to accept or reject students for pull-out remedial assistance, based on available space, student need, and time available.

Examples of two short referral forms are shown in Boxes 13.2 and 13.3. These types of forms can be duplicated or printed on action paper to provide a copy for the reading teacher and the classroom teacher. Notice that they are very brief. Also notice that they include a place for the signatures of both teachers. This insures that important communication transpires.

Box 13.3   *Reading Lab Referral*

Name _____

Teacher _____ Grade _____

Assistance Needed: _____
_____

Projected Length of time: _____
_____

Additional Information: _____
_____
_____

                              _____
                              Reading Teacher

                              _____
                              Classroom Teacher

Scheduling

Scheduling of the remedial pull-out program can be a complex task. A remedial program should not take the place of classroom reading instruction but should supplement the classroom program by providing additional reading instructional time. In fact, some federal and state guidelines require and carefully monitor this distinction between supplementing and supplanting classroom reading instruction. It is also advisable, when possible, to avoid scheduling remedial reading instruction during recess, lunch, physical education, art, or music. These activities are often the ones that provide the remedial reading student with opportunities for success and social development that she or he does not receive in the regular classroom.

To plan a teaching schedule for a remedial program, first determine the amount of time to be allocated to direct services to children; then compile a master schedule for all grade levels and block out those times that would conflict with classroom reading instruction. Then schedule in 30- to 45-minute class periods, making sure you have left some periods unassigned if you plan to conduct flexible, short-term skills groups, a drop-in lab, special testing, or resource work (see Table 13.2). Each class period should enable you to accommodate between five and eight children, depending on their skill levels and needs. In some cases, you may choose to see the same children every day; in others, twice or three times per week will be sufficient.

At first it is difficult to determine which children can best be served by a remedial program. Use the guidelines you have established for referral and always communicate to the classroom teacher the reasons for accepting or rejecting students into the program. When students in need cannot be accommodated, take time to talk with the classroom teacher about possible future openings, along with techniques for helping the children in the classroom and ways in which you might support the teacher's efforts.

Once you have established the schedule for remedial instruction, there are three useful ways to insure that teachers and children adhere to the schedule:

1. Post a master schedule on the door of the remedial reading classroom. At a glance, teachers, children, and administrators will know your instructional, consultative, and resource times.
2. Send a personalized note to each teacher listing the names of students served from that classroom and the time each is to leave for and return from remedial instruction.

Table 13.2

	M	*T*	*W*	*TH*	*F*
8:00–8:45	grade 5	new-student testing	grade 5	new-student testing	grade 5
8:45–9:15	C l a s	s r o o m	R e s o	u r c e	W o r k
9:15–10:30	grade 3	grade 3	consulting	grade 3	grade 3
10:30–11:15	grade 1	consulting	grade 1	consulting	grade 1
11:15–12:00	grade 4	grade 2	grade 4	grade 2	grade 4
12:00–12:45	L	U	N	C	H
12:45–1:45	resource grade 4—content area reading	grade 6	resource grade 4—content-area reading	grade 6	resource grade 4—content-area reading
1:45–2:30	intermediate lab	primary lab	intermediate lab	primary lab	intermediate lab

3. Give each student a 3″ × 5″ card with his or her name, days, and times for special reading help. Have each student tape this card in a special place (inside the desk, on a notebook, etc.) so he or she will be aware of scheduled instruction.

Record Keeping

Just as record keeping is important for keeping track of students' activities, (see chapter 12) so is it important for keeping track of teachers' activities. When planning, it is useful to have a master weekly planning schedule indicating groups of children and weekly objectives. In some cases this might resemble a traditional lesson plan book. In others, it might be much more general (see Table 13.3). Systematic records will help you coordinate materials, will become a long-

Table 13.3 — Instructional Plan January 4–8

	1/4	1/5	1/6	1/7	1/8
8:00–8:45	grade 5 predicting outcomes		grade 5 hypothesizing from text		grade 5 hypothesizing from experience
8:45–9:15	grade 3 Demonstration Teaching & Observations				
9:15–10:30	grade 3 reading for details	grade 3 related details		grade 3 main ideas and supporting details	grade 3 unstated main ideas
10:30–11:15	grade 1 initial consonant sounds b and k		grade 1 sight words with beginning consonants b and k		grade 1 initial consonants in cloze sentences
11:15–12:00	grade 4 multimeaning words	grade 2 vocabulary, semantic mapping	grade 4 multimeaning words in text	grade 2 vocabulary, semantic mapping	grade 4 multimeaning words dictionary
12:00–12:45					
12:45–1:45	grade 4 SQ3R—overview purpose	grade 6 fact/opinion	grade 4 SQ3R-S—skimming, scanning	grade 6 substantiating facts	grade 4 skimming, scanning in social studies
1:45–2:30					

term record of skills taught, and will serve as a check on the articulation of students' instructional programs.

In the same way that a plan helps a teacher to focus attention and energy, it can be a useful organizational tool to help children recognize goals and monitor their own learning. A modified version of the teacher plan can be provided for each student (see Box 13.4). The teacher can write in the objectives for the week, and students can review these to set expectations, or, when instruction is differentiated, each student can consult his or her calendar before beginning work. Another use of this plan involves having students reflect on the day's lesson by summarizing what they have learned.

Box 13.4   *June*

6	7	8	9	10
Some words have more than one meaning	Sometimes the sentence can help me figure out the meaning of a word			

Some teachers prefer to give students a blank calendar for the month and then use one of the previously mentioned procedures week by week. Students can keep their plans in individual file folders where they also keep their daily work. File folders are a good way to help students organize and a handy way to accumulate samples of their work to share with parents and classroom teachers. At the end of the week or the month, the calendar and the contents of the file folder serve as a communication tool to classroom teachers and parents about instruction in the special reading class. There are many other teacher-made forms that can be used in a pull-out program (see Figure 13.1). These brief notes reinforce to the students and classroom teachers the need for co-ordinated efforts.

More formal cumulative records are often required when working with students on a pull-out basis. These records provide verification of student need and documentation of progress. Although the reading teacher will probably keep these records for pupils who are currently in the program, they should also be filed in the child's cumulative folder when special help is terminated or at the end of the school year. In this way classroom teachers have easy access to the records, and the information becomes part of the child's historical record when he or she moves on. An example of a cumulative special-reading record card is shown in Figure 13.2. Although some schools and school districts have specific required forms, others don't provide any systematic format. When a cumulative record is not provided, the reading teacher should develop one to

Figure 13.1 *Note.* Reprinted by permission of K. Patterson, School District 12, Denver, CO.

Student Name ____________________

Reading Teacher ____________________

Date	Standardized Test: Name, Level, Form	Standardized Test: Vocabulary	Standardized Test: Comprehension	Standardized Test: Total			IRI (Instructional Level): Word Recognition	IRI (Instructional Level): Oral Reading	IRI (Instructional Level): Silent Reading	IRI (Instructional Level): Listening	Other Tests								

DOLCH WORD LISTS	Date	Date	Date
Preprimer	/40	/40	/40
Primer	/52	/52	/52
1st	/41	/41	/41
95 Nouns	/95	/95	/95
2nd	/45	/45	/45
3rd	/42	/42	/42

Basal Reading Inventory	Date	Date	Date
Word Recog.			
Comp.			

DIAGNOSTIC ANALYSIS

Date

____

____

____

____

____

Figure 13.2

meet the diagnostic and prescriptive needs of the remedial program. It should include a place to record formal and informal diagnostic test results and sufficient space for the reading specialist to summarize qualitative and quantitative information.

Another more formal record and communication tool is the special-reading report card. Unlike the cumulative record card, which is more summative in nature, including pre- (diagnostic) and postremediation information, the report card provides a formative, ongoing record of the student's progress while in the remedial class. This type of report cements the bond among classroom teacher, parent, and remedial reading teacher. There are many different forms for reading report cards (see Boxes 13.5 and 13.6), but all should provide the classroom teacher and the parent with descriptive information about a student's progress.

Communicating

The success of a remedial pull-out program is greatly determined by the type and amount of communication between the classroom teacher and the remedial reading teacher. We have already considered some important aspects of communication in relation to the referral process, scheduling, and record keeping. If communication is automatically built into the remedial program, the potential for misunderstanding is greatly reduced. But, in addition to these structured forms of communication, the reading teacher must take time to informally talk with the classroom teacher about students in the remedial program. Not only is it important for you to share with the classroom teacher a student's progress, but it is also important to listen to the classroom teacher's assessment of how the student seems to be functioning in the classroom. Remedial instruction cannot be considered effective unless its benefits can be directly observed in the classroom. The time spent conferencing with teachers should be spent talking and listening; the exchange should be equal, both professionals sharing and growing from the other's knowledge. While individual student's needs are being discussed, the door opens for sharing teaching strategies that might be useful with others and suggestions about how the developmental and remedial programs can support each other. This type of interaction with classroom teachers is commonly called *conferencing*. We will discuss it in more depth in the next section.

THE READING CONSULTANT AS MANAGER

As a reading consultant (or a reading resource teacher), you will need to work with teachers to implement new strategies and materials, identify and solve difficulties at the student, classroom, and building levels, and spearhead efforts to increase awareness of current reading research. You will be a model, a teacher,

Box 13.5   *Special-Reading Report Card*

STUDENT INFORMATION   ACTION TAKEN (Date _____)

Name _____

Classroom Teacher _____   _____
                                           Signature—Reading Teacher
Date _____
                                           _____
Reading Level: _____   Signature—Classroom Teacher

Reason for Referral: _____

_____

COMMENTS

Report No. 1: _____ Date _____

_____

_____

_____

Report No. 2: _____ Date _____

_____

_____

_____

Report No. 3: _____ Date _____

_____

_____

_____

Report No. 4: _____ Date _____

_____

_____

_____

Box 13.6

SPECIAL-READING PROGRESS REPORT
_____ SCHOOL

NAME _____

REPORTING PERIOD _____

GRADE _____

CLASSROOM TEACHER _____

SPECIAL-READING TEACHER _____

WORD IDENTIFICATION SKILLS:

COMPREHENSION SKILLS:

STUDY SKILLS:

COMMENTS:

---

a supplier of materials, and a support person. Your interactions with teachers could take the form of conferencing about individual students, planning and modeling lessons, or observing lessons and providing feedback.

This role requires more than expertise in reading; it demands well-developed interpersonal skills. Perhaps the most difficult aspect of a consultative role is building credibility and providing opportunities for teachers to get to know you in a way that encourages them to seek your help. It is a long and sometimes tedious process, one which many times takes 2 to 3 years to develop into a positive, working relationship. In this section we explore techniques for organization, scheduling, record keeping, and effective communication in the reading consultant role.

Organization Guidelines

Just as responsibilities and activities need to be clearly established in a remedial pull-out program, so must they be well thought out and systemized in the consultative role. One way to establish guidelines is to meet with the faculty and discuss how you might assist them. Sometimes individual teachers or entire grade levels have special requests. You will need to decide whether you are willing to provide different support for specific needs or whether you will offer the same assistance to all.

An important point to keep in mind is that, as a consultant, your goal is to work with staff members so that *they* become more effective reading teachers. Although at times you might directly intervene in the classroom, there should be a clear understanding that the ultimate responsibility for reading instruction belongs to the classroom teacher.

This raises some interesting questions; for example, as a reading consultant, are you responsible for working in the classroom with one reading group? If you are, for what length of time should you continue this work? What should be the teacher's responsibility for this group while you are there? How will the classroom teacher benefit from this experience? These are the kinds of questions you need to consider before you offer carte blanche assistance to all faculty members. Then these issues need to be discussed clearly and openly with the teachers involved.

Once you have clarified the guidelines of your consultative position, you should communicate them in writing to other members of the faculty. This can be done by distributing a brief description of your job responsibilities (Box 13.7). Your published Bill of Fare can then be used as an opening for discussion about the reading program. It should be made clear that your support assumes a team effort and that both the classroom teacher and you have a right to expect to grow professionally from the relationship. For example, if you gather materials for a classroom teacher, you should expect feedback on their use and hope that the classroom teacher would share with you other new materials she or he had discovered throughout the year. If you agree to model a reading lesson, it should be expected that the classroom teacher would help in planning the lesson and then observe and provide feedback on the lesson. In all cases, shared responsibility for reading instruction should be the framework in which the reading consultant operates.

But what happens when faculty members prefer that the reading teacher provide remediation only through a pull-out program? The best recommen-

---

Box 13.7	*Reading Resource Bill of Fare*

1. Gather materials for classroom instruction
2. Provide new teaching suggestions
3. Offer small-group instruction
4. Help with grouping
5. Prepare sample lessons
6. Model teach
7. Observe lessons and provide feedback
8. Team teach
9. Handle other special requests

dation is to take small steps and be patient. If teachers don't seek your help, offer to help them by testing children, finding material to teach a particular lesson, or teaching a reading group. Stop by their rooms and show them some interesting materials and offer to let them try them for a time. At this stage, you need to pursue any opportunity to get your foot in the door, to establish credibility and willingness to share.

R. D. Robinson and Pettit (1978) suggested the following strategies that might be useful in expanding your role:

Level One: If you have been given little or no time for responsibilities beyond those of a referral teacher, you might consider the following suggestions as a possible beginning to an expanded role.

1. Assume your share of school-related duties normally assigned to the regular teaching staff (recess supervision, lunchroom duty, etc.). While these activities are not directly related to reading instruction, your willingness to take on a part of these chores will help you gain the confidence of other faculty members.
2. Communicate regularly with teachers concerning the progress their students are making in your reading room.
3. Demonstrate new reading materials and techniques at faculty meetings.
4. Develop reading-related programs for parent/teacher meetings and other community groups.
5. Encourage the development of your local IRA council through active participation in its activities and programs.

Level Two: The suggestions at this level are based on the assumption that you have received some encouragement to expand your influence in the total reading curriculum. At least one period a day would be required for implementing these suggestions.

1. Visit, on request, a teacher's reading class with the understanding that you are not there to criticize but rather to provide assistance in developing the best reading program possible.
2. Assist the teacher in the interpretation of standardized reading test results, with emphasis on implications for classroom application.
3. Provide leadership for such total school reading activities as curriculum studies, textbook selection committees, and library improvements.
4. Share the latest developments in reading research as they relate to classroom procedures.
5. Supply the principal and other administrative personnel information they need to help them make the best policy decisions for the school's reading program.

Level Three: Activities at this level presuppose a strong commitment from the school to the idea of having the reading teacher assume a leading role in the reading program. Probably at least half or more of her/his time would be required to carry through adequately on these suggestions.

1. Teach a demonstration class illustrating a particular aspect of reading instruction (skills activity, directed reading lesson, content strategies, etc.).
2. Arrange, at a teacher's request, a parent conference to discuss some aspect of the classroom reading program or a particular reading problem.
3. Provide instruction for teachers on the use and interpretation of informal reading tests, with emphasis on implications for classroom application.
4. Suggest to teachers a specific program of remedial reading instruction for use in their classrooms (p. 926).

Scheduling

Many of the recommendations for scheduling made in the section, The Remedial Teacher as Manager, also apply to the reading consultant. However, as a reading consultant, it is important to reserve consultation time in the morning and during teachers' planning periods. In the morning, when most classes have reading instruction, you will probably be working in the classroom modeling, teaching, and observing reading lessons. During planning times you will want to remain free to consult with classroom teachers.

If possible, it is advisable to vary your consultant time each day so you can respond to classroom requests from many grade levels and consultation requests from many teachers. Before school, at lunch time, and after school also provide options for meeting with teachers. Although it is tempting to respond to questions posed in passing in the hall, it is usually a good idea to ask the teacher when he or she might have a few minutes to talk with you. This strategy eliminates the notion of the quick fix for reading problems, gives you time to prepare, and reinforces the principle of shared responsibility. A brief written request form like that in Box 13.8 will facilitate this process.

Record Keeping

Although most schools do not require a record of consultative activities, a log of your work recorded on $3'' \times 5''$ cards or in journal format is valuable for several reasons: (a) It documents how you have been spending your time so that those who might be resistant to your role see its value, (b) it helps you keep track of those teachers with whom you have worked and aids you in determining where your next efforts should be concentrated, (c) it becomes a resource file for you to use to refer teachers to their colleagues who are trying new or similar techniques. This enables you to step out of the role of authority and into that of facilitator.

Communicating

Whether you are conducting a formal conference with a teacher or simply informally discussing reading concerns, your interpersonal communication skills will have a tremendous impact on your success or failure in the

Box 13.8 _____ *Elementary School*

READING RESOURCE REQUEST FOR _____

Date Requested _____ Date Needed _____

Teacher _____

Service(s) requested: _____

_____

_____

Available for planning conference on _____

or _____

Additional information/comments: _____

_____

_____

consultative role. When people feel secure, supported, and unthreatened, they are more willing to take risks. As a reading consultant, you will be asking teachers to take risks: to try new techniques, to admit difficulties and ask for help, and to open their classrooms to others. It is important to recognize the apprehension with which most teachers approach the consultant-teacher relationship.

While conducting conferences with classroom teachers we recommend you be aware of the following factors:

Climate. The initial comments made within a conference often establish the tone for the rest of the conference and sometimes for future interactions. The reading consultant's statements should release tension and communicate appreciation for the opportunity to work together. This includes expressions of support and encouragement, stated in a comfortable, relaxed tone.

Target. When a conference is held, its purpose and anticipated outcomes should be clear at the outset. To make them so, the reading teacher might encourage the classroom teacher to reiterate the question(s) to be discussed. The classroom teacher should be given the opportunity to revise the original purpose and suggest others. By attention to target setting, there is less likelihood that the classroom teacher will be dissatisfied or disappointed with the conference, because he or she will have contributed to the agenda.

Responsive Feedback.   The reading teacher should help the classroom teacher clarify ideas by asking questions that encourage the latter to reflect, analyze, and evaluate. Remarks should be specific and help the teacher to think about the situation at hand in a new way. These comments should always be descriptive rather than judgmental, so that they encourage problem solving rather than defensive behavior on the part of the classroom teacher. The reading teacher should try to use praise judiciously and authentically to support the classroom teacher's ideas or performance.

Closure.   At the end of a conference, the reading teacher should review the major outcomes of the session and encourage the classroom teacher to do the same. At this time the reading teacher should also establish a time line for any follow-up activities and communicate continued support.

These guidelines for conferencing provide a useful framework for consulting with classroom teachers. Conferencing is one of the most difficult tasks for reading consultants, because many reading teachers who find themselves in, or aspire to, the consultative role have never had any formal training in or experience interacting with teachers in this manner. We recommend that you use the suggestions just given as a framework in which to develop your personal style and techniques for conferencing with classroom teachers.

SUMMARY

In this chapter we have discussed the different roles of the reading specialist. In general there are three: the remedial reading teacher, the consultant, and the resource person. The remedial reading teacher works with small groups of students in a pull-out format. In this role the reading specialist is directly responsible for instruction of a small number of remedial and corrective reading students. As a consultant, the reading specialist works primarily with classroom teachers, providing them with ideas, materials, and instructional support for working with all children within the context of the regular classroom. Finally, the resource teacher's role is a hybrid of the other two. The resource teacher works directly with a few problem readers in a lab or clinical environment and also with classroom teachers.

Guidelines were provided for identifying and clarifying the role of reading specialist. Finally, organizational, scheduling, record-keeping, and communication aspects of the remedial teacher and the consultant roles were discussed in depth.

14

QUESTIONS TO TEACH BY

Although it would seem that the purpose of education is to find answers, there are some who assert that the questions are just as important. Einstein once said, "Joy in looking and comprehending is nature's most beautiful gift" (1964, p. 114).

With this in mind we recommend that you use certain questions as a framework for diagnosis and instruction and as a framework for assessing your own effectiveness as a reading teacher. If you can answer the questions about to be listed, you can rest assured that you are approaching reading diagnosis and instruction with a good deal of forethought. However, we are not suggesting that, once you have answered these questions, you can or should approach instruction complacently. Instead, the questions should serve as a vehicle for self-evaluation. Occasionally return to them to see if and how your answers have changed. Over time, they should. As you learn more about diagnosis and instruction, you might make dramatic shifts in some basic beliefs about reading. As research on reading and instruction becomes more sophisticated, new techniques will emerge and old ones will drop from use.

Perhaps a good operating principle for reading teachers is to remember that a moderate amount of uncertainty is a useful tool. If you use the following questions as a framework within which to teach, you will always have enough healthy uncertainty to maintain the razor's edge as a diagnostician and teacher:

1. What is my model of reading? How do I think the reading process really works?

2. What evidence do I use to select the instructional activities I prescribe? Is the evidence a product of sound thinking on my part?

3. What evidence do I use to determine whether my instruction is effective? Am I sensitive to change or lack of change in student behavior?

4. What am I not considering that could be a key to solving students' reading problems? Does my model take into account all of the variables I know or believe have an effect on reading performance?

The information in this text was designed to help you begin answering these questions. We have attempted to provide you with a sound theoretical base and suggestions for translating that theory into practice. However, we know that ultimately it is not the information presented in textbooks such as this one that makes for good reading instruction. Rather it is the commitment and effort of individual teachers. We encourage your persistence in both of these traits and hope that this text has served and will serve as a useful resource.

Appendix A
REVIEWS OF
SELECTED TESTS

BOTEL READING INVENTORY is both an individual and a group achievement test. It has two forms and is for students in grades one through twelve. It measures vocabulary, word attack, and spelling. It is published by Follett Publishing Company, 1010 W. Washington Boulevard, Chicago, Illinois 60607.

CALIFORNIA ACHIEVEMENT TESTS: READING is a group achievement test. It has two forms and is for students in grades one through twelve. It measures comprehension, vocabulary, word attack, and spelling. It is published by California Test Bureau, CTB/McGraw-Hill, Del Monte Research Park, Monterey, California 93940.

DIAGNOSTIC READING TESTS is both an individual and a group diagnostic test. It has four forms and is for students in grades kindergarten to eight. It measures speed, comprehension, vocabulary, and word attack. It is published by The Committee on Diagnostic Reading Tests, Mountain Home, North Carolina 28758.

DOREN DIAGNOSTIC READING TEST is a group diagnostic test. It has one form and is for students in grades three through seven. It measures vocabulary and word attack. It is published by Educational Test Bureau, 720 Washington Avenue, SE, Minneapolis, Minnesota 55414.

DURRELL ANALYSIS OF READING DIFFICULTIES is an individual diagnostic test. It has one form and is for students in grades one through six. It measures speed, comprehension, vocabulary, word attack, and spelling. It is published by The Psychological Corporation, 757 Third Avenue, New York, New York 10017.

GATES MACGINITE READING TESTS is a group survey test. It has two forms and is for students in grades one through twelve. It measures speed, vocabulary, and comprehension. It is published by Riverside Publishing Company, 8420 Bryn Mawr, Chicago, Illinois 60631.

GATES MCKILLOP READING DIAGNOSTIC TESTS is an individual diagnostic test. It has two forms and is for students in grades one through six. It measures speed, vocabulary, word attack, spelling, and auding. It is published by Teachers College Press, 1234 Amsterdam Avenue, New York, New York 10027.

GILMORE ORAL READING TEST is an individual diagnostic test. It has two forms and is for students in grades one through six. It measures speed, vocabulary, comprehension, and word attack. It is published by Harcourt Brace Jovanovich, 757 Third Avenue, New York, New York 10017.

GRAY ORAL READING TEST is an individual diagnostic test. It has four forms and is for students in grades one through eight. It measures speed, vocabulary, comprehension, and auding. It is published by Bobbs-Merrill Educational Publishing, 4300 West Sixty-second Street, Indianapolis, Indiana 46206.

IOWA TEST OF BASIC SKILLS is a group achievement test. It has two forms and is for students in grades one through nine. It measures vocabulary and comprehension. It is published by Houghton Mifflin Company, 1 Beacon Street, Boston, Massachusetts 02107.

METROPOLITAN ACHIEVEMENT TESTS: READING is a group achievement test. It has four forms and is for students in grades one through twelve. It measures comprehension, vocabulary, and auding. It is published by The Psychological Corporation, 757 Third Avenue, New York, New York 10017.

MONROE-SHERMAN GROUP DIAGNOSTIC READING APTITUDE AND ACHIEVEMENT TESTS is a group diagnostic test. It has one form and is for students in grades three through nine. It measures speed, comprehension, vocabulary, word attack, and spelling. It is published by Nevins Publishing Company, 810 North Avenue West, Pittsburgh, Pennsylvania 15233.

PEABODY INDIVIDUAL ACHIEVEMENT TEST is an individual achievement test. It has two forms and is for students in grades kindergarten through twelve. It measures vocabulary, comprehension, and spelling. It is published by American Guidance Service, Inc., Publishers Building, Circle Pine, Minnesota 55014.

SPACHE DIAGNOSTIC READING SCALES is an individual diagnostic test. It has four forms and is for students in grades one through eight. It measures vocabulary and comprehension and has a supplementary phonics test. It is published by California Test Bureau, CTB/McGraw-Hill, Del Monte Research Park, Monterey, California 93940.

STANFORD ACHIEVEMENT TESTS: READING is a group achievement test. It has four forms and is for students in grades two through ten. It measures vocabulary and comprehension as well as other skills such as word study. It is published by The Psychological Corporation, 757 Third Avenue, New York, New York 10017.

STANFORD DIAGNOSTIC READING TEST is a group diagnostic test. It has four forms and is for students in grades two through eight. It measures vocabulary, comprehension, phonetic analysis, and structural analysis. It is published by The Psychological Corporation, 757 Third Avenue, New York, New York 10017.

WOODCOCK READING MASTERY TEST is an individual survey test. It has one form and is for students in grades kindergarten through twelve. It measures letter identification, word identification, word attack, word comprehension, and passage comprehension. It is published by American Guidance Service, Inc., Publishers Building, Circle Pine, Minnesota 55014.

Appendix B
NEWBERY MEDAL BOOKS

1922   Van Loon, Hendrik. *The Story of Mankind.*
1923   Lofting, Hugh. *The Voyages of Doctor Dolittle.*
1924   Hawes, Charles. *The Dark Frigate.*
1925   Finger, Charles J. *Tales from Silver Lands.*
1926   Chrisman, Arthur. *Shen of the Sea.*
1927   James, Will. *Smoky, the Cowhorse.*
1928   Mukerji, Dhan Gopal. *Gay Neck, the Story of a Pigeon.*
1929   Kelly, Eric P. *The Trumpeter of Krakow.*
1930   Field, Rachel. *Hitty, Her First Hundred Years.*
1931   Coatsworth, Elizabeth. *The Cat Who Went to Heaven.*
1932   Armer, Laura Adams. *Waterless Mountain.*
1933   Lewis, Elizabeth Foreman. *Young Fu of the Upper Yangtze.*
1934   Meigs, Cornelia. *Invincible Louisa.*
1935   Shannon, Monica. *Dobry.*
1936   Brink, Carol Ryrie. *Caddie Woodlawn.*
1937   Sawyer, Ruth. *Roller Skates.*
1938   Seredy, Kate. *The White Stag.*
1939   Enright, Elizabeth. *Thimble Summer.*
1940   Daugherty, James. *Daniel Boone.*
1941   Sperry, Armstrong. *Call It Courage.*
1942   Edmonds, Walter. *The Matchlock Gun.*
1943   Gray, Elizabeth Janet. *Adam of the Road.*

1944   Forbes, Esther. *Johnny Tremain.*

1945   Lawson, Robert. *Rabbit Hill.*

1946   Lenski, Lois. *Strawberry Girl.*

1947   Bailey, Carolyn Sherwin. *Miss Hickory.*

1948   DuBois, William Pene. *The Twenty-One Balloons.*

1949   Henry, Marguerite. *King of the Wind.*

1950   DeAngeli, Marguerite. *The Door in the Wall.*

1951   Yates, Elizabeth. *Amos Fortune, Free Man.*

1952   Estes, Eleanor. *Ginger Pye.*

1953   Clark, Ann Nolan. *Secret of the Andes.*

1954   Krumgold, Joseph. *. . . and now Miguel.*

1955   DeJong, Meindert. *The Wheel on the School.*

1956   Latham, Jean Lee. *Carry on, Mr. Bowditch.*

1957   Sorensen, Virginia. *Miracles on Maple Hill.*

1958   Keith, Harold. *Rifles for Watie.*

1959   Speare, Elizabeth George. *The Witch of Blackbird Pond.*

1960   Krumgold, Joseph. *Onion John.*

1961   O'Dell, Scott. *Island of the Blue Dolphins.*

1962   Speare, Elizabeth George. *The Bronze Bow.*

1963   L'Engle, Madeleine. *A Wrinkle in Time.*

1964   Neville, Emily. *It's Like This, Cat.*

1965   Wojciechowska, Mai. *Shadow of a Bull.*

1966   de Trevino, Elizabeth Borton. *I, Juan dePareja.*

1967   Hunt, Irene. *Up a Road Slowly.*

1968   Konigsburg, E. L. *From the Mixed-Up Files of Mrs. Basil E. Frankweiler.*

1969   Alexander, Lloyd. *The High King.*

1970   Armstrong, William H. *Sounder.*

1971   Byars, Betsy. *The Summer of the Swans.*

1972   O'Brien, Robert C. *Mrs. Frisby and the Rats of NIMH.*

1973   George, Jean Craighead. *Julie of the Wolves.*

1974   Fox, Paula. *The Slave Dancer.*

1975   Hamilton, Virginia. *M.C. Higgins, the Great.*

1976   Cooper, Susan. *The Grey King.*

1977   Taylor, Mildred D. *Roll of Thunder, Hear My Cry.*

1978   Paterson, Katherine. *Bridge to Terabithia.*

1979   Raskin, Ellen. *The Westing Game.*

1980   Bos, Joan W. *A Gathering of Days: A New England Girl's Journal.*

1981   Paterson, Katherine. *Jacob Have I Loved.*

1982   Willard, Nancy. *A Visit to William Blake's Inn: Poems for Innocent and Experienced Travelers.*

1983   Voigt, Cynthia. *Dicey's Song.*

1984   Cleary, Beverly. *Dear Mr. Henshaw.*

1985   McKinley, Robin. *The Hero and the Crown.*

1986   MacLachlan, Patricia. *Sarah, Plain and Tall.*

Appendix C
CALDECOTT MEDAL BOOKS

1938 Fish, Helen Dean (ed.) *Animals of the Bible*. Illustrated by Dorothy Lathrop.

1939 Handforth, Thomas. *Mei Li*.

1940 d'Aulaire, Ingri and Edgar Parin. *Abraham Lincoln*.

1941 Lawson, Robert. *They Were Strong and Good*.

1942 McCloskey, Robert. *Make Way for Ducklings*.

1943 Burton, Virginia Lee. *The Little House*.

1944 Thurber, James. *Many Moons*. Illustrated by Louis Slobodkin.

1945 Field, Rachel. *Prayer for a Child*. Illustrated by Elizabeth Orton Jones.

1946 Petersham, Maud and Miska. *The Rooster Crows*.

1947 MacDonald, Golden. *The Little Island*. Illustrated by Leonard Weisgard.

1948 Tresselet, Alvin. *White Snow, Bright Snow*. Illustrated by Roger Duvoisin.

1949 Hader, Berta and Elmer Hader. *The Big Snow*.

1950 Politi, Leo. *Song of the Swallows*.

1951 Milhous, Katherine. *The Egg Tree*.

1952 Mordovinoff, Nicholas, ill. (Nicholas, pseud.). William Lipkind (Will, pseud.). *Finders Keepers*.

1953 Ward, Lynd. *The Biggest Bear*.

1954 Bemelmans, Ludwig. *Madeline's Rescue*.

1955 Brown, Marcia. *Cinderella*. (translated from Charles Perrault).

1956 Rojankovsky, Feodor, ill. John Langstaff (retold by). *Frog Went A-Courtin'*.

1957 Simont, Marc, ill. Janice May Udry. *A Tree Is Nice*.

1958 McCloskey, Robert. *Time of Wonder*.

1959   Cooney, Barbara. *Chanticleer and the Fox*. Adapted from The Canterbury Tales.

1960   Ets, Marie Hall, ill. Aurora Labastida (co-author). *Nine Days to Christmas*.

1961   Sidjakov, Nicholas, ill. Ruth Robbins (retold by). *Baboushka and the Three Kings*. Russian folktale.

1962   Brown, Marcia. *Once a Mouse*. Retelling of a fable from the Hitopadesa.

1963   Keats, Ezra Jack. *The Snowy Day*.

1964   Sendak, Maurice. *Where the Wild Things Are*.

1965   Montresor, Beni, ill. Beatrice Schenk deRegniers. *May I Bring a Friend?*

1966   Hogrogian, Nonny, ill. Sorche Nic Leodhas. *Always Room for One More*. Derived from a Scottish nursery rhyme.

1967   Ness, Evaline. *Sam, Bangs, and Moonshine*.

1968   Emberley, Ed, ill. Barbara Emberley (adapted by). *Drummer Hoff*. Based on a 17th Century folk verse—John Ballshotthem.

1969   Shulevitz, Uri, ill. Arthur Ransome (retold by). *The Fool of the World and the Flying Ship*. Russian folktale.

1970   Steig, William. *Sylvester and the Magic Pebble*.

1971   Haley, Gail. *A Story—A Story*. Retelling of an African tale.

1972   Hogrogian, Nonny. *One Fine Day*. Inspired by an Armenian folktale.

1973   Lent, Blair, ill. Arlene Mosel (retold by). *The Funny Little Woman*. Japanese tale.

1974   Zemach, Margot, ill. Harve Zemach (retold by). *Duffy and the Devil*. Cornish tale.

1975   McDermott, Gerald. *Arrow to the Sun*. Adaptation of a Pueblo Indian tale.

1976   Dillon, Leo and Diane Dillon, (retold by). Illustrated by Verna Aardema. *Why Mosquitoes Buzz in People's Ears*. West African tale.

1977   Dillon, Leo and Diane Dillon. *Ashanti to Zulu: African Traditions*. Illustrated by Margaret Musgrove.

1978   Spier, Peter, ill. *Noah's Ark*. Includes Spier's translation of a 17th Century Dutch poem, The Flood, by Jacobus Revius.

1979   Goble, Paul. *The Girl Who Loved Wild Horses*.

1980   Cooney, Barbara. *Ox-Cart Man*. Illustrated by Donald Hall.

1981   Lobel, Arnold. *Fables*.

1982   Van Allsburg, Chris. *Jumanji*.

1983   Brown, Marcia. *Shadow*. Translation of a French poem by Blaise Cendrars.

1984   Provensen, Alice and Martin Provensen. *The Glorious Flight Across the Channel with Louis Blériot*.

1985   Hodges, Margaret, (retold by). Illustrated by Trina Schart Hyman. *Saint George and the Dragon*. (English legend retold from Edmund Spenser's *Faerie Queene*).

1986   Van Allsburg, Chris. *The Polar Express*.

Appendix D
A BIBLIOGRAPHY
OF
PREDICTABLE BOOKS*

Compiled by
Lynn K. Rhodes
University of Colorado-Denver
(Reprinted by permission of the author)

Predictable Trade Books

Alain. *One Two Three Going to Sea*. Englewood Cliffs, N.J.: Scholastic Book Services, 1964.

Aliki. *Go Tell Aunt Rhody*. New York: Macmillan, 1974.

———. *Hush Little Baby*. Englewood Cliffs, N.J.: Prentice-Hall, 1968.

———. *My Five Senses*. New York: Thomas Y. Crowell Co., 1962.

Asch, Frank. *Monkey Face*. New York: Parents Magazine Press, 1977.

Balian, Lorna. *The Animal*. New York: Abingdon Press, 1972.

———. *Where in the World Is Henry?* Scarsdale, New York: Bradbury Press, 1972.

Barchas, Sarah E. *I Was Walking Down the Road*. Englewood Cliffs, N.J.: Scholastic Book Services, 1975.

Baum, Arline and Joseph Baum. *One Bright Monday Morning*. New York: Random House, 1962.

Becker, John. *Seven Little Rabbits*. Englewood Cliffs, N.J.: Scholastic Book Services, 1973.

Beckman, Kaj. *Lisa Cannot Sleep*. New York: Franklin Watts, 1969.

Bellah, Melanie. *A First Book of Sounds*. Racine, Wisc.: Golden Press, 1963.

Boone, Rose, and Mills, Alan. *I Know an Old Lady*. New York: Rand McNally, 1961.

Brand, Oscar. *When I First Came to This Land*. New York: Putnam's Sons, 1974.

Brandenberg, Franz. *I Once Knew a Man*. New York: Macmillan, 1970.

Brown, Marcia. *The Three Billy Goats Gruff*. New York: Harcourt Brace Jovanovich, 1957.

Brown, Margaret Wise. *Four Fur Feet*. New York: William R. Scott, 1961.

———. *Goodnight Moon*. New York: Harper & Row, 1947.

———. *Home for a Bunny*. Racine, Wisc.: Golden Press, 1956.

———. *Where Have You Been?* Englewood Cliffs, N.J.: Scholastic Book Services, 1952.

Carle, Eric. *The Grouchy Ladybug*. New York: Thomas Y. Crowell, 1977.

———. *The Very Hungry Caterpillar*. Cleveland: Collins World, 1969.

———. *The Mixed Up Chameleon*. New York: Thomas Y. Crowell, 1975.

Charlip, Remy. *Fortunately*. New York: Parents' Magazine Press, 1964.

———. *What Good Luck! What Bad Luck!* Englewood Cliffs, N.J.: Scholastic Book Services, 1969.

Cook, Bernadine. *The Little Fish That Got Away*. Reading, Mass.: Addison-Wesley, 1976.

de Regniers, Beatrice Schenk. *Catch a Little Fox*. New York: Seabury Press, 1970.

———. *May I Bring a Friend?* New York: Atheneum, 1972.

———. *The Day Everybody Cried*. New York: The Viking Press, 1967.

———. *Willy O'Dwyer Jumped in the Fire*. New York: Atheneum, 1968.

———. *How Joe the Bear and Sam the Mouse Got Together*. New York: Parents' Magazine Press, 1965.

———. *The Little Book*. New York: Henry Z. Walck, 1961.

Domanska, Janina. *If All the Seas Were One Sea*. New York: Macmillan, 1971.

Duff, Maggie. *Jonny and His Drum*. New York: Henry Z. Walck, 1972.

———. *Rum Pum Pum*. New York: Macmillan, 1978.

Emberley, Barbara. *Simon's Song*. Englewood Cliffs, N.J.: Prentice-Hall, 1969.

Emberly, Ed. *Klippity Klop*. Boston: Little, Brown & Co., 1974.

Ets, Marie Hall. *Elephant in a Well*. New York: Viking Press, 1972.

———. *Play with Me*. New York: Viking Press, 1955.

Flack, Marjorie. *Ask Mr. Bear*. New York: Macmillan, 1932.

Galdone, Paul. *Henny Penny*. Englewood Cliffs, N.J.: Scholastic Book Services, 1968.

———. *The Little Red Hen*. Englewood Cliffs, N.J.: Scholastic Book Services, 1973.

———. *The Three Bears*. Englewood Cliffs, N.J.: Scholastic Book Services, 1972.

———. *The Three Billy Goats Gruff*. New York: Seabury Press, 1973.

———. *The Three Little Pigs*. New York: Seabury Press, 1970.

Ginsburg, Mirra. *The Chick and the Duckling*. New York: Macmillan, 1972.

Greenberg, Polly. *Oh Lord, I Wish I Was a Buzzard*. New York: Macmillan, 1968.

Hoffman, Hilde. *The Green Grass Grows All Around*. New York: Macmillan, 1968.

Hutchins, Pat. *Good-Night Owl*. New York: Macmillan, 1972.

———. *Rosie's Walk*. New York: Macmillan, 1968.

———. *Titch*. New York: Collier Books, 1971.

Keats, Ezra Jack. *Over in the Meadow*. Englewood Cliffs, N.J.: Scholastic Book Services, 1971.

Kent, Jack. *The Fat Cat*. Englewood Cliffs, N.J.: Scholastic Book Services, 1971.

Klein, Leonore. *Brave Daniel*. Englewood Cliffs, N.J.: Scholastic Book Services, 1958.

Kraus, Robert. *Whose Mouse Are You?* New York: Collier Books, 1970.

Langstaff, John. *Frog Went A-Courtin'*. New York: Harcourt Brace Jovanovich, 1955.

———. *Oh, A-Hunting We Will Go*. New York: Atheneum, 1974.

———. *Over in the Meadow*. New York: Harcourt Brace Jovanovich, 1957.

———. *Gather My Gold Together: Four Songs for Four Seasons*. Garden City, N.Y.: Doubleday & Co., 1971.

Laurence, Ester. *We're Off to Catch a Dragon*. Nashville, N.Y.: Abingdon Press, 1969.

Lexau, Joan. *Crocodile and Hen*. New York: Harper & Row, 1969.

Lobel, Anita. *King Rooster, Queen Hen*. New York: Greenwillow Books, 1975.

Lobel, Arnold. *A Treeful of Pigs*. New York: Greenwillow Books, 1979.

Mack, Stan. *10 Bears in My Bed*. New York: Pantheon Books, 1974.

Mayer, Mercer. *If I Had . . .* New York: Dial Press, 1968.

———. *Just for You*. New York: Golden Press, 1975.

McGovern, Ann. *Too Much Noise*. Englewood Cliffs, N.J.: Scholastic Book Services, 1967.

Memling, Carl. *Ten Little Animals*. Racine, Wisc.: Golden Press, 1961.

Moffett, Martha. *A Flower Pot is Not a Hat*. New York: E.P. Dutton & Co., 1972.

Peppe, Rodney. *The House That Jack Built*. New York: Delacorte Press, 1970.

Polushkin, Maria. *Mother, Mother, I Want Another*. New York: Crown Publishers, 1978.

Preston, Edna Mitchell. *Where Did My Mother Go?* New York: Four Winds Press, 1978.

Quackenbush, Robert. *She'll Be Comin' Round the Mountain*. New York: J.B. Lippincott, 1973.

———. *Skip to My Lou*. Philadelphia: J.B. Lippincott, 1975.

Rokoff, Sandra. *Here is a Cat*. Singapore: Hallmark Children's Editions, undated.

Scheer, Jullian and Marvin Bileck. *Rain Makes Applesauce*. New York: Holiday House, 1964.

———. *Upside Down Day*. New York: Holiday House, 1968.

Sendak, Maurice. *Where the Wild Things Are*. Englewood Cliffs, N.J.: Scholastic Book Services, 1963.

Shaw, Charles B. *It Looked Like Spilt Milk*. New York: Harper & Row, 1947.

Shulevitz, Uri. *One Monday Morning*. New York: Charles Scribner's Sons, 1967.

Skaar, Grace. *What Do the Animals Say?* Englewood Cliffs, N.J.: Scholastic Book Services, 1972.

Sonneborn, Ruth A. *Someone is Eating the Sun*. New York: Random House, 1974.

Spier, Peter. *The Fox Went Out on a Chilly Night*. Garden City, N.Y.: Doubleday & Co., 1961.

Stover, Joann. *If Everybody Did*. New York: David McKay, 1960.

Tolstoy, Alexei. *The Great Big Enormous Turnip*. New York: Franklin Watts, 1968.

Welber, Robert. *Goodbye, Hello*. New York: Pantheon Books, 1974.

Wildsmith, Brian. *The Twelve Days of Christmas*. New York: Franklin Watts, 1972.

Wolkstein, Diane. *The Visit*. New York: Alfred A. Knopf, 1977.

Wondriska, William. *All the Animals Were Angry*. New York: Holt, Rinehart and Winston, 1970.

Zaid, Barry. *Chicken Little*. New York: Random House, undated.

Zemach, Harve. *The Judge*. New York: Farrar, Straus, & Giroux, 1969.

Zemach, Margot. *Hush, Little Baby*. New York: E.P. Dutton & Co., 1976.

———. *The Teeny Tiny Woman*. Englewood Cliffs, N.J.: Scholastic Book Services, 1965.

Zolotow, Charlotte. *Do You Know What I'll Do?* New York: Harper & Row, 1958.

*1980 Revision.

Appendix E
NAMES AND ADDRESSES OF PUBLISHERS

Abingdon Press
201 Eighth Ave. South
Nashville, Tenn. 37202

Abrahams Magazine Service
56 E. 13th St.
New York, N.Y. 10003

Academic Press
111 Fifth Ave.
New York, N.Y. 10003

Academic Therapy Publications
20 Commercial Blvd.
Novatio, Calif. 94947

Acropolis Books Ltd.
2400 17th Street, N.W.
Washington, D.C. 20009

Addison-Wesley Publishing
  Company
Jacob Way
Reading, Mass. 01867

Addison-Wesley Testing Service
2725 Sand Hill Rd.
Menlo Park, Calif. 94025

Albert Whitman and Company
560 W. Lake St.
Chicago, Ill. 60606

Allyn and Bacon
7 Wells Ave.
Newton, Mass. 02159

American Council on Education
1 Dupont Circle
Washington, D.C. 20036

American Guidance Service
Publishers' Building
Circle Pines, Minn. 55014

American Printing House for the
  Blind
P.O. Box 6085
Louisville, Ky. 40206

Association for Childhood
   Education International
3615 Wisconsin Ave., N.W.
Washington, D.C. 20016

Audio-Visual Research
1317 Eighth St., S.E.
Waseca, Minn. 56093

Baker and Taylor Company
1515 Broadway
New York, N.Y. 10036

Bantam Books
School and College Marketing
   Division
666 Fifth Ave.
New York, N.Y. 10019

Barnell Loft, Ltd.
958 Church St.
Baldwin, N.Y. 11510

Basic Skills Program
Office of Basic Skills Improvement
Room 1167—Donohoe Building
400 Maryland Ave., S.W.
Washington, D.C. 20202

Bell and Howell
Audio-Visual Products Division
7100 N. McCormick Road
Chicago, Ill. 60645

Benefic Press
1250 Sixth Ave.
San Diego, Calif. 92101

Bobbs-Merrill Educational
   Publishing
4300 W. 62nd St.
P.O. Box 7080
Indianapolis, Ind. 46206

Borg-Warner Educational Systems
600 W. University Drive
Arlington Heights, Ill. 60004

R.R. Bowker Company
1180 Avenue of the Americas
New York, N.Y. 10036

Bowmar Noble Publishers
4563 Colorado Blvd.
Los Angeles, Calif. 90039

Burgless Publishing Company
7108 Ohms Lane
Minneapolis, Minn. 55435

C.C. Publications
P.O. Box 23699
Tigaro, Ore. 97223

Center for Applied Research in
   Education
P.O. Box 130
West Nyack, N.Y. 10995

Charles E. Merrill Publishing
   Company
1300 Alum Creek Drive
Columbus, Ohio 43216

The Children's Book Council
67 Irving Place
New York, N.Y. 10003

Children's Press
1224 W. Van Buren St.
Chicago, Ill. 60607

Clarence L. Barnhart
Box 250
1 Stone Place
Bronxville, N.Y. 10708

College Skills Center
1250 Broadway
New York, N.Y. 10001

The Committee on Diagnostic
   Reading Tests
Mountain Home,
North Carolina 28758

Communacad
Box 541
Wilton, Conn. 06897

Consulting Psychologists Press
577 College Ave.
Palo Alto, Calif. 94306

Coronet
65 E. South Water St.
Chicago, Ill. 60601

Council for Exceptional Children
1920 Association Drive
Reston, Va. 22091

Creative Curriculum
15681 Commerce Lane
Huntington Beach, Calif. 92649

Crown Publishers
1 Park Ave.
New York, N.Y. 10016

CTB/McGraw-Hill
Del Monte Research Park
Monterey, Calif. 93940

Curriculum Associates
5 Esquire Road
North Billerica, Mass. 01862

C. Lucas Dalton
5720 Caruth Haven
Suite 130
Dallas, Texas 75206

Dell Publishing Company
Education Dept.
245 E. 47th St.
New York, N.Y. 10017

DES Educational Publications
25 S. Fifth Ave.
P.O. Box 1291
Highland Park, N.J. 08904

Developmental Learning Materials
7440 Natchez Ave.
Niles, Ill. 60648

Dreier Educational Systems
25 S. Fifth Ave.
P.O. Box 1291
Highland Park, N.J. 08904

A.B. Dick Company
5700 Touhy Ave.
Chicago, Ill. 60648

Dome Press
1169 Logan Ave.
Elgin, Ill. 60120

Doubleday & Company
501 Franklin Ave.
Garden City, N.Y. 11530

EBSCO Curriculum Materials
Box 11521
Birmingham, Ala. 35202

The Economy Company
Box 25308
1901 W. Walnut St.
Oklahoma City, Okla. 73125

EDL/McGraw-Hill
1221 Avenue of the Americas
New York, N.Y. 10020

Educational Activities
P.O. Box 392
Freeport, N.Y. 11520

Educational Progress Division of
    Educational Development
    Corporation
P.O. Box 45663
Tulsa, Okla. 74145

Educational Service
P.O. Box 219
Stevensville, Mich. 49127

Educational Test Bureau
720 Washington Ave., SE
Minneapolis, Minn. 55414

Educational Testing Service
Box 999
Princeton, N.J. 08540

Educators Publishing Service
75 Moulton St.
Cambridge, Mass. 02138

Encyclopedia Britannica Educational
   Corporation
425 N. Michigan Ave.
Chicago, Ill. 60611

E & R Development Company
Vandalia Road
Jacksonville, Fla. 62650

ERIC Clearinghouse on Reading
   and Communication Skills
National Council of Teachers of
   English
1111 Kenyon Road
Urbana, Ill. 61801

Essay Press
P.O. Box 2323
La Jolla, Calif. 92037

Fawcett Books Group
Educational Marketing Dept.
1515 Broadway
New York, N.Y. 10036

Fearon-Pitman Publishers
6 Davis Drive
Belmont, Calif. 94002

Follett Publishing Company
Dept. D.M.
1010 W. Washington Blvd.
Chicago, Ill. 60607

Franklin Watts
730 Fifth Ave.
New York, N.Y. 10019

Frohnhoefer's Books
R.D. 1, Route 9G
Tivoli, N.Y. 12583

Garrard Publishing Company
1607 N. Market St.
Champaign, Ill. 61820

Ginn and Company
P.O. Box 2749
1250 Fairwood Ave.
Columbus, Ohio 43216

Globe Book Company
50 W. 23rd St.
New York, N.Y. 10010

Gorsuch Scarisbrick Publishers
576 Central Ave.
Dubuque, Iowa 52001

Grossett & Dunlap
Education Division
51 Madison Ave.
New York, N.Y. 10010

Grove Press
196 W. Houston St.
New York, N.Y. 10014

E.M. Hale and Company
Harvey House Publishers
128 W. River St.
Chippewa Falls, Wisc. 54729

Harcourt Brace Jovanovich
757 Third Ave.
New York, N.Y. 10017

Harper & Row
10 E. 53rd St.
New York, N.Y. 10022

Hawthorn Books
260 Madison Ave.
New York, N.Y. 10016

Hayden Book Company
50 Essex St.
Rochelle Park, N.J. 07662

D.C. Heath
125 Spring St.
Lexington, Mass. 02173

Heinemann Educational Books
4 Front St.
Exeter, N.H. 03833

Hertzberg-New Method
Vandalia Road
Jacksonville, Ill. 62650

Holt, Rinehart & Winston
CBS Inc.
383 Madison Ave.
New York, N.Y. 10017

Houghton Mifflin
1 Beacon St.
Boston, Mass. 02107

Ideal School Supply Company
11000 S. Lavergne Ave.
Oak Lawn, Ill. 60453

Imperial International Learning
Corporation
P.O. Box 548
Kankakee, Ill. 60901

Incentives for Learning
600 W. Van Buren St.
Chicago, Ill. 60607

Instructional Fair
Box 1650
Grand Rapids, Mich. 49501

Instructor Publications
7 Bank St.
Dansville, N.Y. 14437

International Reading Association
800 Barksdale Road
Newark, Del. 19711

ITA, A Non-Profit Educational
Foundation
Hofstra University
Hempstead, N.Y. 11550

Jamestown Publishers
P.O. Box 6743
Providence, R.I. 02940

Kendall/Hunt Publishing Co.
2460 Kerper Blvd.
Dubuque, Iowa 52001

Kenworthy Educational Service
Box 60
138 Allen St.
Buffalo, N.Y. 14205

Keystone View
Division of Mast Development
Company
2212 E. 12th St.
Davenport, Iowa 52803

Kimbo Educational Publishers
P.O. Box 477
Long Branch, N.J. 07740

The Kingsbury Center
2138 Bancroft Pl., N.W.
Washington, D.C. 20008

The Klamath Printery
628 Oak St.
Klamath Falls, Ore. 97601

Kraus-Thomson Organization, Ltd.
Rte. 100
Millwood, N.Y. 10546

Language Research Associates
P.O. Drawer 2085
Palm Springs, Calif. 92262

Lansford Publishing Company
1088 Lincoln Ave.
P.O. Box 8711
San Jose, Calif. 95155

Learning Arts
P.O. Box 179
Wichita, Kan. 67201

Learning Associates
P.O. Box 561167
Miami, Fla. 33156

The Learning Line
Box 577
Palo Alto, Calif. 94302

Learning Resources Corporation
8517 Production Ave.
San Diego, Calif. 92121

Leswing Press
P.O. Box 3577
San Rafael, Calif. 94901

Library of Congress
National Library Service for the
  Blind and Physically Handicapped
1291 Taylor St., N.W.
Washington, D.C. 20542

Listening Library
1 Park Ave.
Old Greenwich, Conn. 06870

Litton Educational Publishing
7625 Empire Drive
Florence, Ky. 41042

Longman
19 W. 44th St.
New York, N.Y. 10036

The Macmillan Company
Front and Brown Sts.
Riverside, N.J. 08370

McCormick-Mathers Publishing
  Company, A Division of Litton
  Educational Publishing
7625 Empire Drive
Florence, Ky. 41042

McDougal, Littell & Company
P.O. Box 1667-C
Evanston, Ill. 60204

McGraw-Hill Book Company
1221 Avenue of the Americas
New York, N.Y. 10020

McGraw-Hill Ryerson Ltd.
330 Progress Ave.
Scarborough, Ontario
Canada M1P 2Z5

Mast Development Company
2212 E. 12th St.
Davenport, Iowa 52803

Media Materials
Department MDR
2936 Remington Ave.
Baltimore, Md. 21211

G. & C. Merriam Company
47 Federal St.
Springfield, Mass. 01101

Charles E. Merrill Publishing
  Company
1300 Alum Creek Drive
Columbus, Ohio 43216

Midwest Publications
P.O. Box 448
Pacific Grove, Calif. 93950

Milton Bradley Company
Springfield, Mass. 01101

Montana Reading Publications
517 Remrock Road
Billings, Mont. 59102

William Morrow & Company
105 Madison Ave.
New York, N.Y. 10016

National Association for the Deaf
814 Thayer Ave.
Silver Springs, Md. 20910

National Council of Teachers
of English
1111 Kenyon Road
Urbana, Ill. 61801

National Public Radio
2025 M Street, N.W.
Washington, D.C. 20036

National Textbook Company
8259 Viles Center Road
Skokie, Ill. 60077

NCS/Educational Systems Division
4401 W. 76th St.
Minneapolis, Minn. 55435

Nevins Publishing Company
810 North Avenue West
Pittsburgh, Penn. 15233

W.W. Norton & Company
500 Fifth Ave.
New York, N.Y. 10036

Open Court Publishing Company
Box 599
LaSalle, Ill. 61301

Parents Magazine Press
685 Third Avenue
New York, N.Y. 10017

Phonovisual Products
12216 Parklawn Drive
P.O. Box 2007
Rockville, Md. 20852

Pitman Learning (formerly Fearon-
Pitman Publishers)
6 Davis Drive
Belmont, Calif. 94002

Plays
8 Arlington St.
Boston, Mass. 02116

Prentice-Hall
Educational Book Division
Englewood Cliffs, N.J. 07632

Pro-Ed
5341 Industrial Oaks Blvd.
Austin, Tex. 78735

Programs for Achievement in
Readings
Abbott Park Place
Providence, R.I. 02903

Pruett Publishing Company
3235 Prairie Ave.
Boulder, Colo. 80301

The Psychological Corporation
757 Third Ave.
New York, N.Y. 10017

Psychological Test Specialists
Box 9229
Missoula, Mont. 59807

Publishers Test Service
2500 Garden Road
Monterey, Calif. 93940

G.P. Putnam's Sons
Coward McCann & Geoghegan
200 Madison Ave.
New York, N.Y. 10016

Rand McNally and Company
Box 7600
Chicago, Ill. 60680

Random House
201 E. 50th St.
New York, N.Y. 10022

Reader's Digest Services
Educational Division
Pleasantville, N.Y. 10570

The Reading Laboratory
P.O. Box 681
South Norwalk, Conn. 06854

Resources
Instructional Communication
Technology, Inc.
Huntington Station, N.Y. 11746

Riverside Publishing Company
8420 Bryn Mawr
Chicago, Ill. 60631

Santillana Publishing Company
575 Lexington Ave.
New York, N.Y. 10022

Scarecrow Press
52 Liberty St.
Box 656
Metuchen, N.J. 08840

Scholastic Book Services
904 Sylvan Ave.
Englewood Cliffs, N.J. 07632

Scott, Foresman and Company
1900 E. Lake Ave.
Glenview, Ill. 60025

Simon & Schuster
Simon & Schuster Building
1230 Avenue of the Americas
New York, N.Y. 10020

Slosson Educational Publications
P.O. Box 280
East Aurora, N.Y. 14052

Smithsonian Institution
475 L'Enfant Plaza
Suite 4800
Washington, D.C. 20560

SRA
Science Research Associates
155 N. Wacker Drive
Chicago, Ill. 60606

Steck-Vaughn Company
Box 2028
Austin, Tex. 78767

Stoelting Company
1350 S. Kostner Ave.
Chicago, Ill. 60623

Strine Publishing Company
P.O. Box 149
York, Pa. 17405

Sunburst Communications
Room U 23
39 Washington Ave.
Pleasantville, N.Y. 10570

SVE
Society for Visual Educational Inc.
1345 Diversey Parkway
Chicago, Ill. 60614

Teachers College Press
Teachers College
Columbia University
1234 Amsterdam Ave.
New York, N.Y. 10027

Teaching Resources Corporation
50 Pond Park Road
Hingham, Mass. 02043

University of Chicago Press
5801 South Ellis Ave.
Chicago, Ill. 60637

University of Illinois Press
54 E. Gregory Drive
P.O. Box 5081
Station A
Champaign, Ill. 61820

University of Nebraska Press
318 Nebraska Hall
901 N. 17th St.
Lincoln, Neb. 68588

The Viking Press
Viking Penguin, Inc.
625 Madison Ave.
New York, N.Y. 10022

J. Weston Walch, Publisher
321 Valley St.
Portland, Me. 04104

Webster Division of McGraw-Hill
  Book Company
1221 Avenue of the Americas
New York, N.Y. 10020

Weekly Reader
Long Hill Road
Middletown, Conn. 06457

Weekly Reader/Secondary Unit
  Books
1250 Fairwood Ave.
P.O. Box 16618
Columbus, Ohio 43216

Western Psychological Services
12031 Wilshire Blvd.
Los Angeles, Calif. 90025

William C. Brown Company,
  Publishers

2460 Kerper Blvd.
Dubuque, Iowa 52001

World Book-Childcraft
    International
Merchandise Mart Plaza
Chicago, Ill. 60654

The H.W. Wilson Company
950 University Ave.
Bronx, N.Y. 10452

Richard L. Zweig Associates
20800 Beach Blvd.
Huntington Beach, Calif. 92648

REFERENCES

AKELAITIS, A. J. (1944). A study of gnosis, praxis and language following sectioning of the corpus collosum and anterior commisure. *Journal of Neurosurgery, 1*, 94–102.

ALEXANDER, P. (1984). Training analogical reasoning skills in the gifted. *Roeper Review, 6*, 191–194.

ALEXANDER, P., GOETZ, E., PALMER, D., & MANGANO, N. (1983). Examining the effects of direct instruction in analogical reasoning on reading comprehension. In J. Niles & L. Harris (Eds.), *Searching for meaning in reading/ language processing and instruction.* Rochester, NY: National Reading Conference.

ALLEN, A. R., & BORAKS, N. (1978). Peer tutoring: putting it to the test. *Reading Teacher, 31*, 274–280.

ALLEN, P. D., & WATSON, D. J. (1976). *Findings of research in miscue analysis: Classroom implications.* Urbana, IL: National Council of Teachers of English.

ALLEN, R. V. (1976). *Language experience in communication.* Boston: Houghton Mifflin.

ANDERSON, C. A., & BOWMAN, M. J. (1976). Education and economic modernization in historical perspective. In L. Stone (Ed.), *School and society: Studies in the history of education.* Baltimore: Johns Hopkins University Press.

ANDERSON, J. R. (1976). *Language, memory and thought.* Hillsdale, NJ: Lawrence Erlbaum.

ANDERSON, J. R. (1980). *Cognitive psychology and its implications.* San Francisco: W. H. Freeman & Company Publishers.

ANDERSON, J. R. (1983). *The architecture of cognition.* Cambridge, MA: Harvard University Press.

ANDERSON, L., EVERTSON, C., & EMMER, E. (1980). Dimensions in classroom management derived from recent research. *Journal of Curriculum Studies, 12*, 343–356.

ANDERSON, R. C., HIEBERT, E. H., SCOTT, J. A., & WILKINSEN, I. A. (1985). *Becoming a nation of readers.* Washington, DC: National Institute of Education.

ANDERSON, R. C., & PEARSON, P. D. (1984). A schema-theoretic view of basic processes in reading comprehension. In P. D. Pearson, R. Barr & M. Kamil (Eds.), *Handbook of Reading Research.* New York: Longman.

ANDERSON, T. H. (1978). *Study skills and learning strategies.* University of Illinois. Urbana, IL: Center for the Study of Reading.

ASHER, S. (1980). Topic interest and children's reading comprehension. In R. Spiro, B. Bruce, & W. Brewer (Eds.), *Theoretical issues in reading comprehension*. Hillsdale, NJ: Lawrence Erlbaum.

ASHTON-WARNER, S. (1963). *Teacher*. New York: Simon & Schuster.

ASKER, W. (1923). Does knowledge of grammar function? *School and Society, 17*, 107–111.

BAIN, A. (1869). *English composition and rhetoric*. New York: Prentice-Hall, Appleton-Century-Crofts.

BAIRD, J. R., & WHITE, R. T. (1982). Promoting self-control of learning. *Instructional Science, 11*, 227–247.

BAKER, L., & BROWN, A. L. (1984). Metacognitive skills and reading. In P. D. Pearson, R. Barr, & M. Kamil (Eds.). *Handbook of Reading Research*. New York: Longman.

BAKER, L., & STEIN, N. L. (1981). The development of prose comprehension skills. In C. M. Santa & B. L. Hayes (Eds.), *Children's prose comprehension*. Newark, DE: International Reading Association.

BARR, R. (1975). How children are taught to read: Grouping and pacing. *School Review, 83*, 479–498.

BARTEL, N. R. (1975). Problems in language development. In D. D. Hammill & N. R. Bartel (Eds.), *Children with learning disabilities*. Boston, MA: Allyn & Bacon.

BAUMANN, J. F. (1984, November). Implication for reading instruction from the research on teacher and school effectiveness. *Journal of Reading, 28*, 109–113.

BEAN, R. M. (1979). The role of the reading specialist: A multifaceted role. *Reading Teacher, 32*, 409–413.

BEAN, R. M., & EICHELBERGER, R. T. (1985). Changing the role of reading specialists: From pull-out to in-class programs. *Reading Teacher, 38*, 648–653.

BEAN, R. M., & WILSON, R. M. (1981). *Effecting change in school reading programs: The resource role*. Newark, DE: International Reading Association.

BECK, I. (1984). Developing comprehension: The impact of the directed reading lesson. In R. C. Anderson, J. Osborn, & R. J. Tierney (Eds.), *Learning to read in American schools: Basal readers and content text*. Hillsdale, NJ: Lawrence Erlbaum.

BECK, I., PERFETTI, C., & MCKEOWN, M. (1982). Effects of long-term vocabulary instruction on lexical access and reading comprehension. *Journal of Educational Psychology, 74*, 506–521.

BECKER, W. C., DIXON, R., & ANDERSON-INMAN, L. (1980). *Morphographic and root word analysis of 26,000 high frequency words*. Eugene, OR: University of Oregon.

BEEBE, B. F. (1968). *African elephants*. New York: David McKay.

BELDIN, H. O. (1970). Informal reading testing: Historical review and review of the research. In W. Durr (Ed.), *Reading difficulties, correction and remediation*. Newark, DE: International Reading Association.

BELLEZZA, F. S. (1981). Mnemonic devices: Classification, characteristics and criteria. *Review of Educational Research, 51*, 247–275.

BEREITER, C., & ENGLEMAN, S. (1967). *Teaching disadvantaged children in the preschool*. Englewood Cliffs, NJ: Prentice-Hall.

BERLINER, D. C. (1979). Tempus educare. In P. L. Peterson & H. J. Walberg (Eds.), *Research on Teaching*. Berkeley, CA: McCutchan.

BERLINER, D. C. (1981). Academic learning time and reading achievement. In J. T. Guthrie (Ed.), *Comprehension and teaching: Research reviews*. Newark, DE: International Reading Association.

BERLINER, D. C. (1984). The half-full glass: A review of research on teaching. In P. L. Hosford (Ed.), *Using what we know about teaching*. Alexandria, VA: Association for Supervision and Curriculum Development.

BERRY, M. F., & EISENSON, J. (1956). *Speech disorders: principles and practices of therapy*. New York: Prentice-Hall, Appleton-Century-Crofts.

BETTENCOURT, E. M., GILLETT, M. H., GALL, M. D., & HULL, R. E. (1983). Effects of teacher enthusiasm training on student on-task behavior and achievement. *American Education Research Journal, 20*, 435–450.

BEVER, T. G., LACKNER, J. R., & KIRK, R. (1969). The underlying structures of sentences are the primary units of immediate speech processing. *Perception and Psychophysics, 5*, 225–231.

BLOOMFIELD, L., & BARNHART, C. (1961). *Let's read: A linguistic approach*. Detroit, MI: Wayne State University.

BOAST, W. M. (1974). *Message design.* Dubuque, IA: Kendall/Hunt.

BODEK, N. (1984/85). Werner Erhard on transformation and productivity: An interview. *Revision, 7,* 30–38.

BORAAS, J. (1917). *Formal English grammar and the practical mastery of English.* Unpublished doctoral dissertation, University of Minnesota.

BORMUTH, J. (1968). The cloze readability procedure. *Elementary English, 45,* 429–436.

BORTNICK, R., & LOPARDO, G. S. (1973). An instructional application of the cloze procedure. *Journal of Reading, 16,* 296–300.

BRANSFORD, J. D., & FRANKS, J. J. (1971). The abstraction of linguistic ideas. *Cognitive Psychology, 2,* 331–350.

BRANSFORD, J. D., & JOHNSON, M. K. (1972). Contextual prerequisites for understanding: Some investigations of comprehension and recall. *Journal of Verbal Learning and Verbal Behavior, 11,* 717–726.

BRANSFORD, J. D., & JOHNSON, M. K. (1973). Considerations of some problems of comprehension. In W. C. Chase (Ed.), *Visual information processing.* New York: Academic Press.

BREWER, W. F. (1980). Literary theory, rhetoric and stylistics: Implications for psychology. In R. J. Spiro, B. C. Bruce, & W. F. Brewer (Eds.), *Theoretical issues in reading comprehension.* Hillsdale, NJ: Lawrence Erlbaum.

BRIGGS, T. H. (1913). Formal English grammar as a discipline. *Teachers College Record, 14,* 1–93.

BROADBENT, D. E. (1958). *Perception and communication.* London: Pergamon Press.

BROPHY, J. (1983). Classroom organization and management. *The Elementary School Journal, 83,* 265–286.

BROWN, A. (1980). Metacognitive development and reading. In R. J. Spiro, B. C. Bruce, & W. F. Brewer (Eds.), *Theoretical issues in reading comprehension.* Hillsdale, NJ: Lawrence Erlbaum.

BROWN, A., & DAY, J. (1983). Macrorules for summarizing texts: The development of expertise. *Journal of Verbal Learning and Verbal Behavior, 22,* 1–14.

BROWN, A., & SMILEY, S. (1977). Rating the importance of structural units of prose passages: A problem of metacognitive development. *Child Development, 48,* 1–8.

BROWN, R. (1972). *Psycholinguistics: Selected papers.* New York: Macmillan Publishing Co., Free Press.

BROWN, R. (1973). *A First Language.* Cambridge, MA: Harvard University Press.

BROWN, R., & MCNEILL, D. (1966). The tip of the tongue phenomenon. *Journal of Verbal Learning and Verbal Behavior, 5,* 325–337.

BRUCE, B. C. (1980). Plans and social actions. In R. J. Spiro, B. C. Bruce, & W. F. Brewer (Eds.), *Theoretical issues in reading comprehension.* Hillsdale, NJ: Lawrence Erlbaum.

BRUNER, J. (1973). The ontogenesis of speech acts. *Journal of Child Language, 2,* 10–19.

BRYDEN, M. P., & LEY, R. G. (1983). Right-hemispheric involvement in the perception and expression of emotion in normal humans. In K. Heilman & P. Satz (Eds.), *Neuropsychology of Human Emotion.* New York: Guilford Press.

BRYEN, D. N. (1983). *Inquiries into child language.* Boston: Allyn & Bacon.

BURKE, C. L. (1980). Reading interview. In B. R. Farr & D. J. Strickler (Eds.). *Reading comprehension: An instructional videotape series* (Resource Guide). Bloomington, IN: Indiana University Press.

BURNS, P. C., ROE, B. D., & ROSS, E. P. (1984). *Teaching reading in today's elementary schools.* Boston: Houghton Mifflin.

BUROS, O. K. (Ed.). (1975). *Reading tests and reviews II.* Highland Park, NJ: Gryphon Editions.

BUROS, O. K. (Ed.). (1978). *The eighth mental measurements yearbook.* Highland Park, NJ: Gryphon Editions.

BUSSIS, A., CHITTENDON, E., & AMAREL, M. (1976). *Beyond surface curriculum.* Boulder, CO: Westview Press.

CARROLL, J. M., & BEVER, T. G. (1976). Sentence comprehension: A case study in the relation of knowledge and perception. In E. C. Carterette & M. P. Friedman (Eds.), *Handbook and perception, vol. VII: Language and speech.* New York: Academic Press.

CATHERWOOD, C. (1932). *A study of relationships between knowledge of rules and abilities to correct grammatical errors and between identification of sentences and knowledge of subject and predicate.* Unpublished master's thesis, University of Minnesota.

CHAFE, W. L. (1970). *Meaning and the structure of language.* Chicago: University of Chicago Press.

CHEYNEY, A. B. (1984). *Teaching reading skills through the newspaper.* Newark, DE: International Reading Association.

CHOMSKY, N. (1957). *Syntactic structures.* The Hague: Mouton.

CHOMSKY, N. (1965). *Aspects of a theory of syntax.* Cambridge, MA: MIT Press.

CHOMSKY, N. (1968). *Language and mind.* New York: Harcourt Brace Jovanovich.

CHOMSKY, N., & HALLE, M. (1968). *The sound pattern of English.* New York: Harper & Row.

CIPOLLA, C. M. (1969). *Literacy and development in the west.* Baltimore: Penguin.

CLARKE, M., LOSOFF, A., McCRACKEN, M. D., & ROOD, D. S. (1984). Linguistic relativity and sex/gender studies: Epistemological and methodological considerations. *Language Learning, 34,* 47–67.

CLARKE, M., LOSOFF, A., & ROOD, D. S. (1982). Untangling referent and reference in linguistic relativity studies: A response from Clark et al. *Language Learning, 32,* 209–217.

CLIFFORD, G. J. (1984). Buch und lesen: Historical perspective in literacy and schooling. *Review of Educational Research, 54,* 472–500.

CLOWARD, R. (1967). Studies in tutoring. *Journal of Experimental Education, 36,* 14–25.

COHEN, P. (1968). The effect of literature on vocabulary and reading achievement. *Elementary English, 45,* 209–13; 217.

COLLINS, M. L. (1978). Effects of enthusiasm training on preservice elementary teachers. *Journal of Teacher Education, 29,* 53–57.

CONANT, E. H. (1973). *Teacher and paraprofessional work productivity.* Lexington, MA: D.C. Heath.

CONDON, J. C. (1968). *Semantics and communication.* New York: Macmillan.

COSKY, M. (1976). The role of letter recognition in word recognition. *Perception and Psychophysics, 14,* 111–119.

CRYSTAL, D. (1976). *Child language, learning and linguistics.* London: Edward Arnold.

CULLINAN, B. E. (1974). Issues in Black English and reading. In B. E. Cullinan (Ed.), *Black dialects and reading.* Newark, DE: International Reading Association.

CULVER, R. (1982). How to develop a locally-relevant basic sight word list. *Reading Teacher, 35,* 596–597.

CURRY, J. F. (1980). How Am I doing? Assessing the components of a managed curriculum. In D. Lapp (Ed.), *Making reading possible through effective classroom management.* Newark, DE: International Reading Association.

CUTWRIGHT, P. A. (1934). A comparison of methods of securing correct language use. *Elementary School Journal, 34,* 681–690.

DALE, E., & CHALL, J. (1958). *Readability: An appraisal of research and application.* Columbus, OH: Ohio State University Press.

DALLMAN, M. (1982). *The teaching of reading.* New York: Holt, Rinehart and Winston.

D'ANGELO, E. J. (1980). *Process and thought in composition.* Cambridge, MA: Winthrop Publications.

DAVEY, B. (1983). Think aloud: Modeling the cognitive process of reading comprehension. *Journal of Reading, 37,* 104–112.

DAVIS, J. F. (1978). *Developing inferential comprehension.* Paper presented at the meeting of the International Reading Association, Houston, TX.

DAWSON, M. E. (Ed.). (1974). *Are there unwelcome guests in your classroom?* Washington, DC: Association for Childhood Education International.

DAY, J. D. (1980). *Training summarization skills: A comparison of teaching materials.* Unpublished doctoral dissertation, University of Illinois.

deBEAUGRANDE, R. (1980). *Text, discourse and process.* Norwood, NJ: Ablex.

DECHANT, E. V., & SMITH, H. P. (1977). *Psychology in teaching reading.* Englewood Cliffs, NJ: Prentice-Hall.

deGROOT, A. D. (1965). *Thought and choice in chess.* The Hague: Mouton.

DEIGHTON, L. C. (1959). *Vocabulary development in the classroom.* New York: Columbia University Press.

DeSTEFANO, J. S. (1973). Register: A concept to combat negative teacher attitudes toward Black English. In J. A. DeStefano (Ed.), *Language, society and education: A profile of black English.* Worthingham, OH: Charles A. Jones.

DISHAW, M. (1978). *Descriptions of allocated time to content areas for the A-B period. Technical note. Beginning teacher evaluation study.* San Francisco: Far West Laboratory of Education Research and Development.

DiSTEFANO, P., DOLE, J., & MARZANO, R. (1984). *Elementary language arts.* New York: John Wiley & Sons.

DiSTEFANO, P., NOE, M., & VALENCIA, S.

(1981). Measurement of the effects of purpose and passage difficulty in reading flexibility. *Journal of Educational Psychology, 73,* 602–606.

DIXON, R. (1977). *Morphographic spelling program.* Eugene, OR: Englemann-Becker.

DIXON, R., & ENGELMANN, J. (1979). *Corrective spelling through morphographs.* Chicago: Science Research Associates.

DOLCH, E. W. (1936). A basic sight vocabulary. *Elementary School Journal, 36,* 456–60.

DOLE, J. A. (1981). Between language and culture: An Alaskan example. *Bilingual Journal, 6,* 10–12.

DORE, J. (1974). A pragmatic description of early language development. *Journal of Psycholinguistic Research, 3,* 343–350.

DOUGLAS, J. (1976). *Investigative social research.* Beverly Hills, CA: Sage.

DUFF, R. E., & SWICK, K. (1974). Primary level tutors as an instructional resource. *Reading Improvement, 11,* 39–44.

DUNN, R., & DUNN, K. (1978). *Teaching students through their individual learning styles: A practical approach.* Reston, VA: Reston Publishing Co.

DURKIN, D. (1986). *Children who read early.* New York: Teacher's College Press.

DURRELL, D. D., & CATTERSON, J. H. (1980). *Durrell analyses of reading difficulty.* New York: Psychological Corporation.

DYER, W. W. (1976). *Your erroneous zone.* New York: Funk and Wagnalls.

EBBINGHAUS, H. (1897). Ueber eine neue methode zur prufung geistiger fahigkeiten und ihre anwendung bei schulkindern. *Zeitsch fur Psychologie und Physiologie der Sinnesorgane, 13,* 401–457.

EDUCATION COMMISSION OF THE STATES. (1982). *The information society: Are high school graduates ready?* Denver.

EHRI, L. C., DEFFNER, N. D., & WILCE, L. S. (1984). Pictorial mnemonics for phonics. *Journal of Educational Psychology, 76,* 880–893.

EINSTEIN, A. (1964). *Ideas and opinions.* New York: Bonanza Books.

EKWALL, E. E. (1977). *Locating and correcting reading difficulties.* Columbus, OH: Charles E. Merrill.

EKWALL, E. E., & SHANKER, J. L. (1983). *Diagnosis and remediation of the disabled reader.* Boston: Allyn & Bacon.

ELKONIAN, D. B. (1973). USSR. In J. Downing (Ed.), *Comparative reading.* New York: Macmillan.

EMMER, E. T., EVERTSON, C. M., & ANDERSON, L. (1980). Effective management at the beginning of the school year. *Elementary School Journal, 80,* 219–231.

EMMER, E. T., EVERTSON, C. M., SANFORD, J. P., CLEMENTS, B. S., & WORSHAM, M. E. (1984). *Classroom management for secondary teachers.* Englewood Cliffs, NJ: Prentice-Hall.

ESTES, T. (1984, May). Paper presented at the Conference on Reading Research, Atlanta.

EVERTSON, C. M., EMMER, E. T., CLEMENTS, B. S., SANFORD, J. P., & WORSHAM, M. E. (1984). *Classroom management for elementary teachers.* Englewood Cliffs, NJ: Prentice-Hall.

FETTERMAN, D. M. (1984). *Ethnography in educational evaluation.* Beverly Hills, CA: Sage Publications.

FILLMORE, C. (1968). The case for case. In E. Bach & R. Harms (Eds.), *Universals in linguistic theory.* New York: Holt, Rinehart and Winston.

FINN, P. J. (1985). *Helping children learn to read.* New York: Random House.

FISHER, C. W., BERLINER, D. C., FILBY, N., MARLIAVE, R. S., CAHEN, L. S., & DISHAW, M. M. (1980). Teaching behaviors, academic learning time and student achievement: An overview. In C. Denham & A. Lieberman (Eds.), *Time to Learn.* Washington, DC: National Institute of Education.

FISHER, C. W., FILBY, N., MARLIAVE, R. S., CAHEN, L. S., DISHAW, M. M., MOORE, J. E., & BERLINER, D. C. (1978). *Teaching behaviors, academic learning time and student achievement. Final report of phase III-B. Beginning Teacher Evaluation Study.* San Francisco: Far West Laboratory of Educational Research and Development.

FITZGERALD, J. (1983). Helping readers gain self-control over reading comprehension. *Reading Teacher, 37,* 249–253.

FLAVELL, J. H. (1976). Metacognitive aspects of problem solving. In L. B. Resnick (Ed.), *The nature of intelligence.* Hillsdale, NJ: Lawrence Erlbaum.

FLESCH, R. (1981). *Why Johnny still can't read.* New York: Harper & Row.

FLOWER, L., & HAYES, J. R. (1984). Images, plans and prose: The representation of meaning in writing. *Written Communication, 1,* 120–160.

FODOR, J. A., BEVER, T. G., & GARRETT, M. F. (1974). *The psychology of language: An introduction to psycholinguistics and generative grammar.* New York: McGraw-Hill.

FOWLER, G. L. (1982). Developing comprehension skills in primary students through the use of story frames. *Reading Teacher, 36,* 176–179.

FREDERIKSEN, C. H. (1975). Representing the logical and semantic structure of knowledge acquired from discourse. *Cognitive Psychology, 7,* 371–458.

FREEDMAN, G., & REYNOLDS, E. G. (1980). Enriching basal reader lessons with semantic webbing. *Reading Teacher, 33,* 677–683.

FRIES, C. (1955). *Linguistics and reading.* New York: Holt, Rinehart and Winston.

FROMM, E. (1968). The nonproductive character orientation. In L. Gorlow & W. Katkovsky (Eds.), *Reading in the psychology of adjustment.* New York: McGraw-Hill.

FRY, E. (1980). The new instant word list. *Reading Teacher, 34,* 284–89.

FRY, E. (1972). *Reading instruction for classroom and clinic.* New York: McGraw-Hill.

FRY, E., POLK, J. K., & FOUNTOUBIDIS, P. (1984). *The reading teacher's book of lists.* Englewood Cliffs, NJ: Prentice-Hall.

FUNKENSTEIN, D. H. (1967). The psychology of fear and anger. *Psychobiology: The biological bases of behavior.* San Francisco: W. H. Freeman & Company Publishers.

GAGE, N. L. (1979). The generality of dimensions of teaching. In P. L. Peterson & H. J. Walberg (Eds.), *Research in teaching.* Berkeley, CA: McCutchan.

GARDINER, M. F., & WALTER, D. O. (1977). Evidence of hemispheric specialization from infant EEG. In S. Harnad, R. W. Doty, L. Goldstein, J. Jaynes, & G. Krauthamer (Eds.), *Lateralization in the nervous system.* New York: Academic Press.

GARDNER, B. T., & GARDNER, R. A. (1971). Two-way communication with an infant chimpanzee. In A. M. Schrier & F. Stollnitz (Eds.), *Behavior of non-human primates.* New York: Academic Press.

GARMAN, D. (1978). So they've dictated a story . . . now what? *Teacher, 69,* 53–54.

GARRETT, M. F., BEVER, T. G., & FODOR, J. A. (1966). The active uses of grammar in speech perception. *Perception and Psychophysics, 1,* 30–32.

GARTON, S., SCHOENFEIDER, P., & SKRIKA, P. (1979). Activities for young word bankers. *Reading Teacher, 32,* 453–57.

GILLET, J. W., & GENTRY, J. K. (1983). Bridges between nonstandard and standard English with extensions of dictated stories. *Reading Teacher, 36,* 360–364.

GLASS, G. V., & SMITH, M. L. (1977). *Pull-out in compensatory education.* Arlington, VA: ERIC Document Reproduction Service, No. ED 160 723.

GOOD, T. L. (1981). Teacher expectations and student perceptions: A decade of research. *Educational Leadership,* 415–422.

GOOD, T. L., & BROPHY, J. E. (1978). *Looking in classrooms.* New York: Harper & Row.

GOOD, T. L., GROUWS, D. A., & EBMEIER, H. (1983). *Active mathematics teaching.* New York: Longman.

GOOD, T. L., & MARSHALL, S. (1984). Heterogenous versus homogeneous groups. In P. Peterson, L. Wilkerson, & M. Hallinan (Eds.), *The social context of instruction: Group organization and group process.* New York: Academic Press.

GOODMAN, J. B. (1977). *Impulsive and reflective behavior: A developmental analysis of attention and cognitive strategies. Dissertation Abstracts International, 34,* 5190B.

GOODMAN, K. (1967). Reading: A psycholinguistic guessing game. *Journal of the Reading Specialist, 4,* 126–135.

GOODMAN, K. (1973). Analysis of oral reading miscues: Applied linguistics. In F. Smith (Ed.), *Psycholinguistics and reading.* New York: Holt, Rinehart & Winston.

GOODMAN, Y. M. (1978). Kid watching: An alternative to testing. *National Elementary School Principal, 57,* 41–45.

GOODMAN, Y. M., & BURKE, C. L. (1972). *Reading miscue inventory.* New York: Macmillan.

GOUGH, P. B. (1976). One second of reading. In H. Singer & R. Ruddell (Eds.), *Theoretical models and processing of reading.* Newark, DE: International Reading Association.

GREENWALD, M., & PEDERSON, C. (1983). Effects of sentence organization instruction in reading comprehension. In J. Niles & L. Harris (Eds.), *Searching for meaning in reading/language processing and instruction.* Rochester, NY: National Reading Conference.

styles: Their nature and effects. In *Student learning styles: Diagnosing and prescribing programs*. Reston, VA: National Association of Secondary School Principals.

GROSS, S., CARR, M. L., DORNSEIF, A., & ROUSE, S. M. (1974). Behavioral objectives in a reading skills program: Grades 4–8. *Reading Teacher, 27*, 787–789.

GUBA, E. G. (1981). Criteria for assessing the trustworthiness of naturalistic inquiries. *Educational Communication and Technology Journal, 29*, 75–92.

GUTHRIE, J. T. (1973). Reading comprehension and syntactic responses in good and poor readers. *Journal of Educational Psychology, 65*, 294.

GUTHRIE, J. T., SEIFERT, M., BURNHAM, N. & CAPLAN, R. (1974). The maze technique to assess, monitor reading comprehension. *Reading Teacher, 28*, 161–168.

HAGERTY, P. (1985). *Thematic units*. Unpublished paper, Denver.

HALL, M. A. (1965). *The development and evaluation of a language experience approach to reading with first grade culturally disadvantaged children*. Unpublished doctoral dissertation, University of Maryland.

HALLIDAY, M. (1975). *Learning how to mean—explorations in the development of language*. London: Edward Arnold.

HALLIDAY, M., & HASAN, R. (1976). *Cohesion in English*. London: Longman.

HAMACHECK, D. E. (1975). *Behavior dynamics in teaching, learning and growth*. Boston: Allyn & Bacon.

HANNA, G. S., & OASTER, T. R. (1978/79). Toward a unified theory of context dependence. *Reading Research Quarterly, 14*, 226–243.

HANSEN, J. (1981). An inferential comprehension strategy to use with primary grade children. *Reading Teacher, 34*, 665–679.

HANSEN, J., & PEARSON, P. D. (1980). *The effects of inference training and practice on young children's comprehension*. Arlington, VA: ERIC Document Reproduction Service, No. ED 186 839.

HARNISCHFEGER, A., & WILEY, D. (1978). *Conceptual and policy issues in elementary school teachers: Learning*. Paper presented at the Annual Meeting of the American Educational Research Association, Toronto.

HARRIS, A. J., & JACOBSON, M. D. (1973). Basic vocabulary for beginning reading. *Reading Teachers, 26*, 392–395.

HART, L. A. (1983). *Human brain and human learning*. New York: Longman.

HARTER, S., & CONNELL, J. P. (1981). A model of the relationship among children's academic achievement and their self-perceptions of competence, control and motivational orientation. Washington, DC: National Institute of Education.

HAYES, D., & TIERNEY, R. (1982). Developing reading knowledge through analogy. *Reading Research Quarterly, 17*, 256–280.

HECKELMAN, R. G. (1969). A Neurological-impress method of remedial reading instruction. *Academic Therapy, 4*, 277–282.

HENDERSON, H. (1984/85). Post-economic policies for post-industrial societies. *Revision, 7*, 20–29.

HERBER, H. (1978). *Teaching reading in the content areas*. Englewood Cliffs, NJ: Prentice-Hall.

HIEBERT, E. H. (1980). Peers as reading teachers. *Language Arts, 57*, 877–881.

HIEBERT, E. H. (1983). An examination of ability grouping for reading instruction. *Reading Research Quarterly, 18*, 232–255.

HILGARD, E. R., ATKINSON, R. C., & ATKINSON, R. L. (1975). *Introduction to psychology*. New York: Harcourt Brace Jovanovich.

HOFFMAN, J. V., & RUTHERFORD, N. L. (1984). Effective reading programs: A critical review of outlier studies. *Reading Research Quarterly, 20*, 79–92.

HOWARDS, M. (1980). *Reading diagnosis and instruction: An integrated approach*. Reston, VA: Prentice-Hall, Reston Publishing.

HOYT, F. S. (1906). The place of grammar in the elementary school curriculum. *Teachers College Record, 7*, 1–34.

HUEY, E. B. (1974). *The psychology and pedagogy of reading*. Boston, MA: MIT Press.

HUGGINS, A. W. & ADAMS, M. J. (1980). Syntactic aspects of reading comprehension. In R. J. Spiro, B. C. Bruce, & W. F. Brewer (Eds.), *Theoretical issues in reading comprehension*. Hillsdale, NJ: Lawrence Erlbaum.

HUNTER, M. (1984). Knowing, teaching and supervision. In P. L. Hosford (Ed.), *Using what we know about teaching*. Alexandria, VA: Association for Supervision and Curriculum Development.

INTERNATIONAL READING ASSOCIATION. (1981). *Guidelines for the professional preparation of reading specialists and allied professions.* New-ark, DE.

JENSEN, A. R. (1980). *Bias in mental testing.* New York: Free Press.

JOHNS, J. (1981). *Advanced reading inventory.* Dubuque, IA: Wm. C. Brown.

JOHNSON, D. D. (1983). *Three sound strategies for vocabulary development.* (Occasional Paper No. 3). Columbus, OH: Ginn and Co.

JOHNSON, D. D. (1974). Word lists that make sense and those that don't. *Learning Magazine, 4,* 60–61.

JOHNSON, D. D., & PEARSON, P. D. (1984). *Teaching reading vocabulary.* New York: Holt, Rinehart and Winston.

JOHNSON-LAIRD, P. N. (1983). *Mental models.* Cambridge, MA: Harvard University Press.

JONGSMA, K. S., & JONGSMA, E. A. (1981). Test review: Commercial informal reading inventories. *Reading Teacher, 34,* 697–705.

JUNG, C. G. (1976). *Psychological types.* Princeton, NJ: Princeton University Press.

KANDEL, I. L. (1950). The new literacy. *School and Society, 72,* 348–349.

KARLSEN, B., MADDEN, R., & GARDNER, E. (1976). *Stanford diagnostic reading test.* New York: Harcourt Brace Jovanovich.

KARWEIT, N. L. (1983). *Time on task: A research review.* Baltimore: Johns Hopkins University Press.

KATZ, E., & BRENT, S. (1968). Understanding connectives. *Journal of Verbal Learning and Verbal Behavior, 7,* 501–509.

KATZ, J., & FODOR, J. A. (1963). The structure of semantic theory. *Journal of Verbal Learning and Verbal Behavior, 39,* 170–210.

KAVALE, K. (1979). Selecting and evaluating tests. In R. Schreiner (Ed.), *Reading tests and teachers: A practical guide.* Newark, DE: International Reading Association.

KIBBY, M. (1985). *Informal procedure for evaluating reading skills.* (Mimeograph). Buffalo: State University of New York.

KINTSCH, W. (1974). *The representation of meaning in memory.* Hillsdale, NJ: Lawrence Erlbaum.

KINTSCH, W. (1979). On modeling comprehension. *Educational Psychologist, 14,* 3–14.

KINTSCH, W., & van DIJK, T. A. (1978). Toward a model of text comprehension and production. *Psychological Review, 85,* 363–394.

KLAUSMEIER, H. J., & GOODWIN, W. (1975).

Learning and human abilities: Educational psychology. New York: Harper & Row.

KLEIN, M. (1984). Teaching comprehension skills in the reading program. In J. F. Baumann & D. D. Johnson (Eds.), *Reading instruction and the beginning teacher.* Minneapolis: Burgess.

KOLB, D. A., RUBIN, I. M., & McINTYRE, J. M. (1974). *Organizational psychology.* Englewood Cliffs, NJ: Prentice-Hall.

KOUNIN, J.S. (1970). *Discipline and group management in classrooms.* New York: Holt, Rinehart and Winston.

KULIK, C. C., & KULIK, J. A. (1982). Effects of ability grouping on secondary school students: A meta-analysis of evaluation findings. *American Educational Research Journal, 19,* 415–428.

LaBERGE, D., & SAMUELS, S. J. (1974). Toward a theory of automatic information processing in reading comprehension. *Cognitive Psychology, 6,* 293–323.

LABOV, W. (1966). *The social stratification of English in New York City.* Washington, DC: Center for Applied Linguistics.

LAND, M. L. (1980, February). *Joint effects of teacher structure and teacher enthusiasm on student achievement.* Paper presented at the annual meeting of the Southwest Educational Research Association, San Antonio, TX.

LANGER, J. A. (1982). Facilitating text processing: The elaboration of prior knowledge. In J. A. Langer & M. T. Burke-Smith (Eds.), *Reader meets author: Bridging the gap.* Newark, DE: International Reading Association.

LARKIN, J. (1981). Enriching formal knowledge: A model for learning to solve textbook problems. In J. Anderson (Ed.), *Cognitive skills and their acquisition.* Hillsdale, NJ: Lawrence Erlbaum.

LASHLEY, K. S. (1951). The problem of serial order in behavior. In L. A. Jeffress (Ed.), *Cerebral mechanisms in behavior.* New York: John Wiley & Sons.

LEE, D., & ALLEN, R. V. (1963). *Learning to read through experience.* New York: Prentice-Hall, Appleton-Century-Crofts.

LEINHARDT, G., & PALLAY, A. (1982). Restrictive education settings: Exile or haven? *Review of Educational Research, 52,* 557–578.

LENNEBERG, E. (1964). *New Directions in the study of language.* Cambridge, MA: MIT Press.

LESLIE, L. & JETT-SIMPSON, M. (1983). The effect of recall instruction and story deletions on children's story comprehension. In J. Niles & L. Harris (Eds.), *Searching for meaning in reading/language processing and instruction.* Rochester, NY: National Reading Conference.

LETTERI, C. A. (1982). Cognitive profile: Relationship to achievement and development. In *Student learning styles and brain behavior.* Reston, VA: National Association of Secondary School Principals.

LEVINE, D. U. (Ed.). (1985). *Important student achievement through mastery learning programs.* San Francisco: Jossey-Bass.

LEWIS, D., & GREENE, J. (1982). *Thinking better.* New York: Holt, Rinehart and Winston.

LIGHTNER, C. (1965). 1930–1945. In R. McDonald, Jr. (Ed.), *Examination of the attitudes of the NCTE toward language.* Urbana, IL: National Council of Teachers of English.

LINDFORS, J. W. (1980). *Children's language and learning.* Englewood Cliffs, NJ: Prentice-Hall Inc.

LINDSAY, P. H., & NORMAN, D. A. (1977). *Human information processing.* New York: Academic Press.

LIPMAN, M. (1985). Thinking skills fostered by philosophy for children. In J. W. Segal, S. F. Chipman, & R. Glaser (Eds.), *Thinking and learning skills.* Hillsdale, NJ: Lawrence Erlbaum.

LIPMAN, M. OSCANYAN, F. S., & SHARP, A. M. (1979). *Philosophical inquiry: An instructional manual to accompany Harry Stottlemeier's discovery.* Upper Montclair, NJ: the Institute for the Advancement of Philosophy for Children.

MAGER, R. F. (1962). *Preparing instructional objectives.* Belmont, CA: Fearon.

MANDLER, J. M., & JOHNSON, N. S. (1977). Remembrance of things parsed: Story structure and recall. *Cognitive Psychology, 9,* 111–151.

MANGIERI, J., & HEIMBERGER, M. (1980). Perceptions of the reading consultant's role. *Journal of Reading, 23,* 527–530.

MANZO, A. V. (1969). The request procedure. *Journal of Reading, 13,* 123–126; 163.

MANZO, A. V. (1970). Reading and questioning: The request procedure. *Reading Improvement, 18,* 215–218.

MARSHALL, N., & GLOCK, M. (1978/79). Comprehension of connected discourse: A study into the relationship between the structure of text and the information recalled. *Reading Research Quarterly, 76,* 10–56.

MARZANO, R. J. (1983). *A quantitative grammar of meaning and structure.* Denver: Midcontinent Regional Educational Laboratory.

MARZANO, R. J. (1984). A cluster approach to vocabulary instruction: A new direction from the research literature. *Reading Teacher, 38,* 168–173.

MARZANO, R. J. (1985). *Basic vocabulary and concept development: A systematic approach.* Denver: Educational Press.

MARZANO, R. J., & DOLE, J. (1985). *Teaching basic relationships and patterns among sentences.* Denver, CO: Midcontinent Regional Educational Laboratory.

MARZANO, R. J., & RILEY, A. (1984). *Selected school effectiveness variables: Some correlates that are not causes.* Denver, CO: Midcontinent Regional Educational Laboratory.

MASLOW, A. (1968). *Toward a psychology of being.* New York: Van Nostrand Reinhold.

MASON, G. E., & PALMATIER, R. A. (1973). Preparation of professionals in reading. *Journal of Reading, 16,* 637–640.

MCCARTHY, B. (1980). *The 4mat system.* Oak Harbor, IL: Excel, Inc.

MCCOMBS, B. (1984). Processes and skills underlying continuing intrinsic motivation to learn: Toward a definition of motivational skills training intervention. *Educational Psychologist, 19,* 199–218.

MCNEIL, J. D. (1984). *Reading comprehension: New directions for classroom practice.* Glenview, IL: Scott, Foresman.

MCNEIL, J. D., & DONANT, L. (1982). Summarization strategy for improving reading comprehension. In J. Niles & L. Miller (Eds.), *New inquiries in reading research instruction.* (31st Yearbook of the National Reading Conference). New York: National Reading Conference.

MCNEILL, D. (1975). Semiotic extension. In R. L. Solso (Ed.), *Information processing and cognition: The Loyola symposium.* Hillsdale, NJ: Lawrence Erlbaum.

MEHRENS, W. A., & LEHMAN, I. J. (1980). *Standardized tests in education.* New York: Holt, Rinehart and Winston.

MEICHENBAUM, D., & GOODMAN, J. (1971). Training impulsive children to talk to themselves. *Journal of Abnormal Psychology, 77,* 115–126.

MEIER, T. R., & CAZDEN, C. B. (1982, May). Focus on oral language and writing from a multicultural perspective. *Language Arts, 59,* 504–512.

MEYER, B. J. (1975). *The organization of prose and its effects on memory.* Amsterdam: North Holland Publishing Co.

MIDCONTINENT REGIONAL EDUCATIONAL LABORATORY. (1981). Kids who team teach. *Noteworthy.* Denver: Author.

MILES, M., & HUBERMAN, A. M. (1984). *Qualitative data analysis.* Beverly Hills, CA: Sage.

MILLER, G. A., BRUNER, J. S., & POSTMAN, L. (1954). Familiarity of letter sequences and tachistoscopic identification. *Journal of Genetic Psychology, 50,* 129–139.

MILLER, G. A., GALANTER, E., & PRIBRAM, K. H. (1960). *Plans and the structure of behavior.* New York: Holt, Rinehart and Winston.

MILLER, W. H. (1978). *Reading diagnosis kit.* West Nyack, NY: The Center for Applied Research in Education.

MINTZ, S. L. (1979, April). *Teacher planning: A simulation study.* Paper presented at the annual meeting of the American Educational Research Association, San Francisco.

MOORE, D. W., READENCE, J. E., & RICKELMAN, R. J. (1982). *Prereading activities for content area reading and learning.* Newark, DE: International Reading Association.

MORAY, N. (1959). Attention in dichotic listening: Affective cues and the influence of instructions. *Quarterly Journal of Experimental Psychology, 11,* 56–60.

MURRAY, L. (1975). *English grammar adapted to the different classes of learners.* York, England: Longman, Rees, Orme, Brown, Green and Longman.

NAGY, W. E. (1985). *Vocabulary instruction: Implications of the new research.* Paper presented at the conference of the National Council of Teachers of English, Philadelphia.

NAGY, W. E., & ANDERSON, R. C. (1984). How many words are there in printed school English? *Reading Research Quarterly, 19,* 304–330.

NAGY, W. E., HERMAN, P. A., & ANDERSON, R. C. (1985). Learning words from context. *Reading Research Quarterly, 20,* (2), 233–253.

NESSELL, D. D., & JONES, M. B. (1981). *The language experience approach to reading.* New York: Teachers College Press.

NICHOLS, J. N. (1983). Using prediction to increase content area interest and understanding. *Journal of Reading, 27,* 219–224.

NICHOLSON, A. (1958). Background abilities related to reading success in first grade. *Journal of Education, 140,* 7–24.

NORTH, C. (1983). *The three bears.* New York: Western Publishing.

NORTON, D. E. (1980). *The effective teaching of language arts.* Columbus, OH: Charles E. Merrill.

O'HARE, F. (1973). *Sentence combining: Improving student writing without formal grammatical instruction.* Urbana, IL: National Council of Teachers of English.

OLSON, A. V. (1958). Growth in word perception abilities as it relates to success in beginning reading. *Journal of Education, 140,* 25–36.

OLSON, D. (1970). Language and thought: Aspects of a cognitive theory of semantics. *Psychological Review, 77,* 257–273.

OLSON, G. M., & CLARK, H. H. (1976). Research methods in psycholinguistics. In E. C. Carterette & M. D. Friedman (Eds.), *Handbook of perception vol. VII: Language and speech.* New York: Academic Press.

OLSON, M. W. (1984, February). A dash of story grammar and presto! A book report. *Reading Teacher, 37,* 458–461.

ORTONY, A. (1984). Understanding figurative language. In P. D. Pearson, R. Barr, & M. Kamil (Eds.), *Handbook of reading research.* New York, NY: Longman.

OTTO, W., & SMITH, R. J. (1970). *Administering the school reading program.* Boston, MA: Houghton Mifflin Co.

OTTO, W., WOLF, A., & ELDRIDGE, R. G. (1984). Managing instruction. In P. D. Pearson, (Ed.), *Handbook of reading research.* New York, NY: Longman.

PAIVIO, A. (1983). Strategies in language learning. In M. Pressley & J. R. Levin (Eds.), *Cognitive strategy research: Educational applications.* New York: Springer-Verlag.

PALINCSAR, A. S., & BROWN, A. L. (1984). Reciprocal teaching of comprehension—fostering and comprehension—monitoring activities. *Cognition and Instruction, 1,* 117–75.

PALMER, S. E. (1975). Visual perception and word knowledge: Notes on a model of sensory-cognitive interaction. In D. A. Norman, D. E. Rumelhart, & the LNR Research Group

(Eds.), *Explorations in Cognition*. San Francisco: W. H. Freeman & Company Publishers.

PARK, C. (1976). The Bay City experiment . . . As seen by the director. *Journal of Teacher Education, 7,* 5–8.

PAUL, R. (1984). Critical thinking: Fundamental to education for a free society. *Educational Leadership, 42,* 4–16.

PEARSON, P. D. (1974/75). The effects of grammatical complexity in children's comprehension, recall and conception of certain semantic relations. *Reading Research Quarterly, 10,* 155–192.

PEARSON, P. D. (1981). Comprehension in text structures. In J. T. Guthrie (Ed.), *Comprehension and teaching: Research reviews.* Newark, DE: International Reading Association.

PEARSON, P. D. (1982). *Asking questions about stories.* (Occasional Paper No. 15). Columbus, OH: Ginn.

PEARSON, P. D. (1984). Direct explicit teaching of reading comprehension. In G. Duff & L. Roehler (Eds.), *Comprehension instruction: Perspectives and suggestions.* New York: Longman.

PEARSON, P. D. (1985). Changing the face of reading comprehension instruction. *Reading Teacher, 38,* 724–738.

PEARSON, P. D., & JOHNSON, D. (1984). *Teaching reading comprehension.* New York: Holt, Rinehart and Winston.

PEARSON, P. D., & KAMIL, M. (1978). *Basic processes and instructional practices in teaching reading.* Champaign/Urbana IL: Center for the Study of Reading, University of Illinois.

PEARSON, P. D., & SPIRO, R. J. (1982). The new buzz word in reading is schema. *Instructor, 91,* 46–48.

PERKINS, D. (1984). Creativity by design. *Educational Leadership, 42,* 18–25.

PERSELL, C. (1977). *Education and inequality: The roots and results of stratification in American schools.* New York: Free Press.

PETERSON, P., WILKINSON, L., & HALLINAN, M. (1984). *The social context of instruction: Group organization and group processes.* New York: Academic Press.

PIAGET, J. (1965). *The language and thought of the child.* London: Routledge and Kegan.

PIKULSKI, J. (1974). A Critical review: Informal reading inventories. *Reading Teacher, 28,* 141–151.

PIKULSKI, J. J. & ROSS, E. (1979). Classroom teachers' perceptions of the role of the reading specialist. *Journal of Reading, 23,* 126–135.

PITKIN, W. L. (1977). X/Y: Some basic strategies of discourse. *College English, 38,* 660–672.

PITMAN, SIR J., & ST. JOHN, J. (1969). *Alphabets and reading.* New York: Pitman.

POPHAM, J. W. (1978). *Criterion-referenced measurement.* Englewood Cliffs, NJ: Prentice-Hall.

POWELL, W. R. (1970). Reappraising the criteria for interpreting informal reading inventories. In D. DeBoer (Ed.), *Reading diagnosis and evaluation.* Newark, DE: International Reading Association.

POWELL, W. R., & DUNKELD, C. G. (1971). Validity of the IRI reading levels. *Elementary English, 48,* 632–642.

PRESSLEY, M., & LEVIN, J. R. (Eds.) (1983a). *Cognitive strategy research: Educational applications.* New York: Springer-Verlag.

PRESSLEY, M., & LEVIN, J. R. (Eds.) (1983b). *Cognitive strategy research: Psychological foundations.* New York: Springer-Verlag.

PRESSLEY, M., LEVIN, J. R., & BRYANT, S. L. (1983). Memory strategy instruction during adolescence: When is explicit instruction needed? In M. Pressley & J. R. Levin (Eds.), *Cognitive strategy research: Psychological foundations.* New York: Springer-Verlag.

RAPHAEL, T. E. (1982). Question-answering strategies for children. *Reading Teacher, 36,* 186–190.

READANCE, J. E., BEAN, T. W., & BALDWIN, R. S. (1981). *Content area reading: An integrated approach.* Dubuque, IA: Kendall/Hunt.

RESEARCH INSTITUTE OF AMERICA. (1985, April). *Personal Report.* New York: Author.

REICHER, G. M. (1969). Perceptual recognition as a function of meaningfulness of stimulus material. *Journal of Experimental Psychology, 81,* 275–280.

RESNICK, L. (in press). *Education and learning to think.* Pittsburgh, PA: Learning Research and Development Center.

REUTER, G. S. (1963). *The length of the school day.* Chicago, IL: American Federation of Teachers.

RHODES, L. K. (1981, February). I can read! Predictable books as resources for reading and writing instruction. *Reading Teacher, 34,* 511–518.

RICHARDSON, A. (1983). Images, definitions and types. In A. A. Scheikh (Ed.), *Imagery: Current theory, research and application.* New York: John Wiley & Sons.

RICHARDSON, D. C., & HAVLICEK, L. L. (1975). High school students as reading instructors. *Elementary School Journal, 75,* 389–393.

RINGLER, L. H., & WEBER, C. K. (1984). *A language-thinking approach to reading.* New York: Harcourt Brace Jovanovich.

ROADY, ROADRUNNER, & YOSHI. (1976). *Reading 720: How it is nowadays.* T. Clymer et al. Lexington, MA: Ginn & Company.

ROBERTSON, J. (1968). Pupil understanding of connectives in reading. *Reading Research Quarterly, 3,* 387–417.

ROBINSON, H. A. (1967). The reading teacher of the past, present and possible future. *Reading Teacher, 20,* 475–482.

ROBINSON, H. A., & RAUCH, S. J. (1985). *Guiding the reading program: A reading consultant's handbook.* Chicago, IL: Science Research Associates.

ROBINSON, R. D., & PETTIT, N. T. (1978). The role of the reading teacher. *Reading Teacher, 31,* 923–927.

ROSENSHINE, B. (1970). Enthusiastic teaching: A research review. *School Review, 78,* 499–514.

ROSENSHINE, B. (1983). Teaching functions in instructional programs. *Elementary School Journal, 83,* 335–352.

ROSENSHINE, B., & STEVENS, R. (1984). Classroom instruction in reading. In P. D. Pearson (Ed.), *Handbook of reading research.* New York: Longman.

ROSS, J., & LAWRENCE, K. A. (1968). Some observations on memory artifice. *Psychonomic Science, 13,* 107–108.

ROSSMILLER, R. A. (1982). *Managing school resources to improve student achievement.* Paper presented at the State Superintendent's Conference for District Administrators. Madison, WI.

RUMELHART, D. E. (1975). Notes on a schema for stories. In D. Bobrow & A. Collins (Eds.), *Representation and understanding: Studies in cognitive science.* New York: Academic Press.

RUMELHART, D. E. (1977). Toward an interactive model of reading. In S. Dornic (Ed.). *Attention and Performance. VI,* Hillsdale, NJ: Lawrence Erlbaum.

RUMELHART, D. E. (1980). Schemata: The building blocks of cognition. In R. J. Spiro, B. C. Bruce, & W. F. Brewer (Eds.), *Theoretical issues in reading comprehension.* Hillsdale, NJ: Lawrence Erlbaum.

RUSSELL, B. (1971). *The conquest of happiness.* New York: Liveright.

SACHS, J. S. (1967). Recognition memory for syntactic and semantic aspects of connected discourse. *Perception and Psychophysics, 2,* 437–442.

SADOW, M. W. (1982). The use of story grammar in the design of questions. *Reading Teacher, 35,* 263–65.

SAGOTSKY, G., PATTERSON, C., & LEPPER, M. (1978). Training children's self-control: A field experiment in self-monitoring and goal setting in the classroom. *Journal of Experimental Psychology, 25,* 242–253.

SALVIA, J., & YSSELDYKE, J. (1981). *Assessment in special and remedial education.* Boston: Houghton Mifflin.

SAMUELS, S. J. (1972). The effects of letter-name knowledge on learning to read. *American Educational Research Journal, 9,* 65–74.

SAMUELS, S. J. (1979). The method of repeated readings. *Reading Teacher, 32,* 403–408.

SAMUELS, S. J. (1981). Characteristics of exemplary reading programs. In J. T. Guthrie (Ed.), *Comprehension and teaching: Research reviews.* Newark, DE: International Reading Association.

SAPIR, E. (1921). *Language: An introduction to the study of speech.* New York: Harcourt Brace Jovanovich.

SCHANK, R., GOLDMAN, J., REIGER, C., & REISBECK, C. (1975). *Conceptual information processing.* Amsterdam: North Holland.

SCHLESINGER, M. (1971). Production of utterances and language acquisition. In D. I. Slobin (Ed.), *The ontogenesis of grammar.* New York: Academic Press.

SCHWARTZ, P., & OGILVY, J. (1979). *The emergent paradigm: Changing patterns of thought and belief values and lifestyles program.* Menlo Park: CA: SRI International.

SHATZ, M. (1977). On the development of communicative understandings: An early strategy for interpreting and responding to messages. In J. Glick & A. Clarke-Stewart (Eds.), *Studies in social and cognitive development.* New York: Gardner Press.

Shavelson, R. J., & Stern, P. (1981). Research on teacher's pedagogical thoughts, judgments, decisions and behavior. *Review of Educational Research, 51*, 455–498.

Sheikh, A. A. (Ed.). (1983). *Imagery: Current theory, research and application.* New York: John Wiley & Sons.

Shepherd, D. (1973). *Comprehensive high school reading methods.* Columbus, OH: Charles Merrill.

Shuy, R. (1969). Bonnie and Clyde tactics in English teaching. *Florida FL Reporter, 7,* 75–82.

Shuy, R. (1977). Sociolinguistics. In R. W. Shuy (Ed.), *Linguistic theory: What can it say about reading?* Newark, DE: International Reading Association.

Shuy, R., Wolfram, W. A., & Riley, W. R. (1968). *Field Techniques in an urban language study.* Washington, DC: Center for Applied Linguistics.

Silvaroli, N. J. (1982). *Classroom reading inventory.* Dubuque, IA: Wm. C. Brown.

Silverstein, S. (1964). *The giving tree.* New York: Harper & Row.

Sinatra, R. (1982). Learning literacy in nonverbal style. In *Student Learning Styles and Brain Behavior.* Reston, VA: National Association of Secondary School Principals.

Singer, H. (1978). Active comprehension. *Reading Teacher, 8,* 901–908.

Skrtic, T. (1983). *The doing of emergent paradigm research into educational organization.* Overland Park, KS: University of Kansas.

Slavin, R. E. (1980). *Using student team learning.* Baltimore, MD: The Johns Hopkins Team Teaching Project.

Slavin, R. E. (1982). *Cooperative learning: Student teams.* Washington, DC: National Education Association.

Slobin, D. I. (1979). *Psycholinguistics.* Glenview, IL: Scott, Foresman.

Smith, E. B., Goodman, K., & Meredith, R. (1976). *Language and thinking in school.* New York: Holt, Rinehart and Winston.

Smith, F. (1975). *Comprehension in learning.* New York: Holt, Rinehart and Winston.

Smith, F. (1982). *Understanding reading.* New York: Holt, Rinehart and Winston.

Smith, H. (1979). Nonverbal communication in teaching. *Review of Educational Research, 49,* 631–672.

Smith, J., & Dauer, V. L. (1984). A comprehension-monitoring strategy for reading content area materials. *Journal of Reading, 28,* 144–147.

Smith, L. A. (1976). Miscue research and readability. In P. D. Allen & D. J. Watson (Eds.), *Findings of research in miscue analysis: Classroom implications.* Urbana, IL: National Council of Teachers of English.

Smith, M. L., & Glass, G. V. (1979). *Relationship of class size to classroom processes, teacher satisfaction and pupil affect: A meta-analysis.* San Francisco: Far West Regional Educational Laboratory.

Snyder, C. (1983). *Memo: To myself when I have a teenage daughter.* New York: Coward-McCann.

Spache, G. (1981). *Diagnostic reading scales* (3rd ed.). Monterey, CA: California Test Bureau. McGraw-Hill.

Sperling, G. (1963). A model for visual memory tasks. *Human Factors, 5,* 19–31.

Sperry, R. W. (1964). The great cerebral commissure. *Scientific American,* 42–57.

Standards for educational and psychological tests. (1974). Washington, DC: American Psychological Association.

Stauffer, R. G. (1969). *Directing maturity as a cognitive process.* New York: Harper & Row.

Stauffer, R. (1970). *The language-experience approach to the teaching of reading.* New York: Harper & Row.

Stein, H., & Glenn, C. G. (1977). An analysis of story comprehension in elementary school children. In R. Freedle (Ed.), *New directions in discourse processing.* Norwood, NJ: Ablex.

Sternberg, R. J. (1977). *Intelligence, information processing and analogical reasoning: The componential analysis of human abilities.* Hillsdale, NJ: Lawrence Erlbaum.

Sternberg, R. J. (1984). What should intelligence tests test: Implications of a triarchic theory of intelligence for intelligence testing. *Educational Researcher, 13,* 5–15.

Strong, W. (1973). *Sentence combining.* New York: Random House.

Suinn, R. M. (1983). Imagery and sports. In A. A. Sheikh (Ed.), *Imagery: Current theory research and application.* New York: John Wiley & Sons.

Swarts, H., Flower, L. S., & Hayes, J. R. (1984). Designing protocol studies of the writing process; An introduction. In R. Beach & L. Bridwell (Eds.), *New direction in composition research*. New York: Guilford Press.

SYLWESTER, R. (1985). Research on memory: Major discoveries, major educational challenges. *Educational Leadership, 42,* 69–75.

SYMONDS, P. M. (1931). Practice versus grammar in the learning of correct English. *Journal of Educational Psychology, 27,* 81–95.

TANNEN, D. (1979). What's in a frame? Surface evidence for underlying expectations. In R. Freedle (Ed.), *New directions in discourse processing*. Norwood, NJ: Ablex.

TAYLOR, B., & SAMUELS, S. J. (1983). Children's use of text in the recall of expository material. *American Educational Research Journal, 20,* 517–528.

TAYLOR, W. (1953). Cloze procedure: A new tool for measuring readability. *Journalism Quarterly, 30,* 415–433.

THATCHER, R. W. (1977). Evoked-potential correlates of hemispheric lateralization during semantic information-processing. In S. Harnad, R. W. Doty, L. Goldstein, J. Jaynes, & G. Krauthamer (Eds.), *Lateralization in the nervous system*. New York: Academic Press.

THORNDYKE, P. W. (1977). Cognitive structures in comprehension and memory of narrative discourse. *Cognitive Psychology, 9,* 77–110.

TIERNEY, R. J., READENCE, J. F., & DISHNER, E. K. (1980). *Reading strategies and practices: Guides for improving instruction*. Boston: Allyn & Bacon.

TOULMIN, S. (1969). *The use of argument*. Cambridge: Cambridge University Press.

TOULMIN, S., RIEKE, R., & JANIK, A. (1979). *An introduction to reasoning*. New York: Macmillan.

TRELEASE, J. (1982). *The read aloud handbook*. New York: Penguin.

TUIMAN, J. J. (1976). Asking reading dependent questions. *Journal of Reading, 14,* 289–292, 336.

TURNER, A., & GREENE, E. (1977). *The construction and use of a propositional text base*. Boulder, CO: The Institute for the Study of Intellectual Behavior.

UNDERWOOD, B. J. (1969). Attributes of memory. *Psychological Review, 76,* 559–573.

VACCA, R. T. (1981). *Content area reading*. Boston: Little, Brown.

VAN DIJK, T. A. (1980). *Macrostructures*. Hillsdale, NJ: Lawrence Erlbaum.

VAN DIJK, T. A., & KINTSCH, W. (1983). *Strategies of discourse comprehension*. New York: Academic Press.

VAN DIJK, T. A., & KINTSCH, W. (1976). Cognitive psychology and discourse: Recalling and summarizing stories. In W. V. Dressler (Ed.), *Trends in text linguistics*. New York: deFruyter.

VENEZKY, R. L. (1974). *Testing in reading: Testing and instructional decision making*. Urbana, IL: National Council of Teachers of English.

VYGOTSKY, L. S. (1962). *Thought and language*. Cambridge, MA: MIT Press.

WABER, B. (1975). *Ira sleeps over*. Boston: Houghton Mifflin.

WALLIS, W. A., & ROBERTS, H. V. (1956). *Statistics: A new approach*. New York: Free Press.

WARREN, W. H., NICKOLAS, D. W., & TRABASSO, T. (1979). Event chains and influences in understanding narratives. In R. O. Freedale (Ed.), *New directions in discourse processing II*. Norwood, NJ: Ablex.

WATERHOUSE, L. (1980). The implications of theories of language and thought in reading. In F. B. Murray (Ed.), *Language awareness and reading*. Newark, DE: International Reading Association.

WATERS, H. S. (1978). Superordinate-subordinate structure in semantic memory: The roles of comprehension and retrieval processes. *Journal of Verbal Learning and Verbal Behavior, 17,* 587–597.

WATSON, D. J. (1978). Reader selected miscues: Getting more from sustained silent reading. *English Education, 10,* 75–85.

WATT, W. C. (1970). On two hypotheses concerning psycholinguistics. In J. R. Hayes (Ed.), *Cognition and the development of language*. New York: John Wiley & Sons.

WEBB, E. J., CAMPBELL, D. T., SCHWARTZ, R. D., & SECHREST, L. (1965). *Unobtrusive measures*. Chicago: Rand McNally.

Webster's ninth new collegiate dictionary. (1983). Springfield, MA: Merriam-Webster.

WHALEY, J. F. (1981). Reader's expectations for story structure. *Reading Research Quarterly, 17,* 90–114.

WHIMBEY, A. (1980). Students can learn to be better problem solvers. *Educational Leadership, 37,* 560–563.

WHITAKER, H. (1981). Dichotomania: An essay on our left and right brains: A research commentary. *Division News. 6*, College Park, MD: University of Maryland.

WHITE, R. (1959). Motivation reconsidered: The concept of competency. *Psychological Review, 66*, 297–333.

WHITE, R. (1960). Competence and the psychosexual stages of development. *Nebraska Symposium on Motivation.* Lincoln, NE: University of Nebraska Press.

WHORF, B. L. (1956). *Language, thought and reality.* Cambridge MA: MIT Press.

WOOD, K. D., & ROBINSON, N. (1983). Vocabulary, language and prediction: A prereading strategy. *Reading Teacher, 36,* 392–395.

WOODS, M. X., & MOE, A. J. (1981). *Analytical reading inventory.* Columbus, OH: Charles E. Merrill.

WYCOFF, W. L. (1973). The effect of stimulus variation in learning from lecture. *Journal of Experimental Education, 41,* 85–96.

YOUNG, R., & BECKER, A. (1980). Toward a modern theory of rhetoric: A tagmemic contribution. In M. Wolf, M. K. McQuillian, & E. Radwin (Eds.), *Thought and language: Language and thought* (Harvard Educational Review Reprint Series #14). Cambridge, MA: Harvard University Press.

ZDENEK, M. (1983). *The right-brain experience.* New York: McGraw-Hill.

INDEX